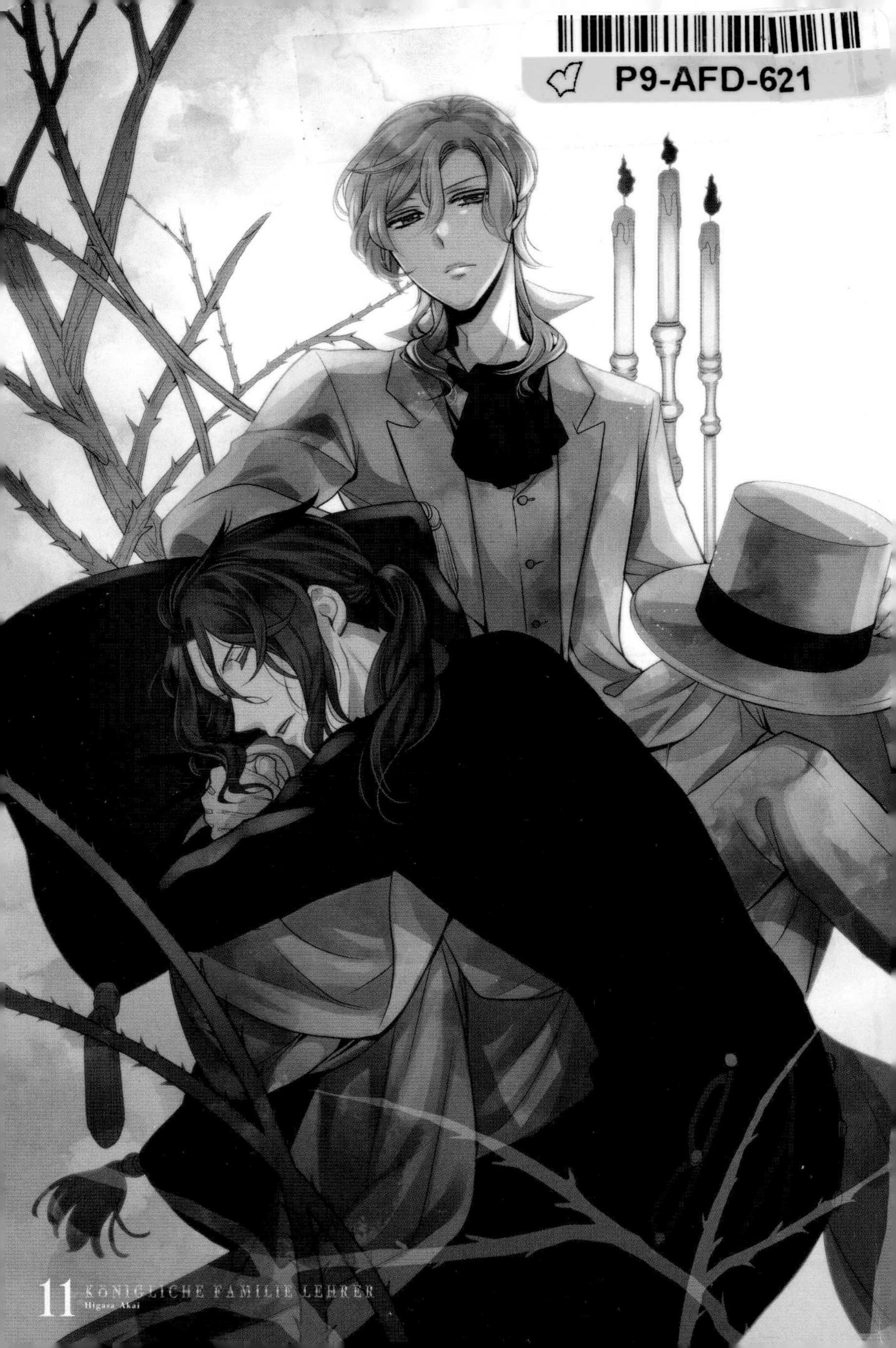
11
KÖNIGLICHE FAMILIE LEHRER
Higasa Akai

Contents

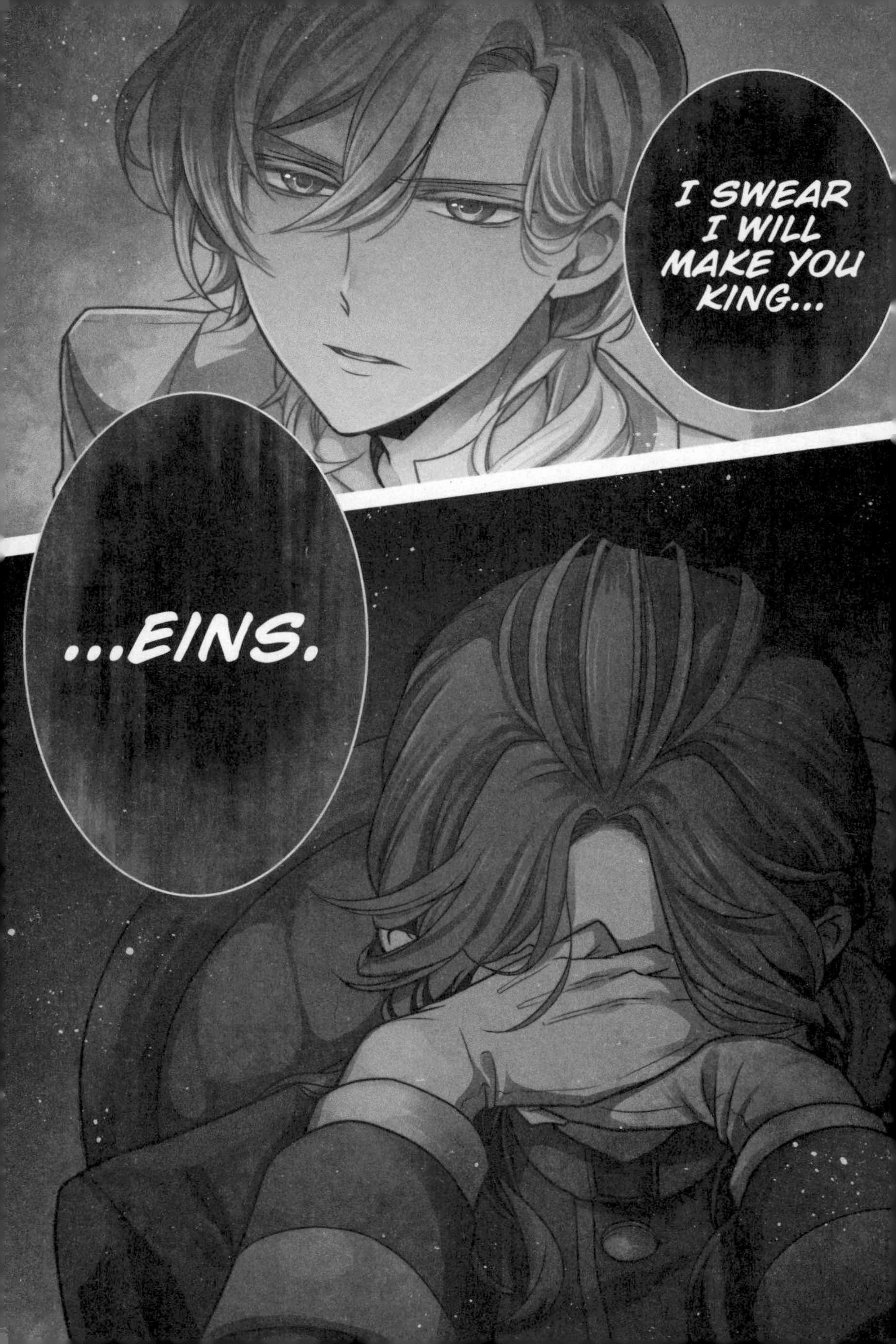
I SWEAR I WILL MAKE YOU KING...
...EINS.

Chapter 60

Pet-Pet S.O.S.!

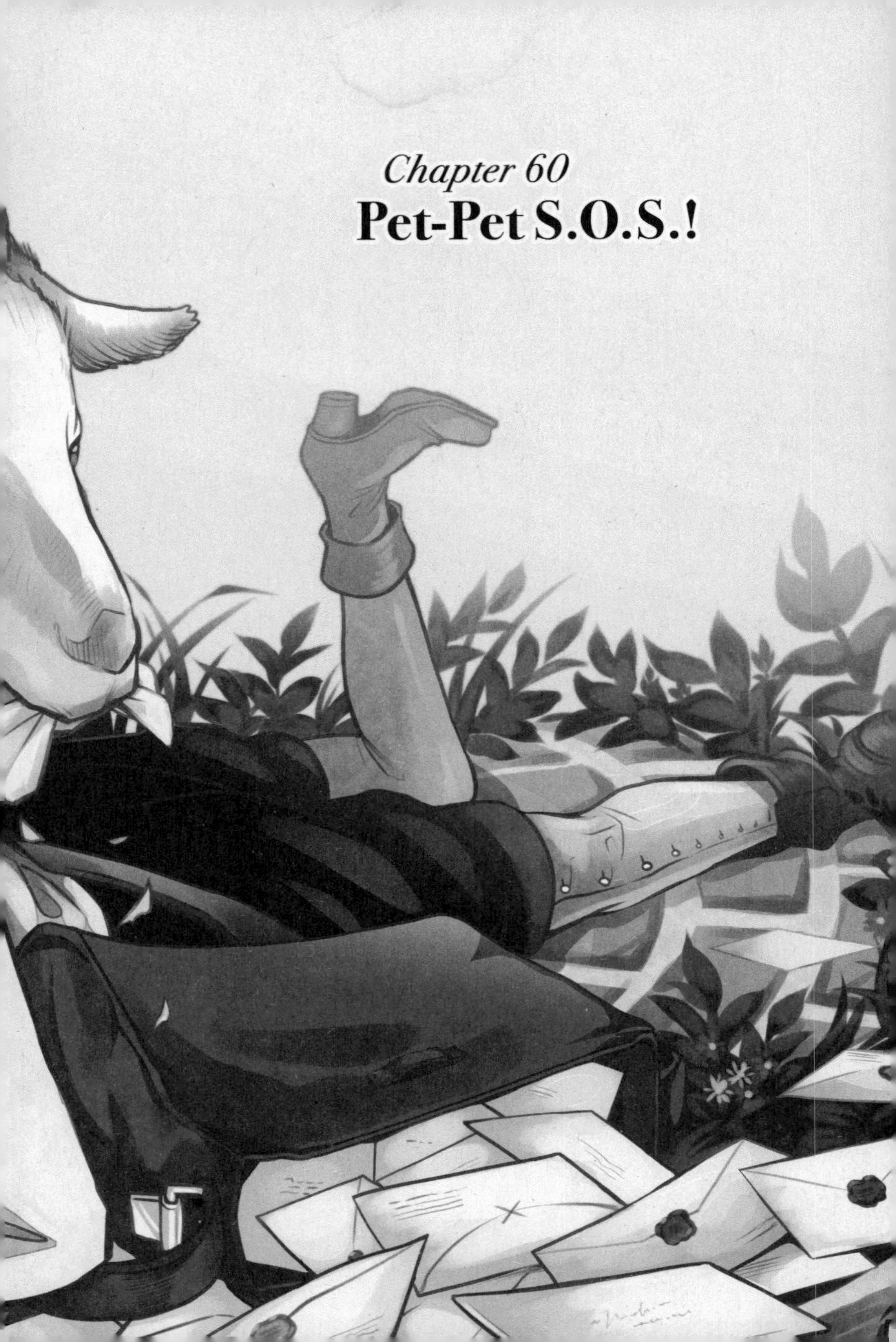

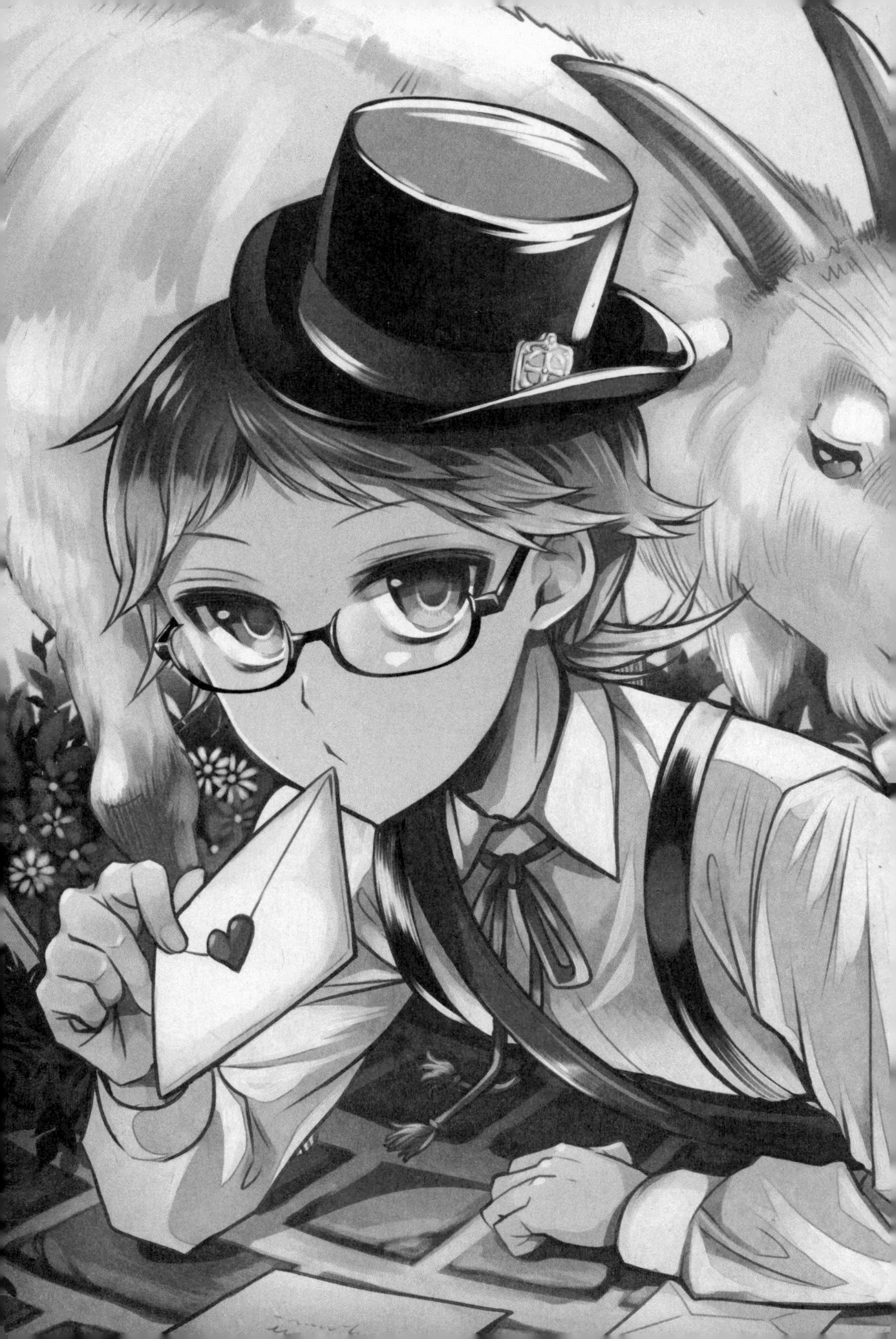

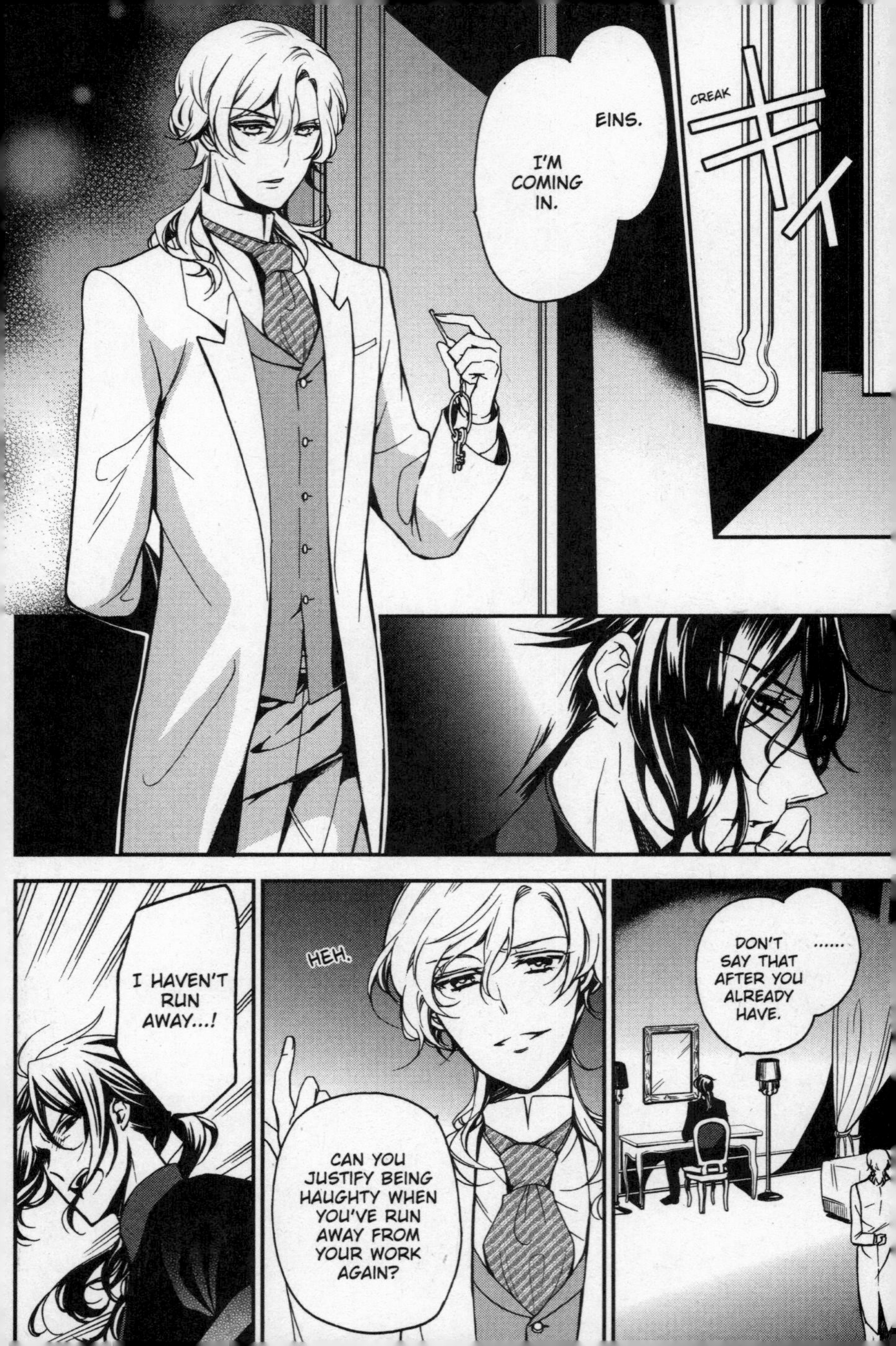
CREAK
EINS. I'M COMING IN.
......
DON'T SAY THAT AFTER YOU ALREADY HAVE.
HEH.
CAN YOU JUSTIFY BEING HAUGHTY WHEN YOU'VE RUN AWAY FROM YOUR WORK AGAIN?
I HAVEN'T RUN AWAY...!

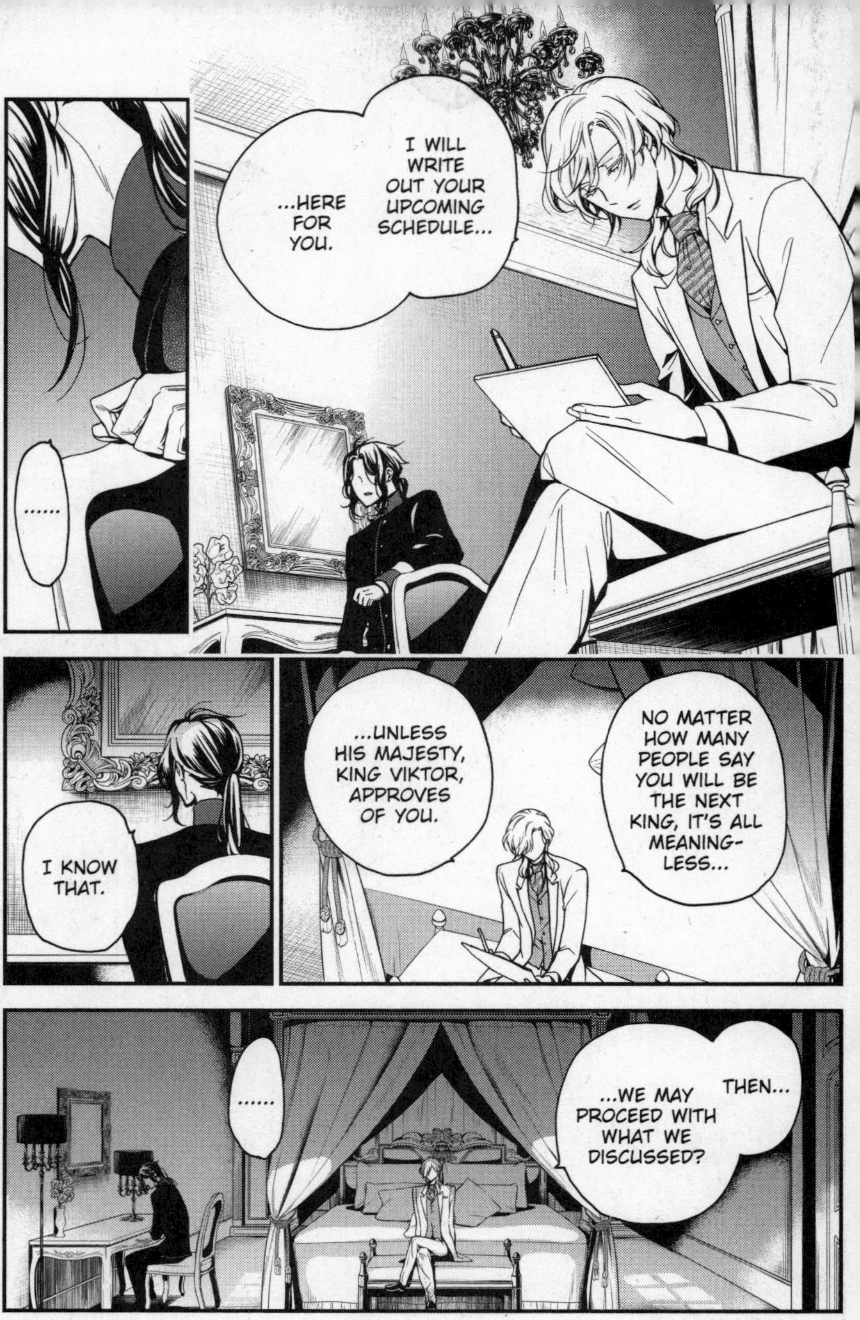
I WILL WRITE OUT YOUR UPCOMING SCHEDULE...
...HERE FOR YOU.
......
NO MATTER HOW MANY PEOPLE SAY YOU WILL BE THE NEXT KING, IT'S ALL MEANING-LESS...
...UNLESS HIS MAJESTY, KING VIKTOR, APPROVES OF YOU.
I KNOW THAT.
THEN...
...WE MAY PROCEED WITH WHAT WE DISCUSSED?
......

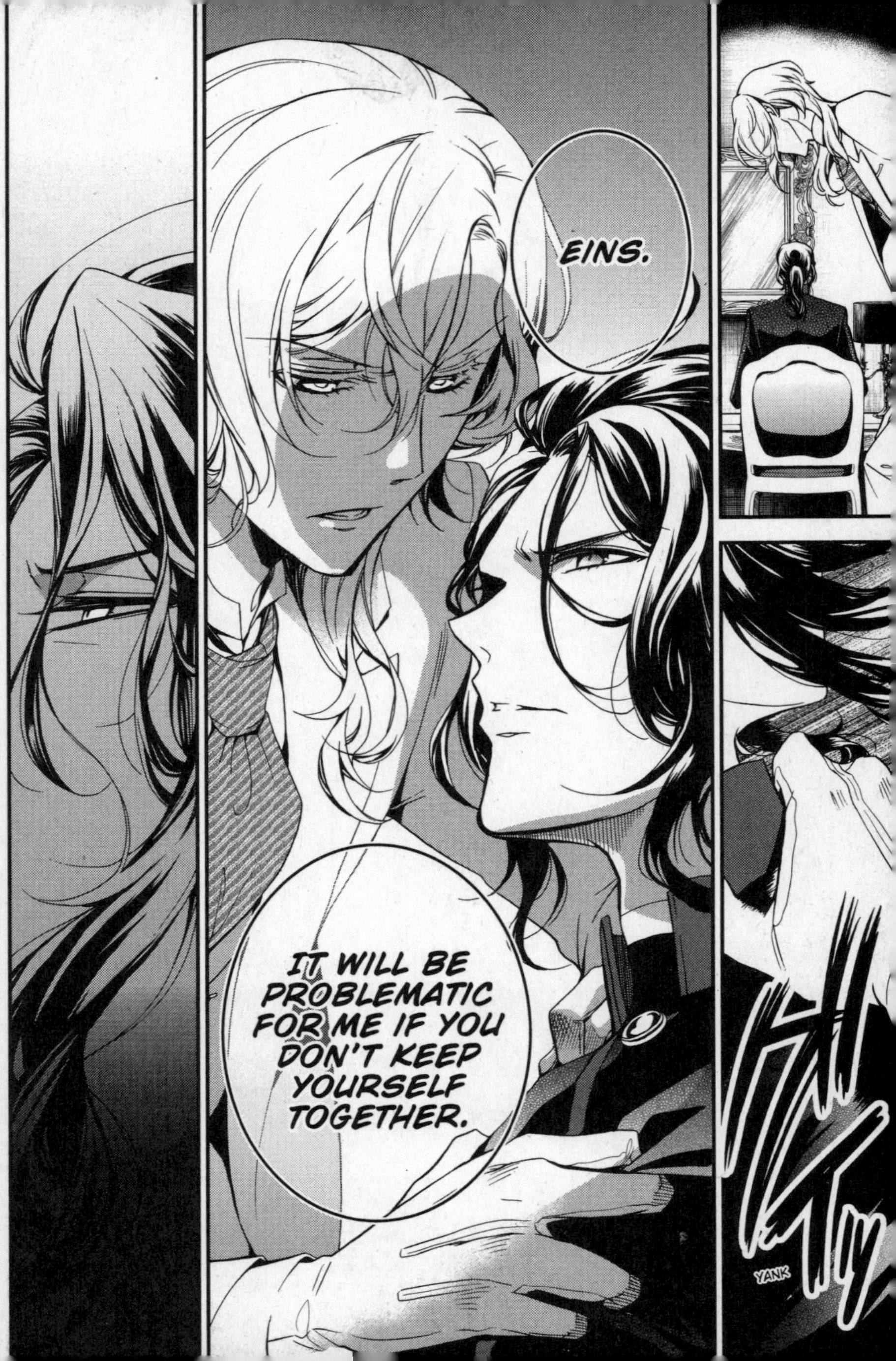
YANK
EINS.
IT WILL BE PROBLEMATIC FOR ME IF YOU DON'T KEEP YOURSELF TOGETHER.

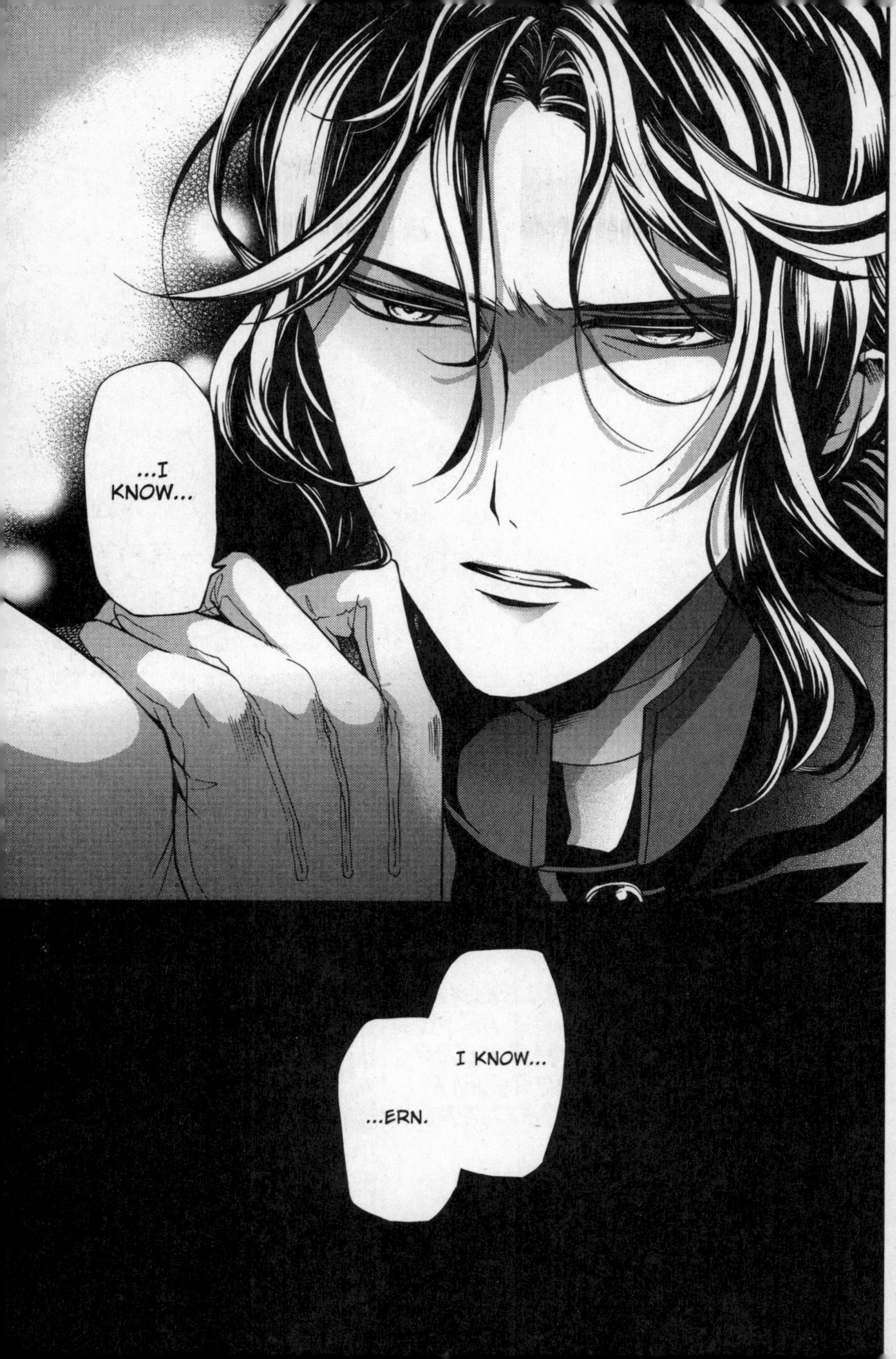
...I KNOW...
I KNOW...
...ERN.

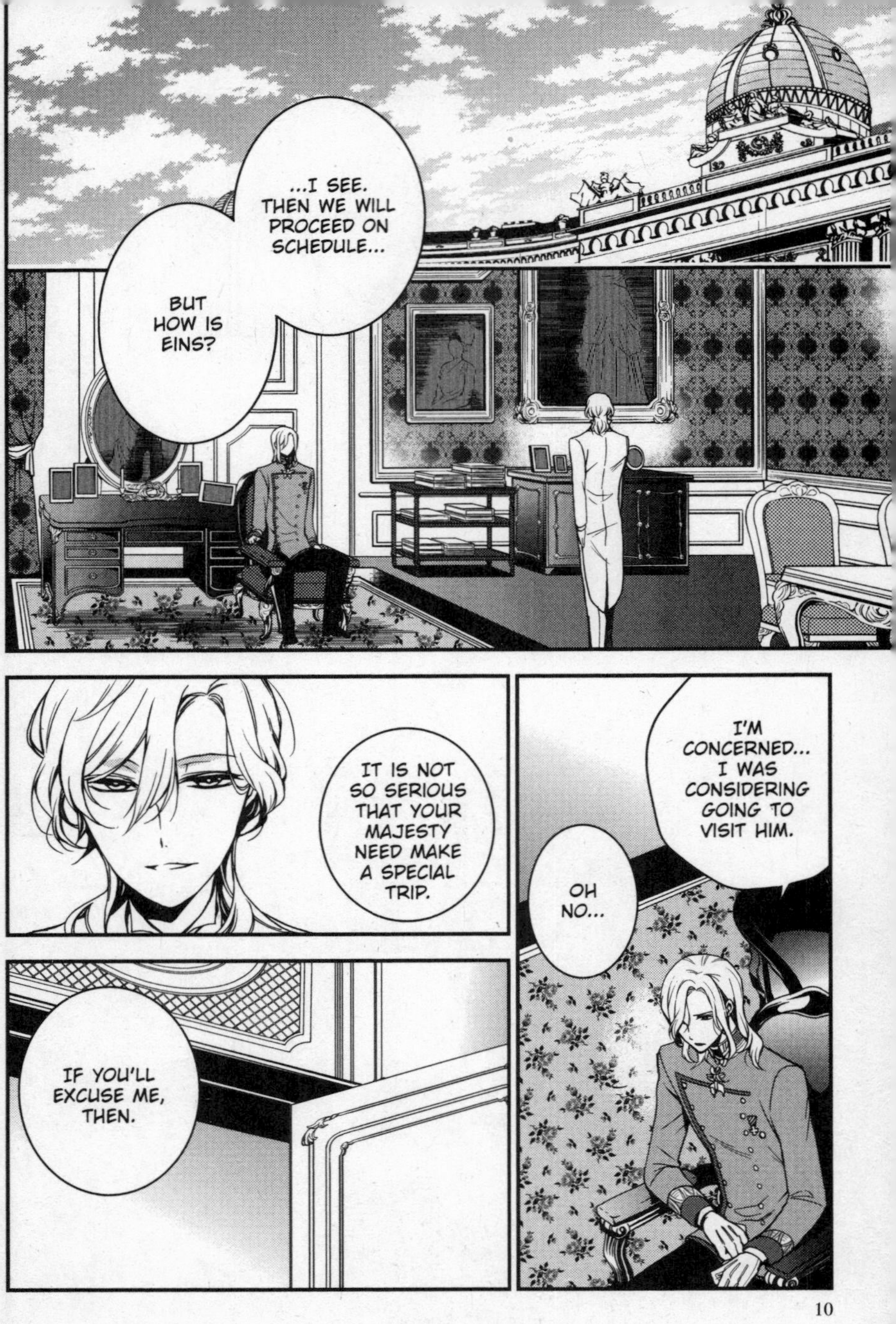
...I SEE. THEN WE WILL PROCEED ON SCHEDULE...
BUT HOW IS EINS?
I'M CONCERNED... I WAS CONSIDERING GOING TO VISIT HIM.
OH NO...
IT IS NOT SO SERIOUS THAT YOUR MAJESTY NEED MAKE A SPECIAL TRIP.
IF YOU'LL EXCUSE ME, THEN.

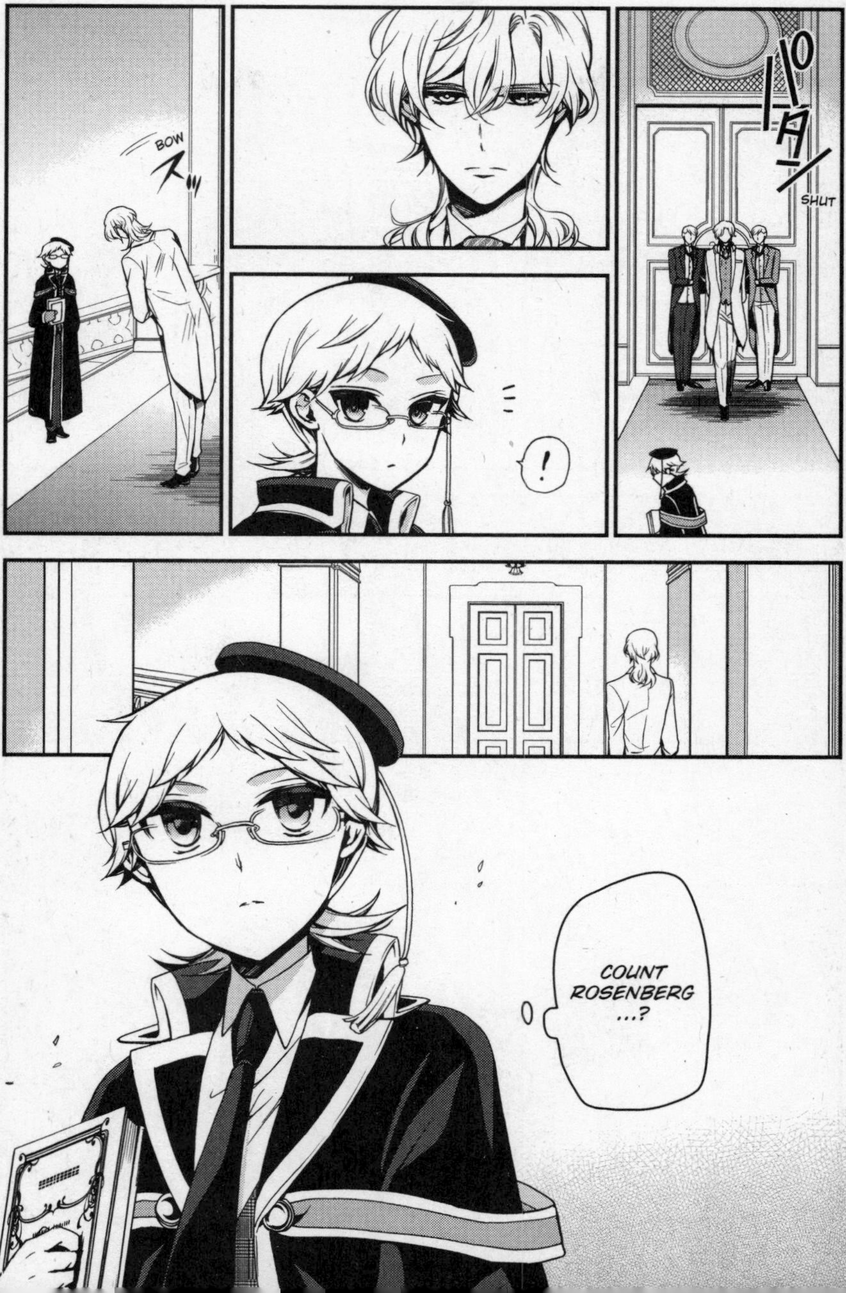
パタン
SHUT
!
BOW
スッ
COUNT ROSENBERG ...?

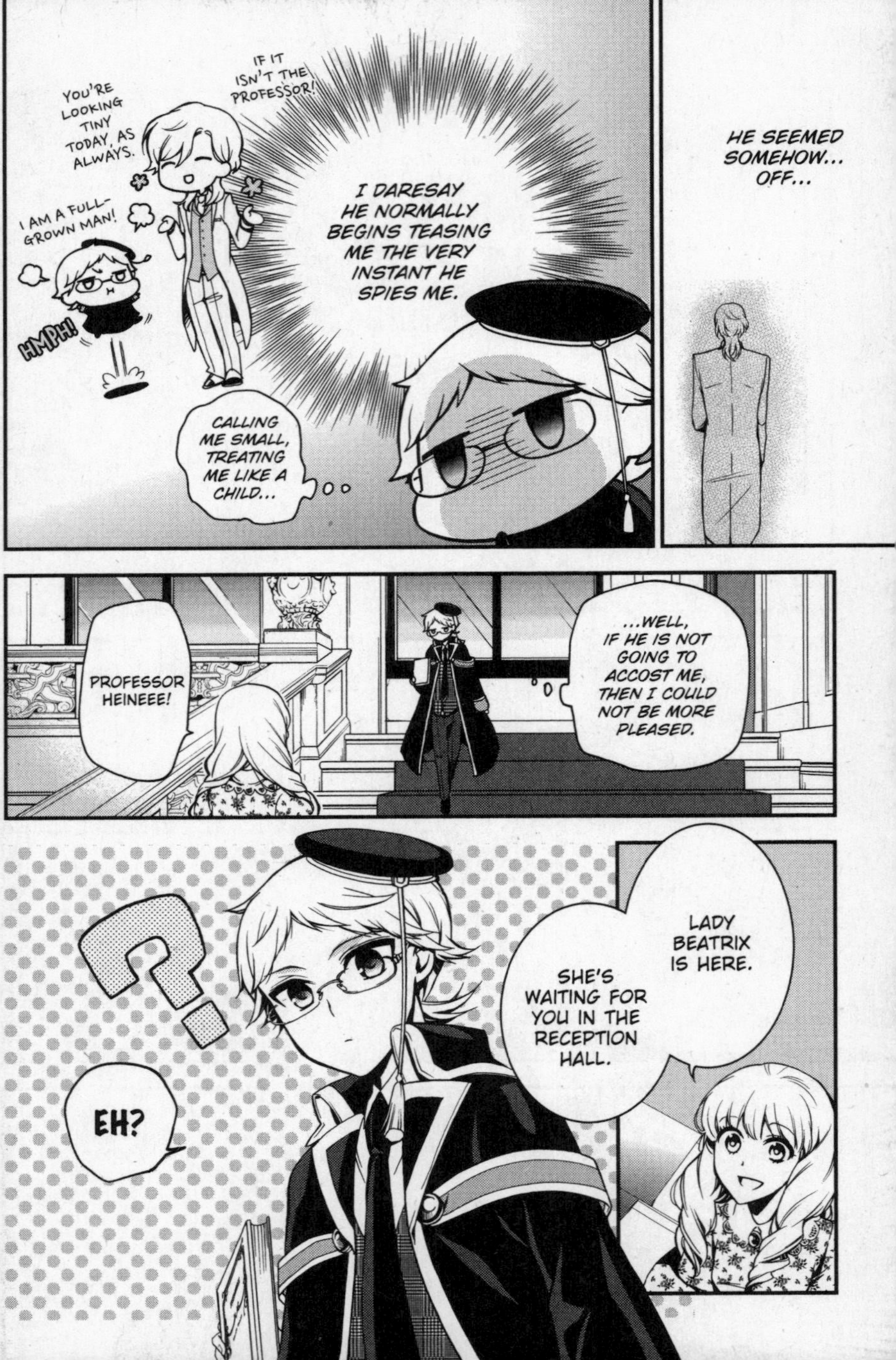
HE SEEMED SOMEHOW... OFF...
IF IT ISN'T THE PROFESSOR!
YOU'RE LOOKING TINY TODAY, AS ALWAYS.
I DARESAY HE NORMALLY BEGINS TEASING ME THE VERY INSTANT HE SPIES ME.
I AM A FULL-GROWN MAN!
HMPH!
CALLING ME SMALL, TREATING ME LIKE A CHILD...
...WELL, IF HE IS NOT GOING TO ACCOST ME, THEN I COULD NOT BE MORE PLEASED.
PROFESSOR HEINEEE!
LADY BEATRIX IS HERE.
SHE'S WAITING FOR YOU IN THE RECEPTION HALL.
EH?

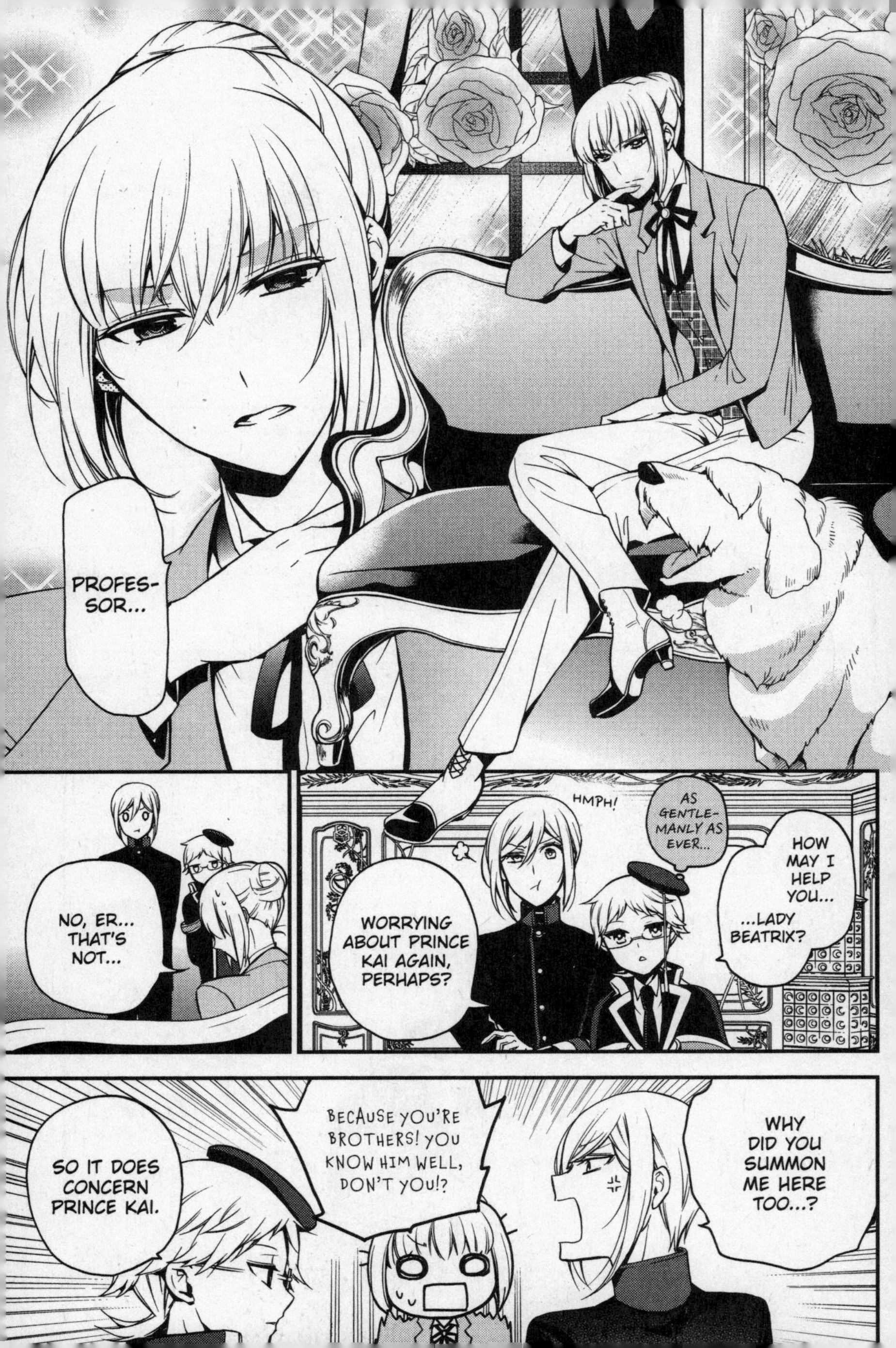
PROFES-SOR...
HOW MAY I HELP YOU...
AS GENTLE-MANLY AS EVER...
HMPH!
...LADY BEATRIX?
WORRYING ABOUT PRINCE KAI AGAIN, PERHAPS?
NO, ER... THAT'S NOT...
WHY DID YOU SUMMON ME HERE TOO...?
BECAUSE YOU'RE BROTHERS! YOU KNOW HIM WELL, DON'T YOU!?
SO IT DOES CONCERN PRINCE KAI.

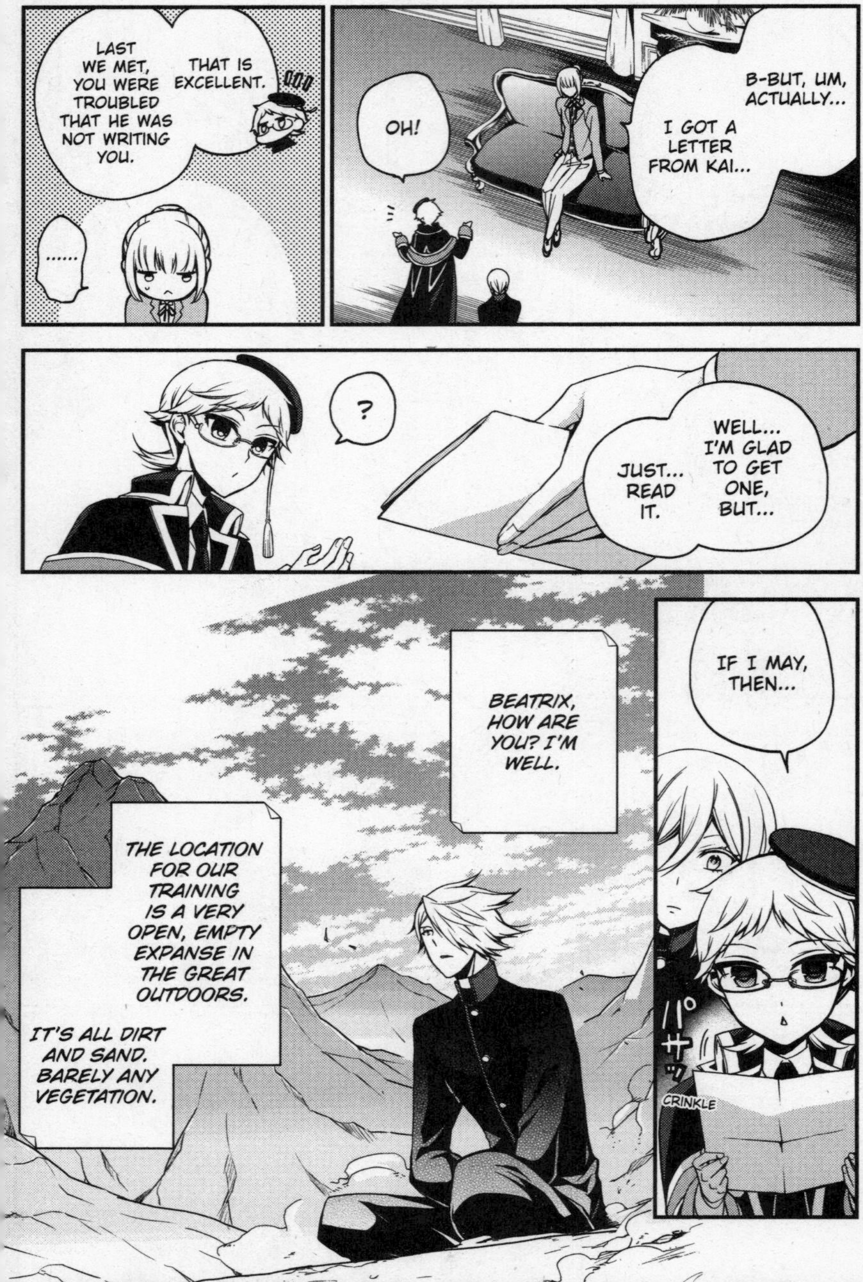
B-BUT, UM, ACTUALLY...
I GOT A LETTER FROM KAI...
OH!
THAT IS EXCELLENT.
LAST WE MET, YOU WERE TROUBLED THAT HE WAS NOT WRITING YOU.
......
WELL... I'M GLAD TO GET ONE, BUT...
JUST... READ IT.
?
IF I MAY, THEN...
CRINKLE
BEATRIX, HOW ARE YOU? I'M WELL.
THE LOCATION FOR OUR TRAINING IS A VERY OPEN, EMPTY EXPANSE IN THE GREAT OUTDOORS.
IT'S ALL DIRT AND SAND. BARELY ANY VEGETATION.

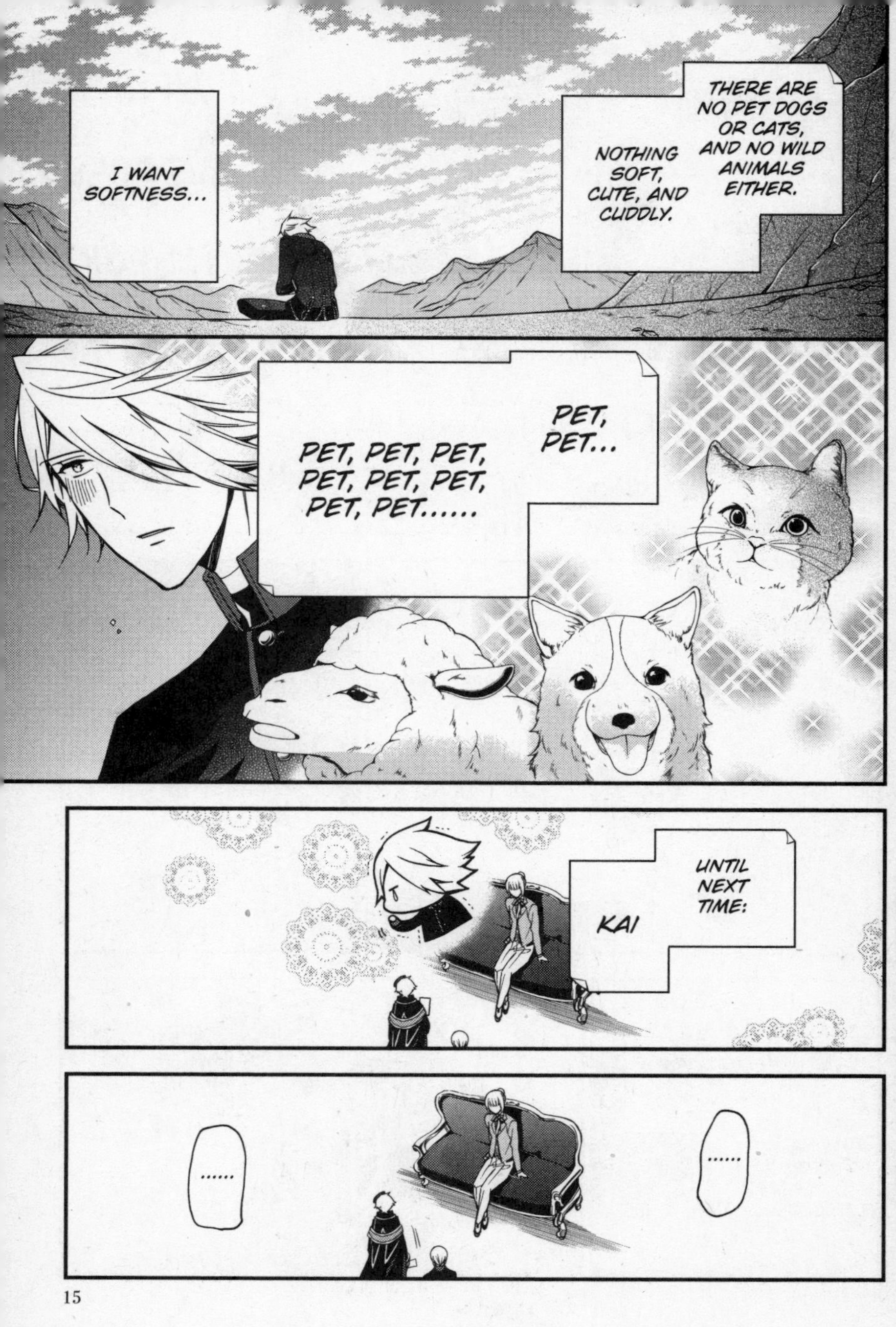
THERE ARE NO PET DOGS OR CATS, AND NO WILD ANIMALS EITHER.
NOTHING SOFT, CUTE, AND CUDDLY.
I WANT SOFTNESS...
PET, PET...
PET, PET, PET, PET, PET, PET, PET, PET......
UNTIL NEXT TIME:
KAI
......
......

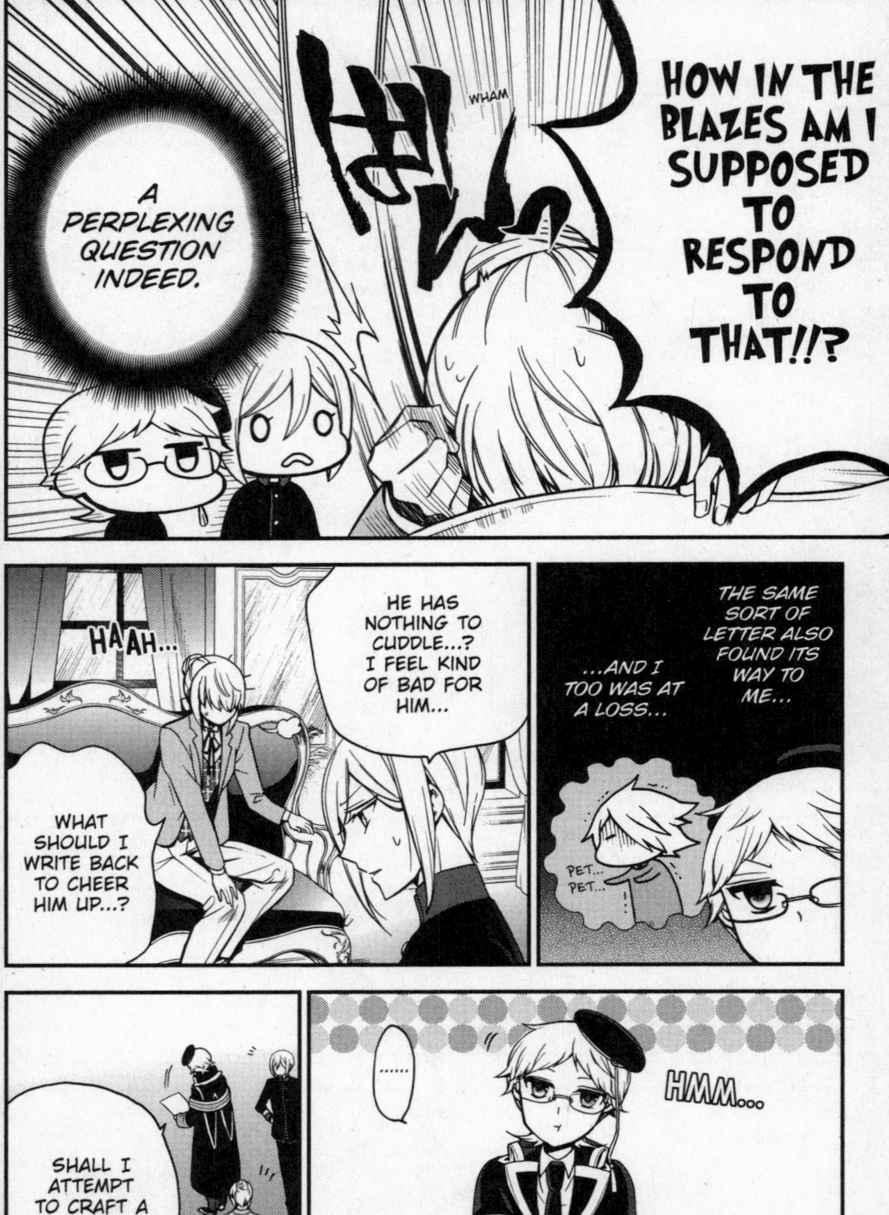
HOW IN THE BLAZES AM I SUPPOSED TO RESPOND TO THAT!!?
WHAM
A PERPLEXING QUESTION INDEED.
THE SAME SORT OF LETTER ALSO FOUND ITS WAY TO ME...
...AND I TOO WAS AT A LOSS...
PET... PET...
HAAH...
HE HAS NOTHING TO CUDDLE...? I FEEL KIND OF BAD FOR HIM...
WHAT SHOULD I WRITE BACK TO CHEER HIM UP...?
HMM...
......
SHALL I ATTEMPT TO CRAFT A RESPONSE?

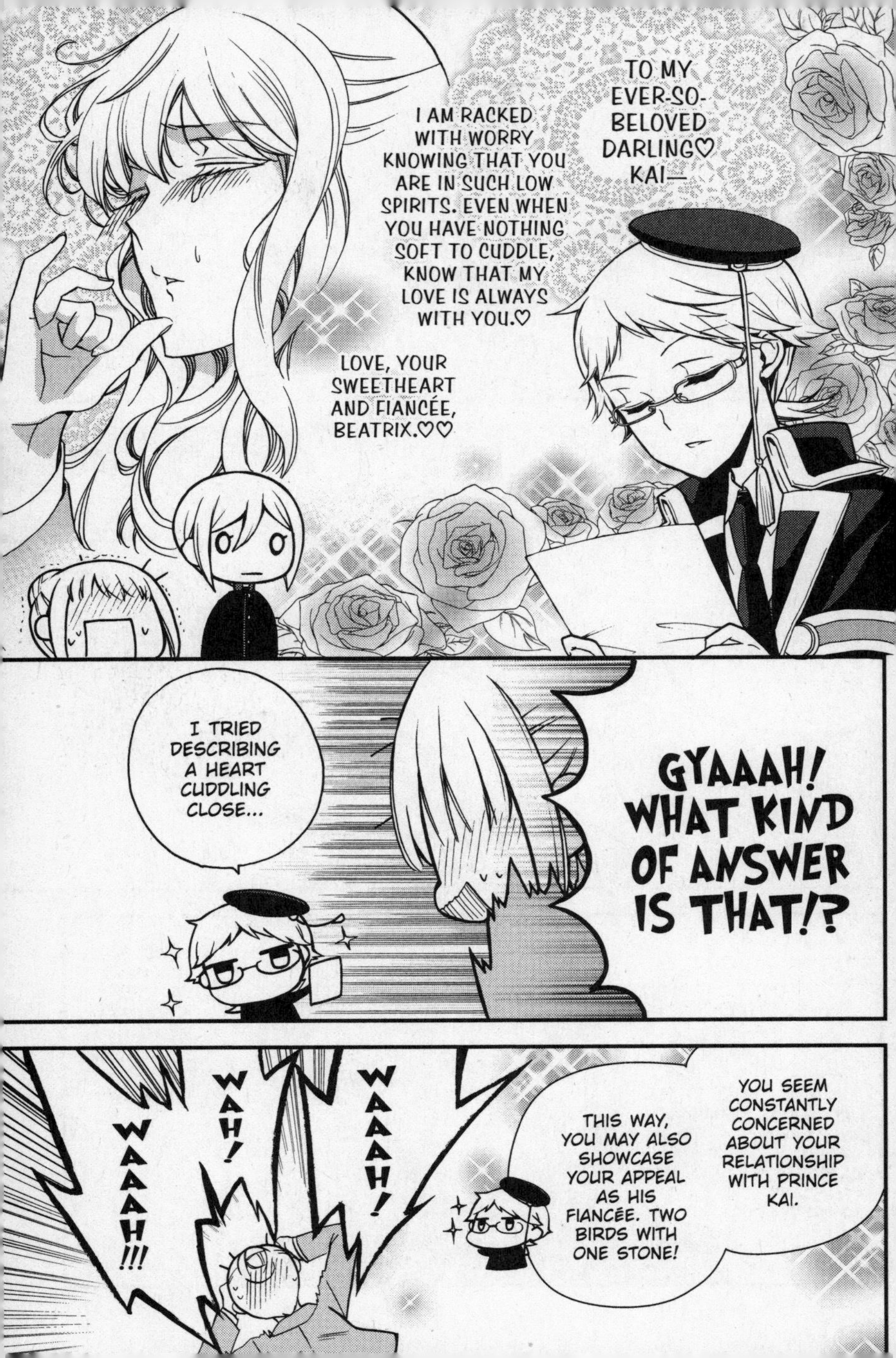
TO MY EVER-SO-BELOVED DARLING♡ KAI—
I AM RACKED WITH WORRY KNOWING THAT YOU ARE IN SUCH LOW SPIRITS. EVEN WHEN YOU HAVE NOTHING SOFT TO CUDDLE, KNOW THAT MY LOVE IS ALWAYS WITH YOU.♡
LOVE, YOUR SWEETHEART AND FIANCÉE, BEATRIX.♡♡
GYAAAH! WHAT KIND OF ANSWER IS THAT!?
I TRIED DESCRIBING A HEART CUDDLING CLOSE...
YOU SEEM CONSTANTLY CONCERNED ABOUT YOUR RELATIONSHIP WITH PRINCE KAI.
THIS WAY, YOU MAY ALSO SHOWCASE YOUR APPEAL AS HIS FIANCÉE. TWO BIRDS WITH ONE STONE!
WAAAH!
WAH!
WAAAH!!!

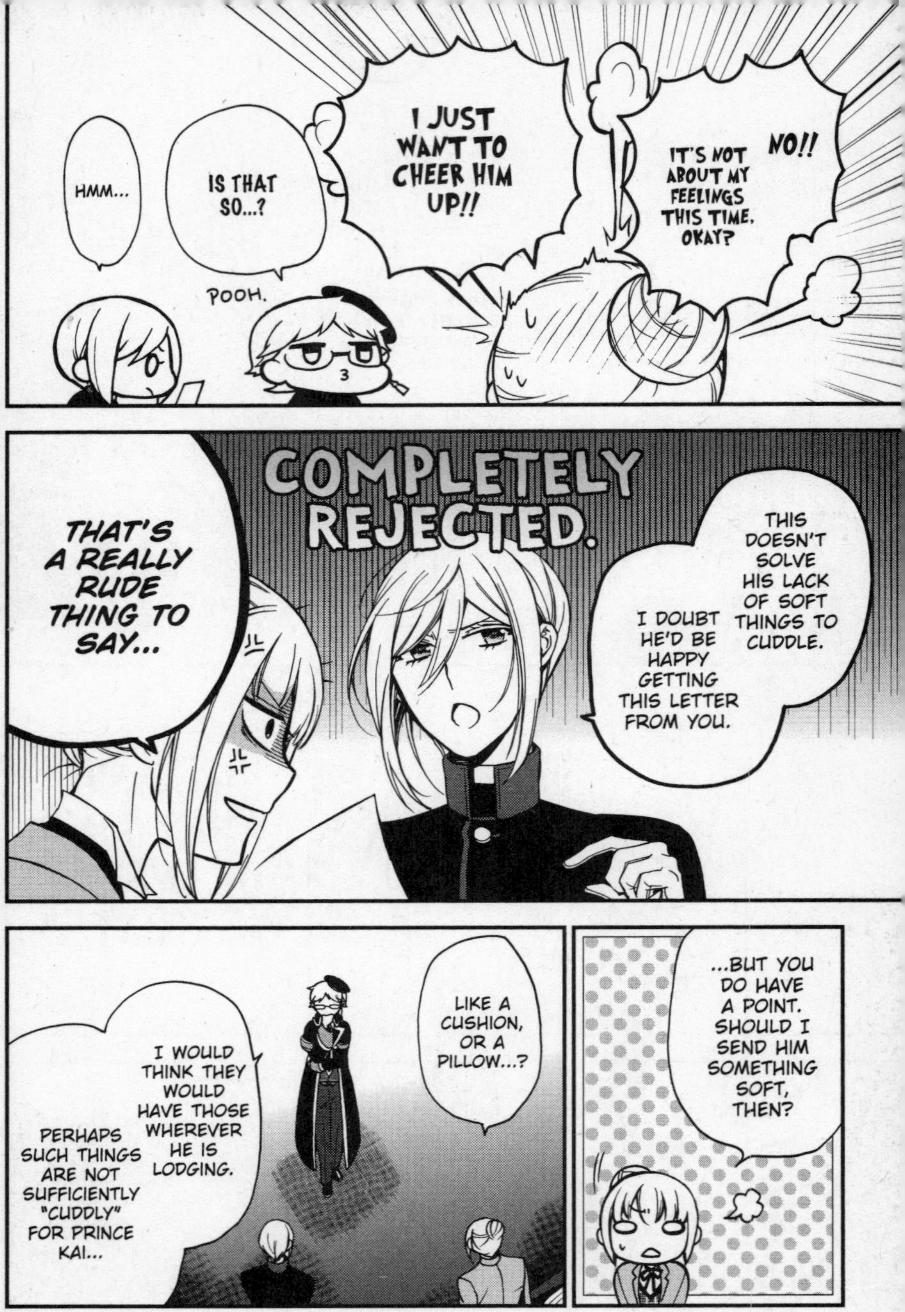
NO!!
IT'S NOT ABOUT MY FEELINGS THIS TIME, OKAY?
I JUST WANT TO CHEER HIM UP!!
IS THAT SO...?
POOH.
HMM...
COMPLETELY REJECTED.
THIS DOESN'T SOLVE HIS LACK OF SOFT THINGS TO CUDDLE.
I DOUBT HE'D BE HAPPY GETTING THIS LETTER FROM YOU.
THAT'S A REALLY RUDE THING TO SAY...
...BUT YOU DO HAVE A POINT. SHOULD I SEND HIM SOMETHING SOFT, THEN?
LIKE A CUSHION, OR A PILLOW...?
I WOULD THINK THEY WOULD HAVE THOSE WHEREVER HE IS LODGING.
PERHAPS SUCH THINGS ARE NOT SUFFICIENTLY "CUDDLY" FOR PRINCE KAI...

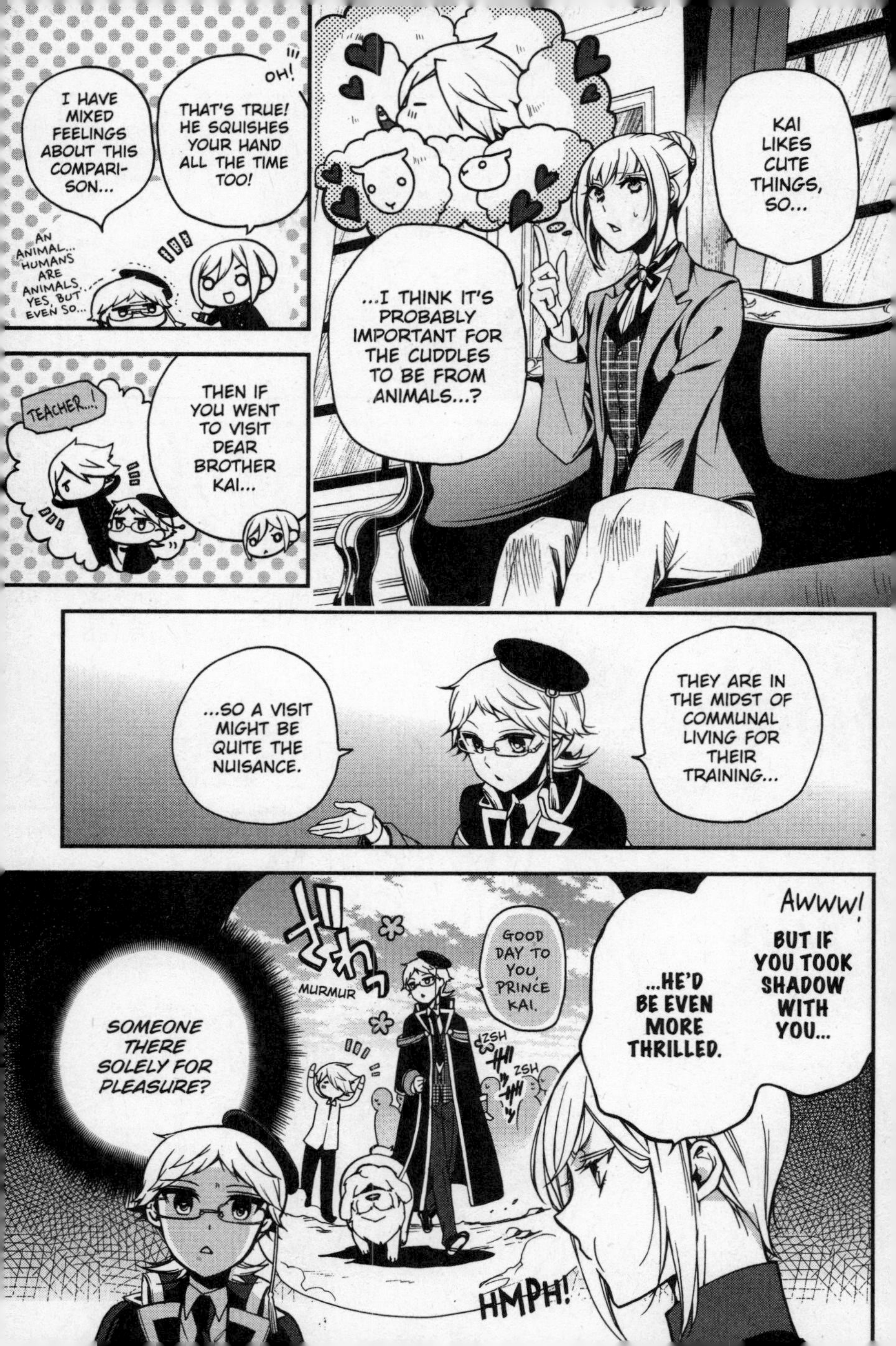
KAI LIKES CUTE THINGS, SO...
...I THINK IT'S PROBABLY IMPORTANT FOR THE CUDDLES TO BE FROM ANIMALS...?
OH!
THAT'S TRUE! HE SQUISHES YOUR HAND ALL THE TIME TOO!
I HAVE MIXED FEELINGS ABOUT THIS COMPARI-SON...
AN ANIMAL... HUMANS ARE ANIMALS, YES, BUT EVEN SO...
THEN IF YOU WENT TO VISIT DEAR BROTHER KAI...
TEACHER...!
THEY ARE IN THE MIDST OF COMMUNAL LIVING FOR THEIR TRAINING...
...SO A VISIT MIGHT BE QUITE THE NUISANCE.
AWWW!
BUT IF YOU TOOK SHADOW WITH YOU...
...HE'D BE EVEN MORE THRILLED.
GOOD DAY TO YOU, PRINCE KAI.
ZSH
ZSH
MURMUR
SOMEONE THERE SOLELY FOR PLEASURE?
HMPH!

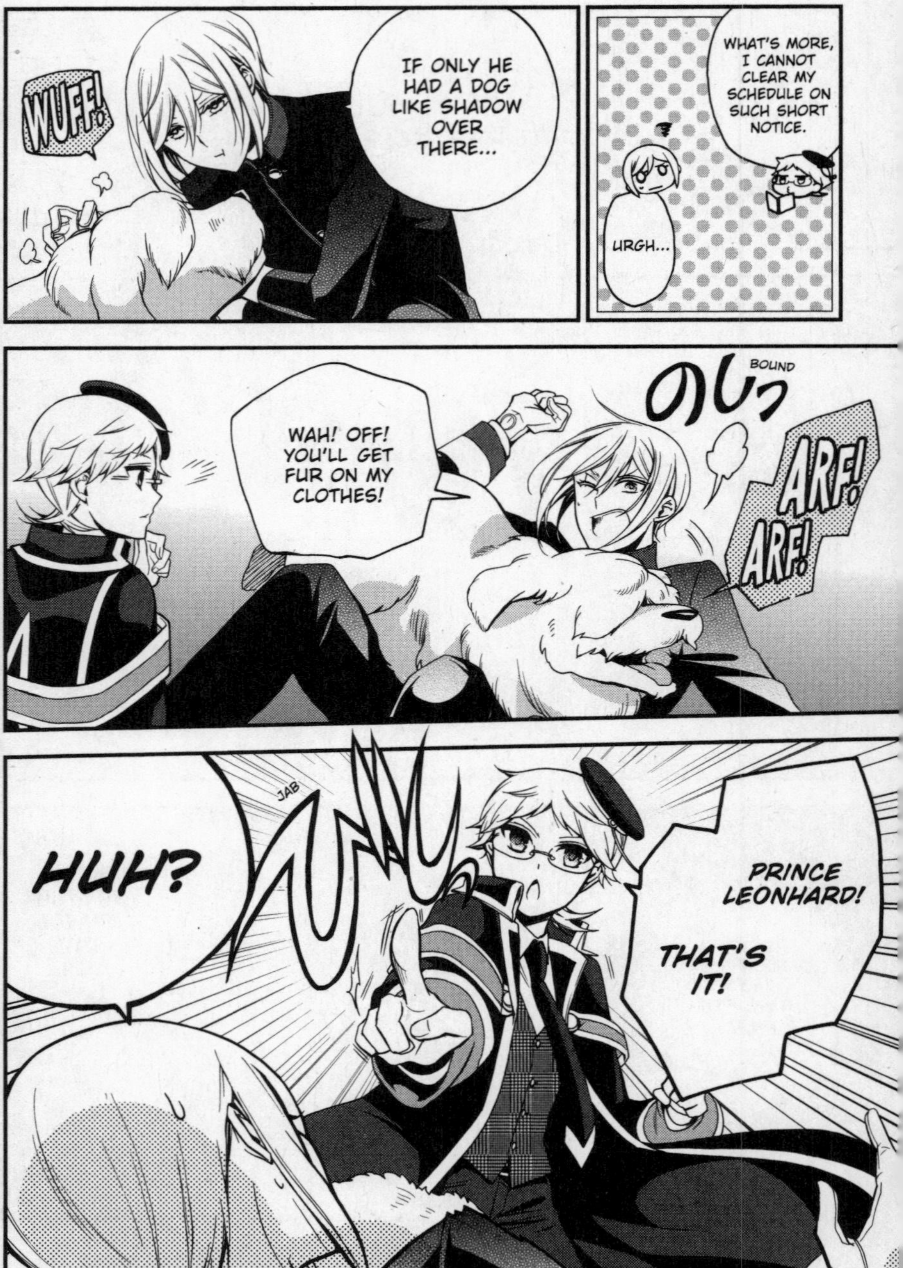
WHAT'S MORE, I CANNOT CLEAR MY SCHEDULE ON SUCH SHORT NOTICE.
URGH...
IF ONLY HE HAD A DOG LIKE SHADOW OVER THERE...
WUFF!
のしっ
BOUND
ARF! ARF!
WAH! OFF! YOU'LL GET FUR ON MY CLOTHES!
PRINCE LEONHARD!
THAT'S IT!
JAB
HUH?

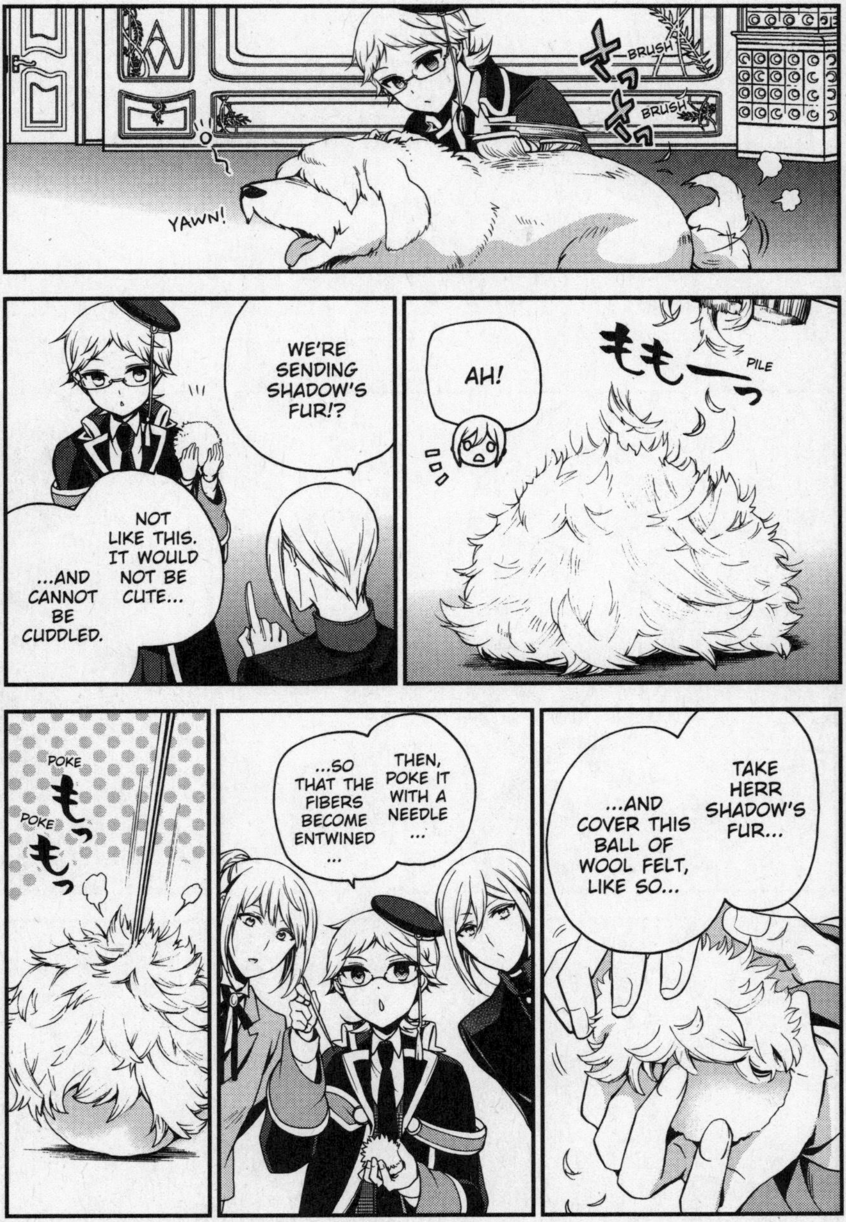
BRUSH
BRUSH
YAWN!
AH!
PILE
WE'RE SENDING SHADOW'S FUR!?
NOT LIKE THIS. IT WOULD NOT BE CUTE...
...AND CANNOT BE CUDDLED.
TAKE HERR SHADOW'S FUR...
...AND COVER THIS BALL OF WOOL FELT, LIKE SO...
THEN, POKE IT WITH A NEEDLE ...
...SO THAT THE FIBERS BECOME ENTWINED ...
POKE
POKE

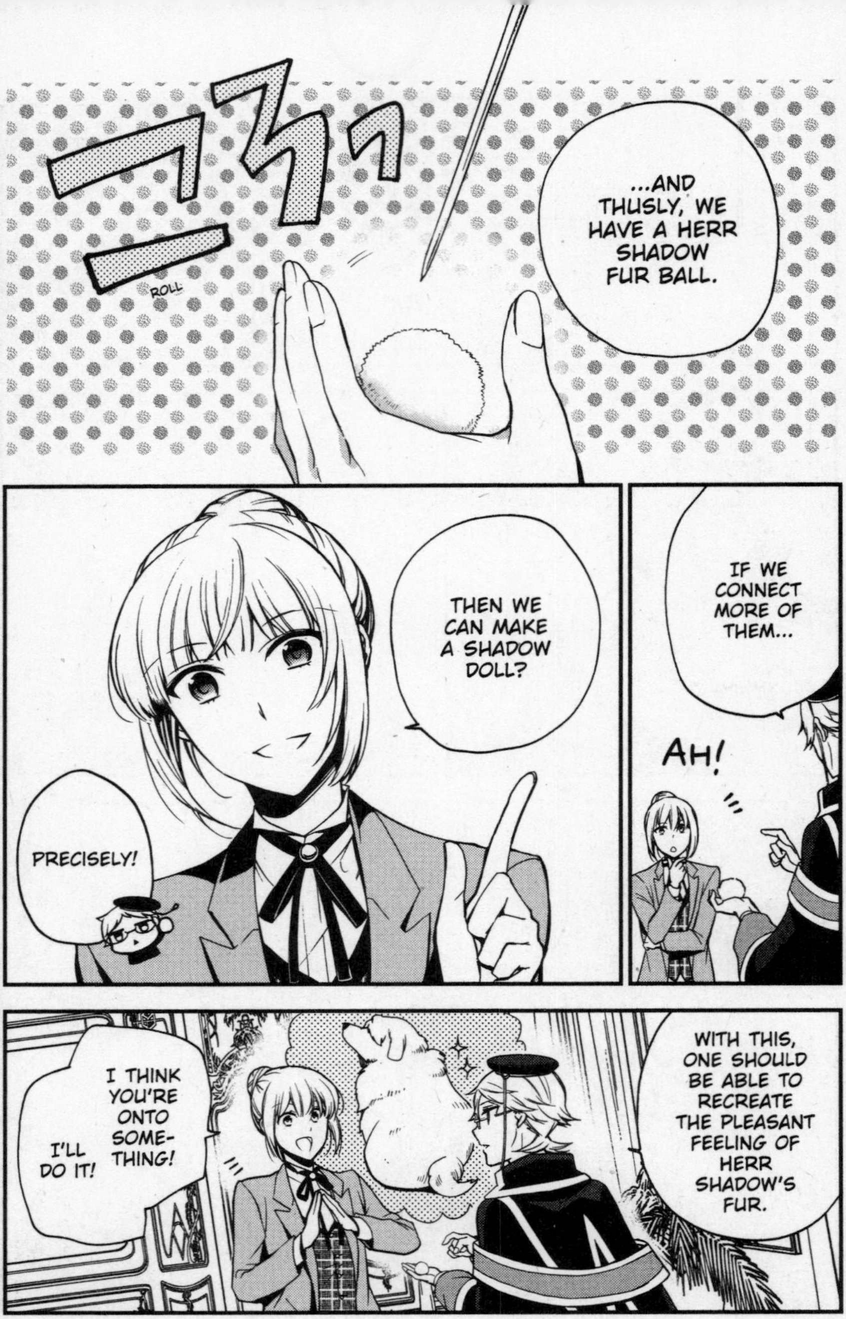
...AND THUSLY, WE HAVE A HERR SHADOW FUR BALL.
ROLL
IF WE CONNECT MORE OF THEM...
AH!
THEN WE CAN MAKE A SHADOW DOLL?
PRECISELY!
WITH THIS, ONE SHOULD BE ABLE TO RECREATE THE PLEASANT FEELING OF HERR SHADOW'S FUR.
I THINK YOU'RE ONTO SOMETHING!
I'LL DO IT!

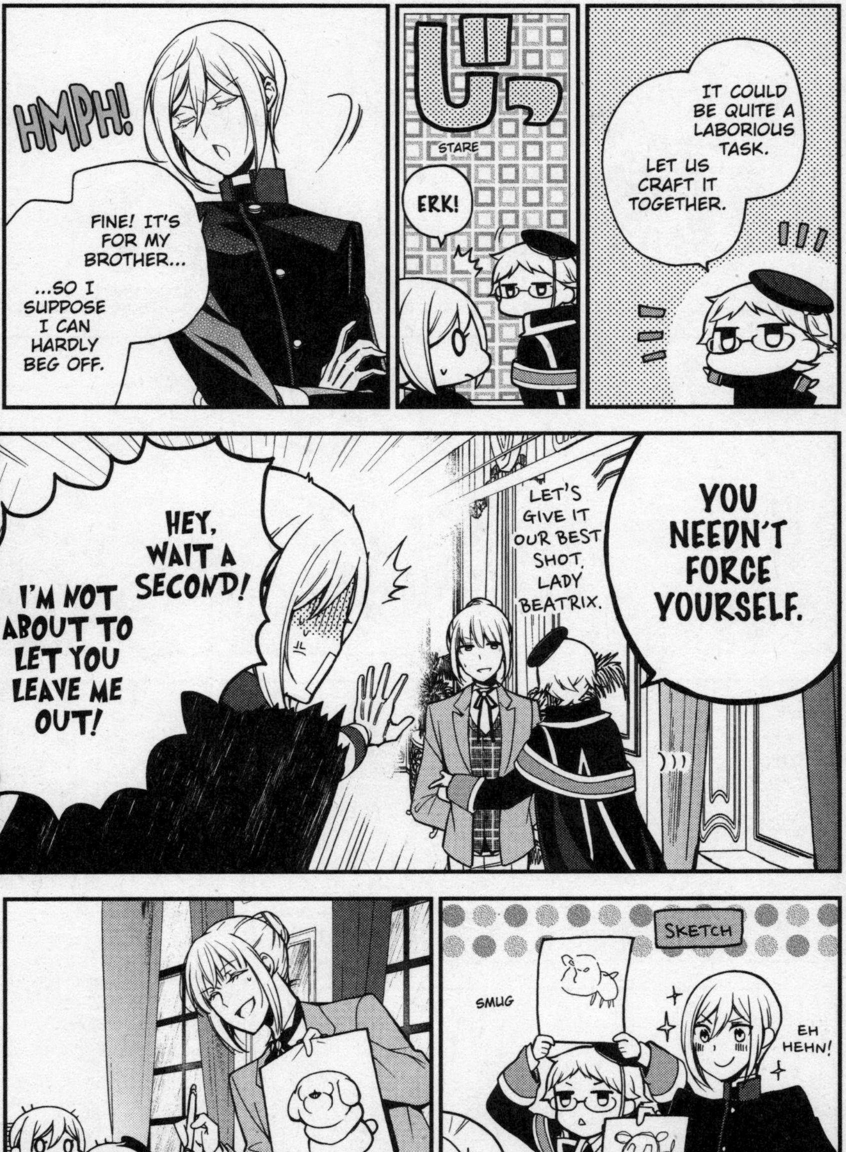
IT COULD BE QUITE A LABORIOUS TASK.
LET US CRAFT IT TOGETHER.
じっ
STARE
ERK!
HMPH!
FINE! IT'S FOR MY BROTHER...
...SO I SUPPOSE I CAN HARDLY BEG OFF.
YOU NEEDN'T FORCE YOURSELF.
LET'S GIVE IT OUR BEST SHOT, LADY BEATRIX.
HEY, WAIT A SECOND!
I'M NOT ABOUT TO LET YOU LEAVE ME OUT!
SKETCH
EH HEHN!
SMUG

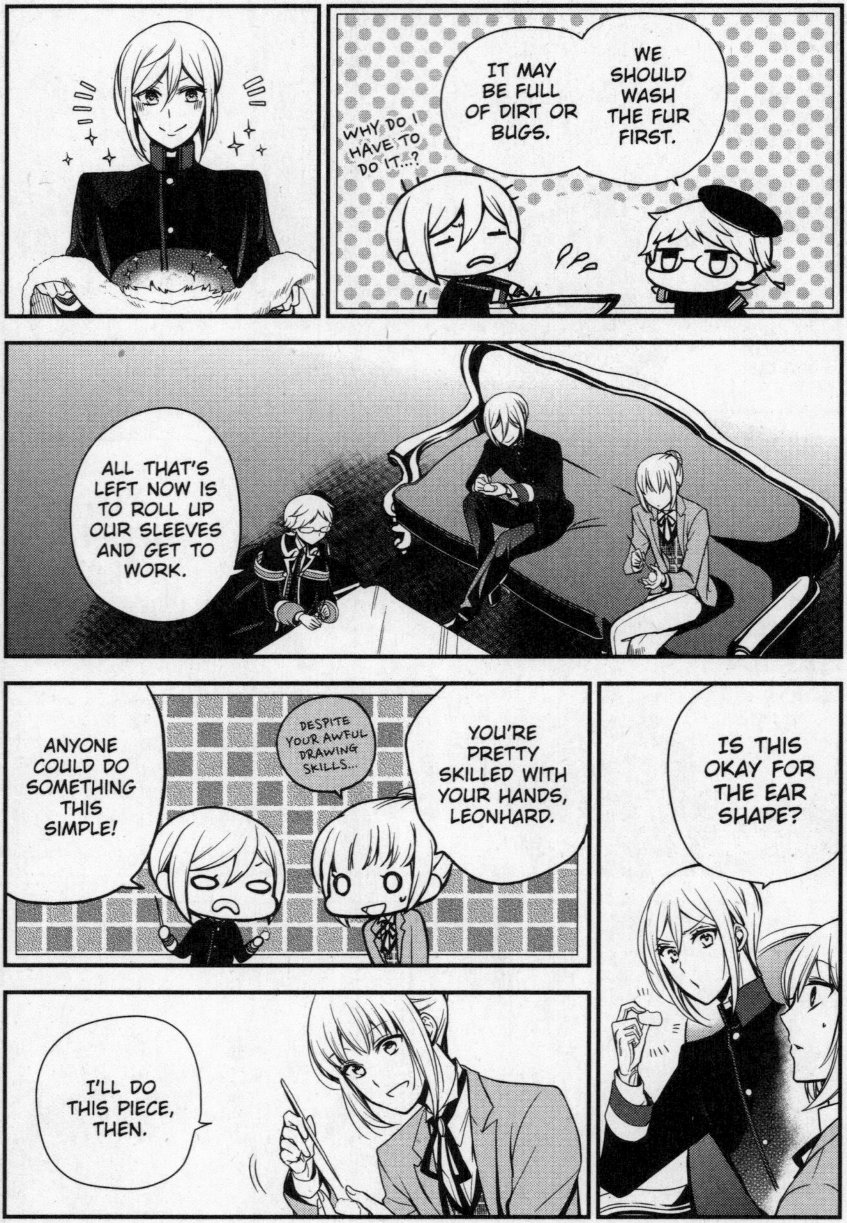
WE SHOULD WASH THE FUR FIRST.
IT MAY BE FULL OF DIRT OR BUGS.
WHY DO I HAVE TO DO IT...?
ALL THAT'S LEFT NOW IS TO ROLL UP OUR SLEEVES AND GET TO WORK.
IS THIS OKAY FOR THE EAR SHAPE?
YOU'RE PRETTY SKILLED WITH YOUR HANDS, LEONHARD.
DESPITE YOUR AWFUL DRAWING SKILLS...
ANYONE COULD DO SOMETHING THIS SIMPLE!
I'LL DO THIS PIECE, THEN.

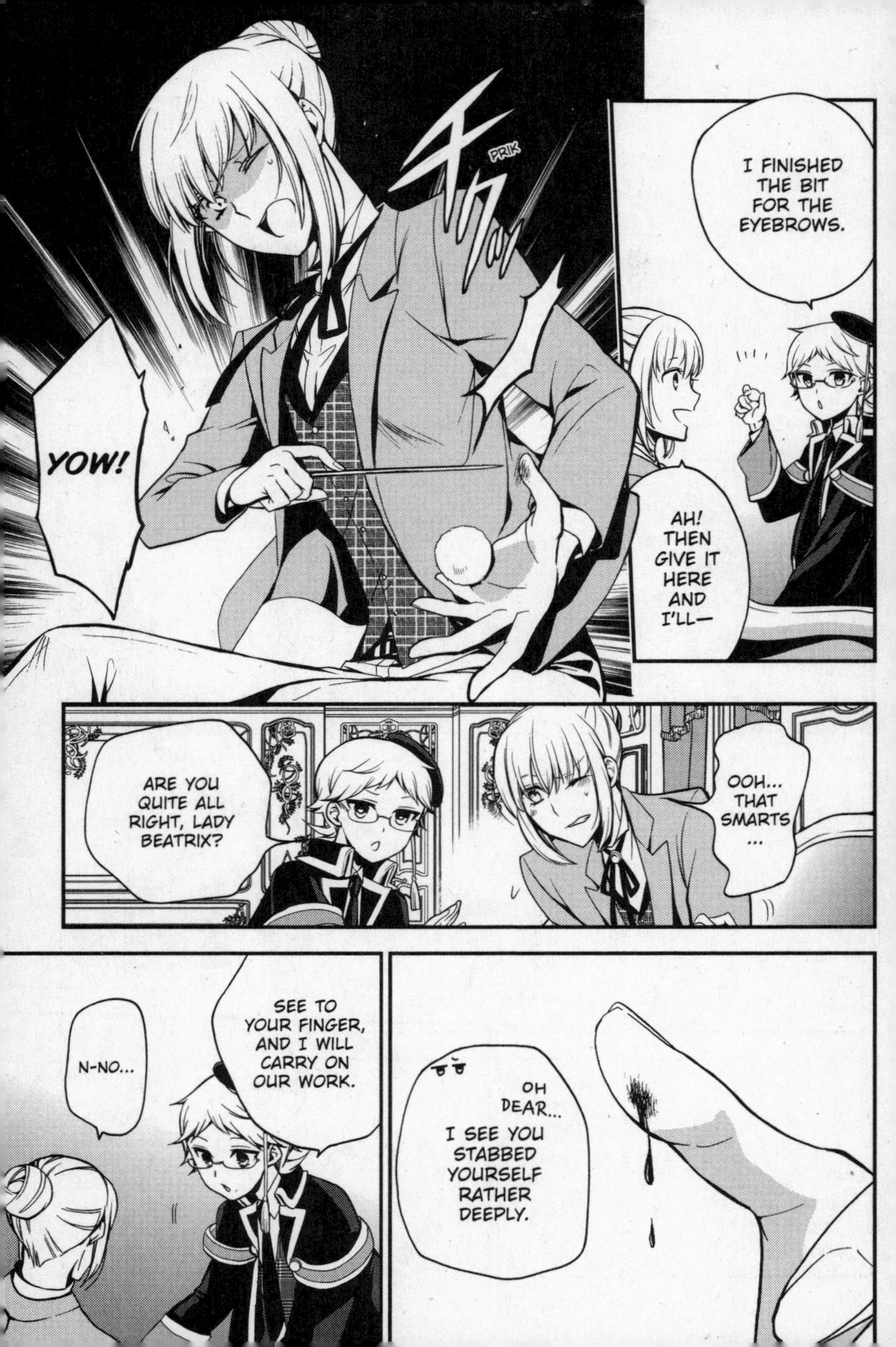
I FINISHED THE BIT FOR THE EYEBROWS.
AH! THEN GIVE IT HERE AND I'LL—
チクッ
PRIK
YOW!
OOH... THAT SMARTS ...
ARE YOU QUITE ALL RIGHT, LADY BEATRIX?
OH DEAR... I SEE YOU STABBED YOURSELF RATHER DEEPLY.
SEE TO YOUR FINGER, AND I WILL CARRY ON OUR WORK.
N-NO...

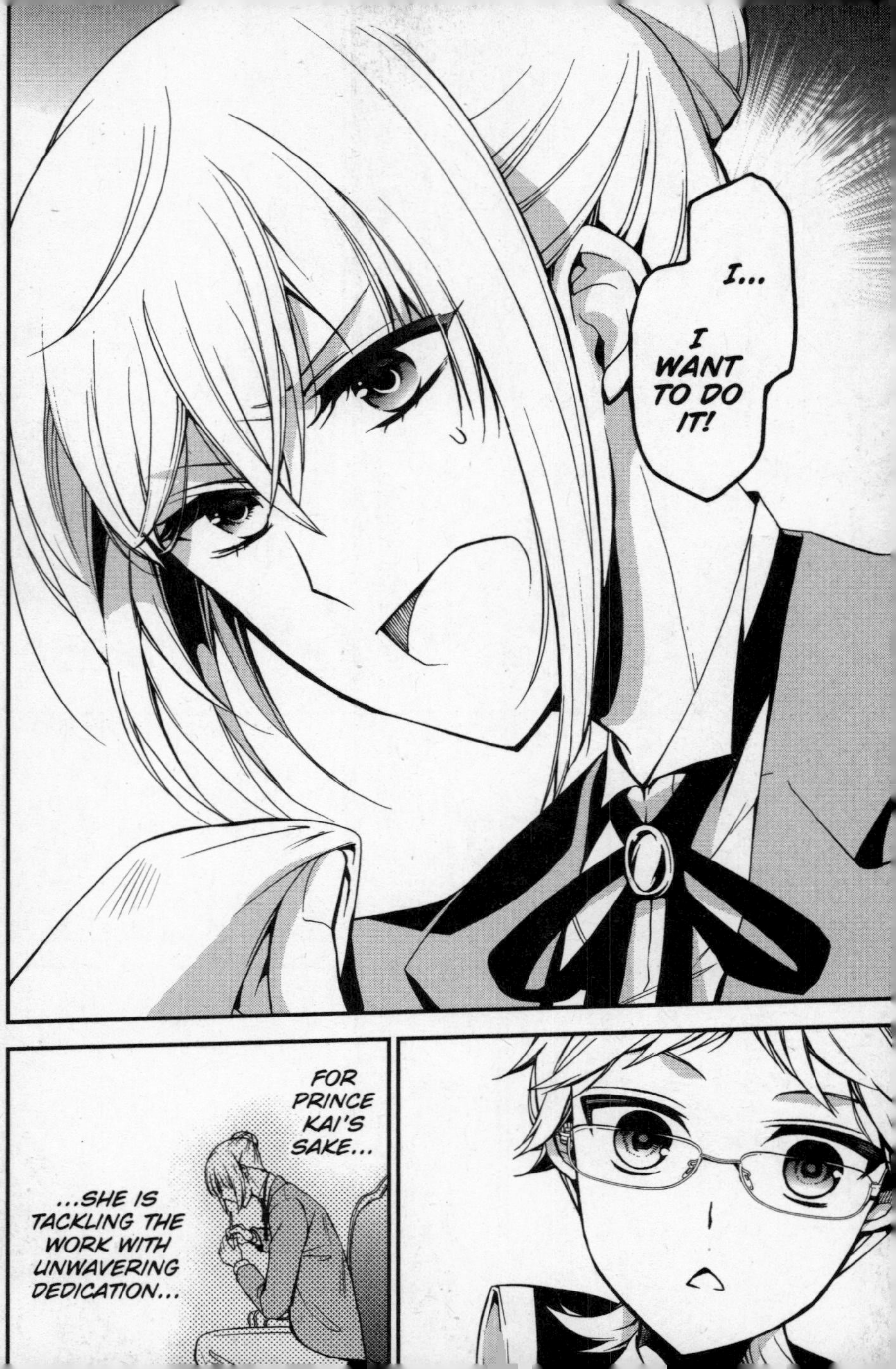
I...
I WANT TO DO IT!
FOR PRINCE KAI'S SAKE...
...SHE IS TACKLING THE WORK WITH UNWAVERING DEDICATION...

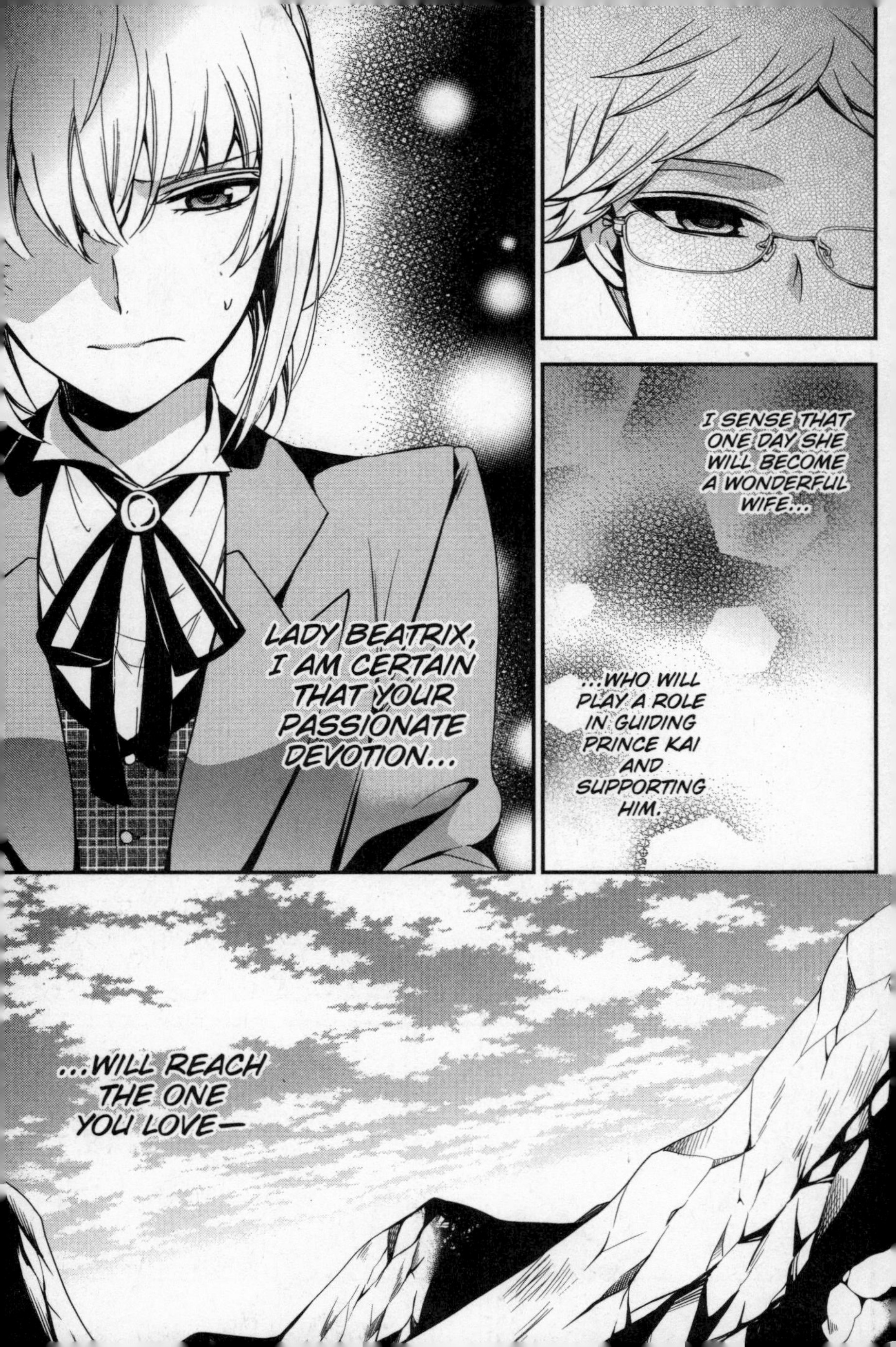
I SENSE THAT ONE DAY SHE WILL BECOME A WONDERFUL WIFE...
...WHO WILL PLAY A ROLE IN GUIDING PRINCE KAI AND SUPPORTING HIM.
LADY BEATRIX, I AM CERTAIN THAT YOUR PASSIONATE DEVOTION...
...WILL REACH THE ONE YOU LOVE—

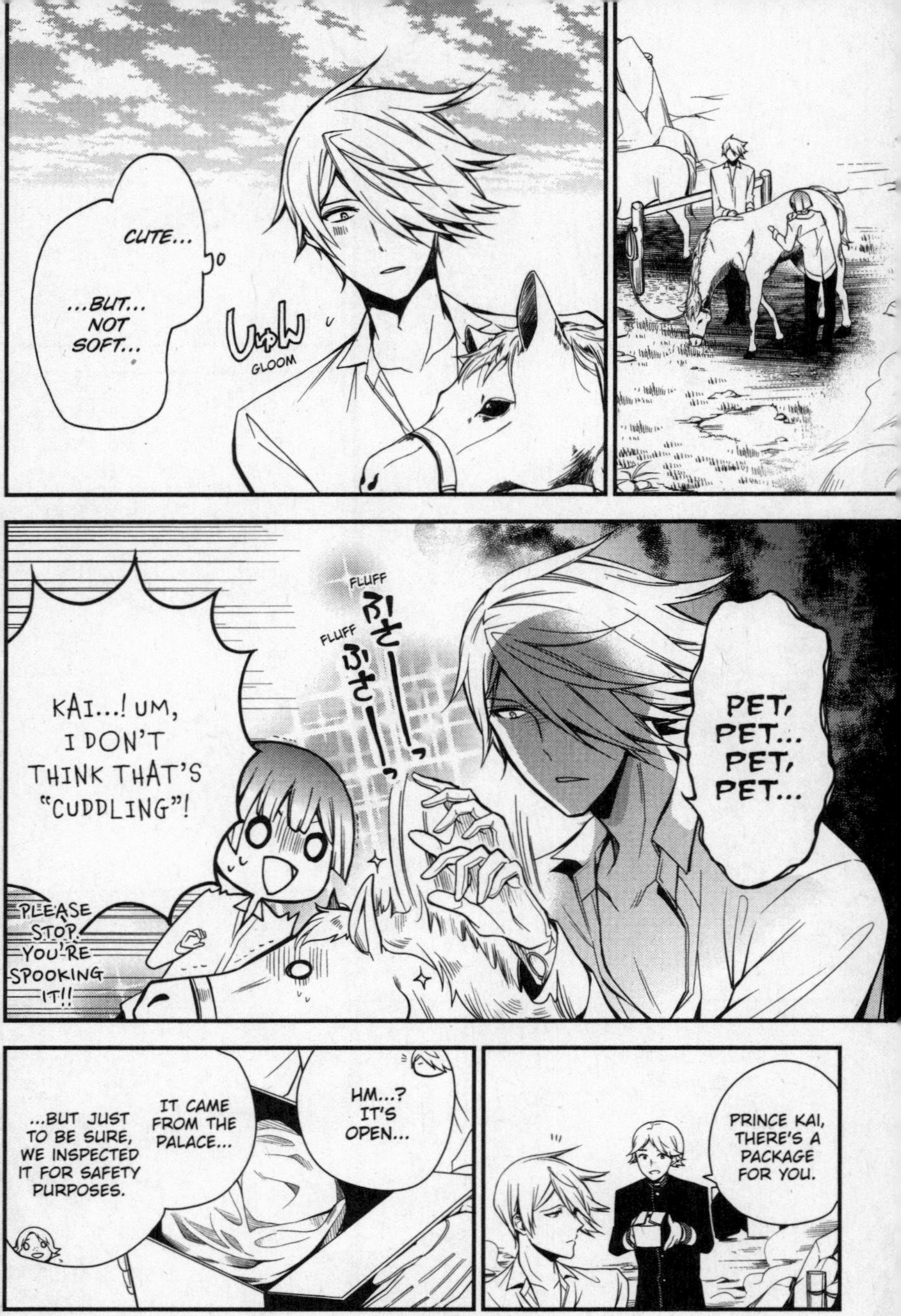
CUTE...
...BUT... NOT SOFT...
しゅん
GLOOM
PET, PET... PET, PET...
ふさーっ
FLUFF
ふさーっ
FLUFF
KAI...! UM, I DON'T THINK THAT'S "CUDDLING"!
PLEASE STOP. YOU'RE SPOOKING IT!!
PRINCE KAI, THERE'S A PACKAGE FOR YOU.
HM...? IT'S OPEN...
IT CAME FROM THE PALACE...
...BUT JUST TO BE SURE, WE INSPECTED IT FOR SAFETY PURPOSES.

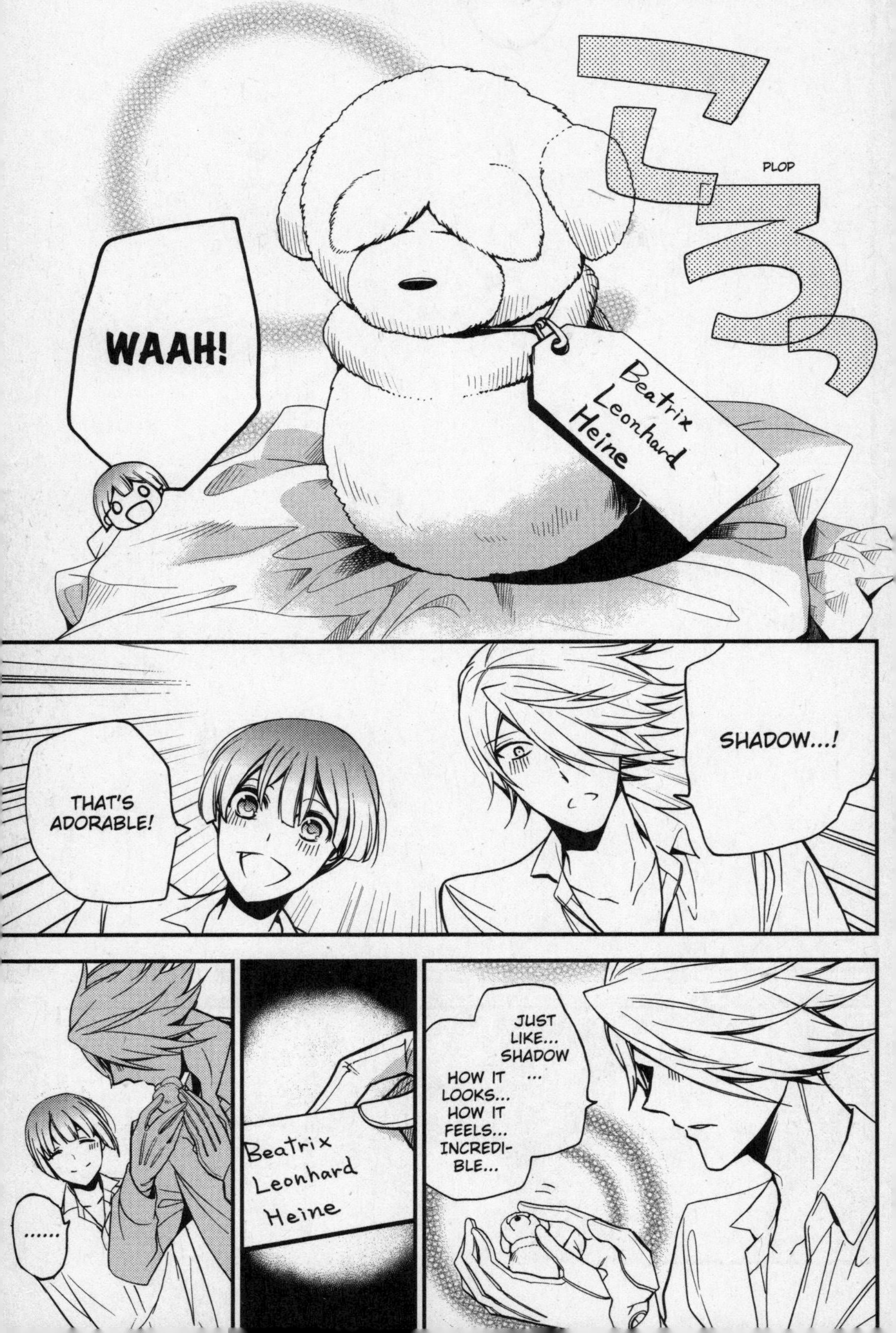
PLOP
Beatrix Leonhard Heine
WAAH!
SHADOW...!
THAT'S ADORABLE!
JUST LIKE... SHADOW ...
HOW IT LOOKS... HOW IT FEELS... INCREDIBLE...
Beatrix Leonhard Heine
......

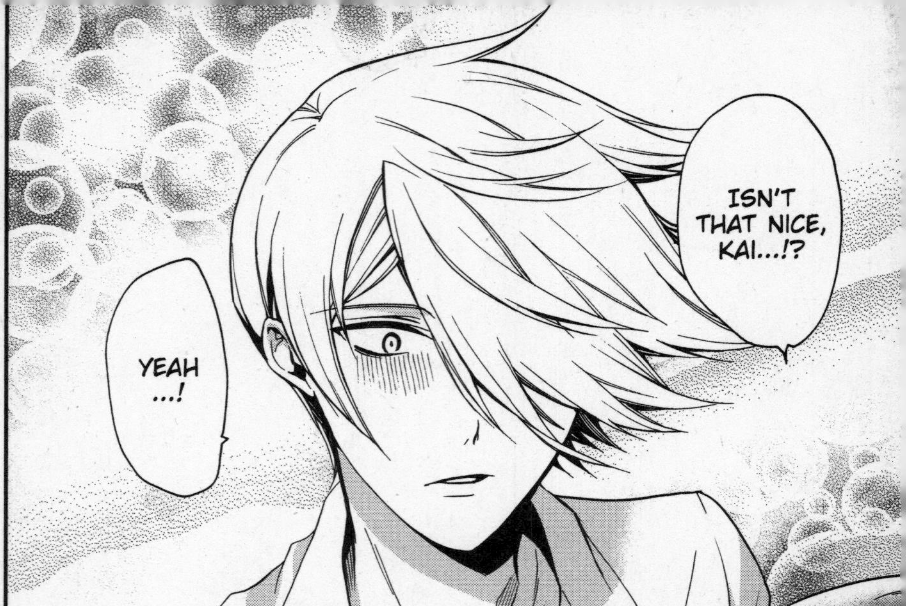
ISN'T THAT NICE, KAI...!?
YEAH...!
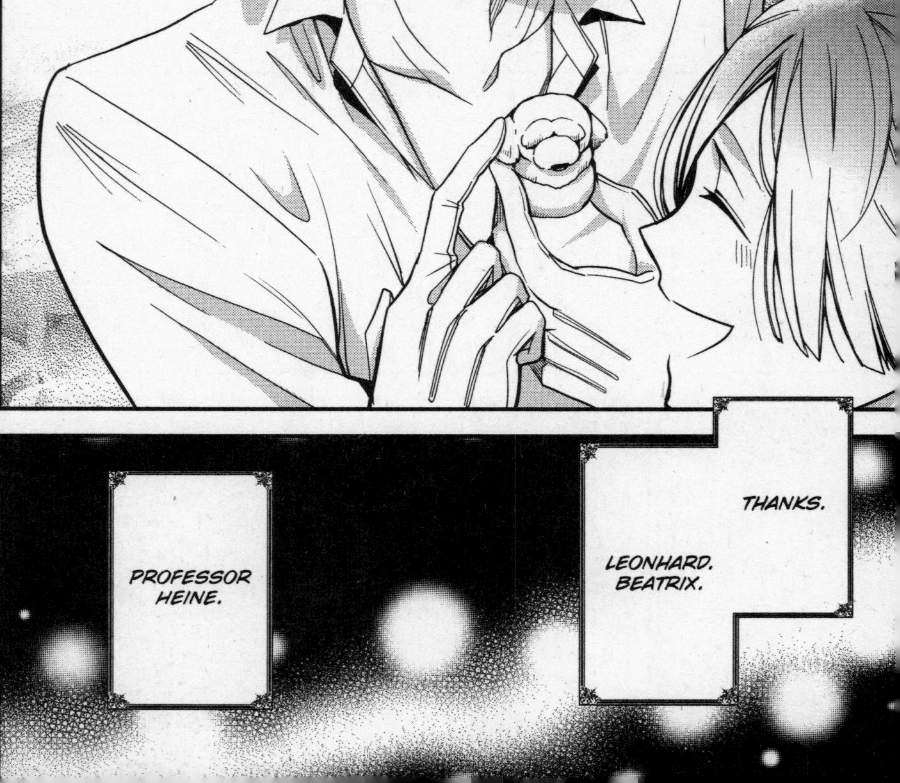
THANKS.
LEONHARD. BEATRIX.
PROFESSOR HEINE.

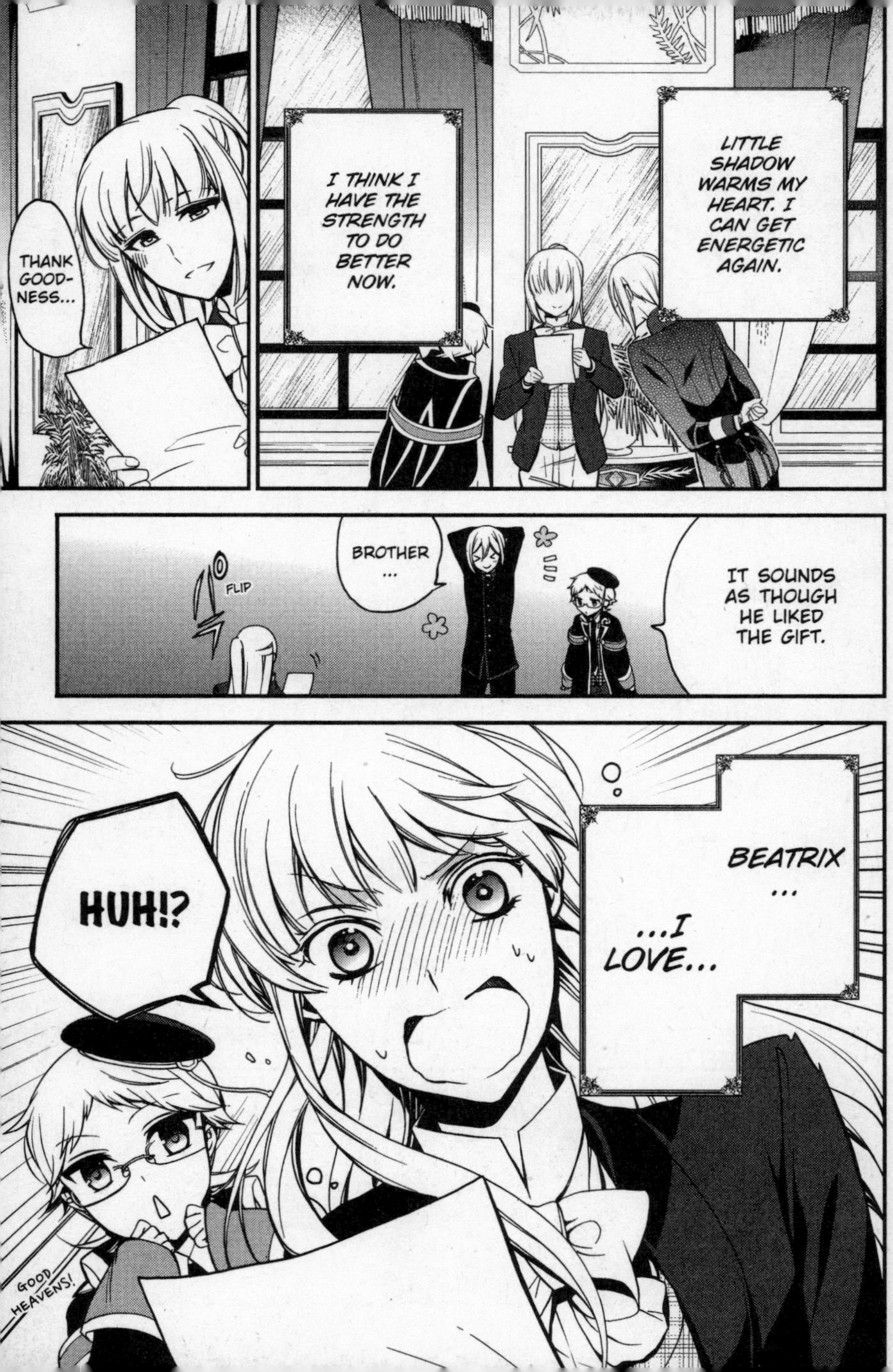

LITTLE SHADOW WARMS MY HEART. I CAN GET ENERGETIC AGAIN.
I THINK I HAVE THE STRENGTH TO DO BETTER NOW.
THANK GOOD-NESS...
IT SOUNDS AS THOUGH HE LIKED THE GIFT.
BROTHER ...
FLIP
BEATRIX ...
...I LOVE...
HUH!?
GOOD HEAVENS!

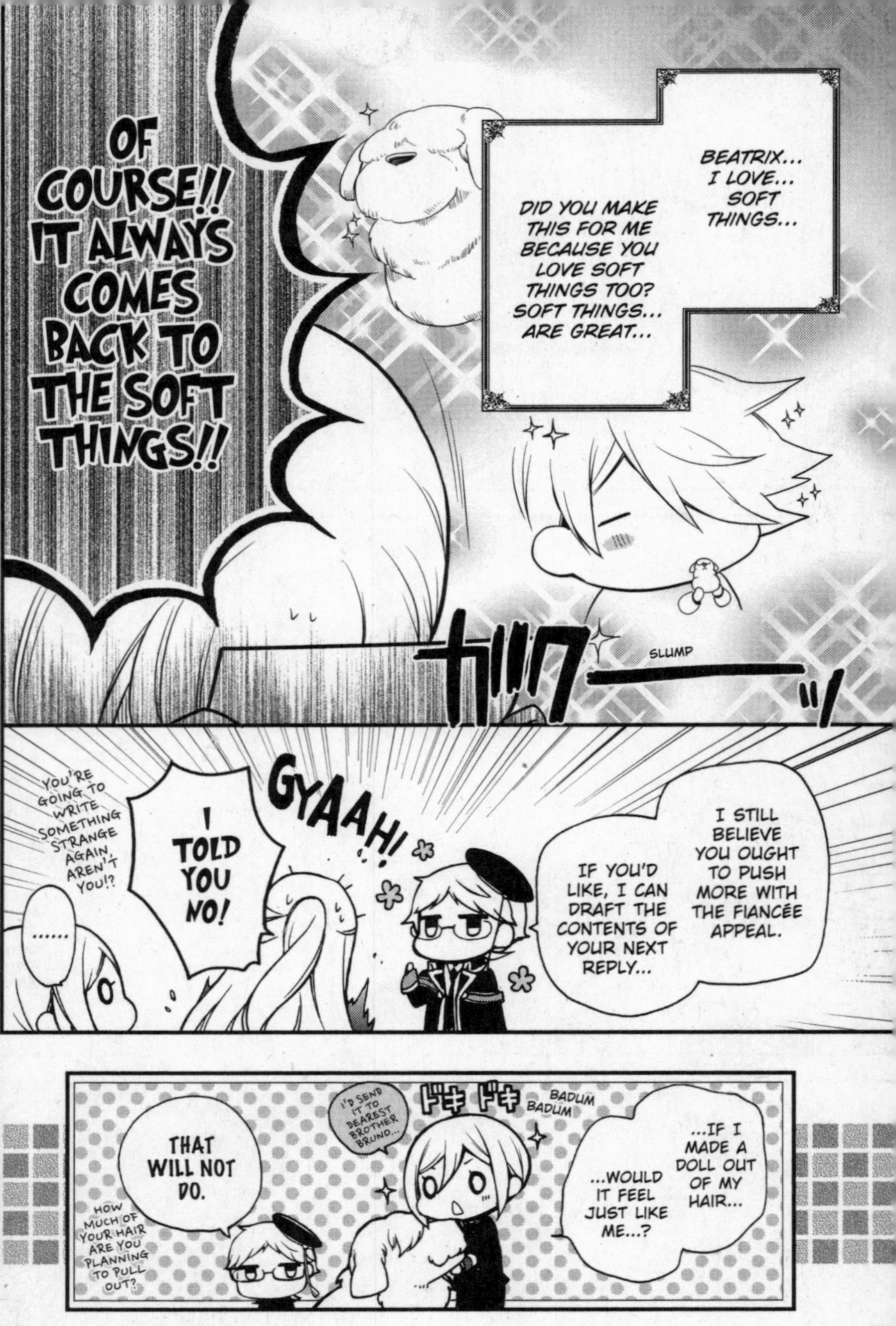
BEATRIX... I LOVE... SOFT THINGS...
DID YOU MAKE THIS FOR ME BECAUSE YOU LOVE SOFT THINGS TOO? SOFT THINGS... ARE GREAT...
OF COURSE!! IT ALWAYS COMES BACK TO THE SOFT THINGS!!
ガクーーーッ
SLUMP
I STILL BELIEVE YOU OUGHT TO PUSH MORE WITH THE FIANCÉE APPEAL.
IF YOU'D LIKE, I CAN DRAFT THE CONTENTS OF YOUR NEXT REPLY...
GYAAH!
I TOLD YOU NO!
YOU'RE GOING TO WRITE SOMETHING STRANGE AGAIN, AREN'T YOU!?
......
...IF I MADE A DOLL OUT OF MY HAIR...
...WOULD IT FEEL JUST LIKE ME...?
ドキドキ
BADUM BADUM
I'D SEND IT TO DEAREST BROTHER BRUNO...
THAT WILL NOT DO.
HOW MUCH OF YOUR HAIR ARE YOU PLANNING TO PULL OUT?

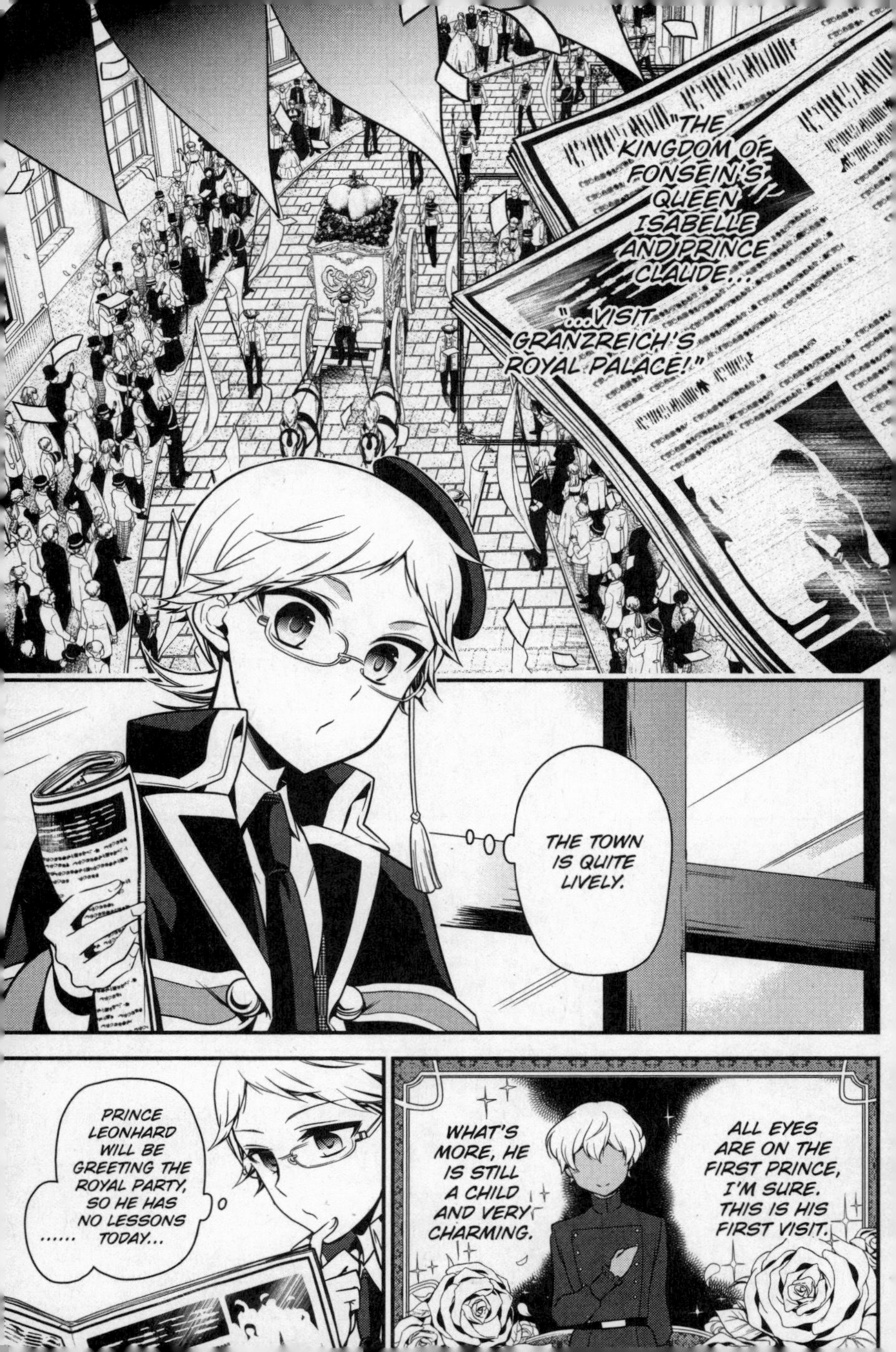
"THE KINGDOM OF FONSEIN'S QUEEN ISABELLE AND PRINCE CLAUDE..."
"...VISIT GRANZREICH'S ROYAL PALACE!"
THE TOWN IS QUITE LIVELY.
ALL EYES ARE ON THE FIRST PRINCE, I'M SURE. THIS IS HIS FIRST VISIT.
WHAT'S MORE, HE IS STILL A CHILD AND VERY CHARMING.
PRINCE LEONHARD WILL BE GREETING THE ROYAL PARTY, SO HE HAS NO LESSONS TODAY...
......

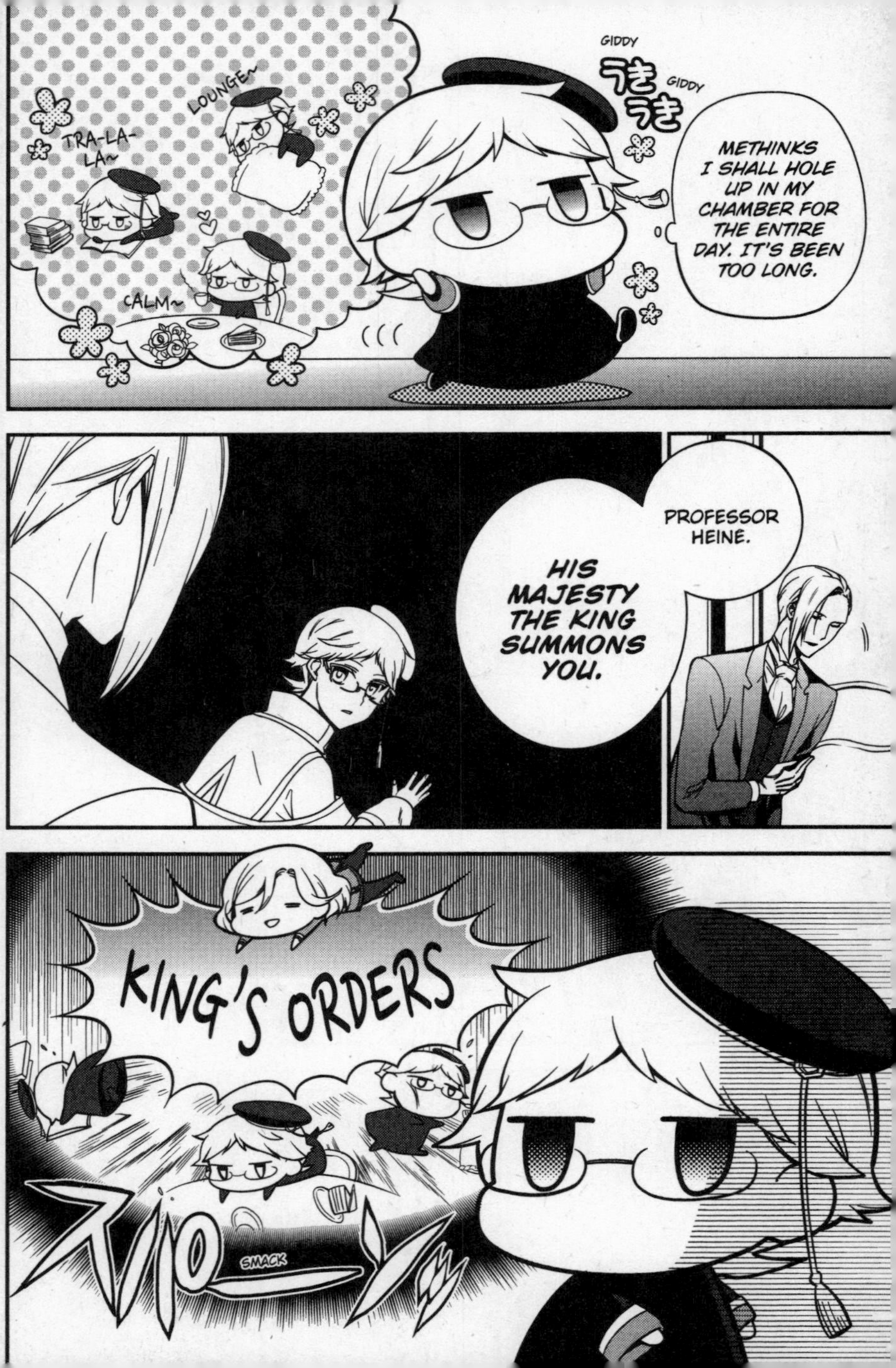
GIDDY
うきうき
GIDDY
METHINKS I SHALL HOLE UP IN MY CHAMBER FOR THE ENTIRE DAY. IT'S BEEN TOO LONG.
LOUNGE~
TRA-LA-LA~
CALM~
PROFESSOR HEINE.
HIS MAJESTY THE KING SUMMONS YOU.
KING'S ORDERS
SMACK

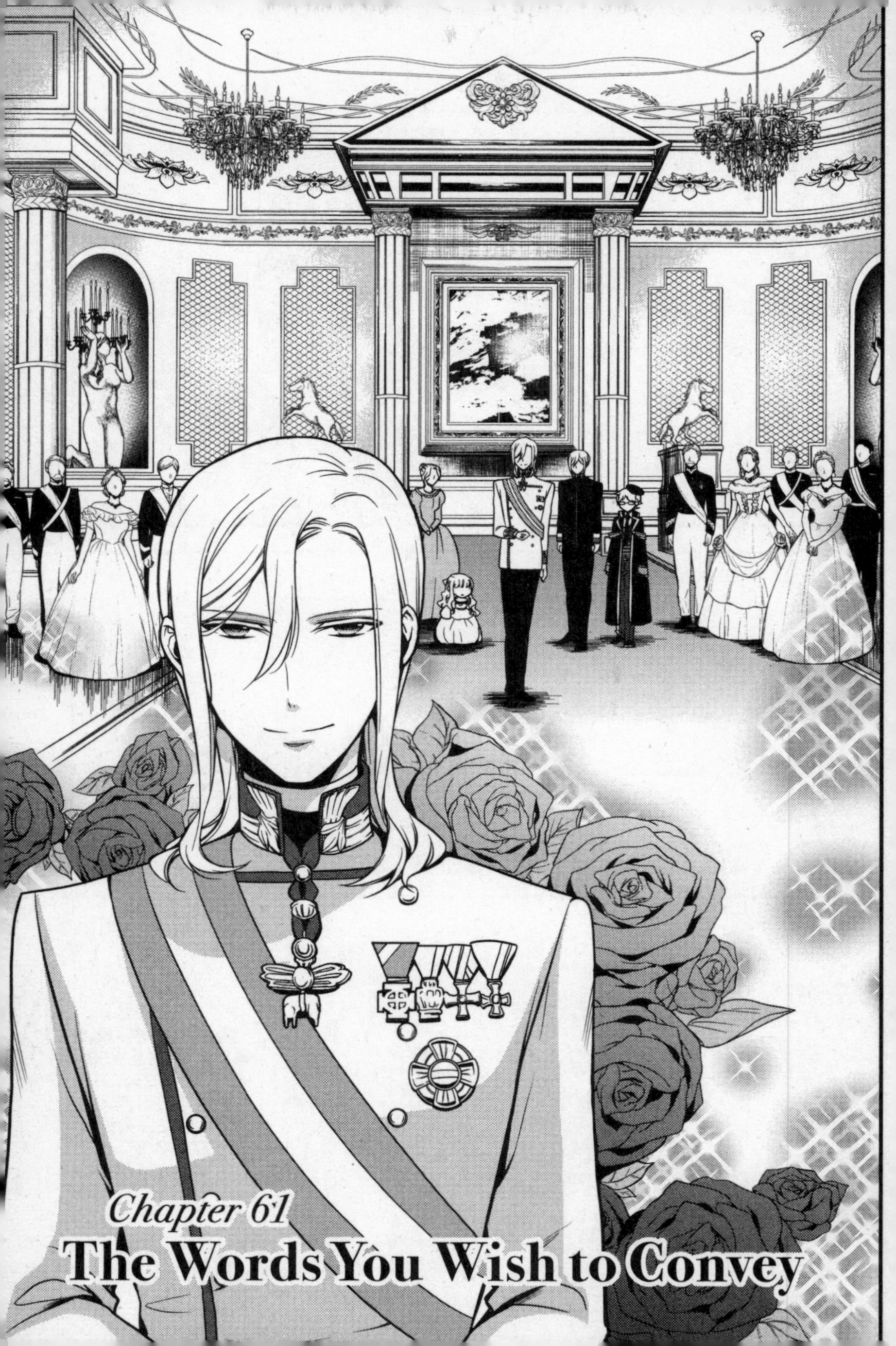
Chapter 61
The Words You Wish to Convey

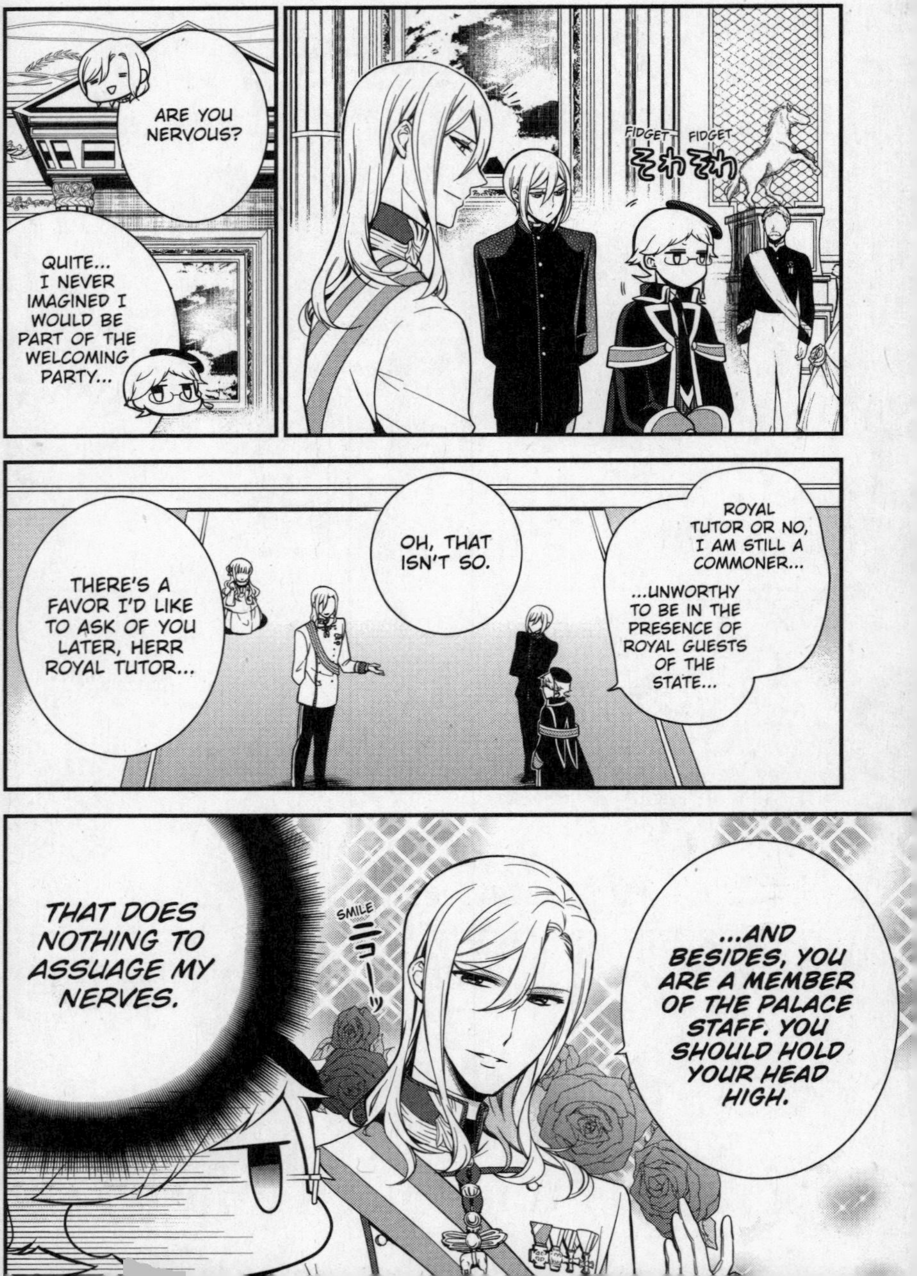
FIDGET FIDGET
そわそわ
ARE YOU NERVOUS?
QUITE... I NEVER IMAGINED I WOULD BE PART OF THE WELCOMING PARTY...
ROYAL TUTOR OR NO, I AM STILL A COMMONER...
...UNWORTHY TO BE IN THE PRESENCE OF ROYAL GUESTS OF THE STATE...
OH, THAT ISN'T SO.
THERE'S A FAVOR I'D LIKE TO ASK OF YOU LATER, HERR ROYAL TUTOR...
...AND BESIDES, YOU ARE A MEMBER OF THE PALACE STAFF. YOU SHOULD HOLD YOUR HEAD HIGH.
SMILE
ニコーッ
THAT DOES NOTHING TO ASSUAGE MY NERVES.

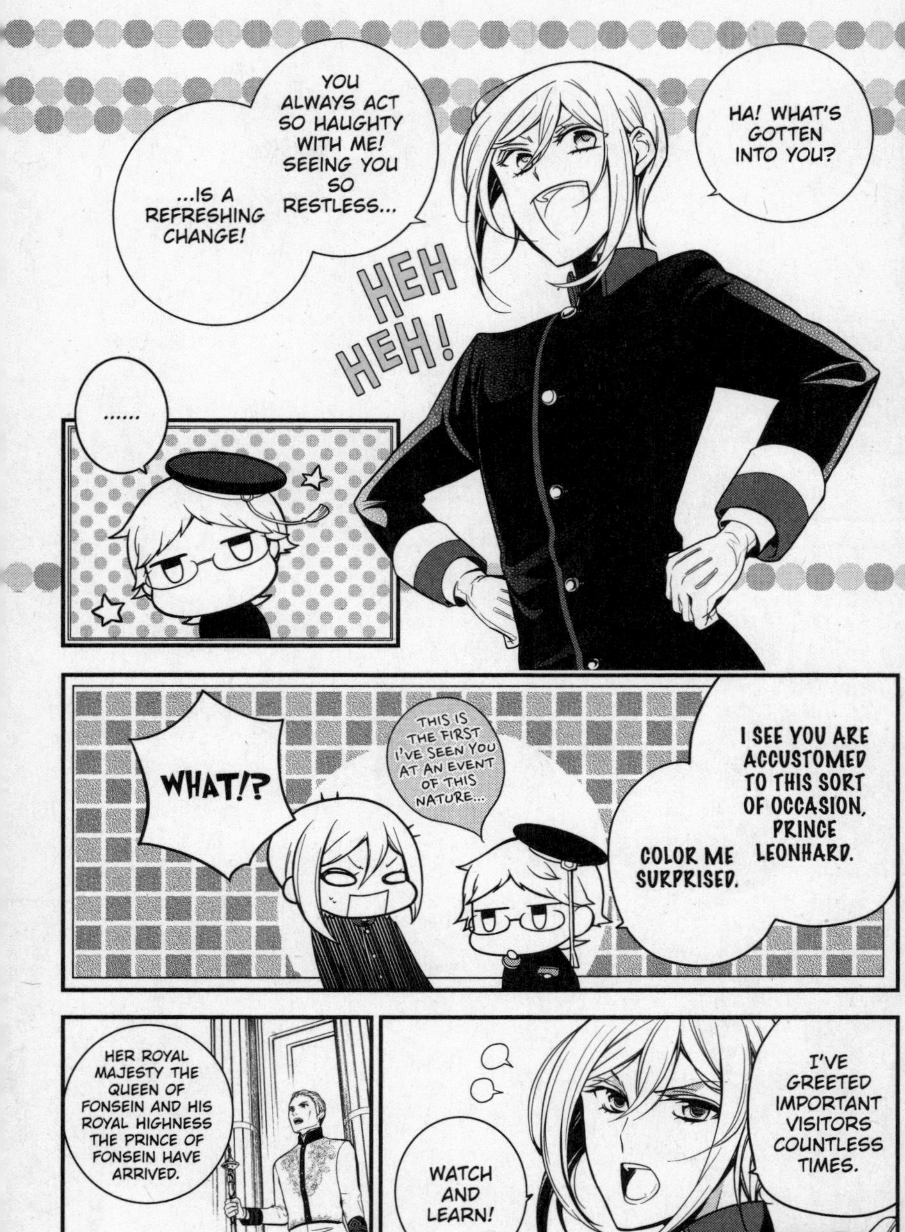
HA! WHAT'S GOTTEN INTO YOU?
YOU ALWAYS ACT SO HAUGHTY WITH ME! SEEING YOU SO RESTLESS...
...IS A REFRESHING CHANGE!
HEH HEH!
......
I SEE YOU ARE ACCUSTOMED TO THIS SORT OF OCCASION, PRINCE LEONHARD.
COLOR ME SURPRISED.
THIS IS THE FIRST I'VE SEEN YOU AT AN EVENT OF THIS NATURE...
WHAT!?
I'VE GREETED IMPORTANT VISITORS COUNTLESS TIMES.
WATCH AND LEARN!
HER ROYAL MAJESTY THE QUEEN OF FONSEIN AND HIS ROYAL HIGHNESS THE PRINCE OF FONSEIN HAVE ARRIVED.

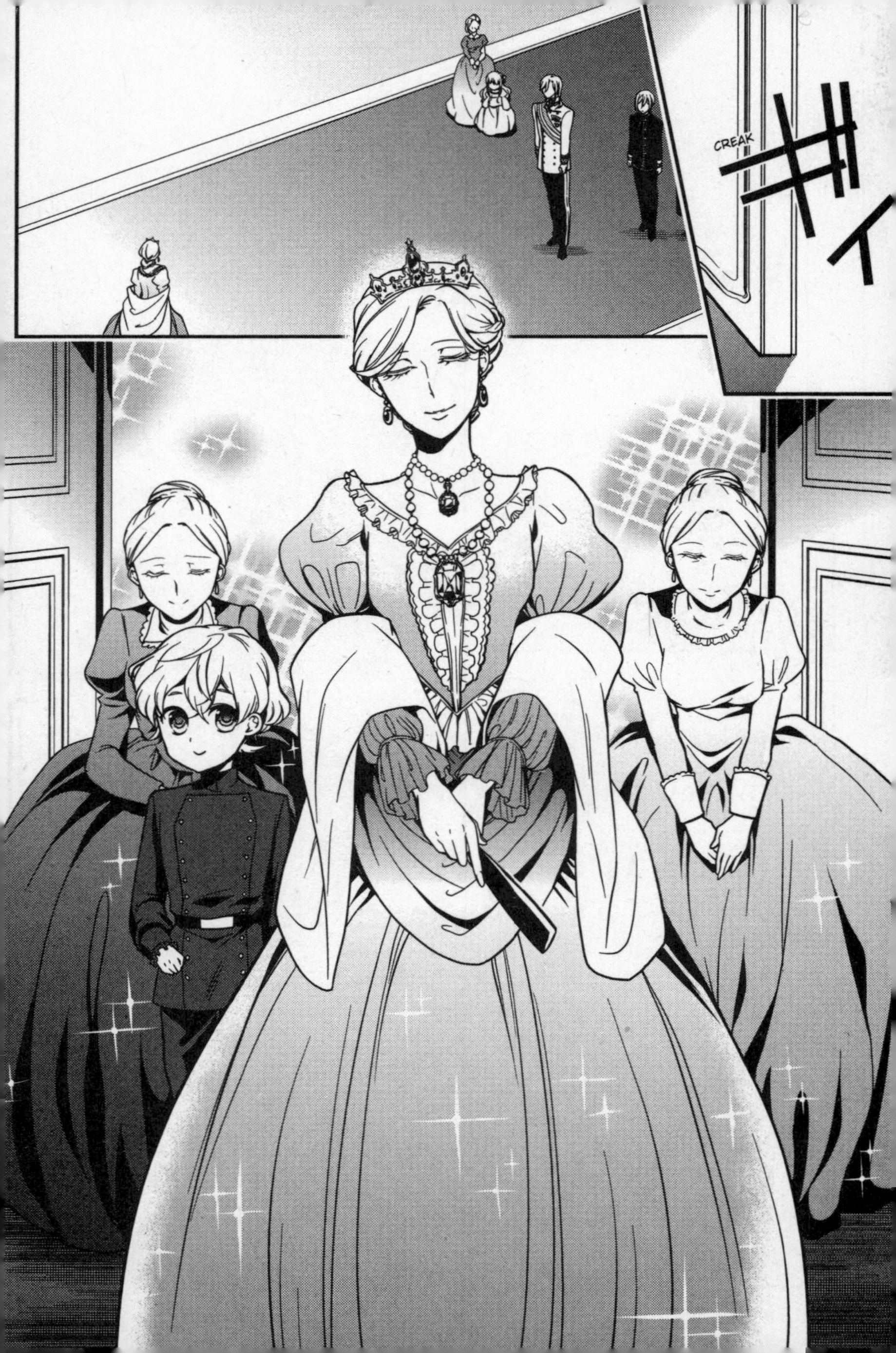
CREAK
ギィ

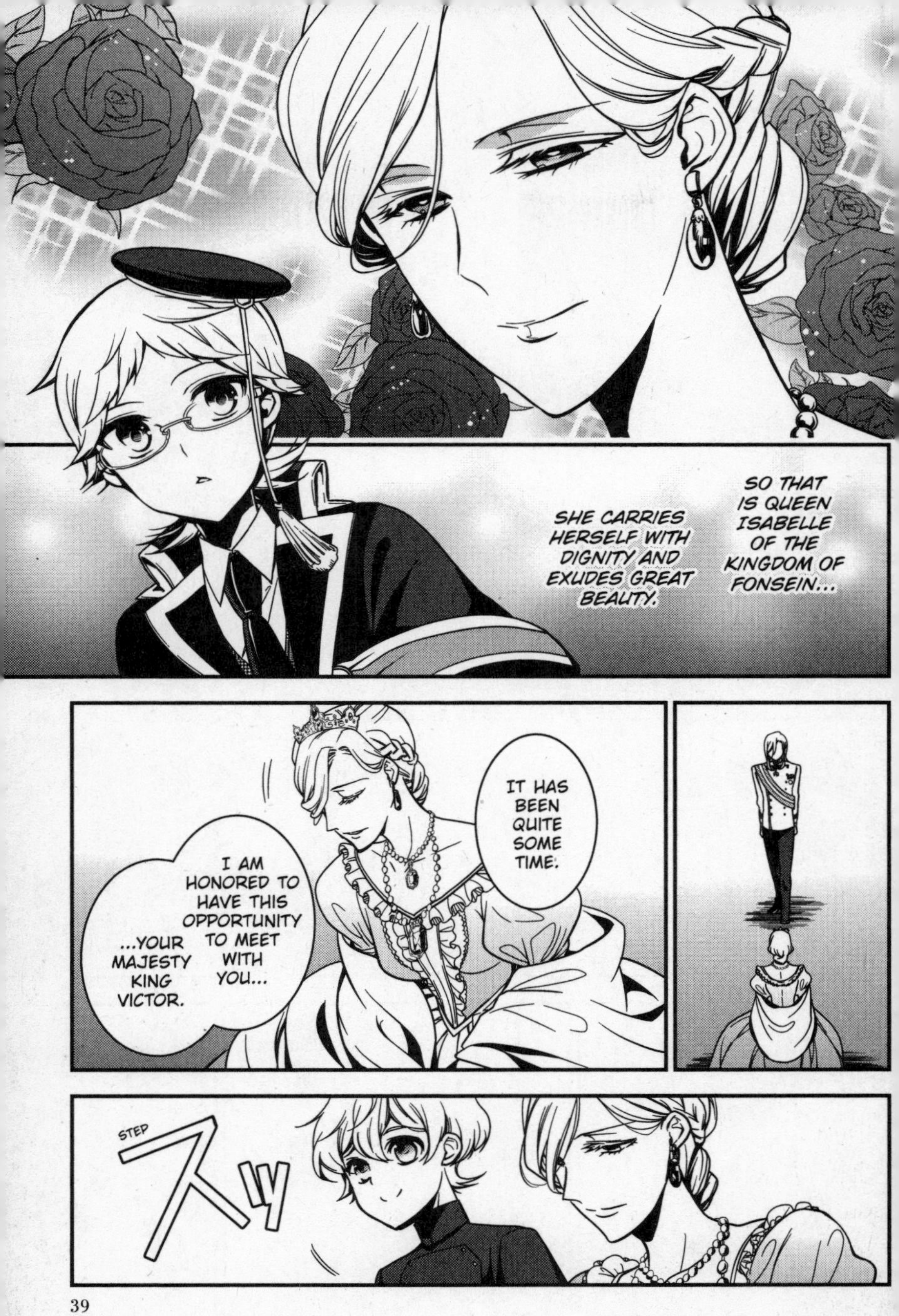
SO THAT IS QUEEN ISABELLE OF THE KINGDOM OF FONSEIN...
SHE CARRIES HERSELF WITH DIGNITY AND EXUDES GREAT BEAUTY.
IT HAS BEEN QUITE SOME TIME.
I AM HONORED TO HAVE THIS OPPORTUNITY TO MEET WITH YOU...
...YOUR MAJESTY KING VICTOR.
スッ
STEP

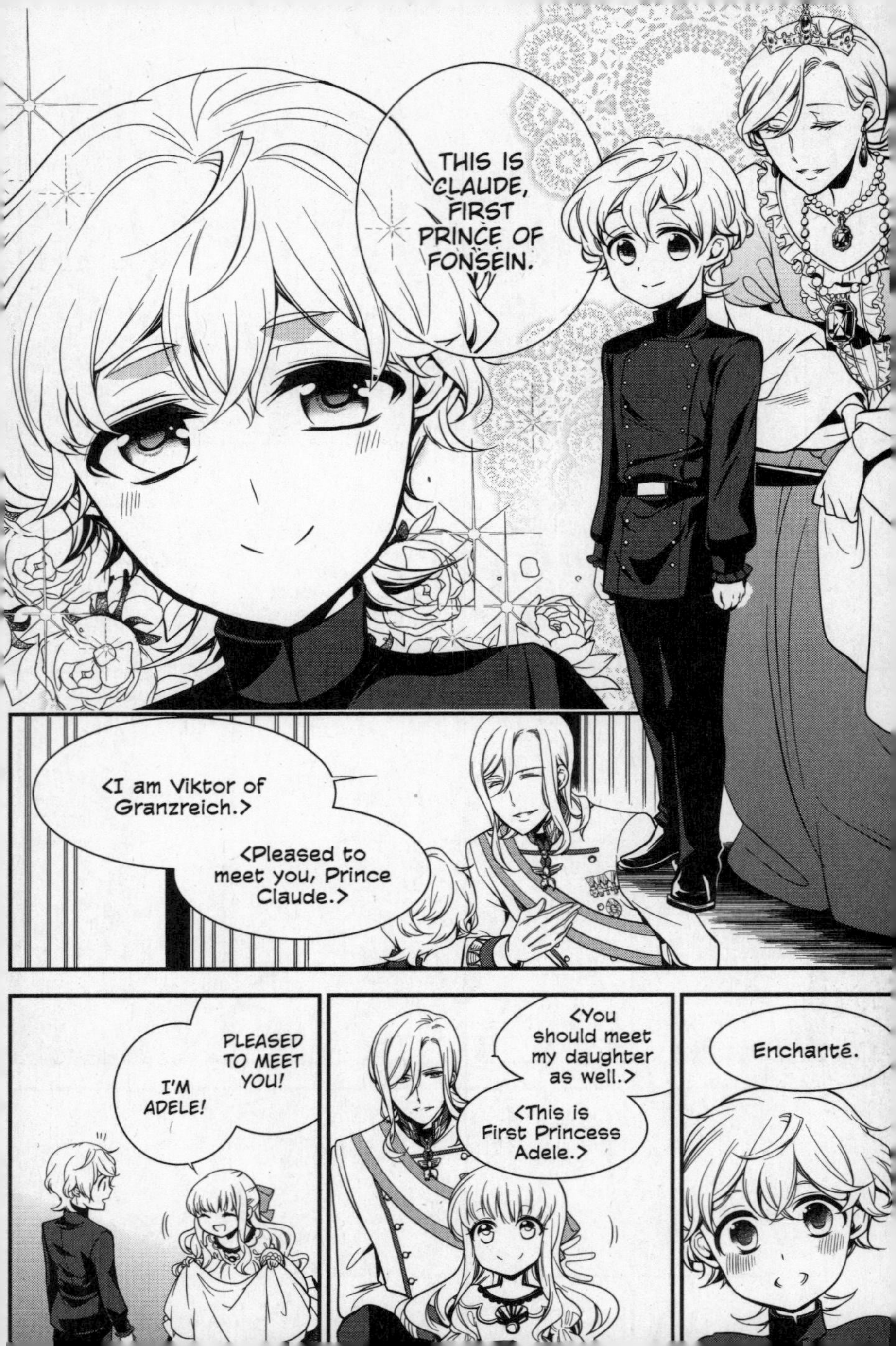
THIS IS CLAUDE, FIRST PRINCE OF FONSEIN.
<I am Viktor of Granzreich.>
<Pleased to meet you, Prince Claude.>
Enchanté.
<You should meet my daughter as well.>
<This is First Princess Adele.>
PLEASED TO MEET YOU!
I'M ADELE!

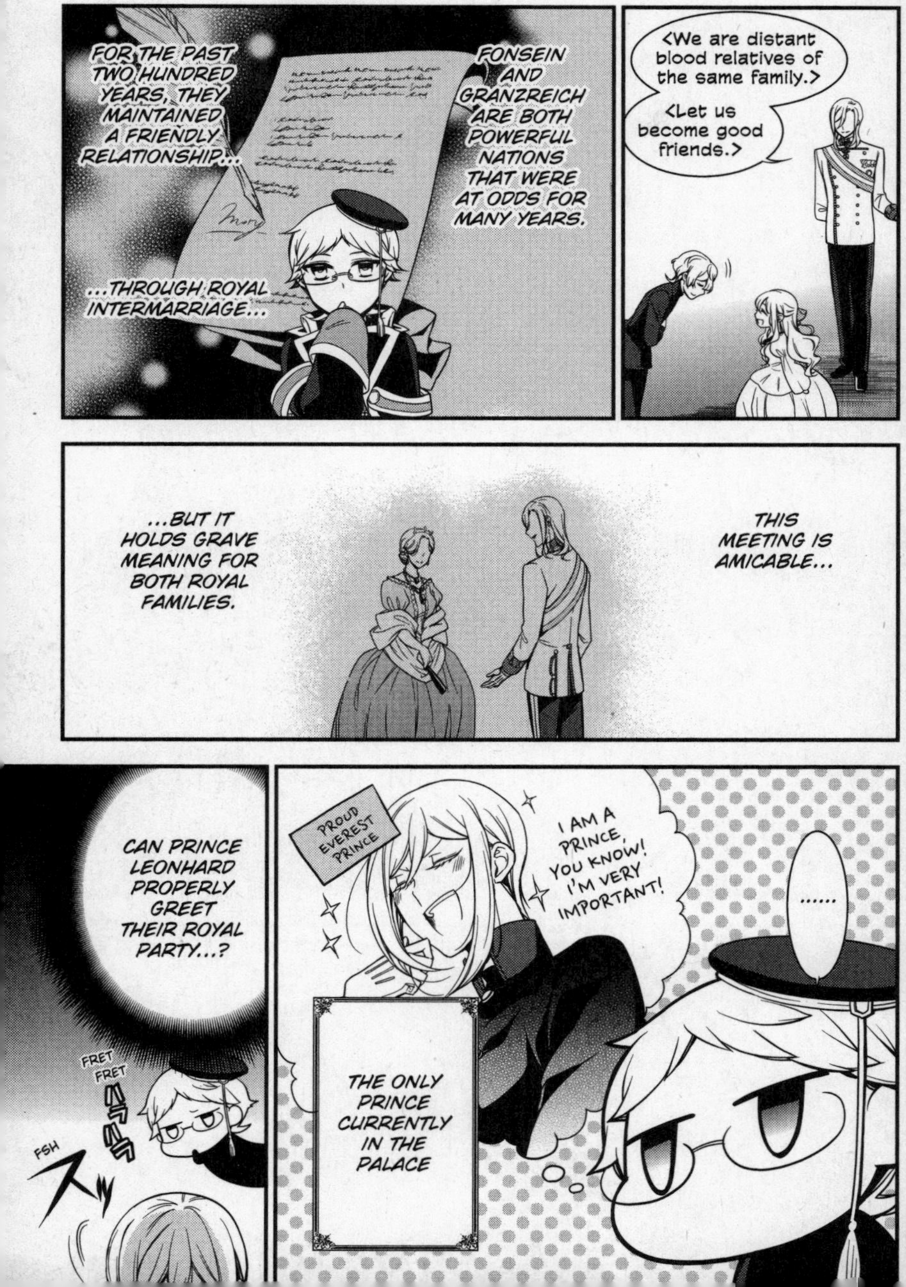
<We are distant blood relatives of the same family.>
<Let us become good friends.>
FONSEIN AND GRANZREICH ARE BOTH POWERFUL NATIONS THAT WERE AT ODDS FOR MANY YEARS.
FOR THE PAST TWO HUNDRED YEARS, THEY MAINTAINED A FRIENDLY RELATIONSHIP...
...THROUGH ROYAL INTERMARRIAGE...
THIS MEETING IS AMICABLE...
...BUT IT HOLDS GRAVE MEANING FOR BOTH ROYAL FAMILIES.
......
I AM A PRINCE, YOU KNOW! I'M VERY IMPORTANT!
PROUD EVEREST PRINCE
THE ONLY PRINCE CURRENTLY IN THE PALACE
CAN PRINCE LEONHARD PROPERLY GREET THEIR ROYAL PARTY...?
FRET FRET
FSH

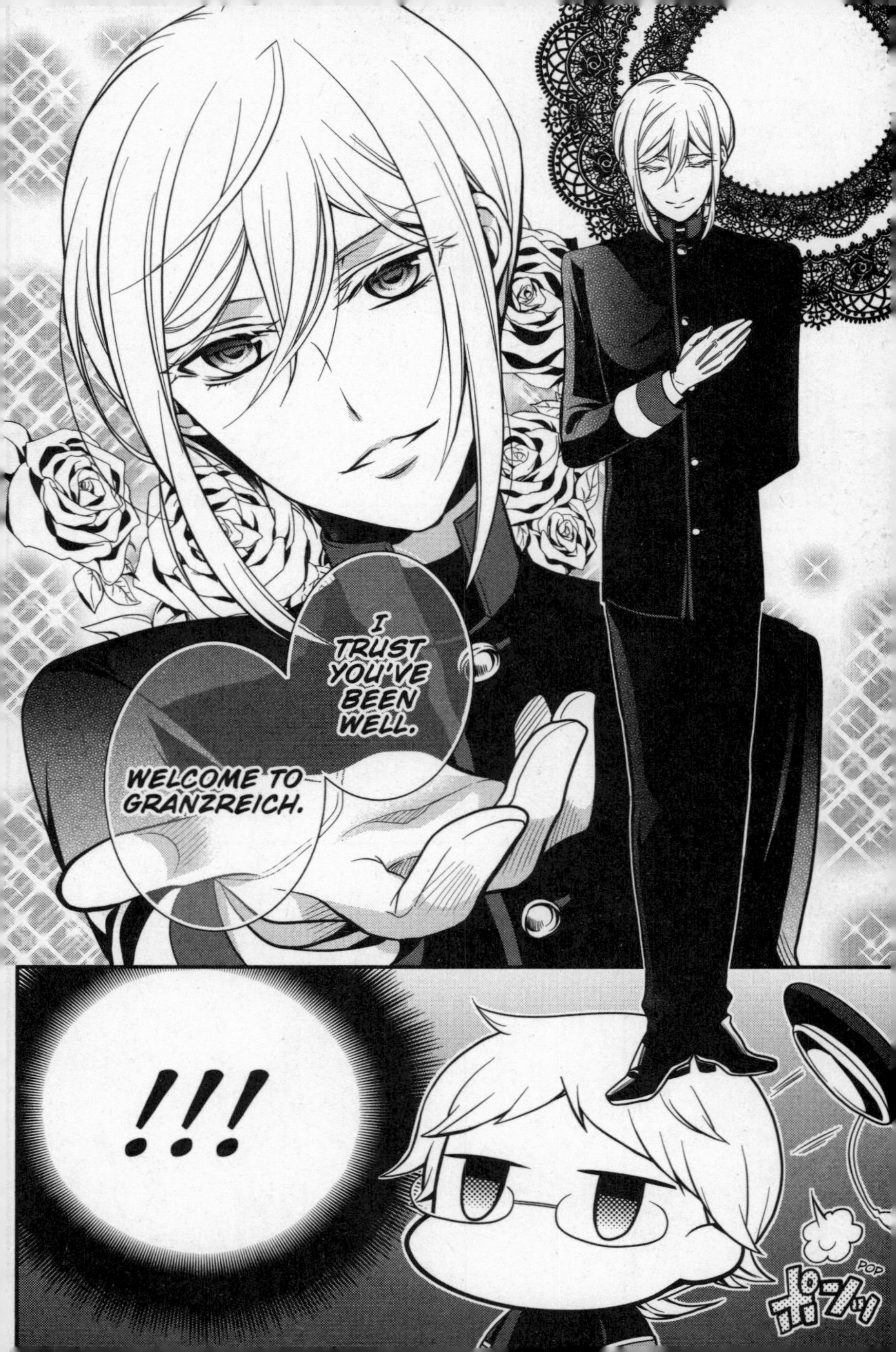
I TRUST YOU'VE BEEN WELL.
WELCOME TO GRANZREICH.
POP
!!!

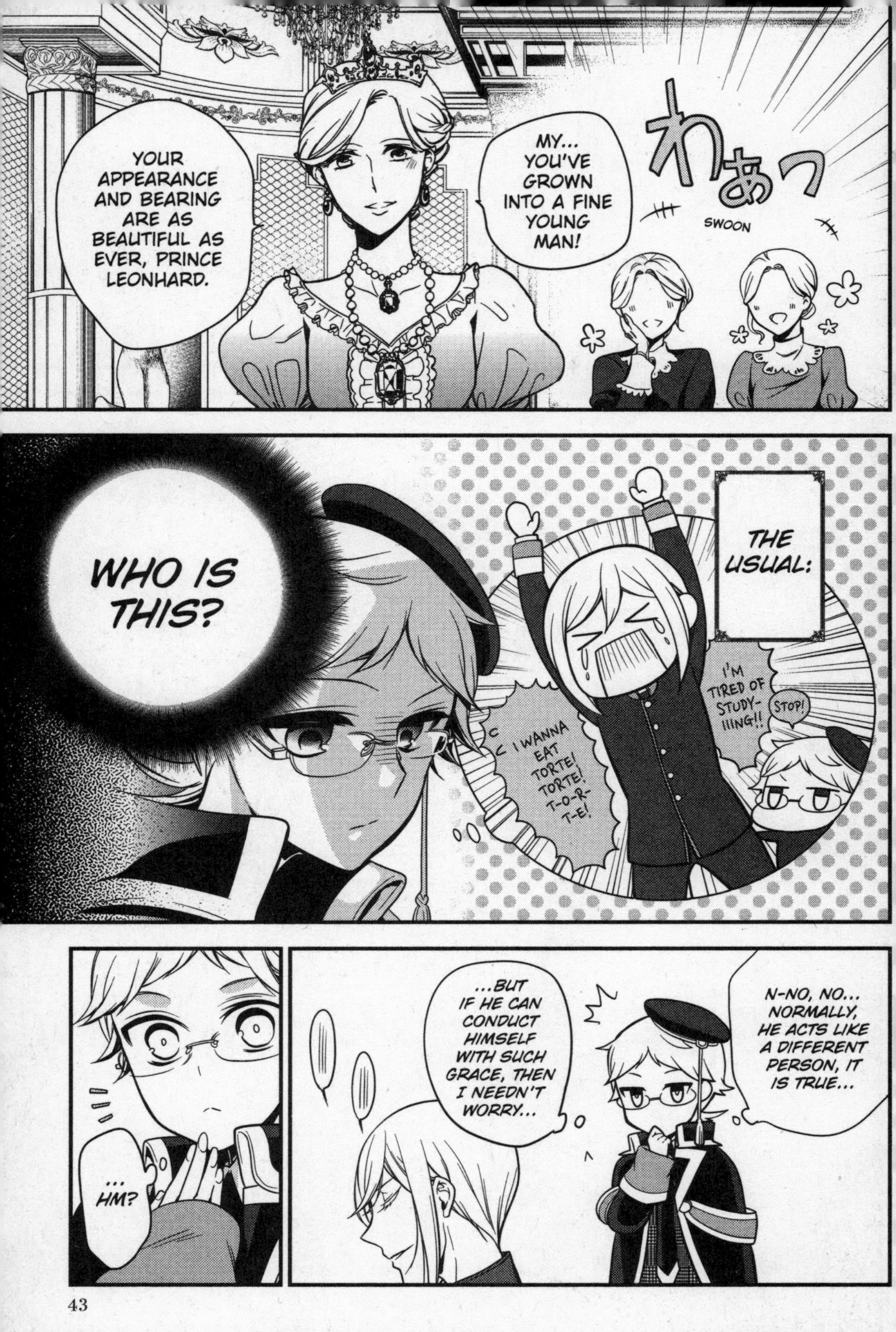
わぁっ
SWOON
MY... YOU'VE GROWN INTO A FINE YOUNG MAN!
YOUR APPEARANCE AND BEARING ARE AS BEAUTIFUL AS EVER, PRINCE LEONHARD.
THE USUAL:
I'M TIRED OF STUDY-IIING!!
STOP!
I WANNA EAT TORTE! TORTE! T-O-R-T-E!
WHO IS THIS?
N-NO, NO... NORMALLY, HE ACTS LIKE A DIFFERENT PERSON, IT IS TRUE...
...BUT IF HE CAN CONDUCT HIMSELF WITH SUCH GRACE, THEN I NEEDN'T WORRY...
... HM?

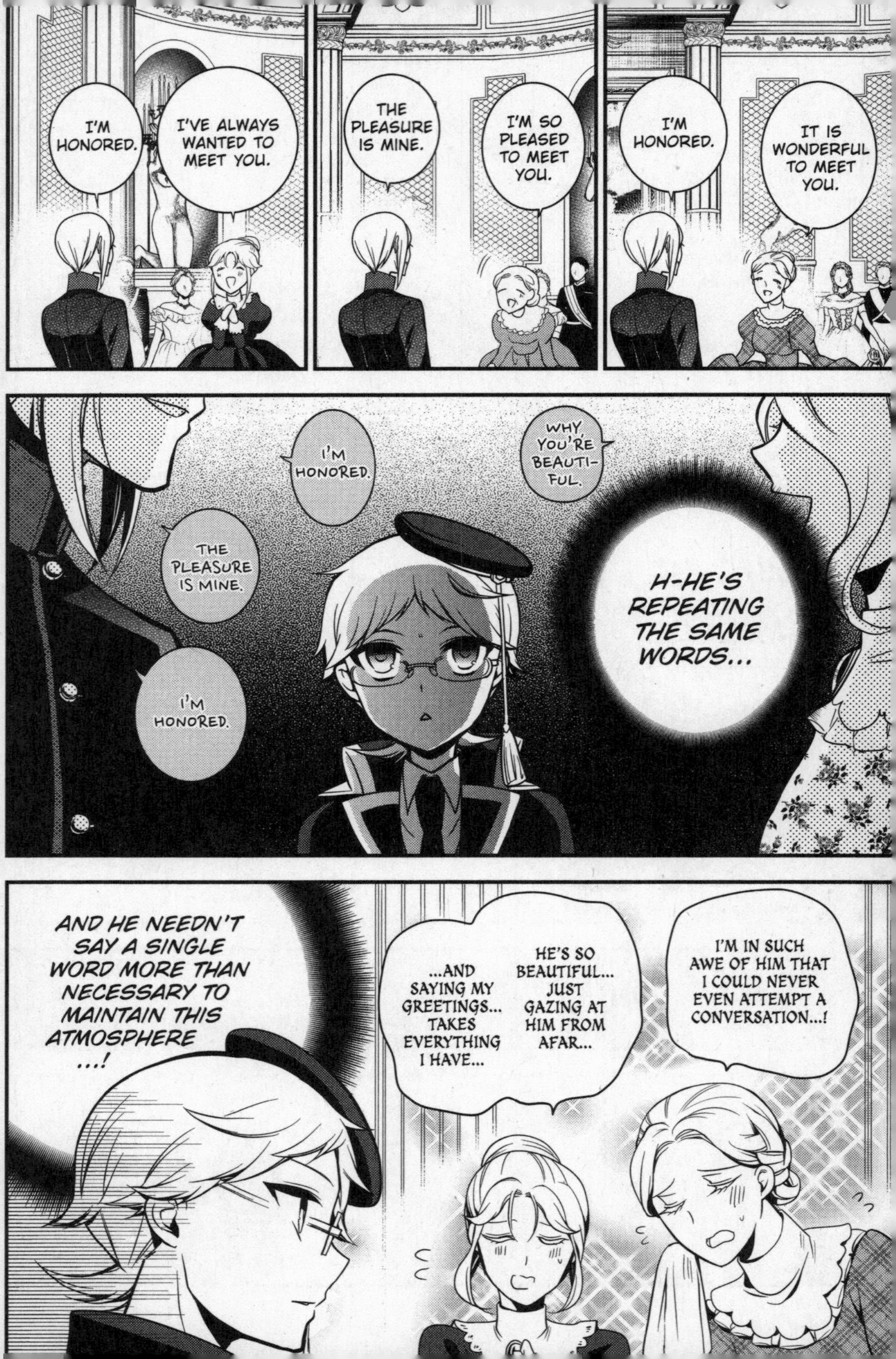
IT IS WONDERFUL TO MEET YOU.
I'M HONORED.
I'M SO PLEASED TO MEET YOU.
THE PLEASURE IS MINE.
I'VE ALWAYS WANTED TO MEET YOU.
I'M HONORED.
WHY, YOU'RE BEAUTI-FUL.
I'M HONORED.
H-HE'S REPEATING THE SAME WORDS...
THE PLEASURE IS MINE.
I'M HONORED.
I'M IN SUCH AWE OF HIM THAT I COULD NEVER EVEN ATTEMPT A CONVERSATION...!
HE'S SO BEAUTIFUL... JUST GAZING AT HIM FROM AFAR...
...AND SAYING MY GREETINGS... TAKES EVERYTHING I HAVE...
AND HE NEEDN'T SAY A SINGLE WORD MORE THAN NECESSARY TO MAINTAIN THIS ATMOSPHERE ...!

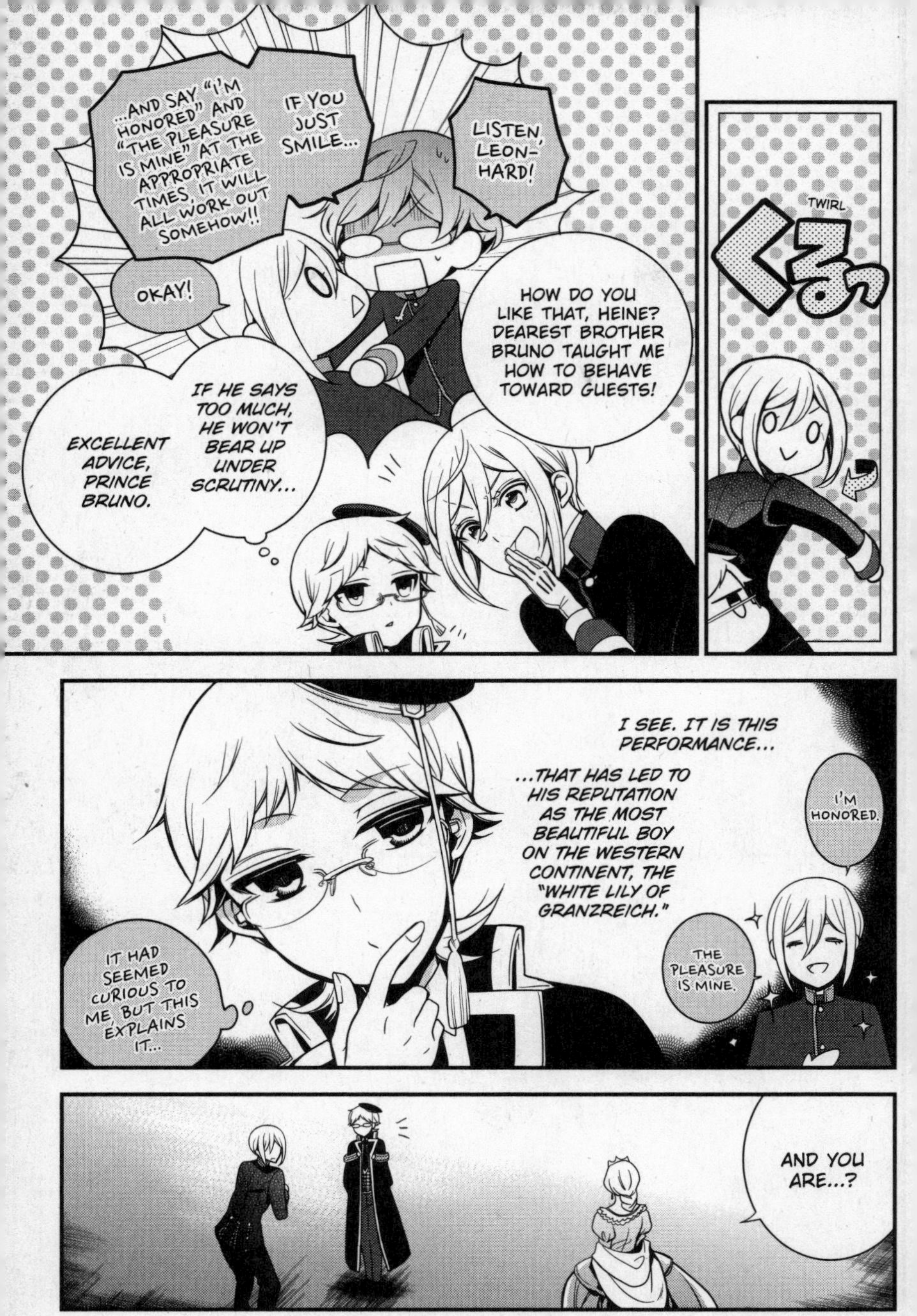
TWIRL
くるっ
LISTEN, LEON-HARD!
IF YOU JUST SMILE...
...AND SAY "I'M HONORED" AND "THE PLEASURE IS MINE" AT THE APPROPRIATE TIMES, IT WILL ALL WORK OUT SOMEHOW!!
OKAY!
HOW DO YOU LIKE THAT, HEINE? DEAREST BROTHER BRUNO TAUGHT ME HOW TO BEHAVE TOWARD GUESTS!
IF HE SAYS TOO MUCH, HE WON'T BEAR UP UNDER SCRUTINY...
EXCELLENT ADVICE, PRINCE BRUNO.
I'M HONORED.
THE PLEASURE IS MINE.
I SEE. IT IS THIS PERFORMANCE...
...THAT HAS LED TO HIS REPUTATION AS THE MOST BEAUTIFUL BOY ON THE WESTERN CONTINENT, THE "WHITE LILY OF GRANZREICH."
IT HAD SEEMED CURIOUS TO ME, BUT THIS EXPLAINS IT...
AND YOU ARE...?

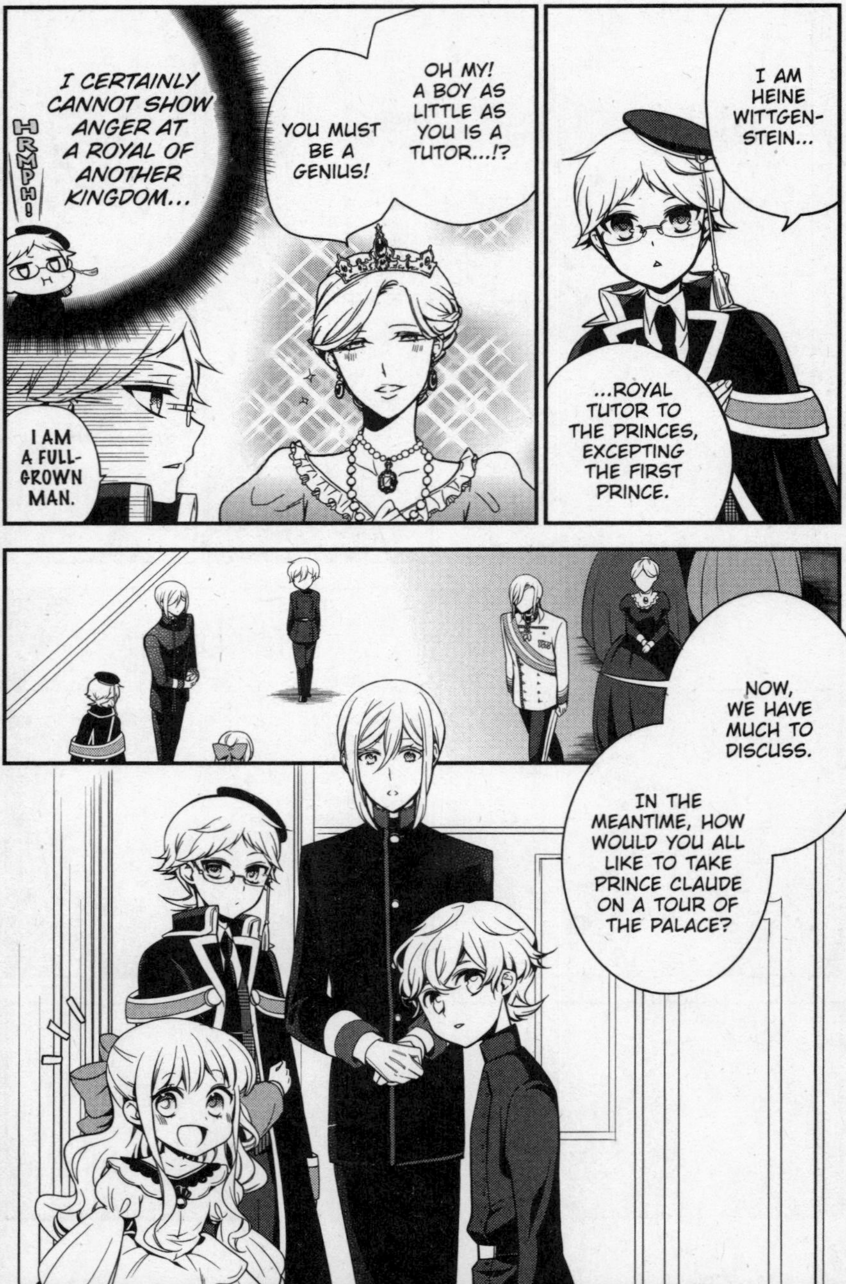
I AM HEINE WITTGEN-STEIN...
...ROYAL TUTOR TO THE PRINCES, EXCEPTING THE FIRST PRINCE.
OH MY! A BOY AS LITTLE AS YOU IS A TUTOR...!?
YOU MUST BE A GENIUS!
I CERTAINLY CANNOT SHOW ANGER AT A ROYAL OF ANOTHER KINGDOM...
HRMPH!
I AM A FULL-GROWN MAN.
NOW, WE HAVE MUCH TO DISCUSS.
IN THE MEANTIME, HOW WOULD YOU ALL LIKE TO TAKE PRINCE CLAUDE ON A TOUR OF THE PALACE?

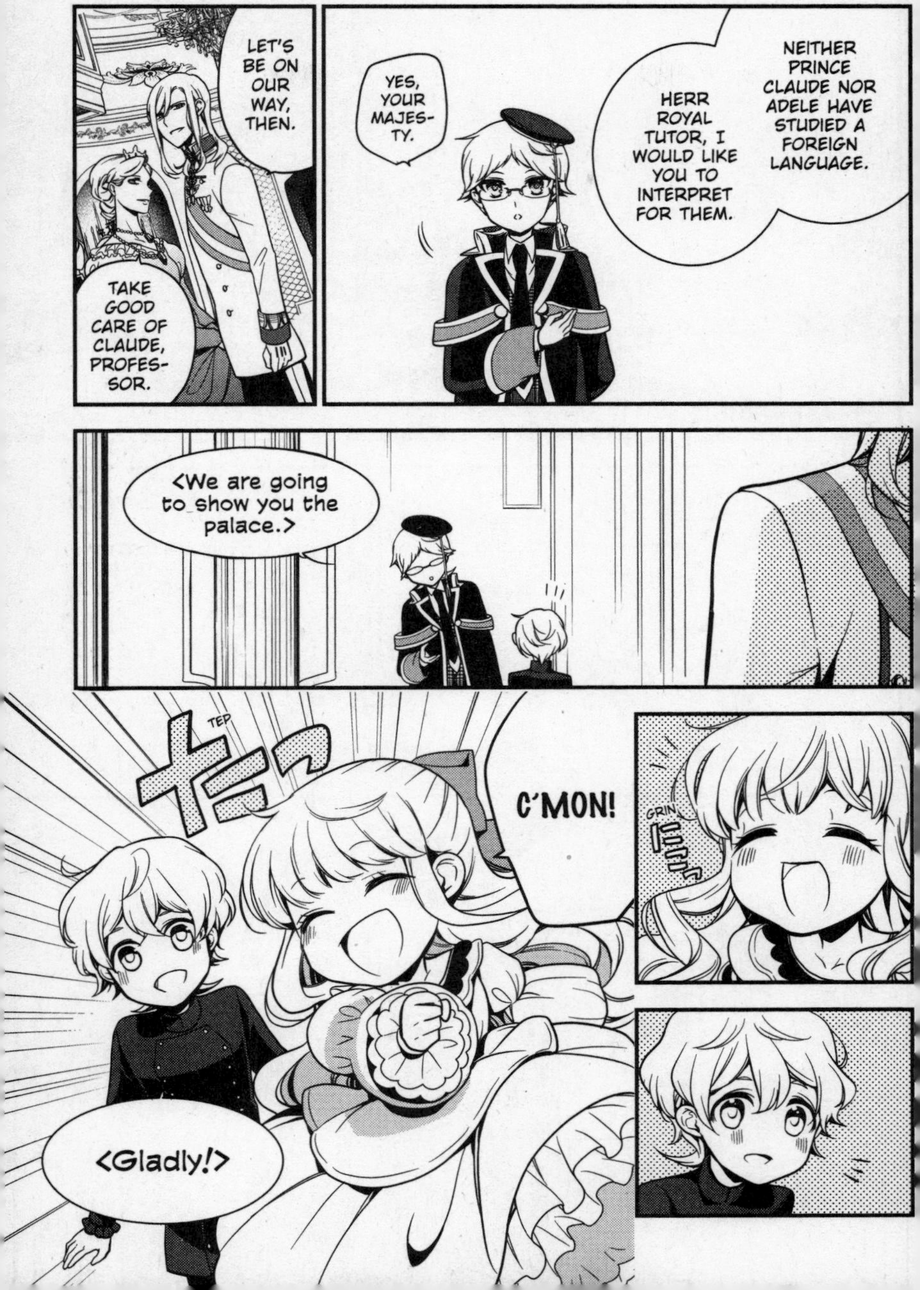
NEITHER PRINCE CLAUDE NOR ADELE HAVE STUDIED A FOREIGN LANGUAGE.
HERR ROYAL TUTOR, I WOULD LIKE YOU TO INTERPRET FOR THEM.
YES, YOUR MAJES-TY.
LET'S BE ON OUR WAY, THEN.
TAKE GOOD CARE OF CLAUDE, PROFES-SOR.
<We are going to show you the palace.>
GRIN
C'MON!
TEP
<Gladly!>

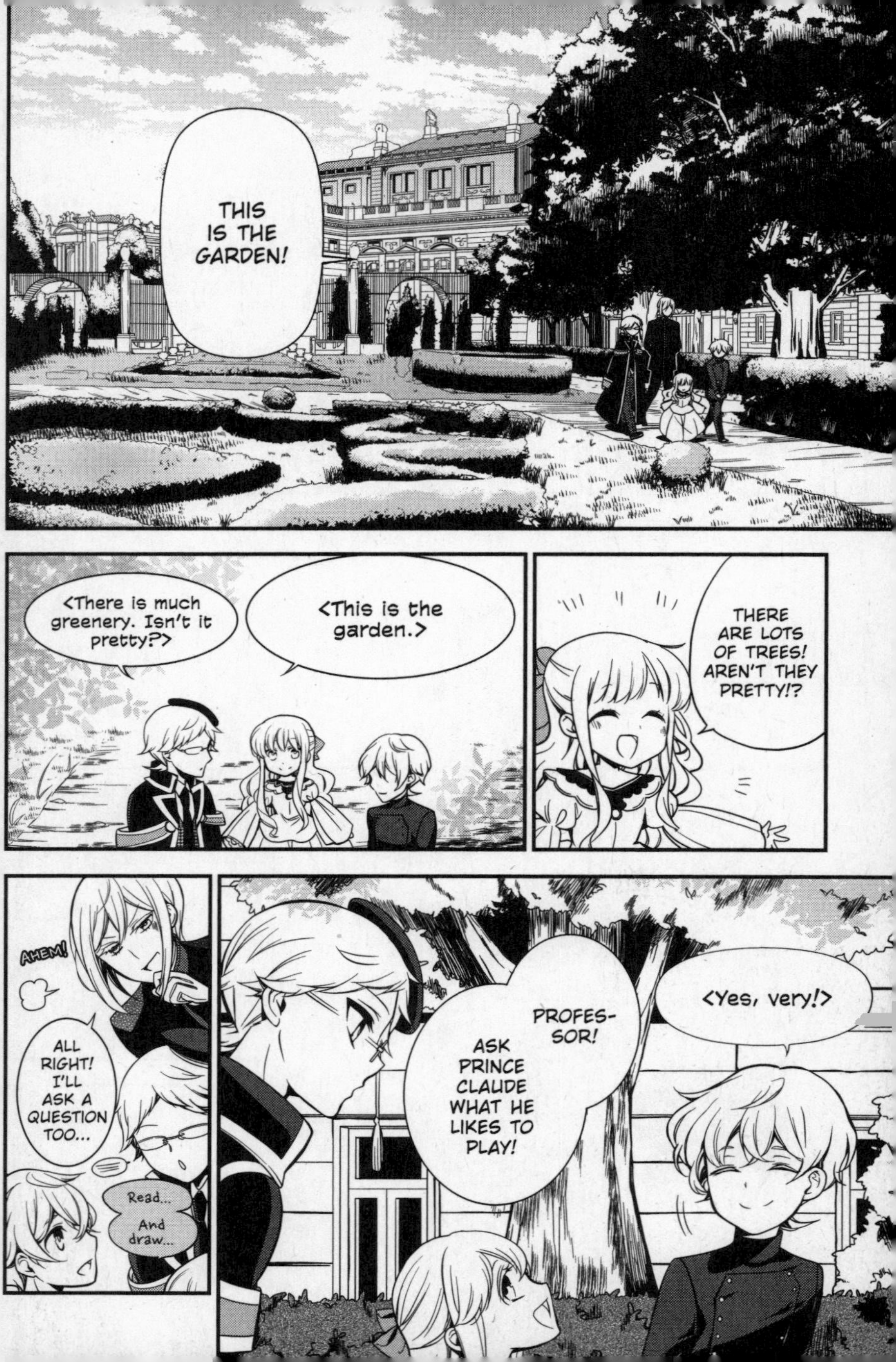
THIS IS THE GARDEN!
THERE ARE LOTS OF TREES! AREN'T THEY PRETTY!?
<This is the garden.>
<There is much greenery. Isn't it pretty?>
<Yes, very!>
PROFESSOR!
ASK PRINCE CLAUDE WHAT HE LIKES TO PLAY!
AHEM!
ALL RIGHT! I'LL ASK A QUESTION TOO...
Read...
And draw...

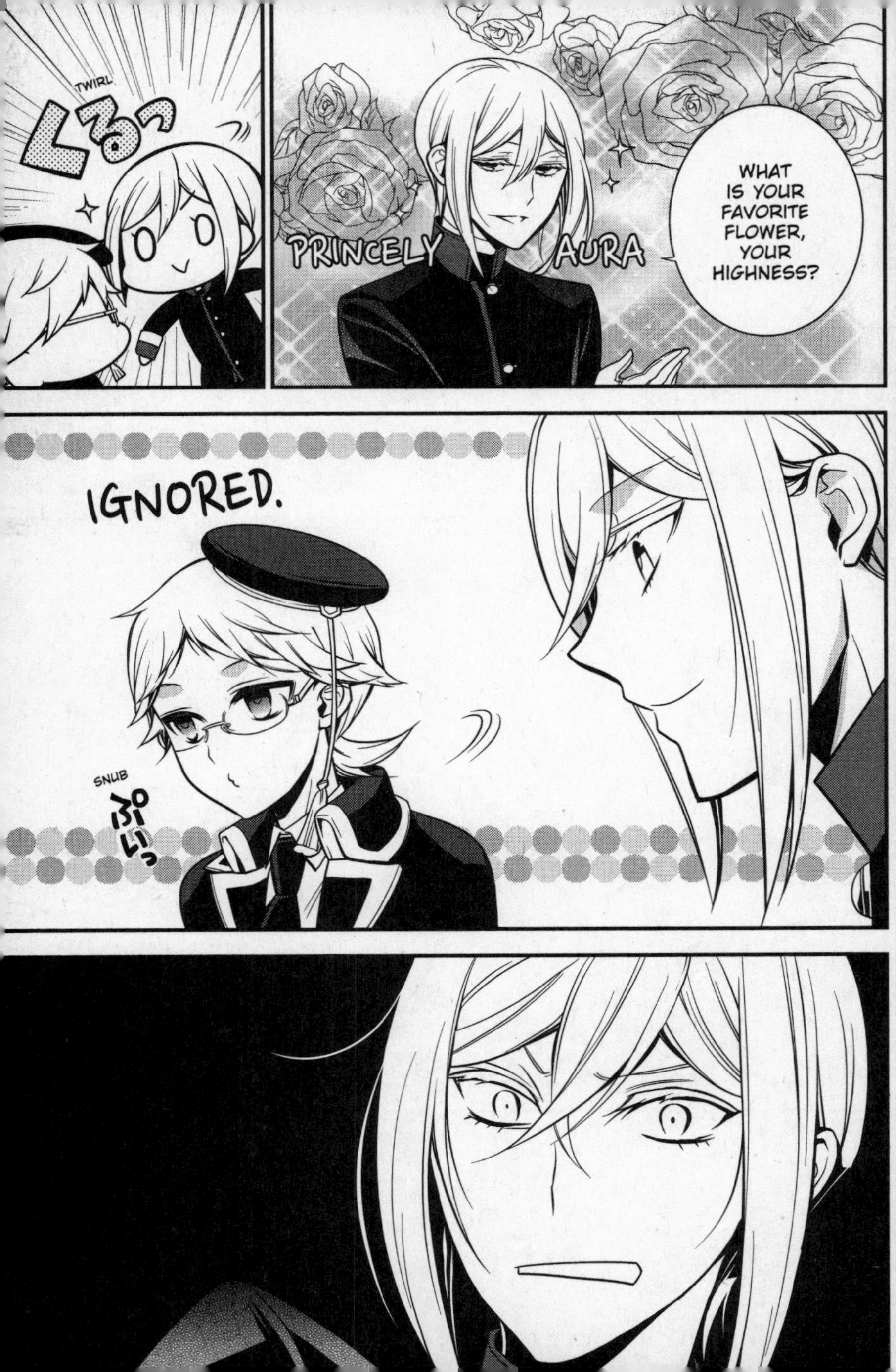
WHAT IS YOUR FAVORITE FLOWER, YOUR HIGHNESS?
PRINCELY AURA
TWIRL
くるっ
IGNORED.
SNUB
ぷいっ

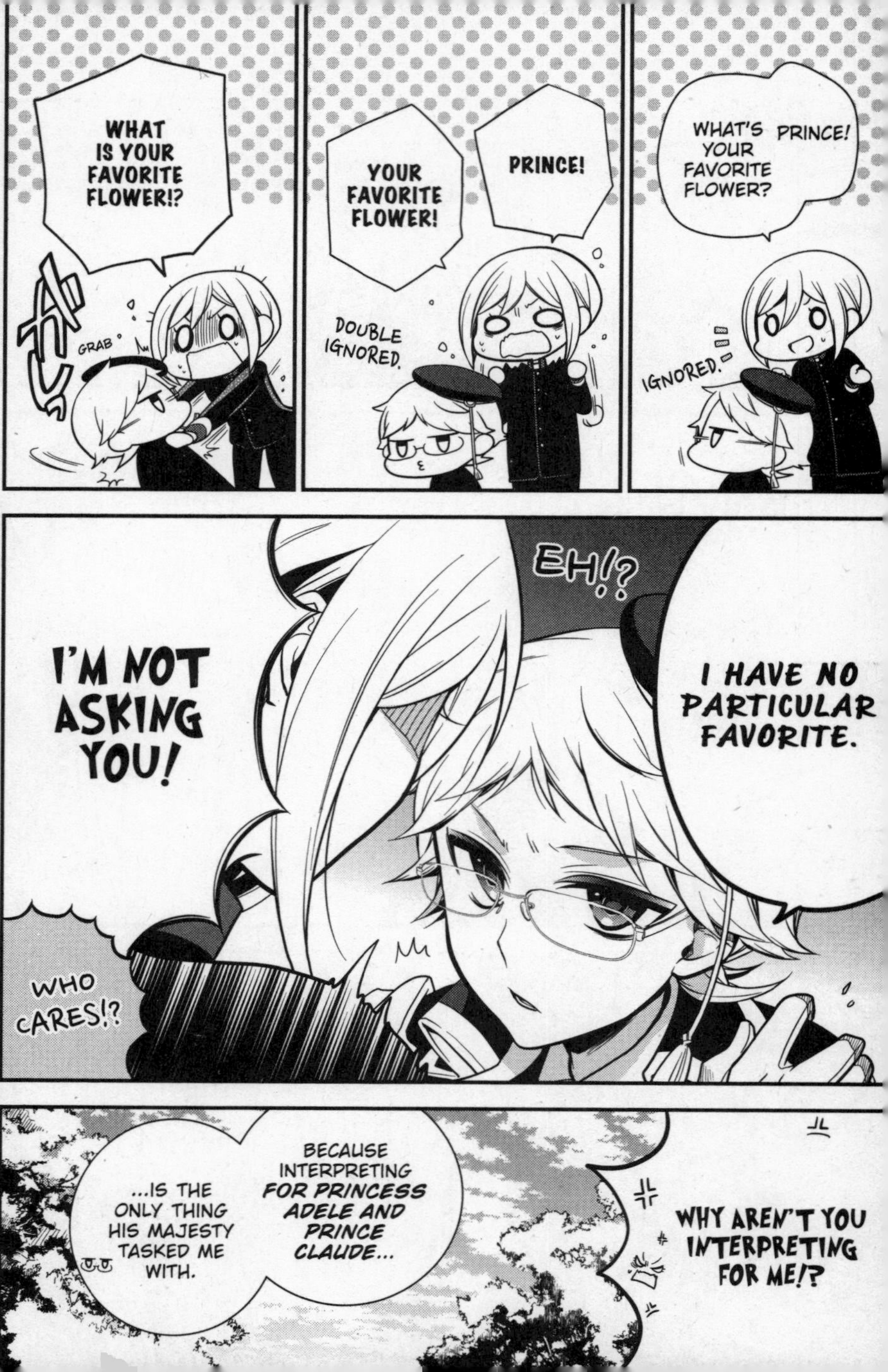
PRINCE! WHAT'S YOUR FAVORITE FLOWER?
IGNORED.
PRINCE!
YOUR FAVORITE FLOWER!
DOUBLE IGNORED.
WHAT IS YOUR FAVORITE FLOWER!?
GRAB
EH!?
I HAVE NO PARTICULAR FAVORITE.
I'M NOT ASKING YOU!
WHO CARES!?
WHY AREN'T YOU INTERPRETING FOR ME!?
BECAUSE INTERPRETING FOR PRINCESS ADELE AND PRINCE CLAUDE...
...IS THE ONLY THING HIS MAJESTY TASKED ME WITH.

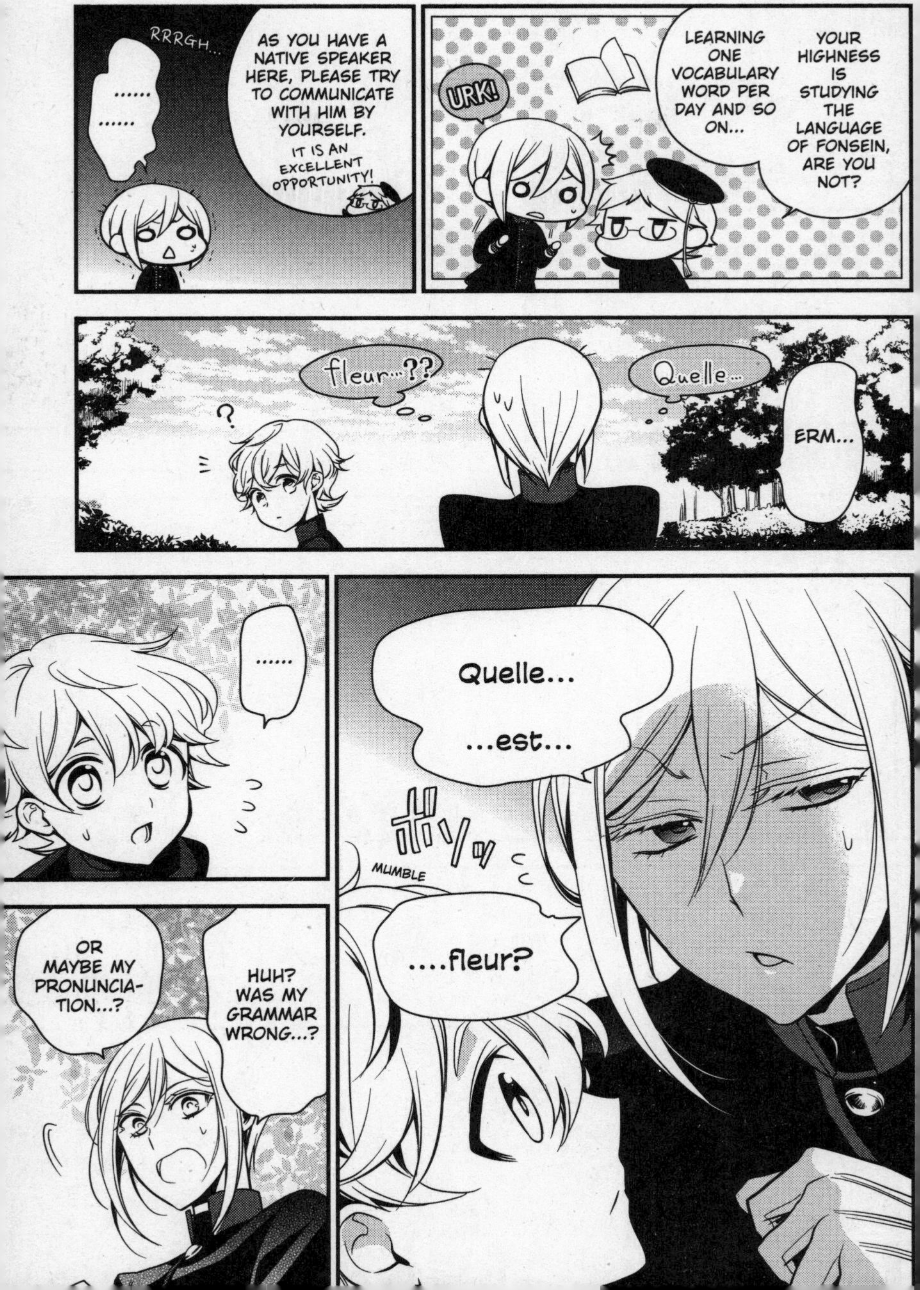
YOUR HIGHNESS IS STUDYING THE LANGUAGE OF FONSEIN, ARE YOU NOT?
LEARNING ONE VOCABULARY WORD PER DAY AND SO ON...
URK!
AS YOU HAVE A NATIVE SPEAKER HERE, PLEASE TRY TO COMMUNICATE WITH HIM BY YOURSELF.
IT IS AN EXCELLENT OPPORTUNITY!
RRRGH...
......
......
ERM...
Quelle...
fleur...??
?
Quelle...
...est...
....fleur?
MUMBLE
......
HUH? WAS MY GRAMMAR WRONG...?
OR MAYBE MY PRONUNCIATION...?

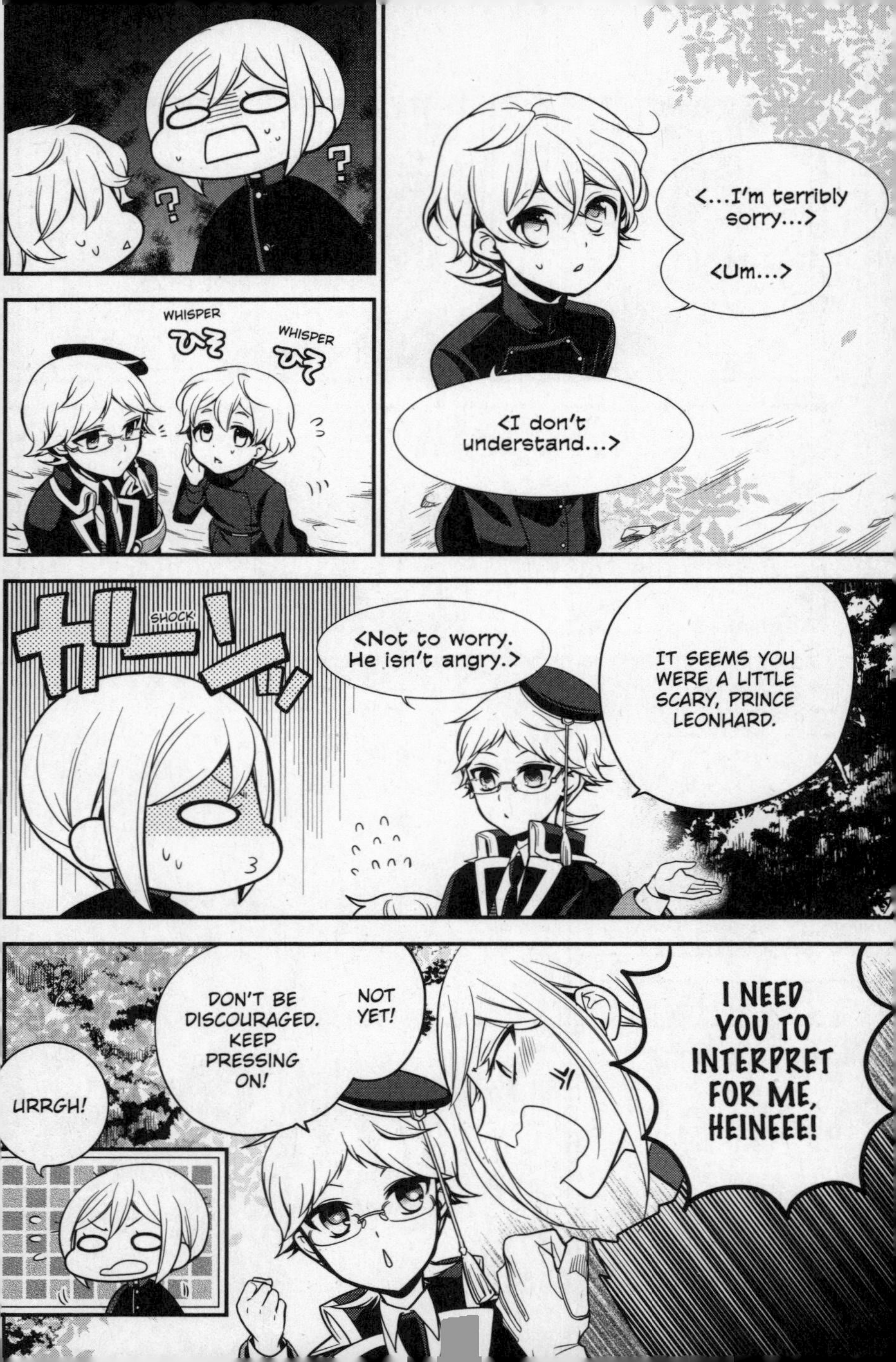
<...I'm terribly sorry...>
<Um...>
<I don't understand...>
WHISPER
ひそ
WHISPER
ひそ
IT SEEMS YOU WERE A LITTLE SCARY, PRINCE LEONHARD.
<Not to worry. He isn't angry.>
SHOCK
ガーン
I NEED YOU TO INTERPRET FOR ME, HEINEEE!
NOT YET!
DON'T BE DISCOURAGED. KEEP PRESSING ON!
URRGH!

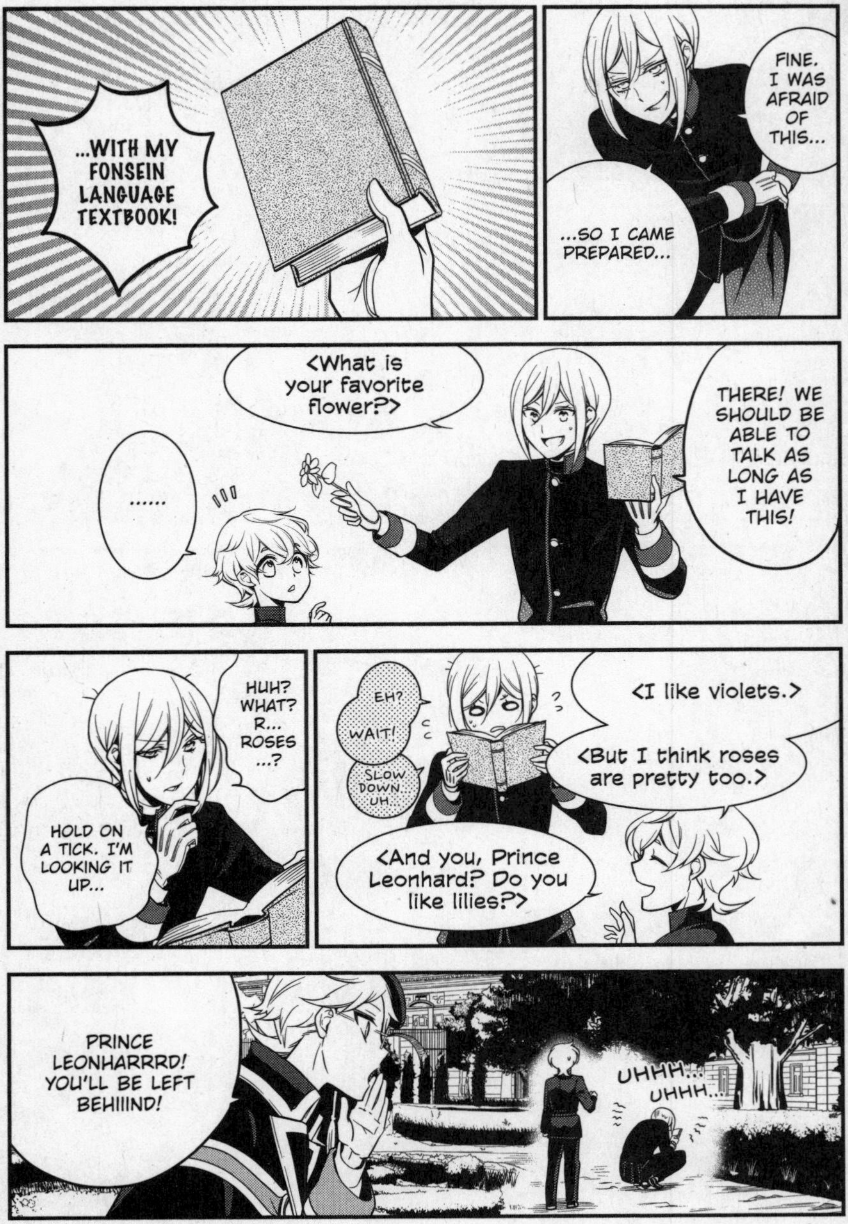

FINE. I WAS AFRAID OF THIS...
...SO I CAME PREPARED...
...WITH MY FONSEIN LANGUAGE TEXTBOOK!
THERE! WE SHOULD BE ABLE TO TALK AS LONG AS I HAVE THIS!
<What is your favorite flower?>
......
<I like violets.>
<But I think roses are pretty too.>
EH?
WAIT!
SLOW DOWN.. UH...
<And you, Prince Leonhard? Do you like lilies?>
HUH? WHAT? R... ROSES ...?
HOLD ON A TICK. I'M LOOKING IT UP...
UHHH... UHHH...
PRINCE LEONHARRRD! YOU'LL BE LEFT BEHIIIND!

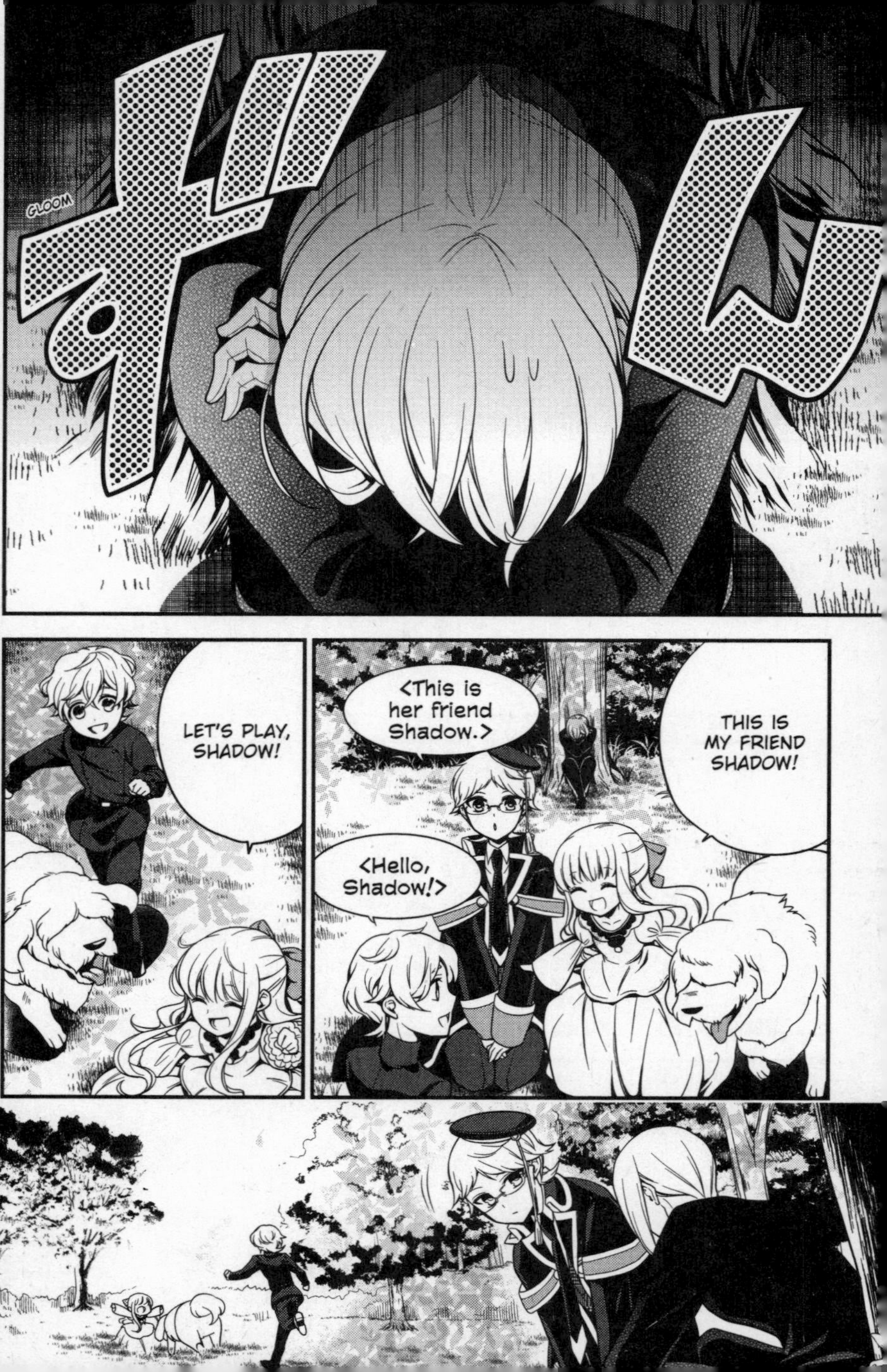
GLOOM
THIS IS MY FRIEND SHADOW!
<This is her friend Shadow.>
<Hello, Shadow!>
LET'S PLAY, SHADOW!

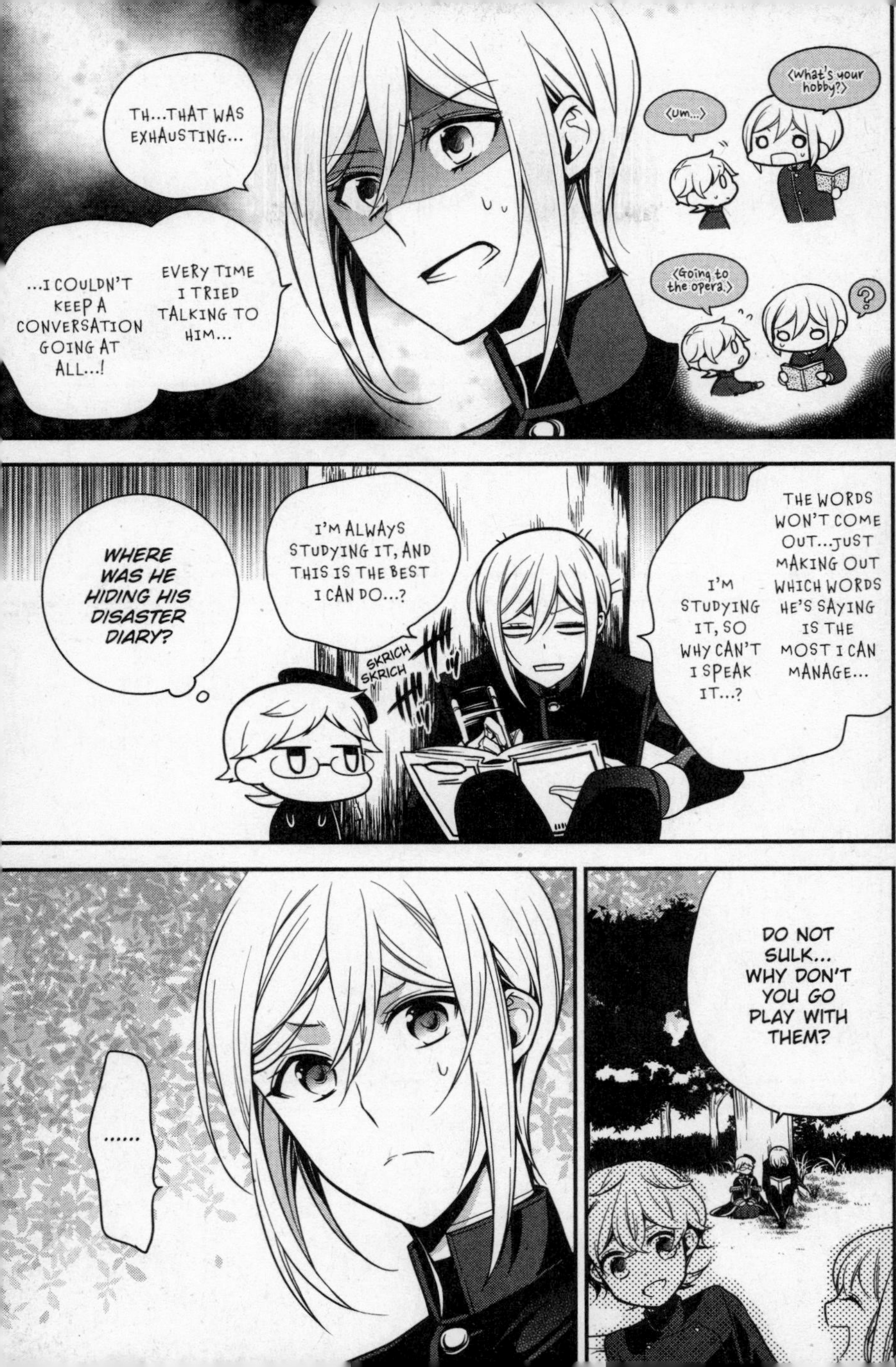

‹What's your hobby?›
‹Um...›
‹Going to the opera.›
TH...THAT WAS EXHAUSTING...
EVERY TIME I TRIED TALKING TO HIM...
...I COULDN'T KEEP A CONVERSATION GOING AT ALL...!
THE WORDS WON'T COME OUT...JUST MAKING OUT WHICH WORDS HE'S SAYING IS THE MOST I CAN MANAGE...
I'M STUDYING IT, SO WHY CAN'T I SPEAK IT...?
I'M ALWAYS STUDYING IT, AND THIS IS THE BEST I CAN DO...?
SKRICH SKRICH
WHERE WAS HE HIDING HIS DISASTER DIARY?
DO NOT SULK... WHY DON'T YOU GO PLAY WITH THEM?
......

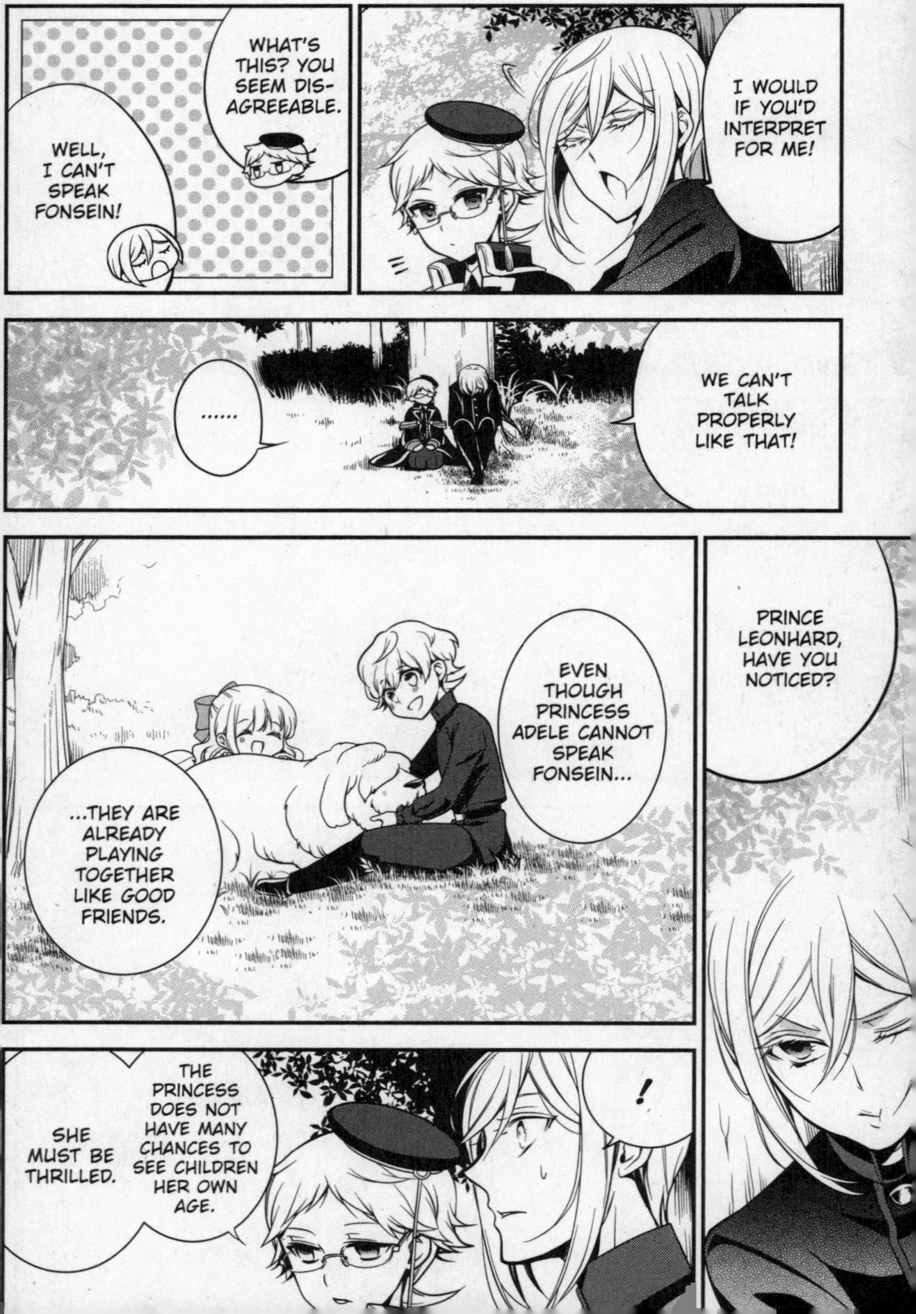
I WOULD IF YOU'D INTERPRET FOR ME!
WHAT'S THIS? YOU SEEM DIS-AGREEABLE.
WELL, I CAN'T SPEAK FONSEIN!
WE CAN'T TALK PROPERLY LIKE THAT!
......
PRINCE LEONHARD, HAVE YOU NOTICED?
EVEN THOUGH PRINCESS ADELE CANNOT SPEAK FONSEIN...
...THEY ARE ALREADY PLAYING TOGETHER LIKE GOOD FRIENDS.
!
THE PRINCESS DOES NOT HAVE MANY CHANCES TO SEE CHILDREN HER OWN AGE.
SHE MUST BE THRILLED.

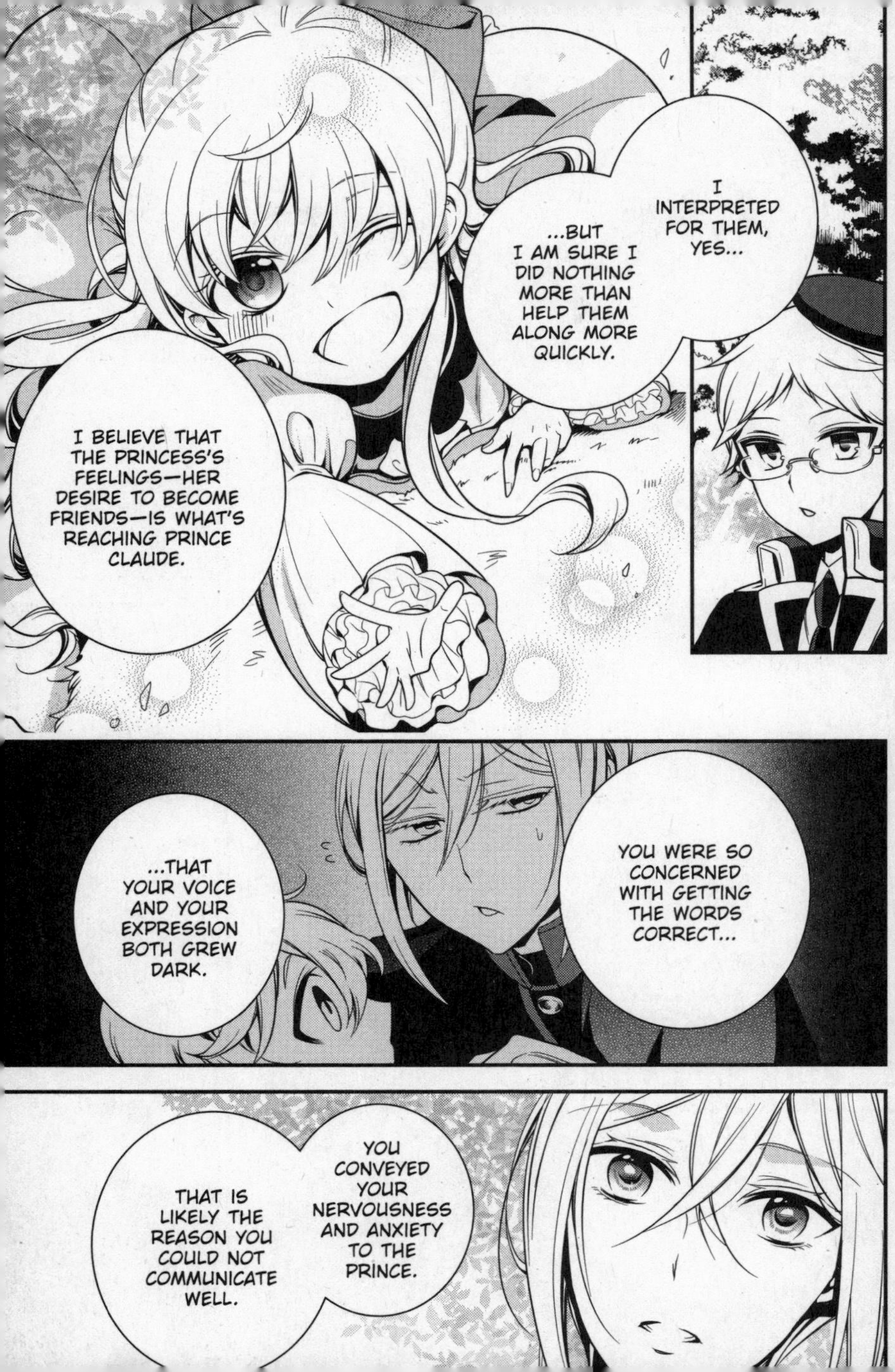
I INTERPRETED FOR THEM, YES...
...BUT I AM SURE I DID NOTHING MORE THAN HELP THEM ALONG MORE QUICKLY.
I BELIEVE THAT THE PRINCESS'S FEELINGS—HER DESIRE TO BECOME FRIENDS—IS WHAT'S REACHING PRINCE CLAUDE.
YOU WERE SO CONCERNED WITH GETTING THE WORDS CORRECT...
...THAT YOUR VOICE AND YOUR EXPRESSION BOTH GREW DARK.
YOU CONVEYED YOUR NERVOUSNESS AND ANXIETY TO THE PRINCE.
THAT IS LIKELY THE REASON YOU COULD NOT COMMUNICATE WELL.

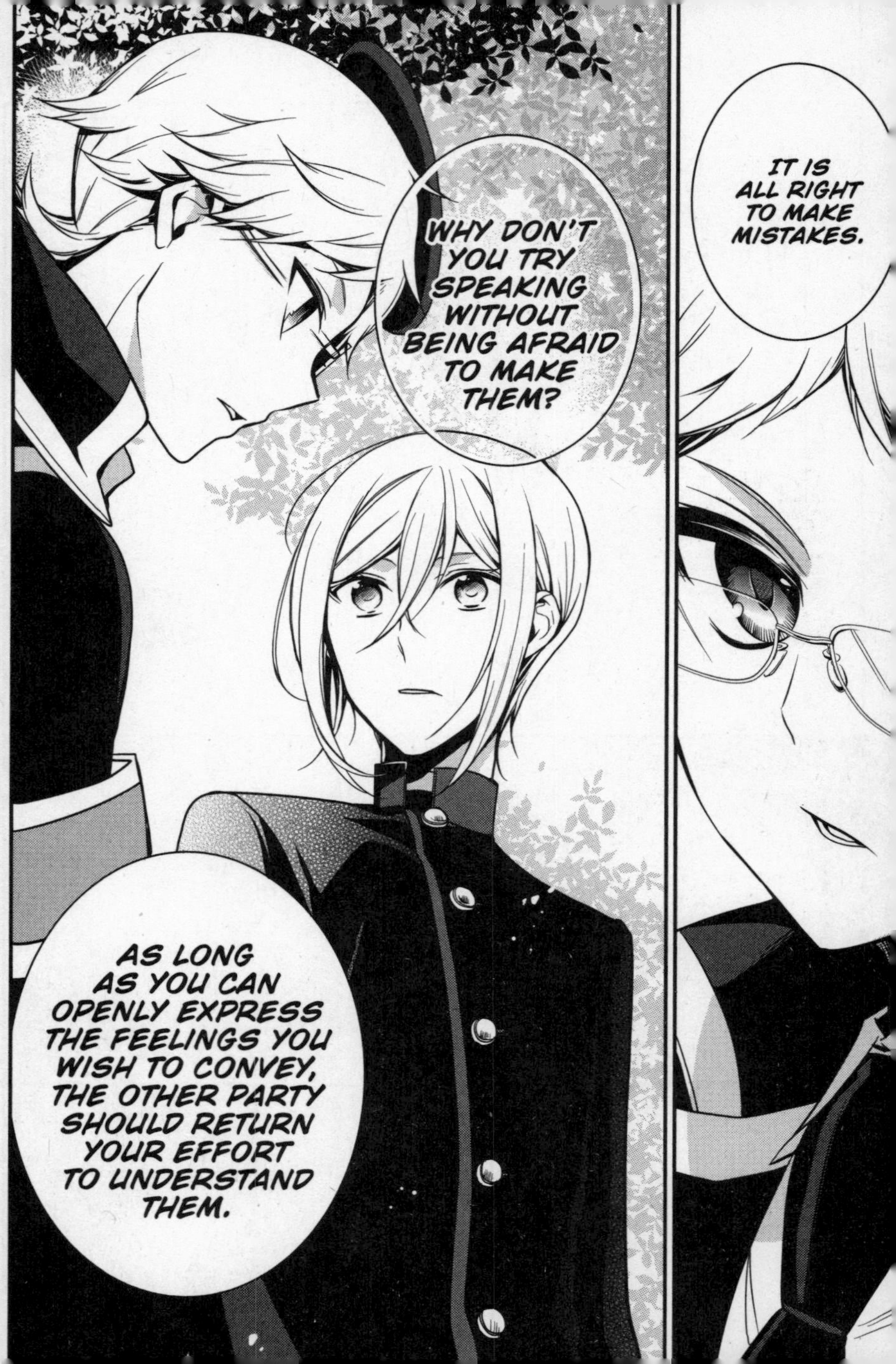
IT IS ALL RIGHT TO MAKE MISTAKES.
WHY DON'T YOU TRY SPEAKING WITHOUT BEING AFRAID TO MAKE THEM?
AS LONG AS YOU CAN OPENLY EXPRESS THE FEELINGS YOU WISH TO CONVEY, THE OTHER PARTY SHOULD RETURN YOUR EFFORT TO UNDERSTAND THEM.

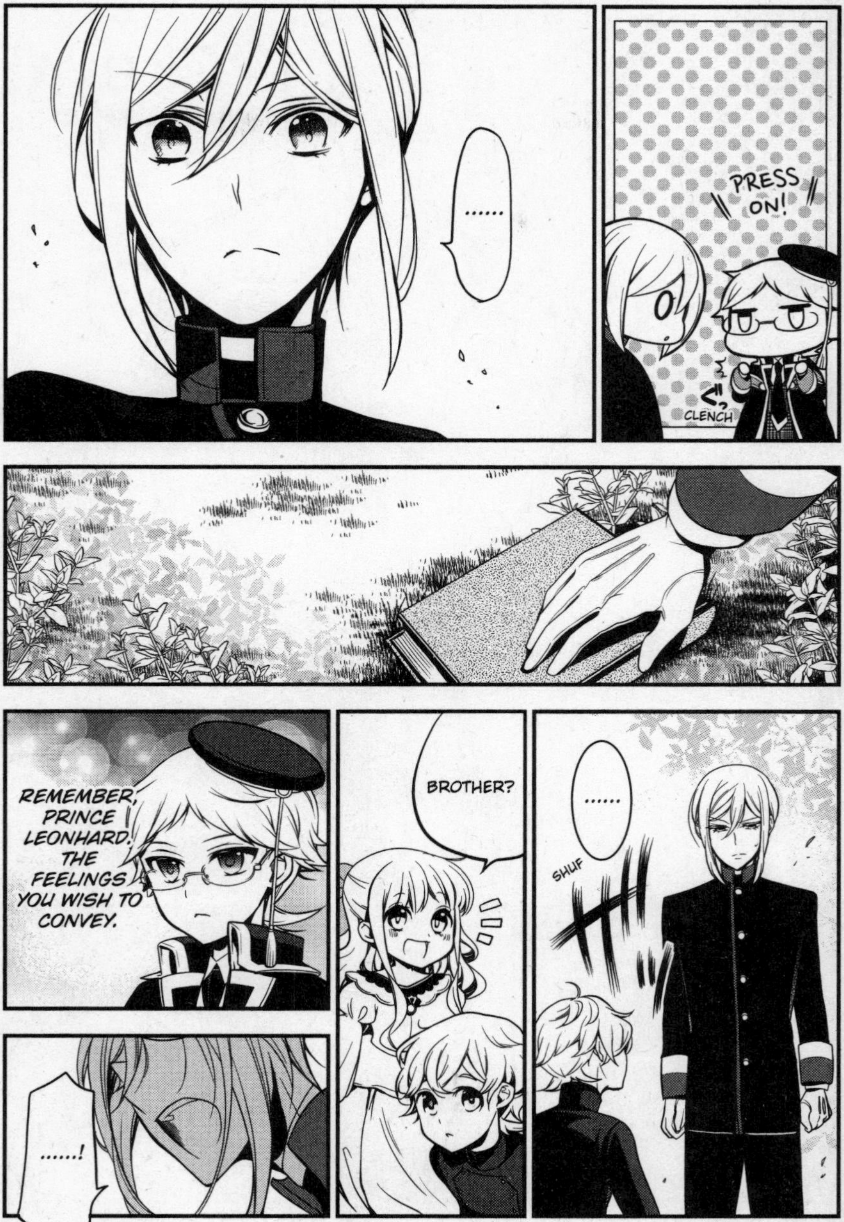
PRESS ON!
CLENCH
......
......
SHUF
BROTHER?
REMEMBER, PRINCE LEONHARD. THE FEELINGS YOU WISH TO CONVEY.
......!

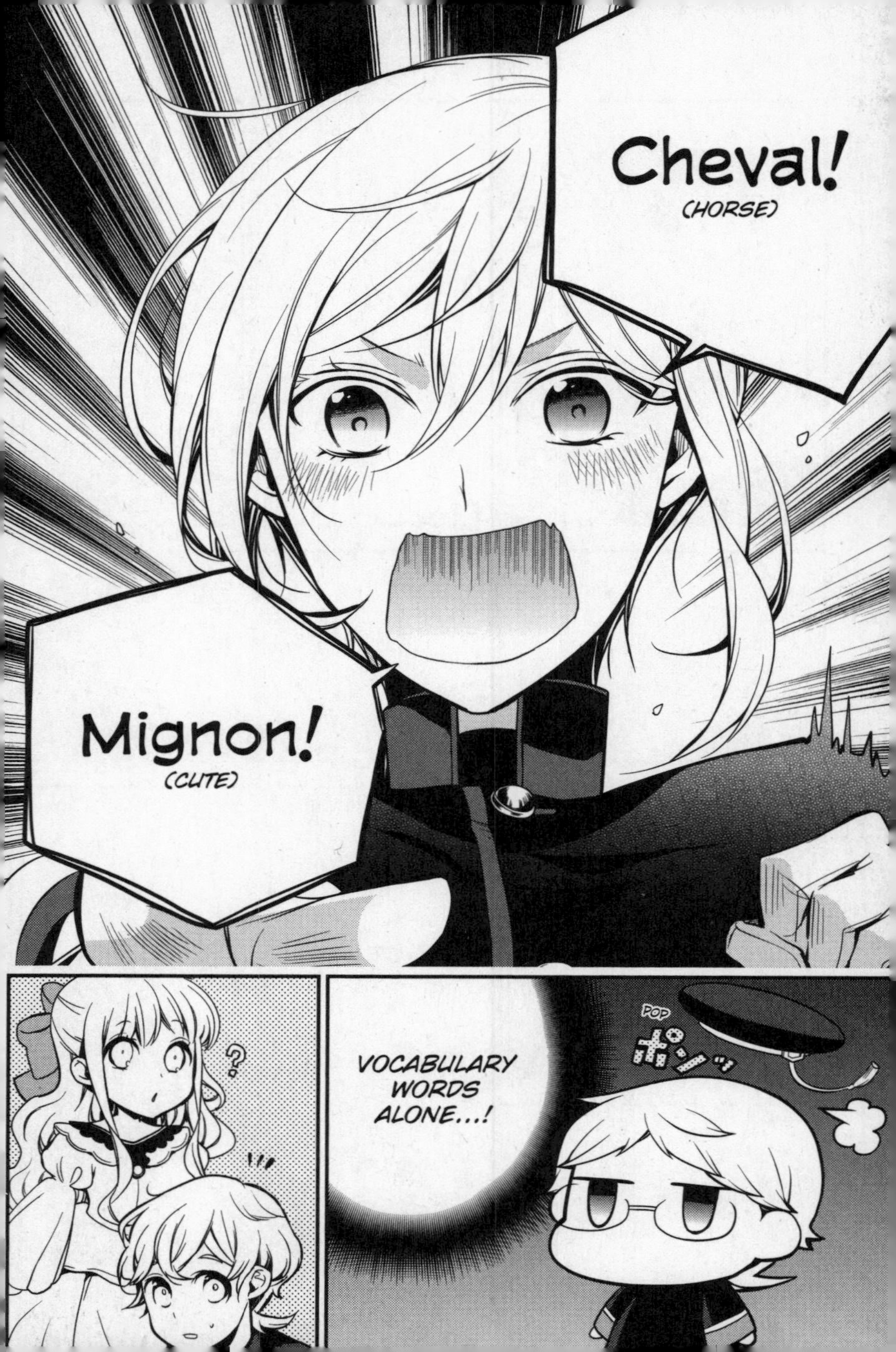
Cheval!
(HORSE)
Mignon!
(CUTE)
POP
ポンッ!
VOCABULARY WORDS ALONE...!

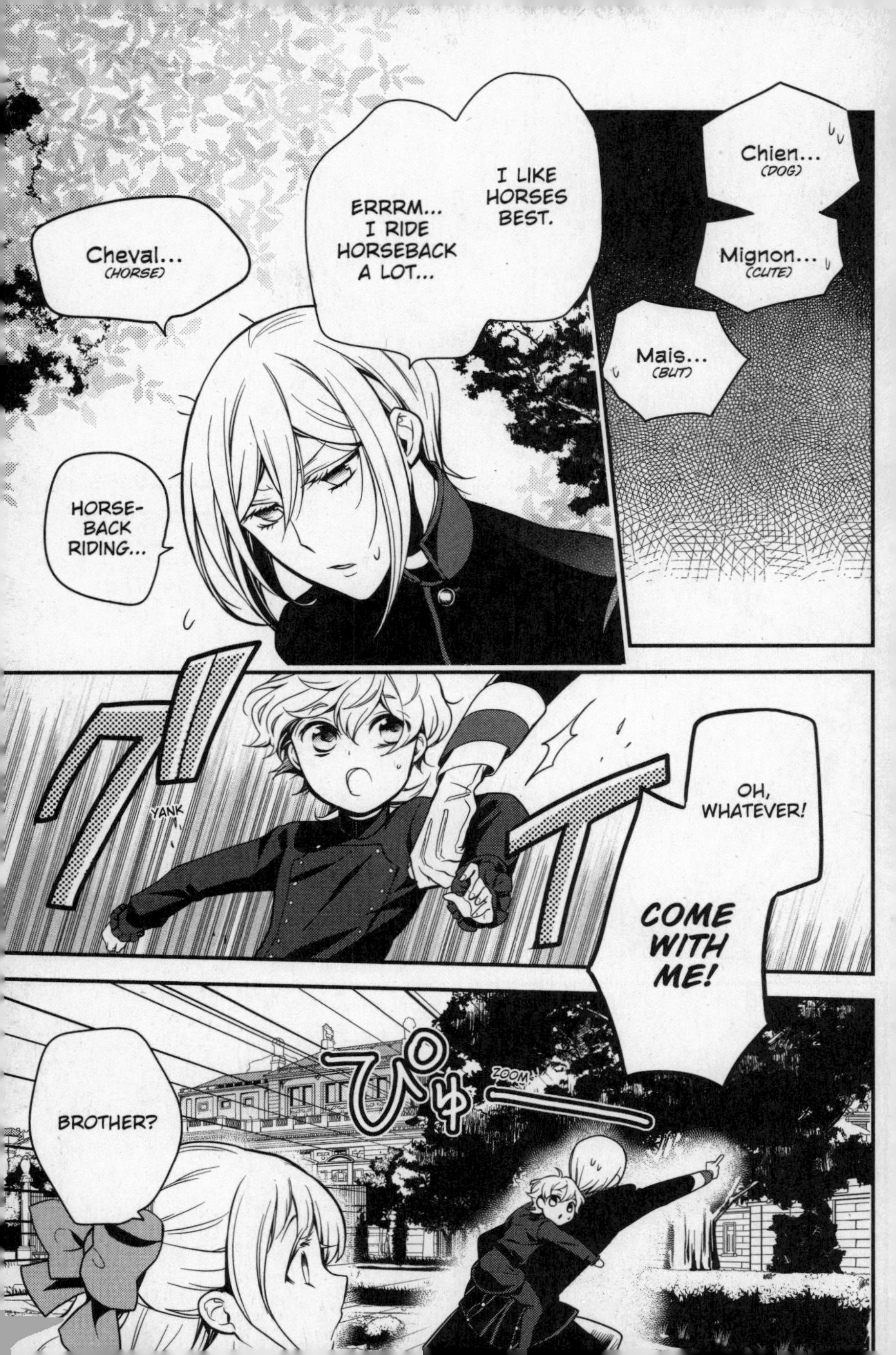
Chien...
(DOG)
Mignon...
(CUTE)
Mais...
(BUT)
I LIKE HORSES BEST.
ERRRM... I RIDE HORSEBACK A LOT...
Cheval...
(HORSE)
HORSE-BACK RIDING...
OH, WHATEVER!
COME WITH ME!
グイ
YANK
ぴゅー
ZOOM
BROTHER?

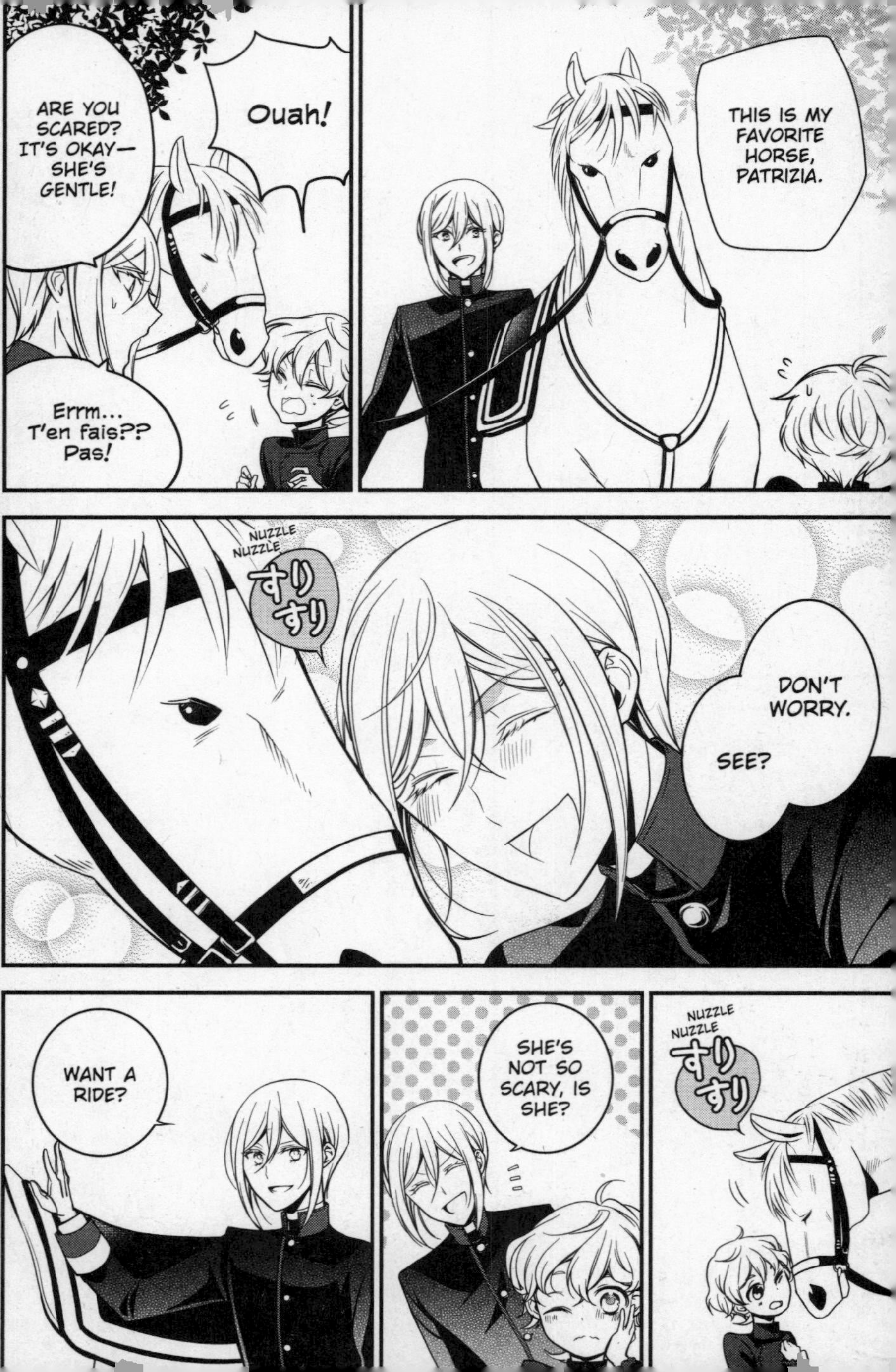
THIS IS MY FAVORITE HORSE, PATRIZIA.
Ouah!
ARE YOU SCARED? IT'S OKAY— SHE'S GENTLE!
Errm... T'en fais?? Pas!
NUZZLE NUZZLE
すりすり
DON'T WORRY.
SEE?
NUZZLE NUZZLE
すりすり
SHE'S NOT SO SCARY, IS SHE?
WANT A RIDE?

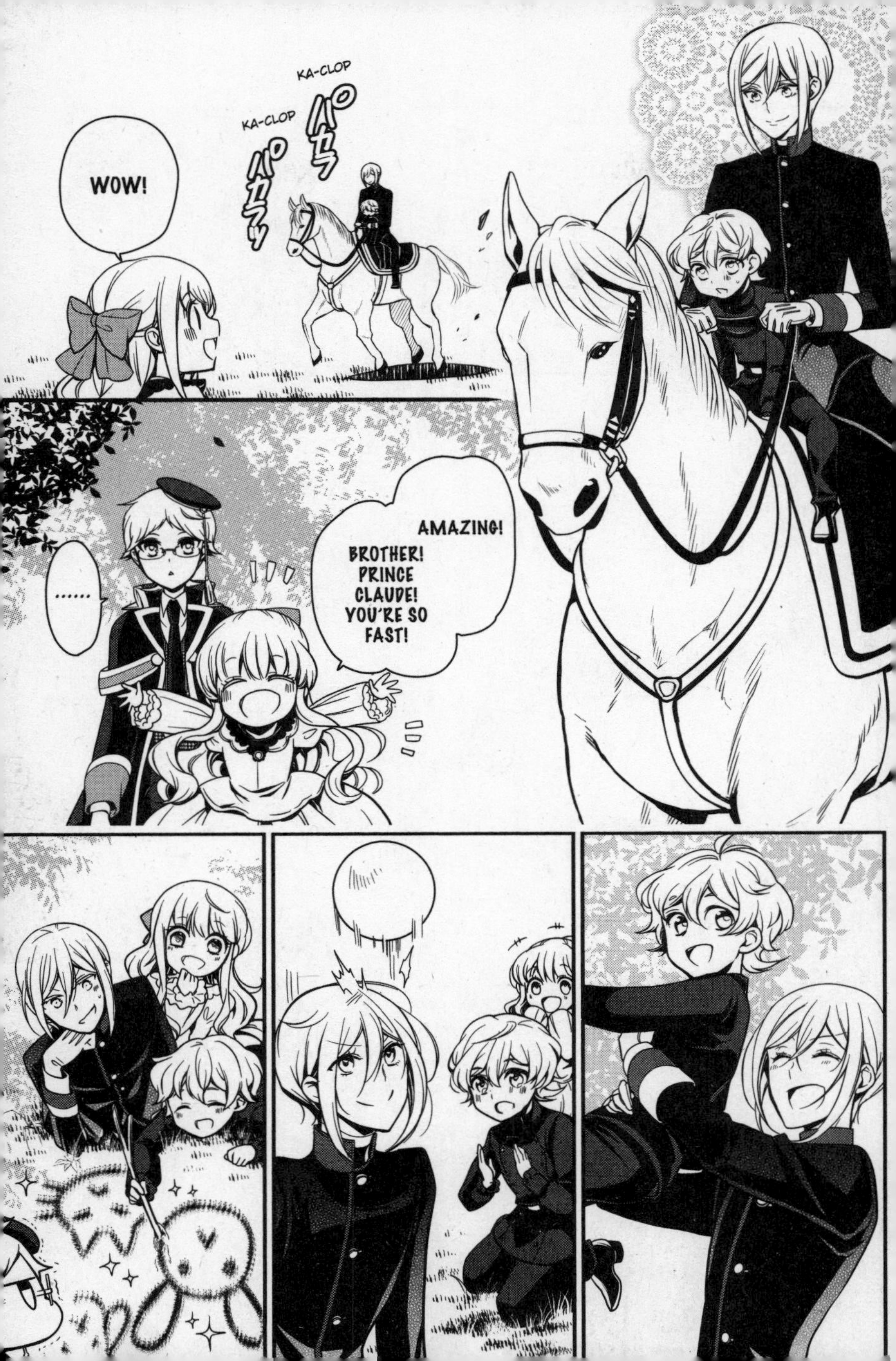
KA-CLOP
パカラ
KA-CLOP
パカラッ
WOW!
AMAZING! BROTHER! PRINCE CLAUDE! YOU'RE SO FAST!
......

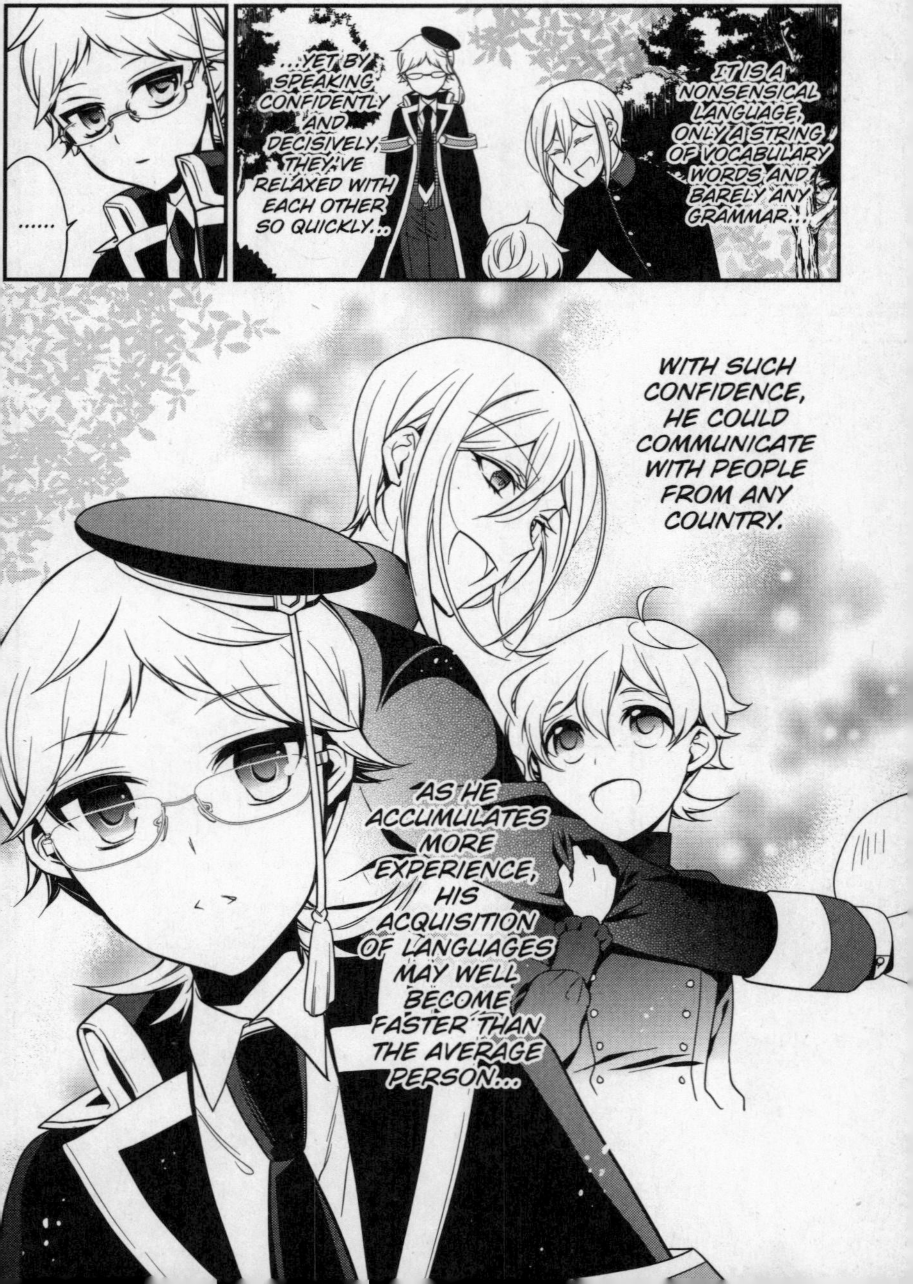
IT IS A NONSENSICAL LANGUAGE, ONLY A STRING OF VOCABULARY WORDS AND BARELY ANY GRAMMAR...
...YET BY SPEAKING CONFIDENTLY AND DECISIVELY, THEY'VE RELAXED WITH EACH OTHER SO QUICKLY...
......
WITH SUCH CONFIDENCE, HE COULD COMMUNICATE WITH PEOPLE FROM ANY COUNTRY.
AS HE ACCUMULATES MORE EXPERIENCE, HIS ACQUISITION OF LANGUAGES MAY WELL BECOME FASTER THAN THE AVERAGE PERSON...

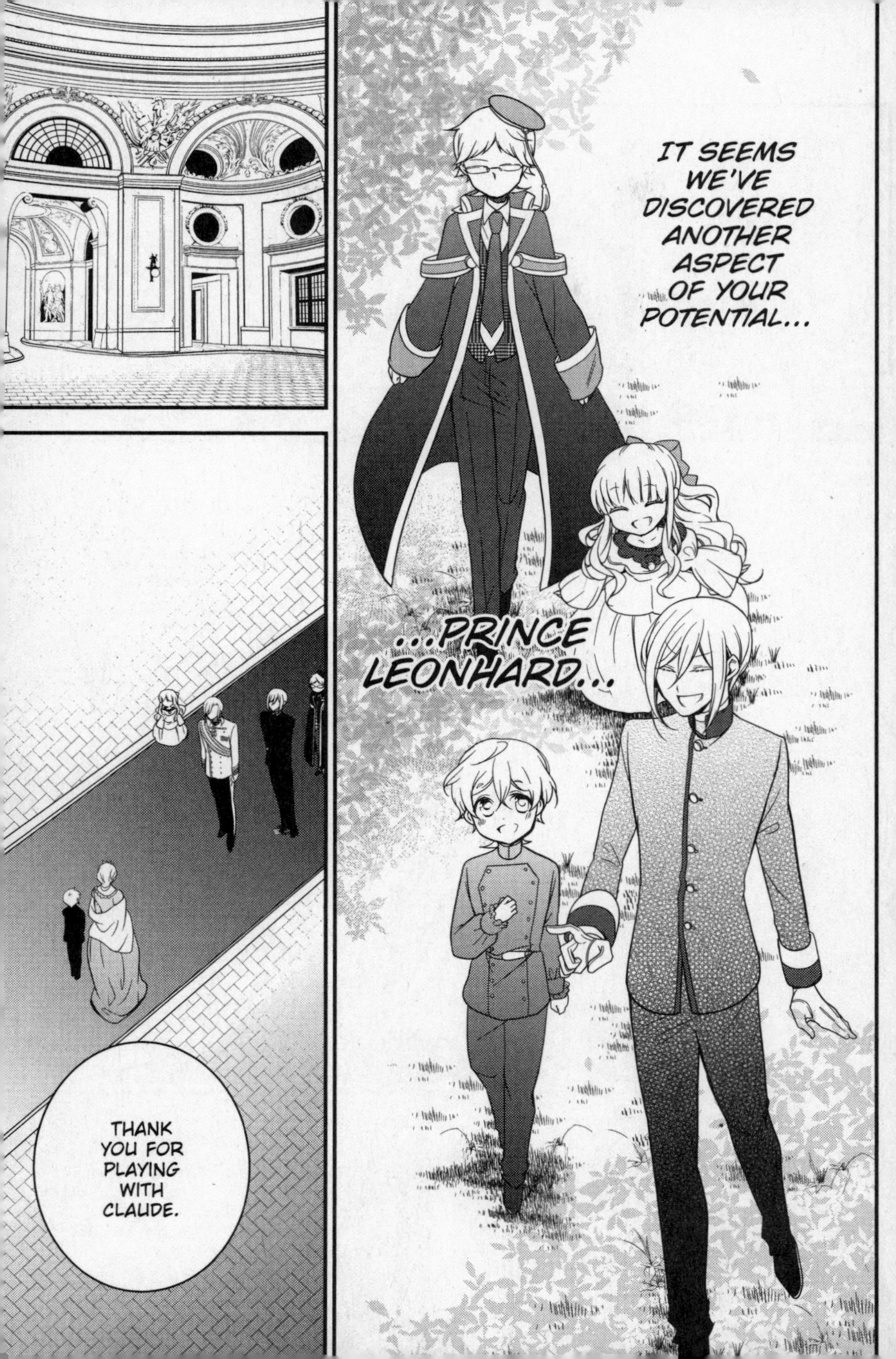
IT SEEMS WE'VE DISCOVERED ANOTHER ASPECT OF YOUR POTENTIAL...
...PRINCE LEONHARD...
THANK YOU FOR PLAYING WITH CLAUDE.

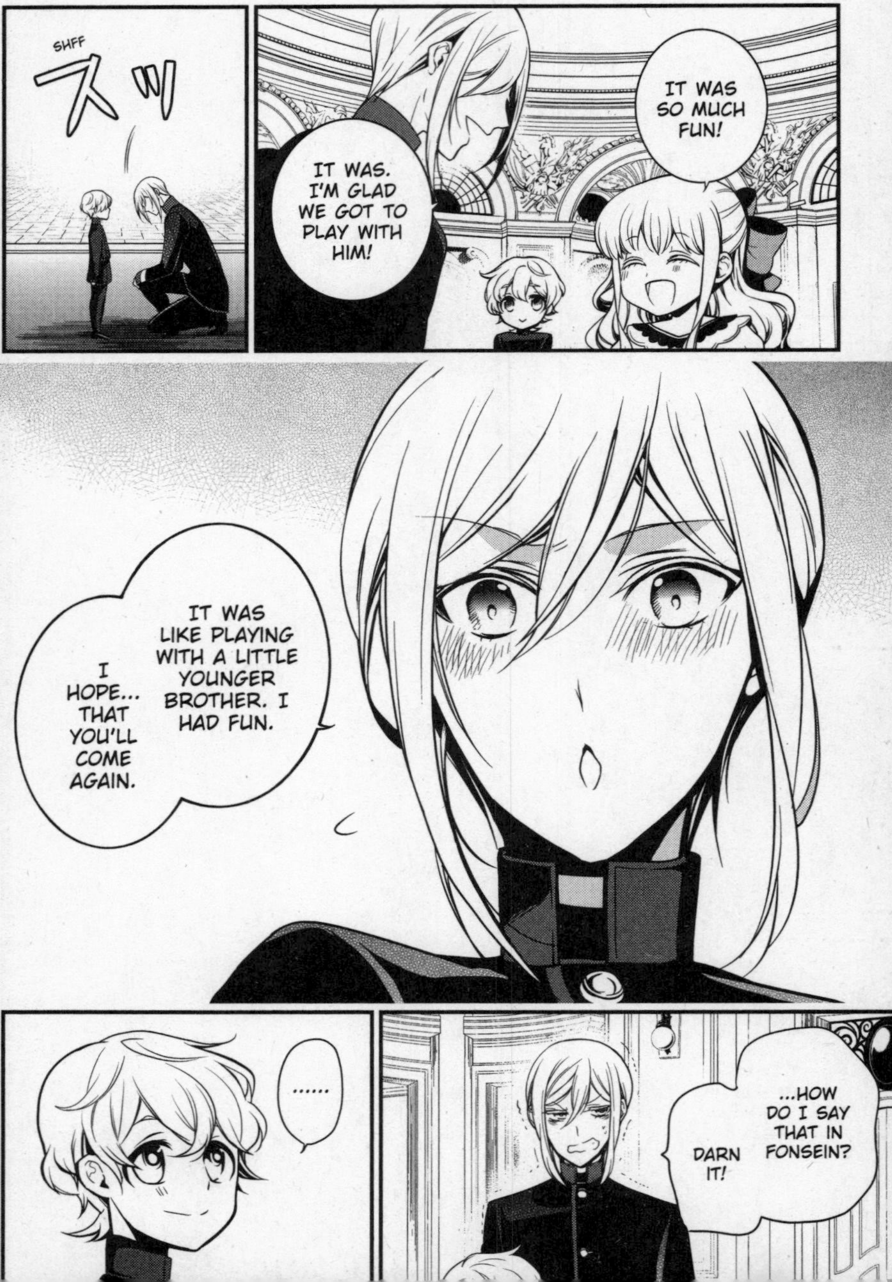
IT WAS SO MUCH FUN!
IT WAS. I'M GLAD WE GOT TO PLAY WITH HIM!
SHFF
スッ
IT WAS LIKE PLAYING WITH A LITTLE YOUNGER BROTHER. I HAD FUN.
I HOPE... THAT YOU'LL COME AGAIN.
...HOW DO I SAY THAT IN FONSEIN?
DARN IT!
......

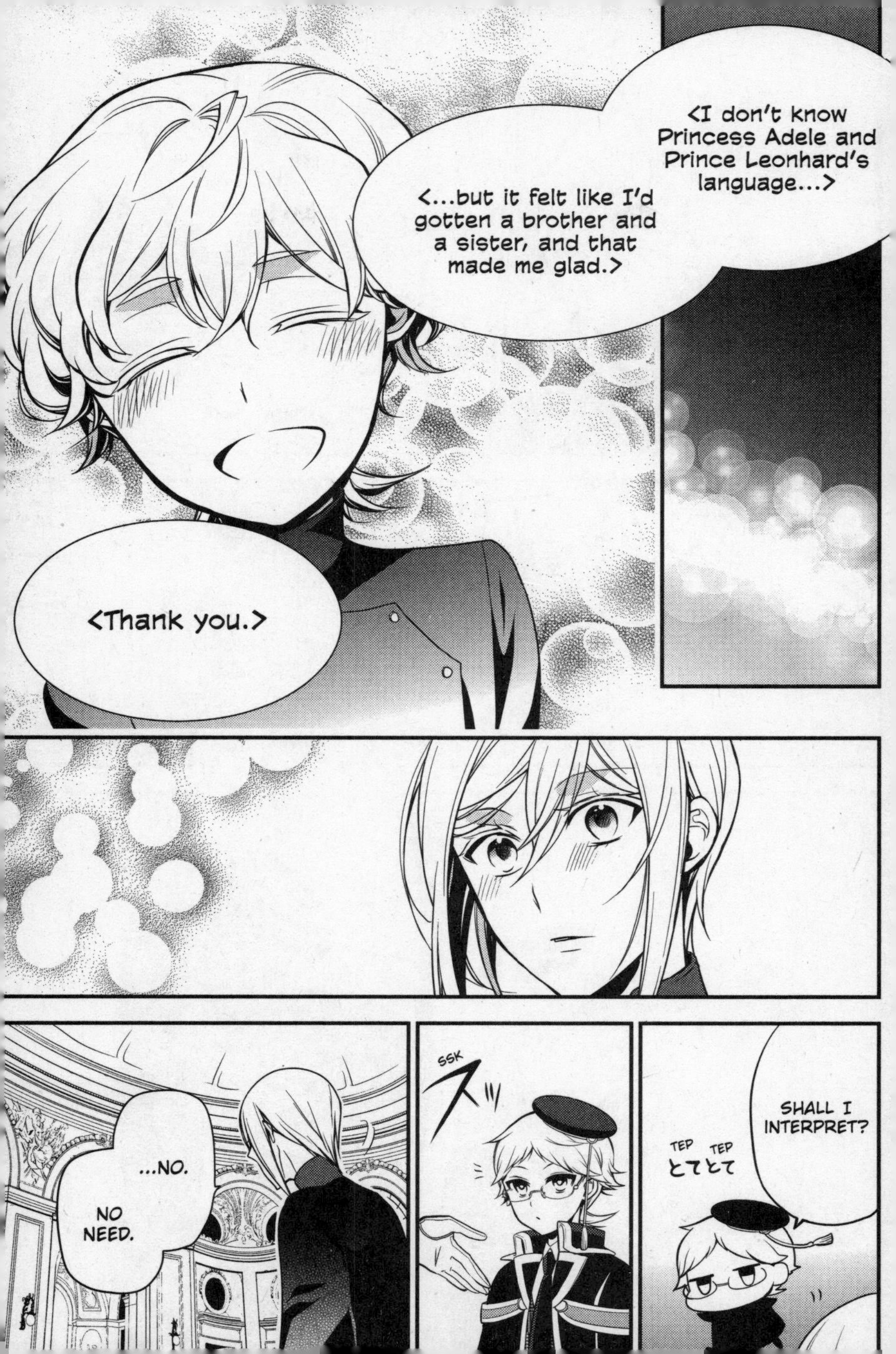

<I don't know Princess Adele and Prince Leonhard's language...>
<...but it felt like I'd gotten a brother and a sister, and that made me glad.>
<Thank you.>
SHALL I INTERPRET?
TEP TEP
とてとて
SSK
...NO.
NO NEED.

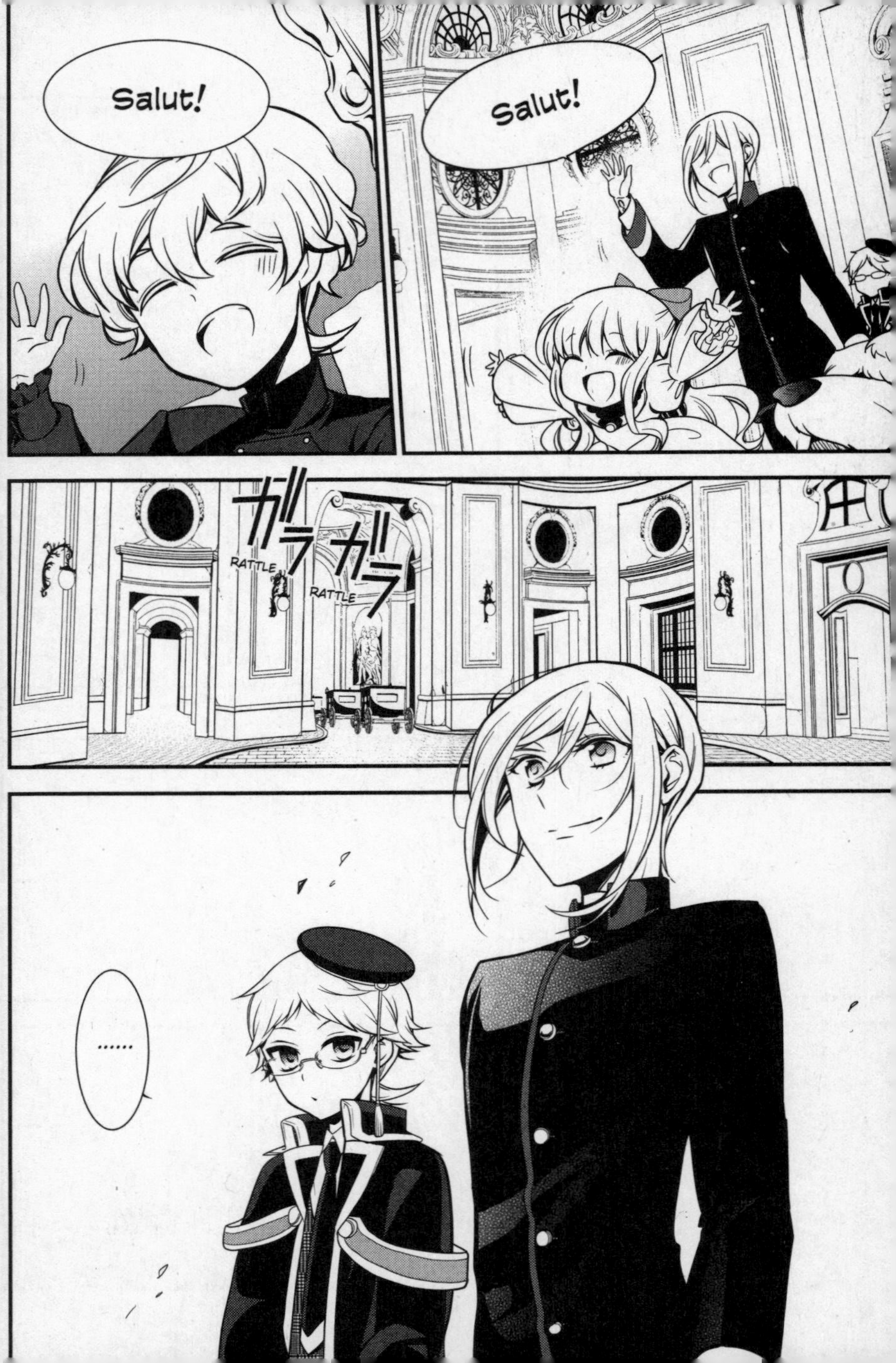
Salut!
Salut!
ガラガラ
RATTLE
RATTLE
......

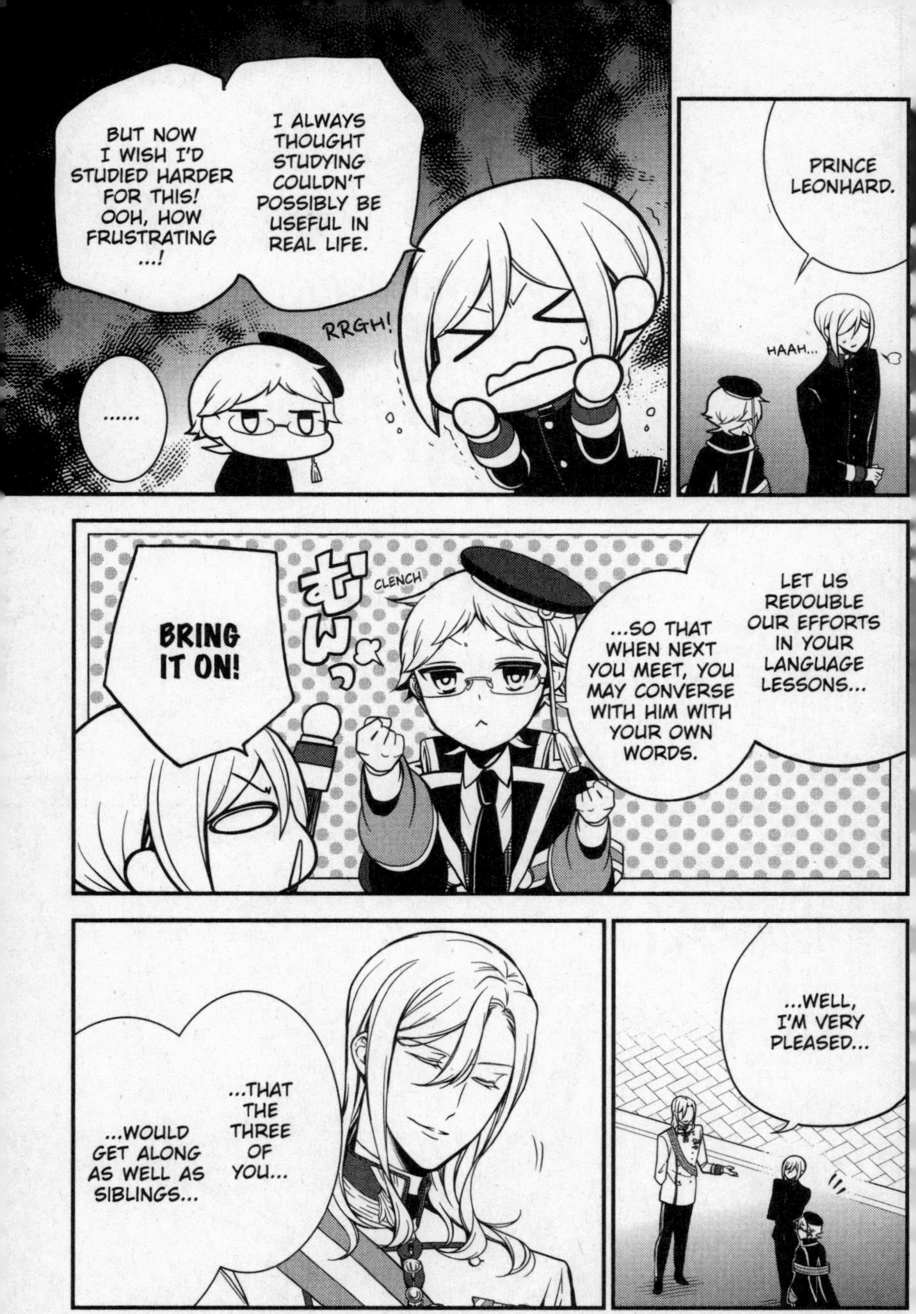
PRINCE LEONHARD.
HAAH...
I ALWAYS THOUGHT STUDYING COULDN'T POSSIBLY BE USEFUL IN REAL LIFE.
BUT NOW I WISH I'D STUDIED HARDER FOR THIS! OOH, HOW FRUSTRATING ...!
RRGH!
......
LET US REDOUBLE OUR EFFORTS IN YOUR LANGUAGE LESSONS...
...SO THAT WHEN NEXT YOU MEET, YOU MAY CONVERSE WITH HIM WITH YOUR OWN WORDS.
むんっ
CLENCH
BRING IT ON!
...WELL, I'M VERY PLEASED...
...THAT THE THREE OF YOU...
...WOULD GET ALONG AS WELL AS SIBLINGS...

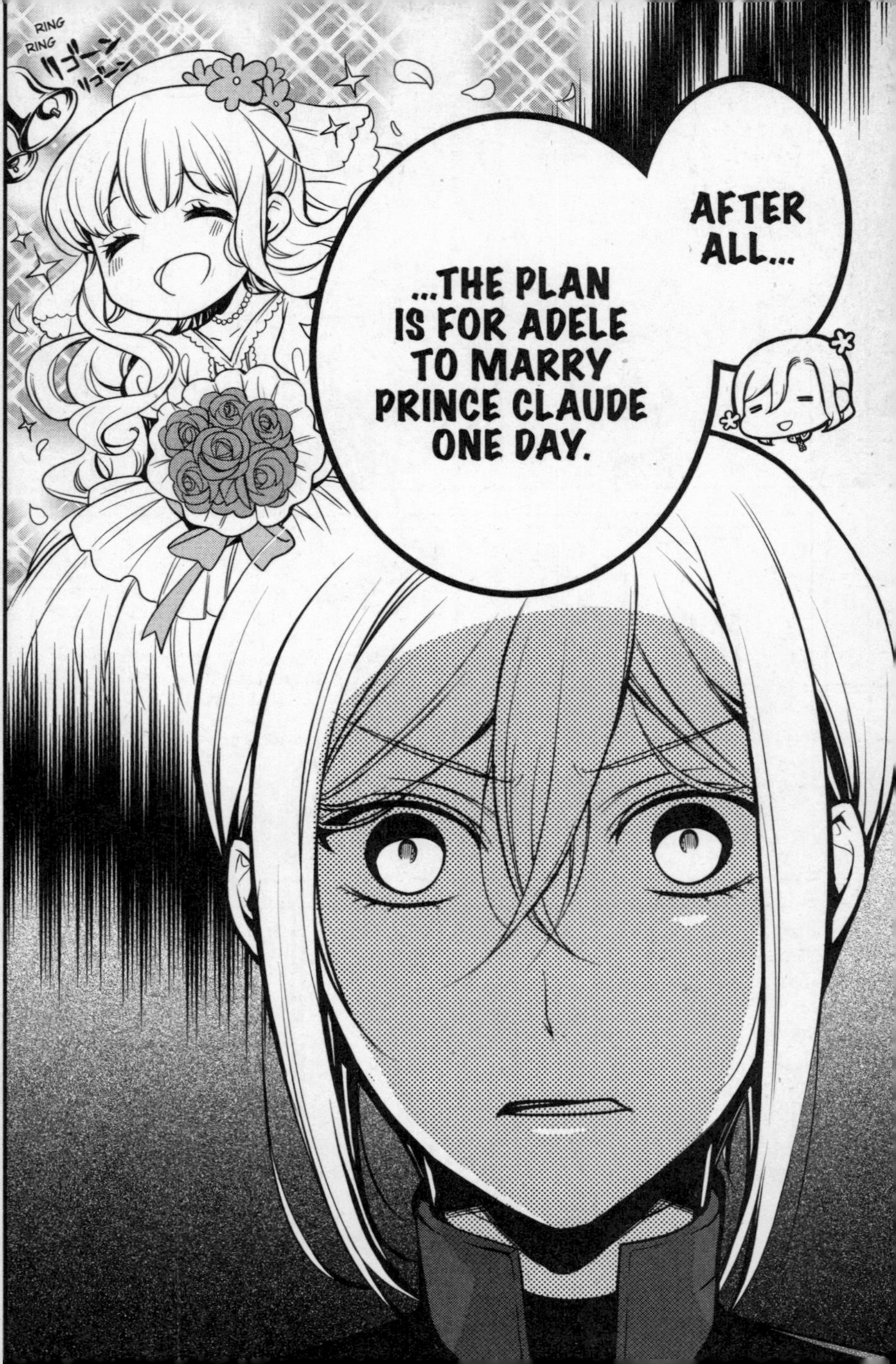
RING RING
リゴーン リゴーン
AFTER ALL...
...THE PLAN IS FOR ADELE TO MARRY PRINCE CLAUDE ONE DAY.

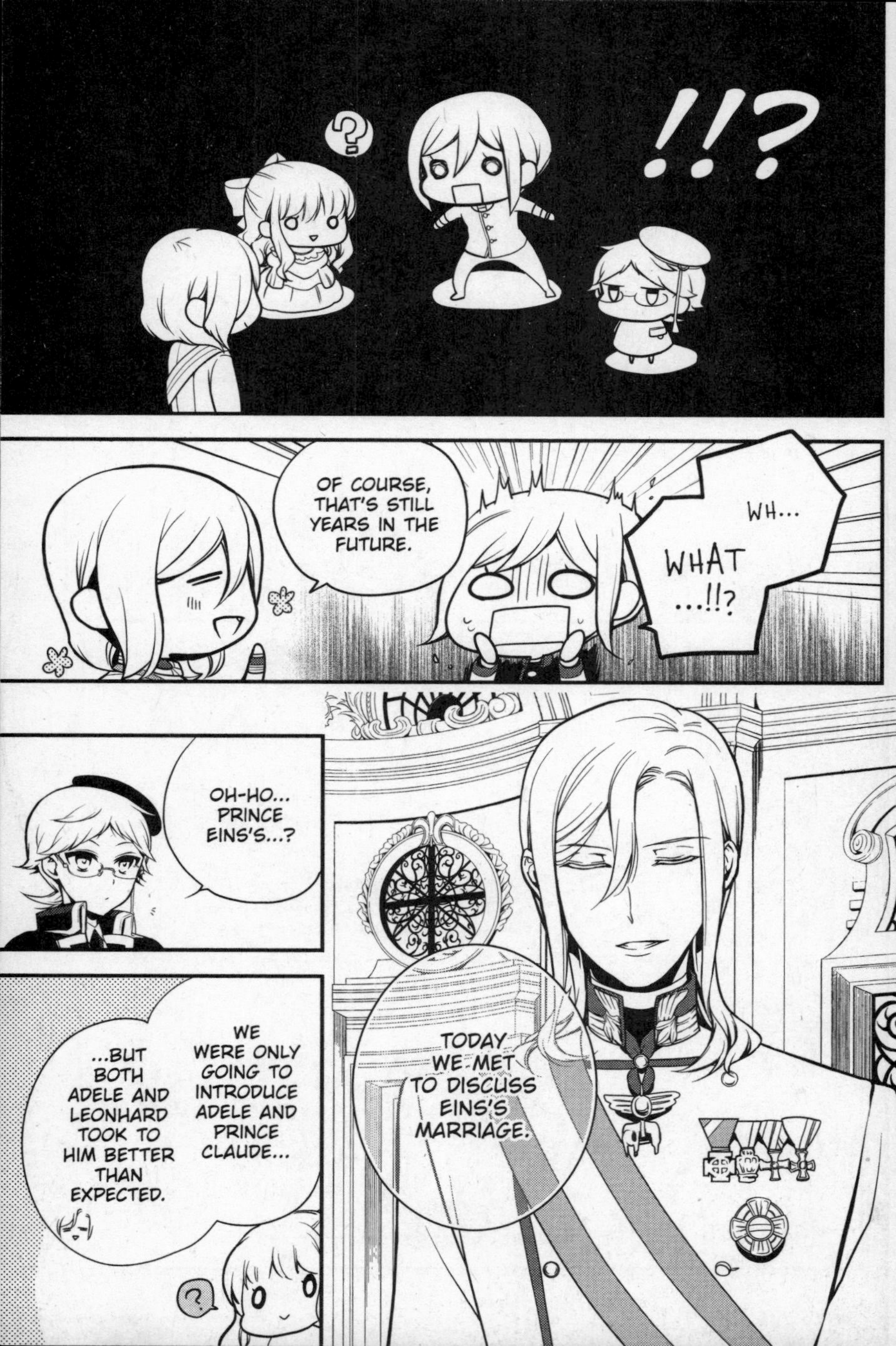
!!?
WH... WHAT ...!!?
OF COURSE, THAT'S STILL YEARS IN THE FUTURE.
TODAY WE MET TO DISCUSS EINS'S MARRIAGE.
OH-HO... PRINCE EINS'S...?
WE WERE ONLY GOING TO INTRODUCE ADELE AND PRINCE CLAUDE...
...BUT BOTH ADELE AND LEONHARD TOOK TO HIM BETTER THAN EXPECTED.

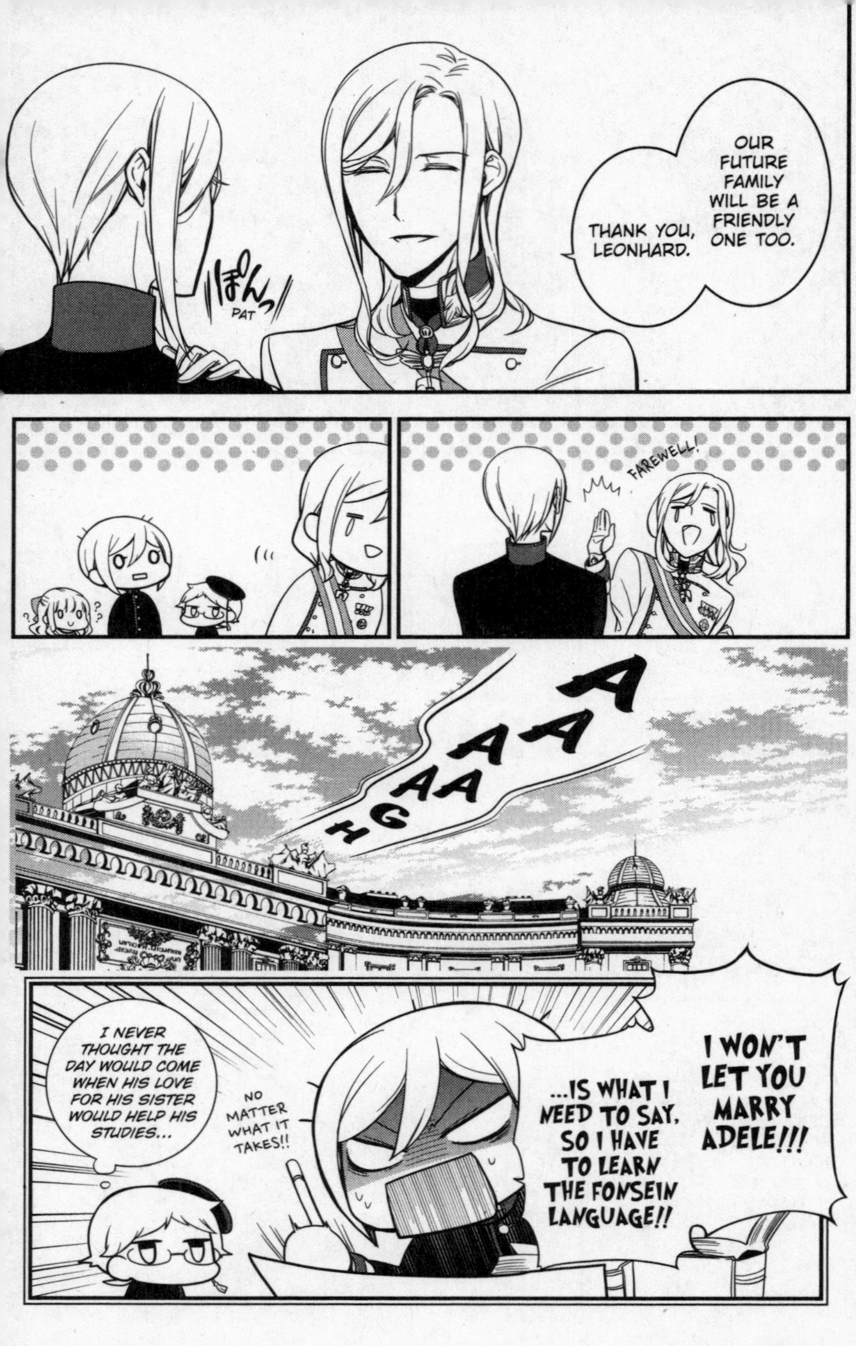
OUR FUTURE FAMILY WILL BE A FRIENDLY ONE TOO.
THANK YOU, LEONHARD.
ぽんっ
PAT
FAREWELL!
AAAAAGH
I WON'T LET YOU MARRY ADELE!!!
...IS WHAT I NEED TO SAY, SO I HAVE TO LEARN THE FONSEIN LANGUAGE!!
NO MATTER WHAT IT TAKES!!
I NEVER THOUGHT THE DAY WOULD COME WHEN HIS LOVE FOR HIS SISTER WOULD HELP HIS STUDIES...

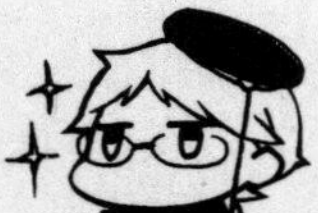

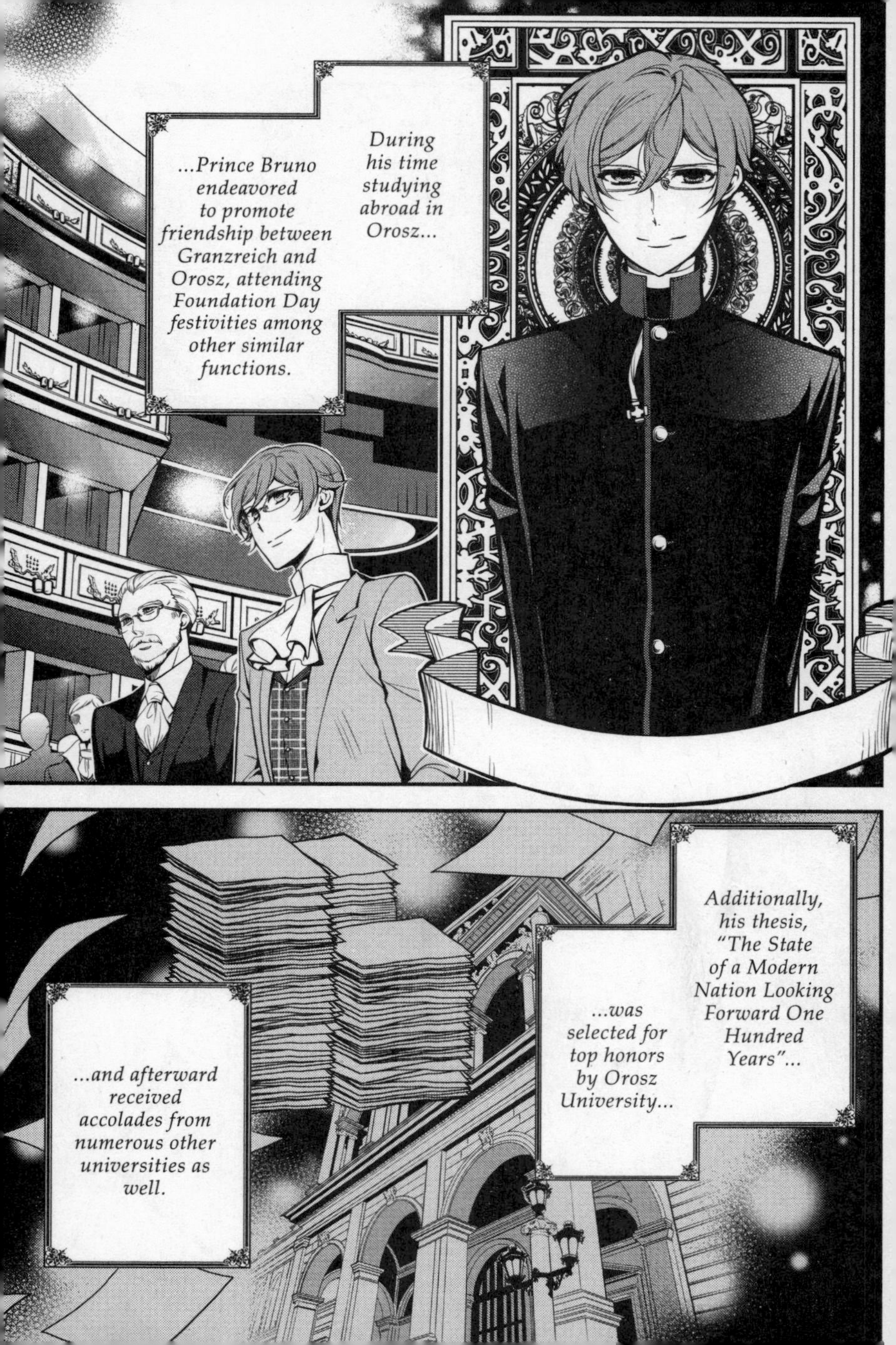
During his time studying abroad in Orosz...
...Prince Bruno endeavored to promote friendship between Granzreich and Orosz, attending Foundation Day festivities among other similar functions.
Additionally, his thesis, "The State of a Modern Nation Looking Forward One Hundred Years"...
...was selected for top honors by Orosz University...
...and afterward received accolades from numerous other universities as well.

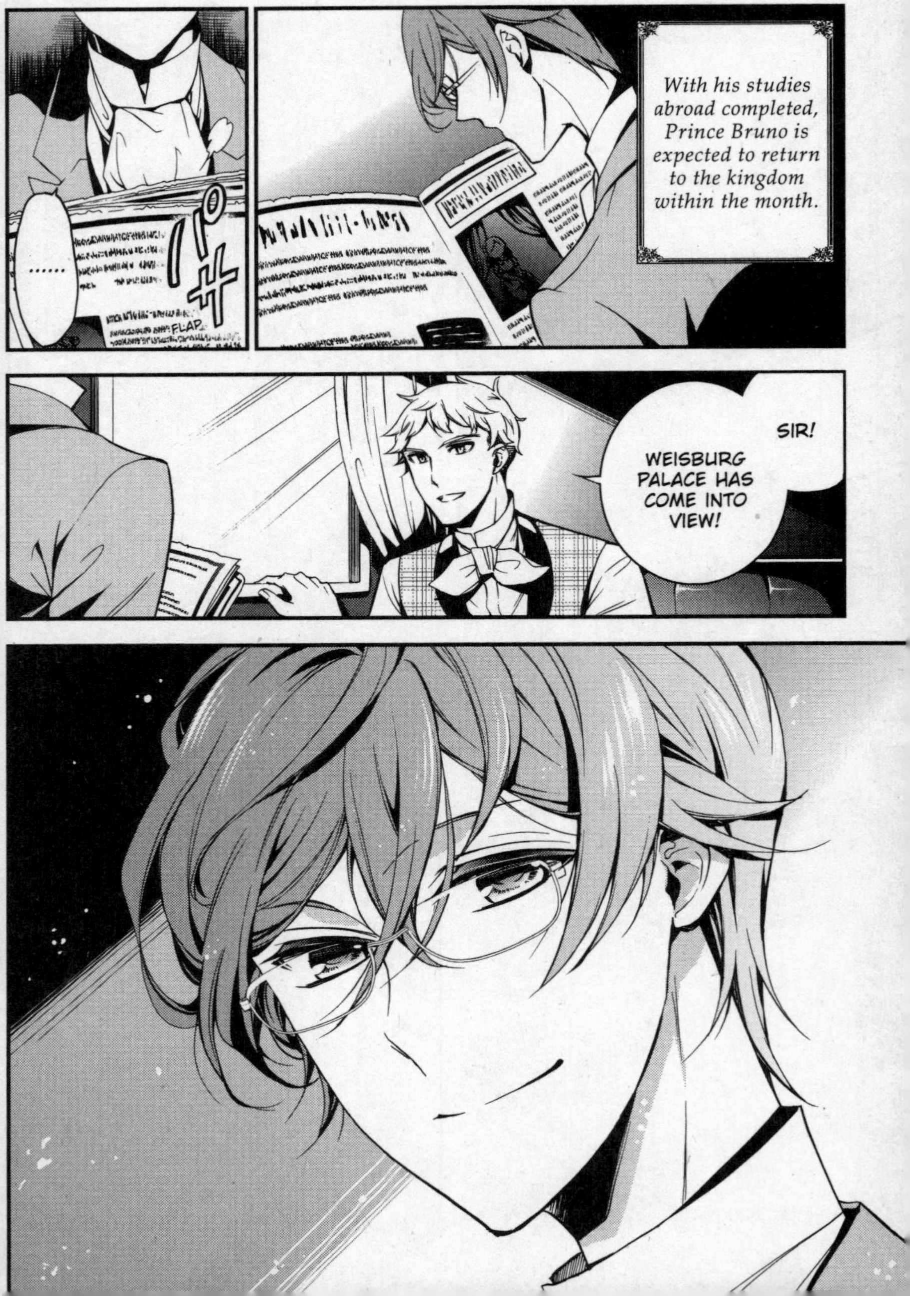
With his studies abroad completed, Prince Bruno is expected to return to the kingdom within the month.
......
FLAP
SIR!
WEISBURG PALACE HAS COME INTO VIEW!

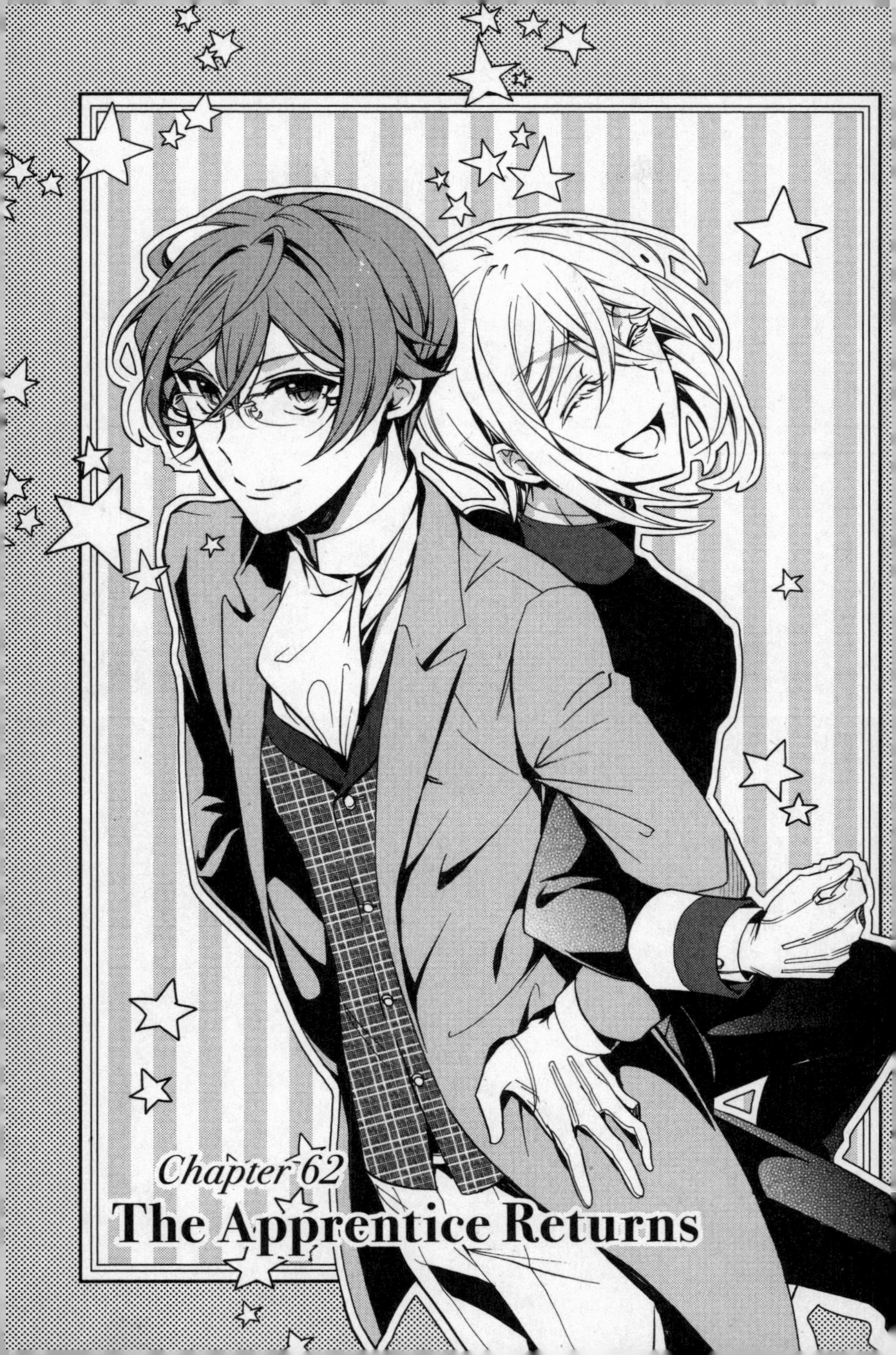
Chapter 62
The Apprentice Returns

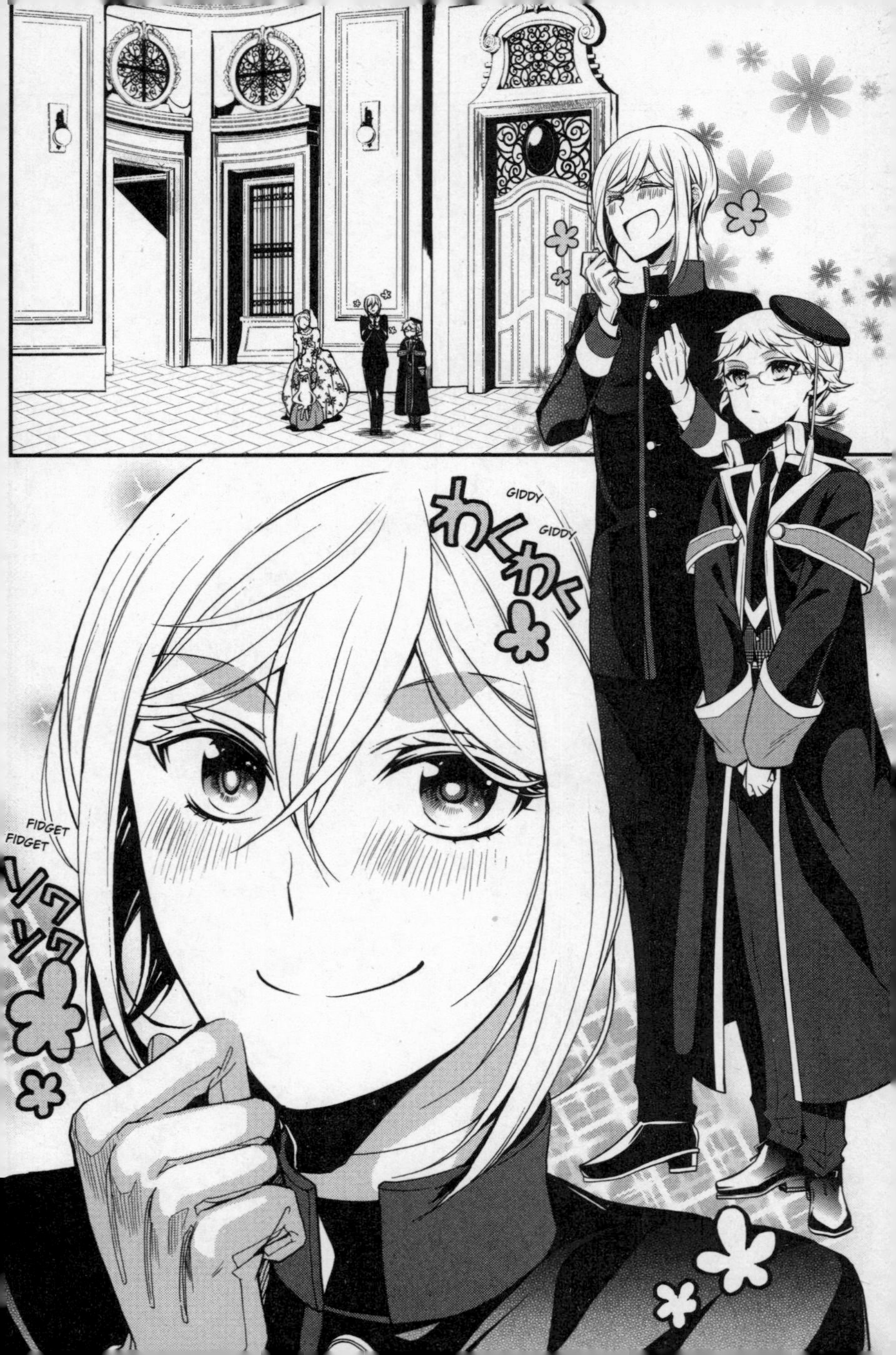
GIDDY GIDDY
わくわく
FIDGET FIDGET
ソワソワ

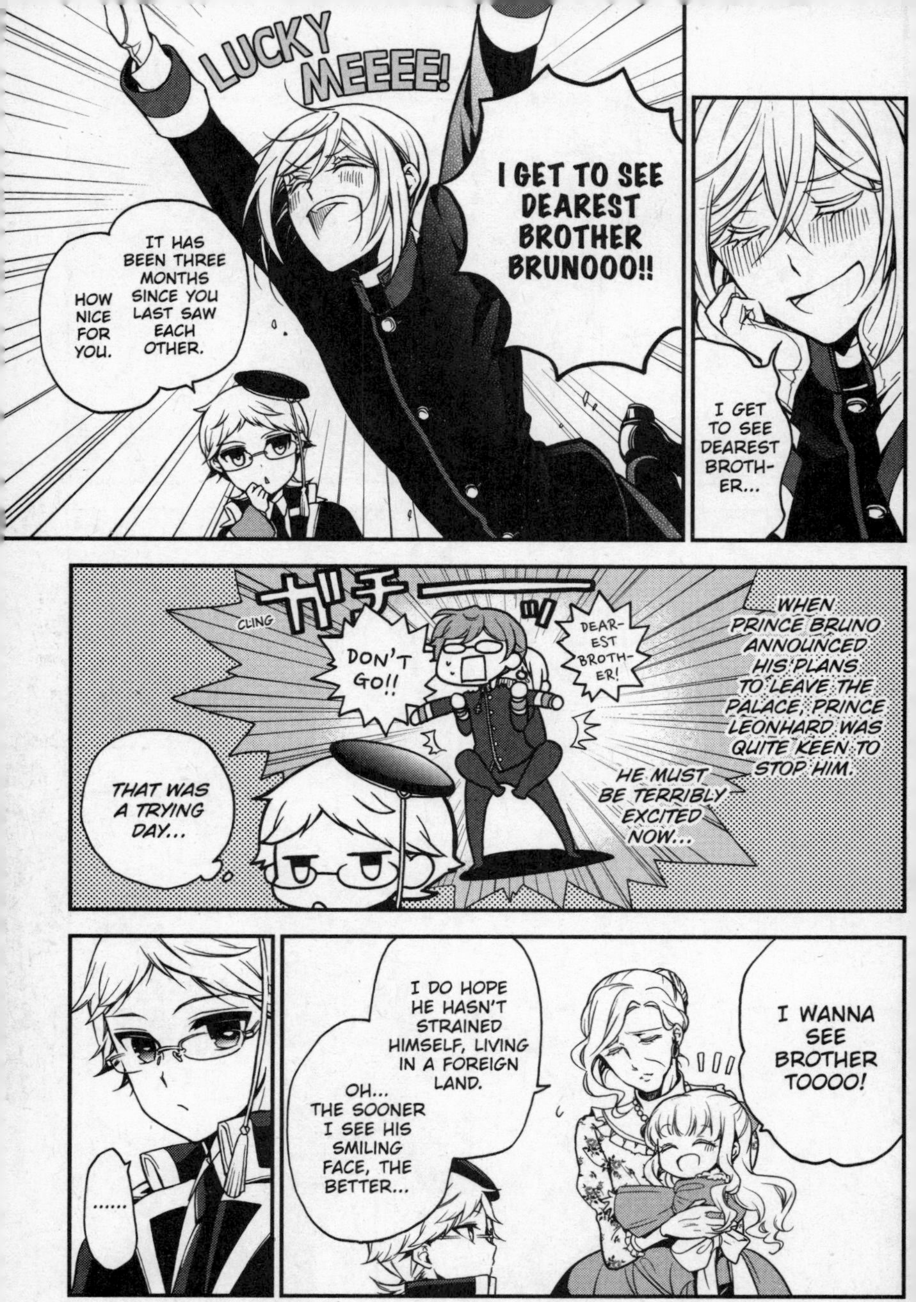
I GET TO SEE DEAREST BROTH-ER...
LUCKY MEEEE!
I GET TO SEE DEAREST BROTHER BRUNOOO!!
IT HAS BEEN THREE MONTHS SINCE YOU LAST SAW EACH OTHER.
HOW NICE FOR YOU.
WHEN PRINCE BRUNO ANNOUNCED HIS PLANS TO LEAVE THE PALACE, PRINCE LEONHARD WAS QUITE KEEN TO STOP HIM.
DEAR-EST BROTH-ER!
ガチー
DON'T GO!!
CLING
HE MUST BE TERRIBLY EXCITED NOW...
THAT WAS A TRYING DAY...
I WANNA SEE BROTHER TOOOO!
I DO HOPE HE HASN'T STRAINED HIMSELF, LIVING IN A FOREIGN LAND.
OH... THE SOONER I SEE HIS SMILING FACE, THE BETTER...
......

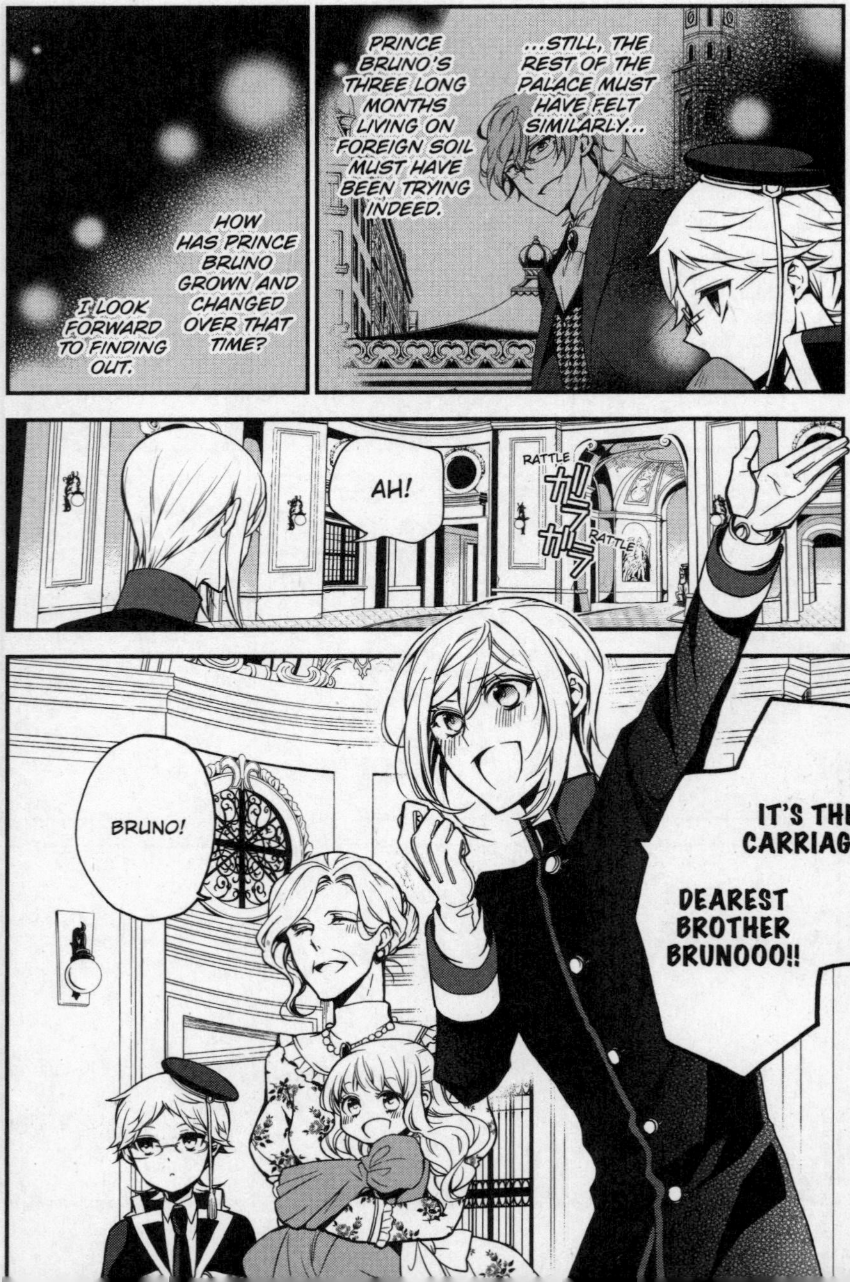
PRINCE BRUNO'S THREE LONG MONTHS LIVING ON FOREIGN SOIL MUST HAVE BEEN TRYING INDEED.
...STILL, THE REST OF THE PALACE MUST HAVE FELT SIMILARLY...
HOW HAS PRINCE BRUNO GROWN AND CHANGED OVER THAT TIME?
I LOOK FORWARD TO FINDING OUT.
RATTLE
RATTLE
AH!
IT'S THE CARRIAGE!
DEAREST BROTHER BRUNOOO!!
BRUNO!

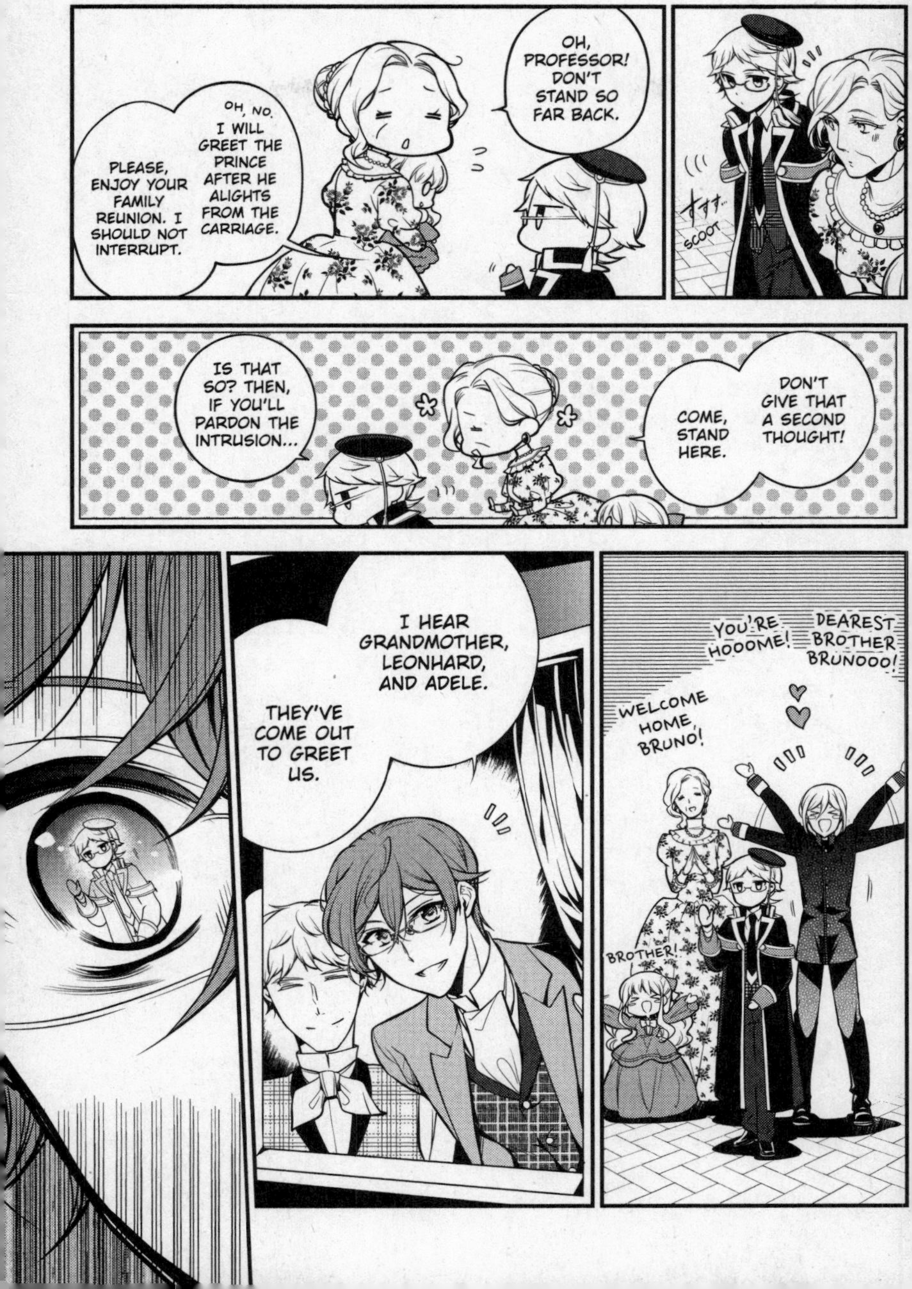

すすす…
SCOOT
OH, PROFESSOR! DON'T STAND SO FAR BACK.
OH, NO. I WILL GREET THE PRINCE AFTER HE ALIGHTS FROM THE CARRIAGE.
PLEASE, ENJOY YOUR FAMILY REUNION. I SHOULD NOT INTERRUPT.
DON'T GIVE THAT A SECOND THOUGHT!
COME, STAND HERE.
IS THAT SO? THEN, IF YOU'LL PARDON THE INTRUSION...
DEAREST BROTHER BRUNOOO!
YOU'RE HOOOME!
WELCOME HOME BRUNO!
BROTHER!
I HEAR GRANDMOTHER, LEONHARD, AND ADELE.
THEY'VE COME OUT TO GREET US.

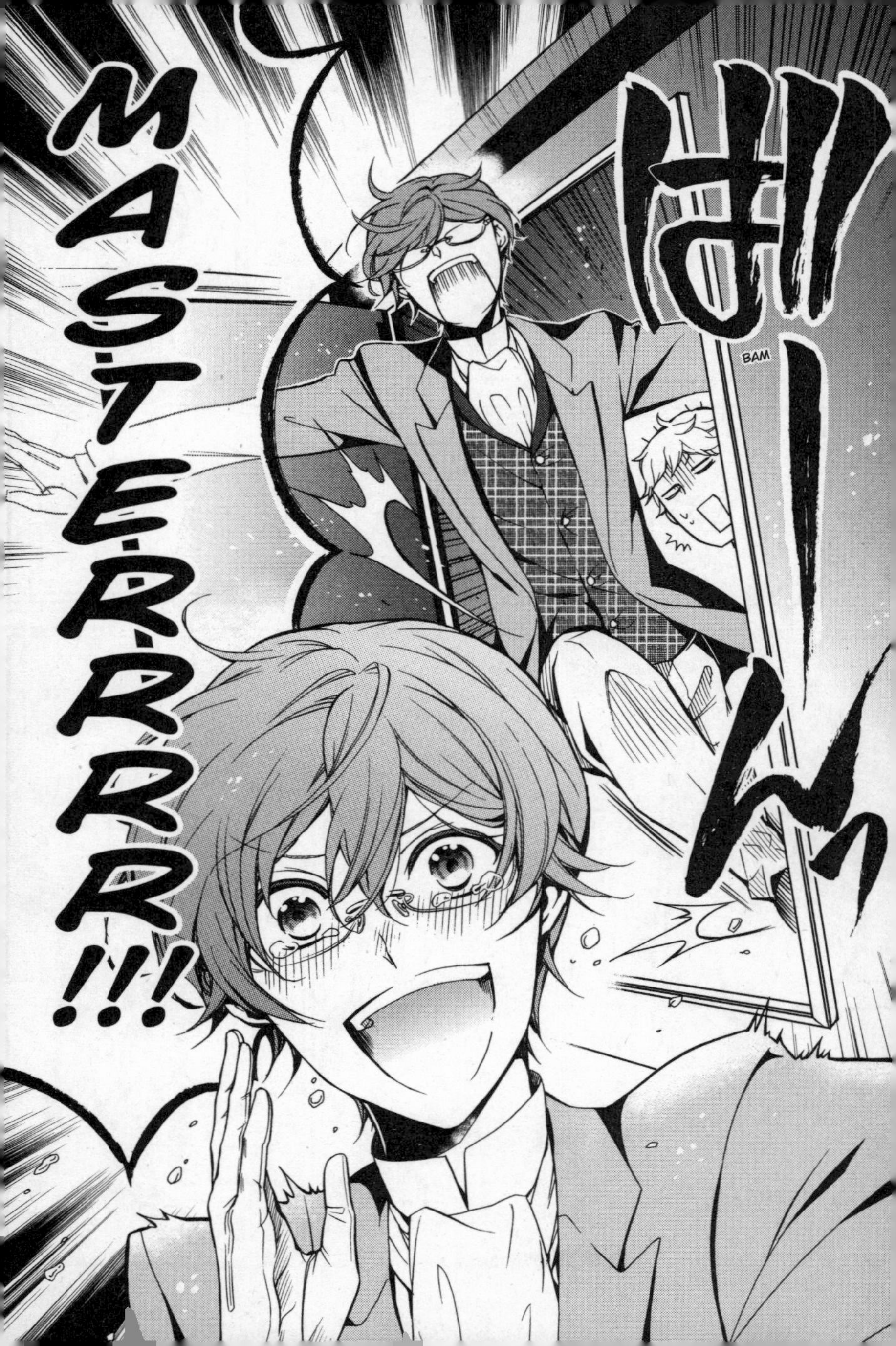
ばーん
BAM
MAS-T-E-R-R-RR!!!

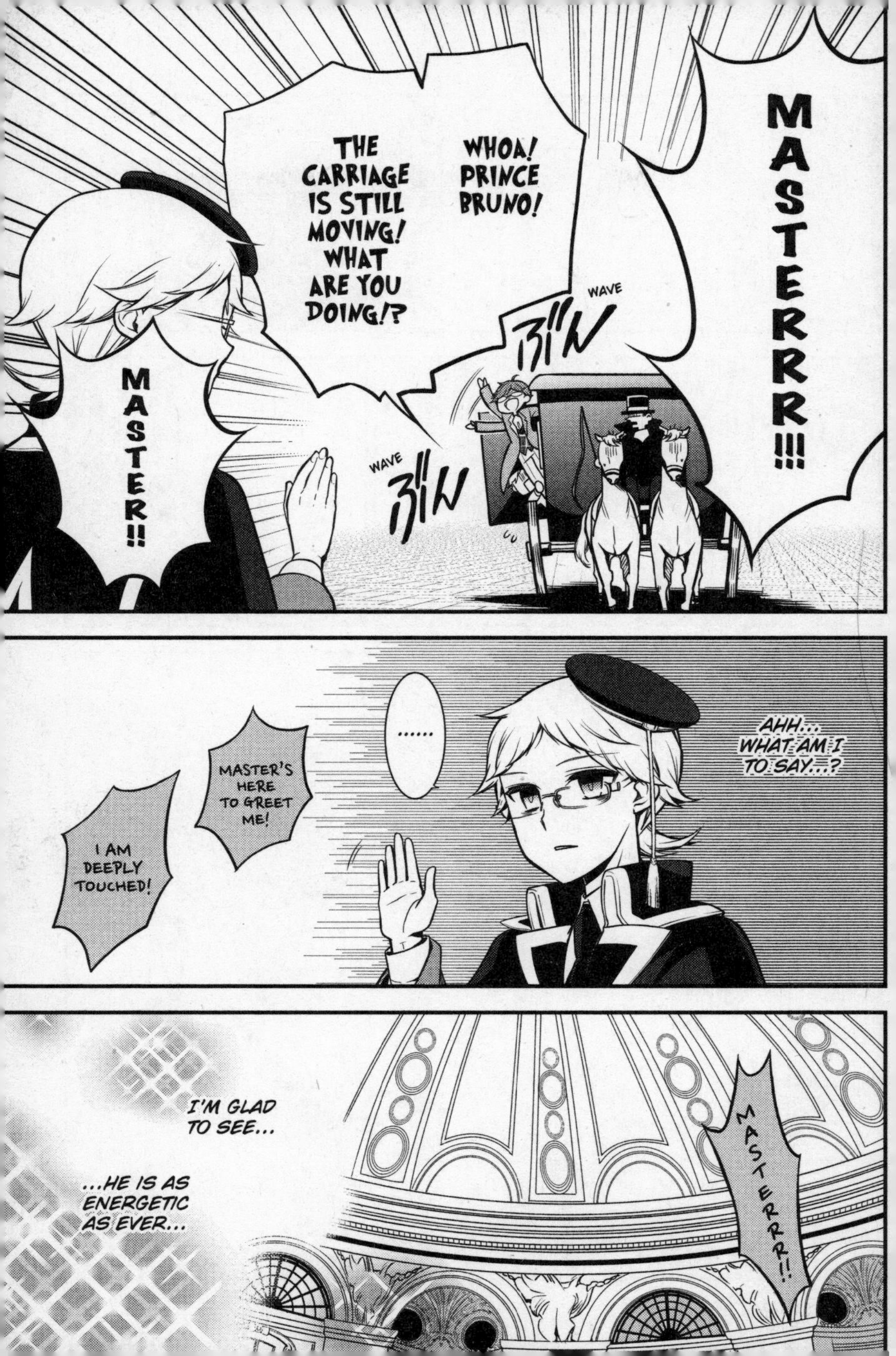
MASTERRR!!!
WHOA! PRINCE BRUNO!
THE CARRIAGE IS STILL MOVING! WHAT ARE YOU DOING!?
WAVE
ぶん
WAVE
ぶん
MASTER!!
AHH... WHAT AM I TO SAY...?
......
MASTER'S HERE TO GREET ME!
I AM DEEPLY TOUCHED!
MASTERRR!!
I'M GLAD TO SEE...
...HE IS AS ENERGETIC AS EVER...

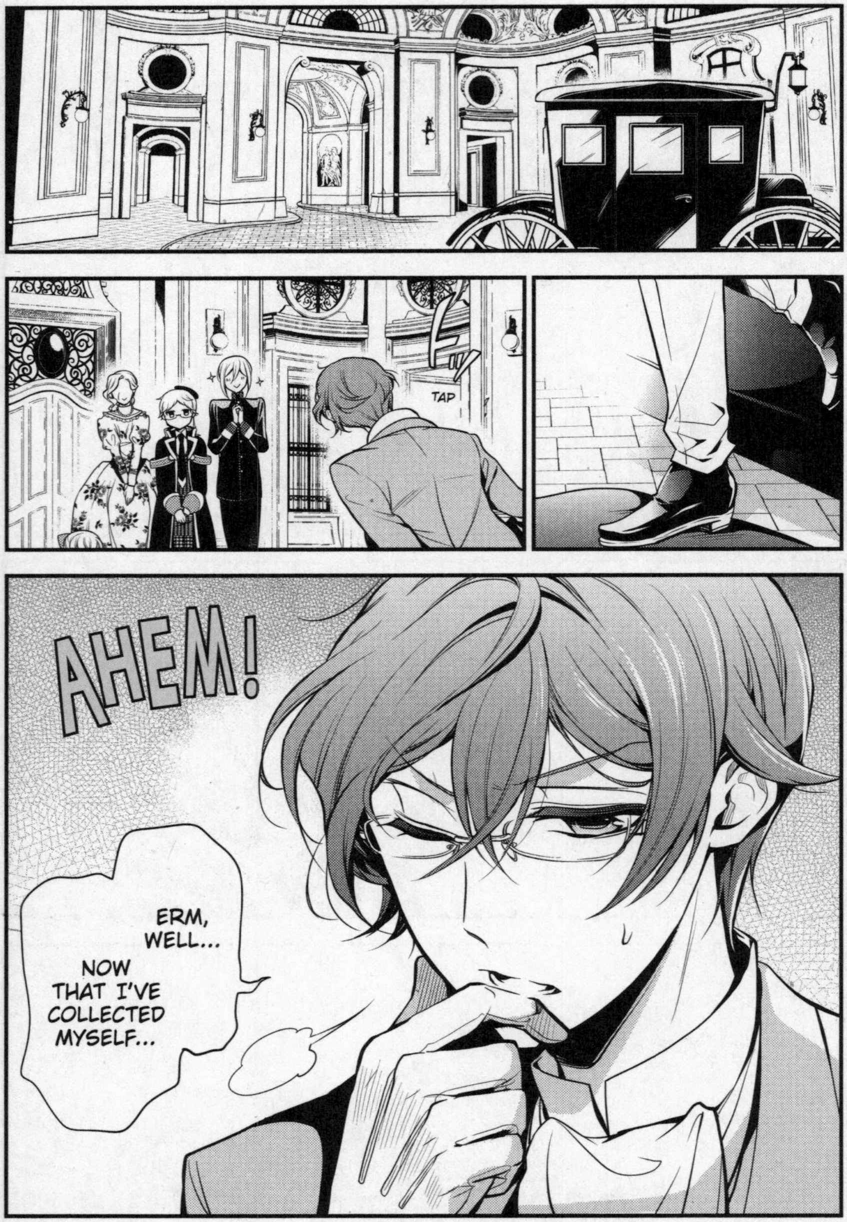
TAP
AHEM!
ERM, WELL... NOW THAT I'VE COLLECTED MYSELF...

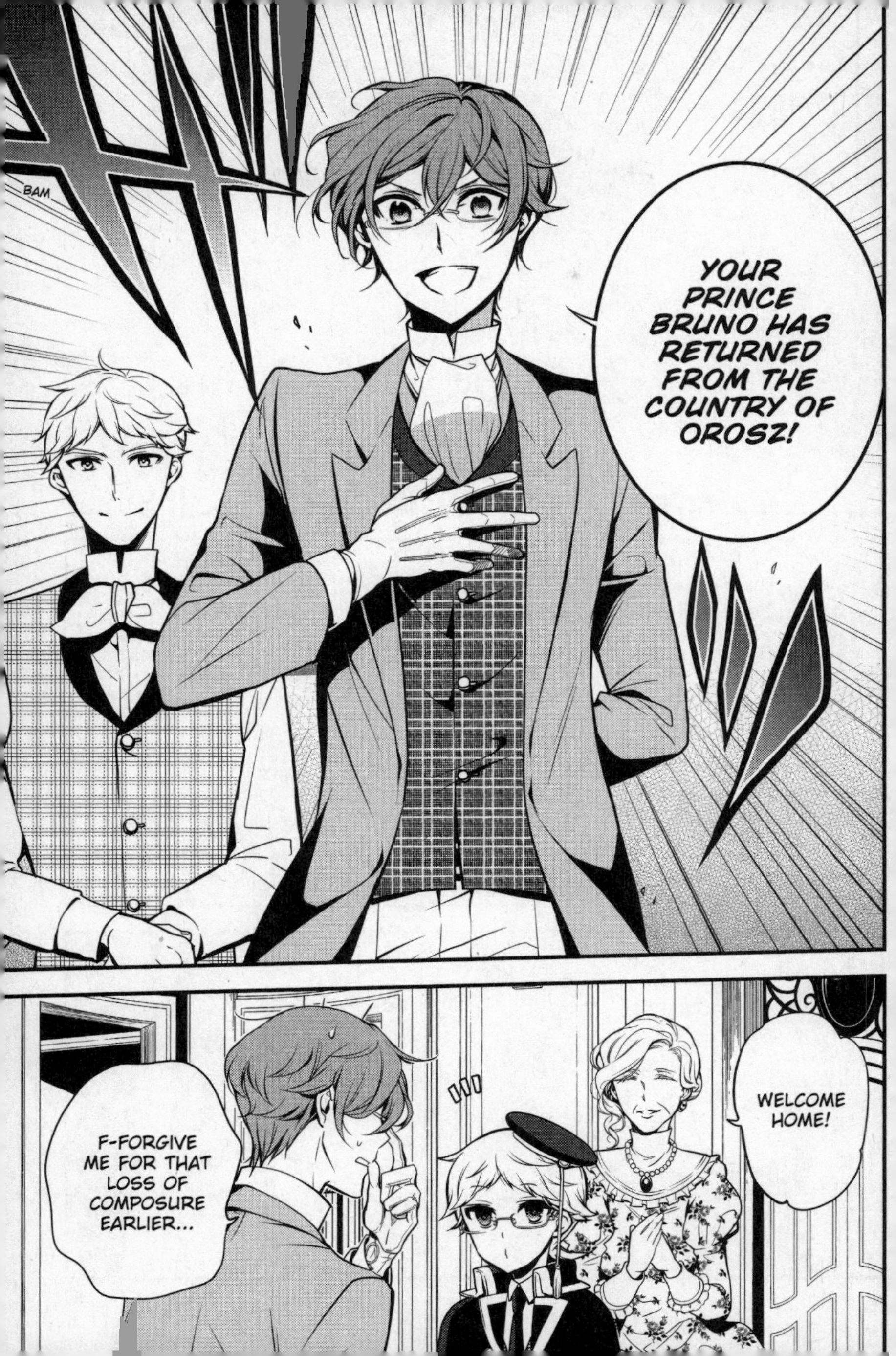
YOUR PRINCE BRUNO HAS RETURNED FROM THE COUNTRY OF OROSZ!
BAM
WELCOME HOME!
F-FORGIVE ME FOR THAT LOSS OF COMPOSURE EARLIER...

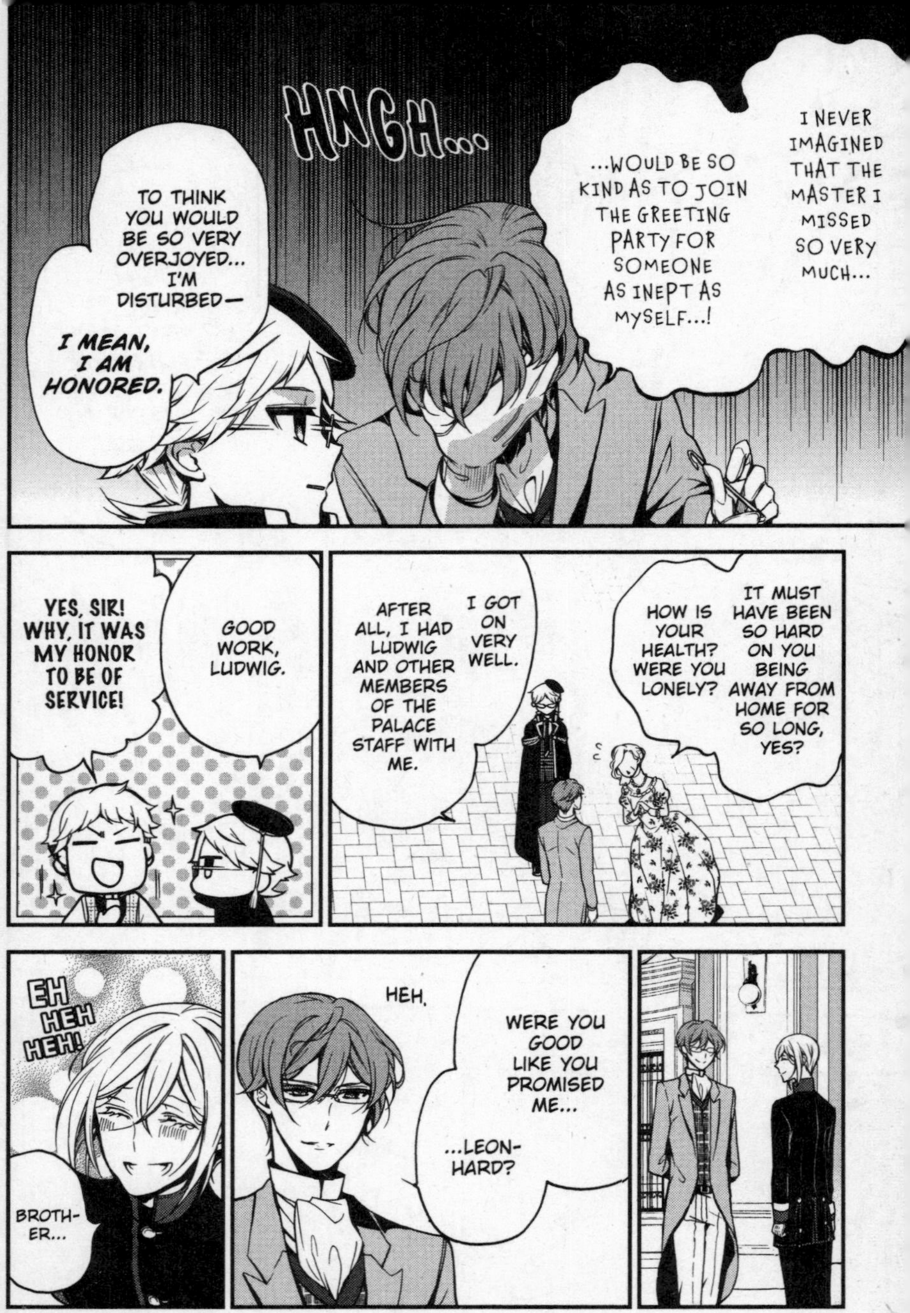
I NEVER IMAGINED THAT THE MASTER I MISSED SO VERY MUCH...
...WOULD BE SO KIND AS TO JOIN THE GREETING PARTY FOR SOMEONE AS INEPT AS MYSELF...!
HNGH...
TO THINK YOU WOULD BE SO VERY OVERJOYED... I'M DISTURBED—
I MEAN, I AM HONORED.
IT MUST HAVE BEEN SO HARD ON YOU BEING AWAY FROM HOME FOR SO LONG, YES?
HOW IS YOUR HEALTH? WERE YOU LONELY?
I GOT ON VERY WELL.
AFTER ALL, I HAD LUDWIG AND OTHER MEMBERS OF THE PALACE STAFF WITH ME.
GOOD WORK, LUDWIG.
YES, SIR! WHY, IT WAS MY HONOR TO BE OF SERVICE!
HEH.
WERE YOU GOOD LIKE YOU PROMISED ME...
...LEON-HARD?
EH HEH HEH!
BROTH-ER...

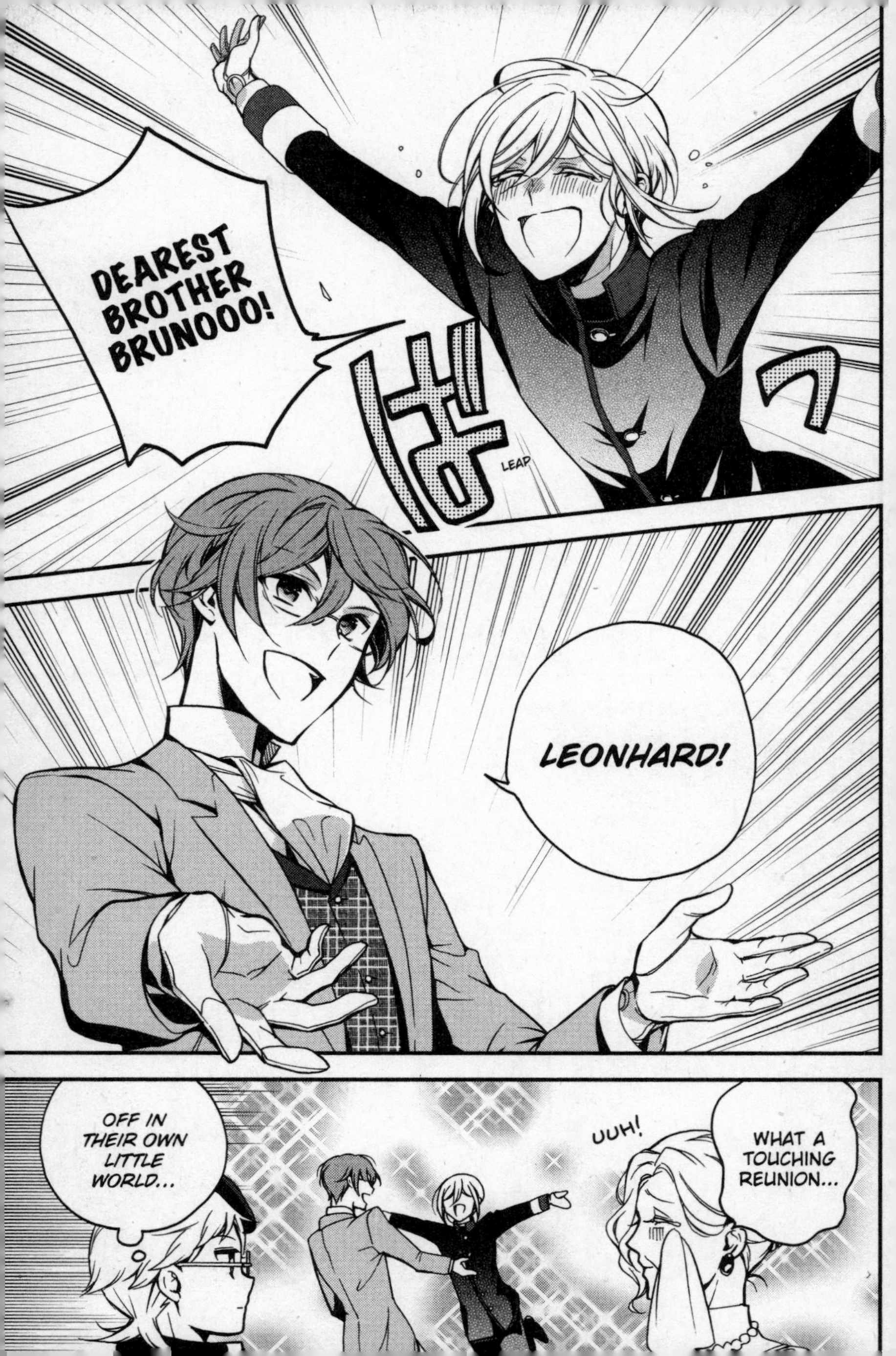
DEAREST BROTHER BRUNOOO!
LEAP
LEONHARD!
WHAT A TOUCHING REUNION...
UUH!
OFF IN THEIR OWN LITTLE WORLD...

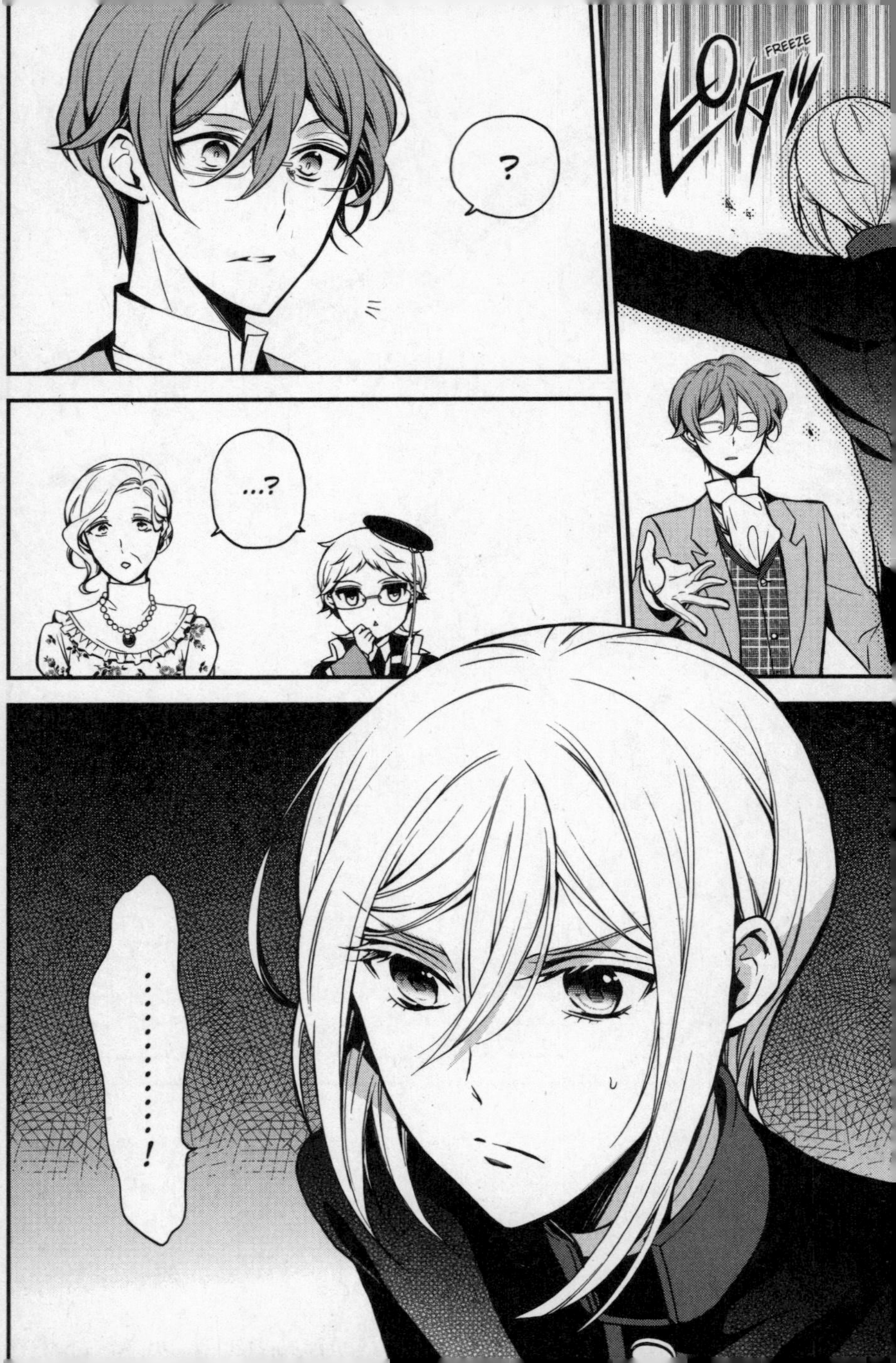
ピタッ
FREEZE
?
...?
.........!

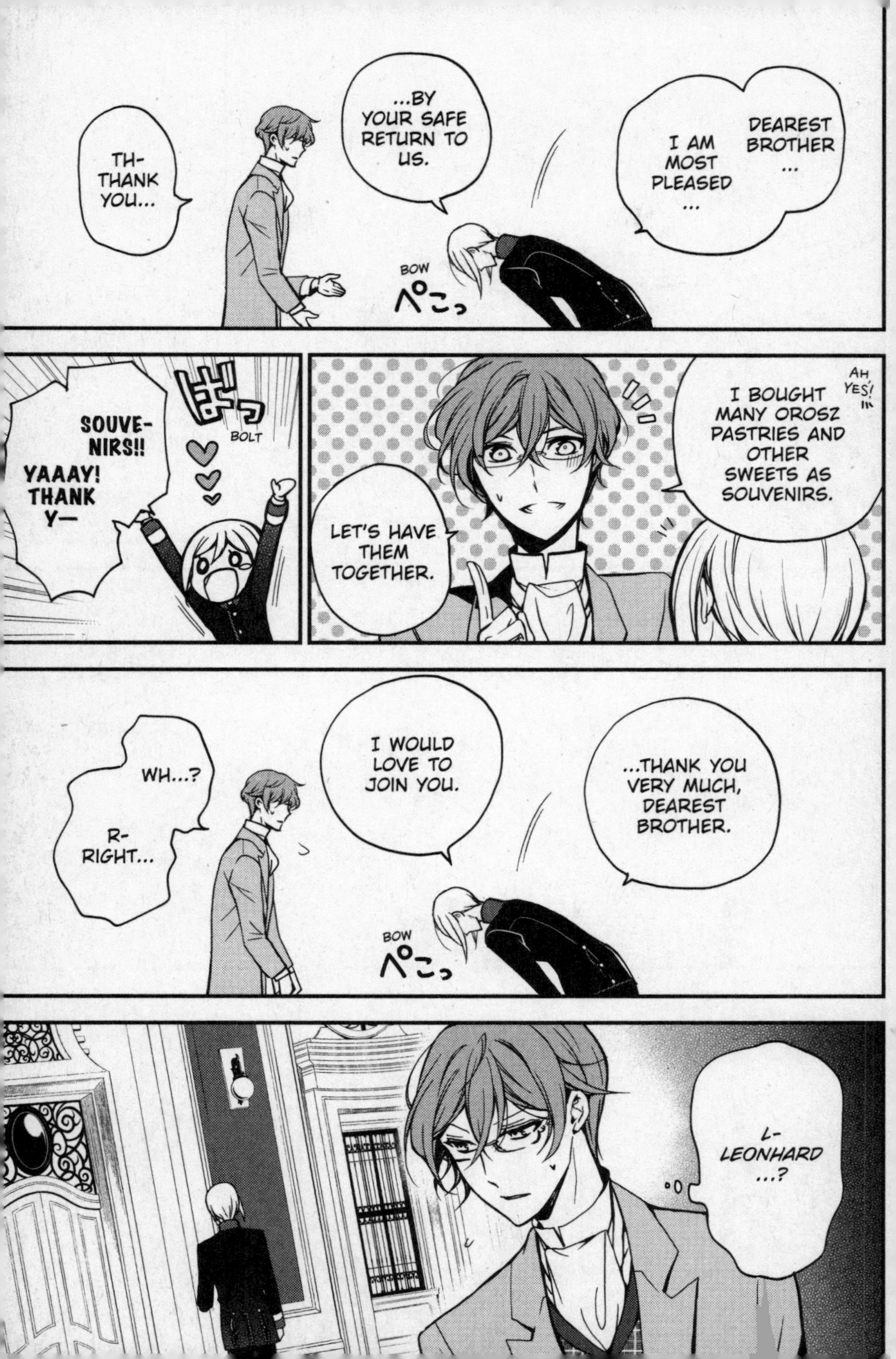
DEAREST BROTHER ... I AM MOST PLEASED ...
...BY YOUR SAFE RETURN TO US.
BOW
ぺこっ
TH-THANK YOU...
AH YES!!
I BOUGHT MANY OROSZ PASTRIES AND OTHER SWEETS AS SOUVENIRS.
LET'S HAVE THEM TOGETHER.
ぼっ
BOLT
SOUVENIRS!! YAAAY! THANK Y—
...THANK YOU VERY MUCH, DEAREST BROTHER.
I WOULD LOVE TO JOIN YOU.
BOW
ぺこっ
WH...?
R-RIGHT...
L-LEONHARD ...?

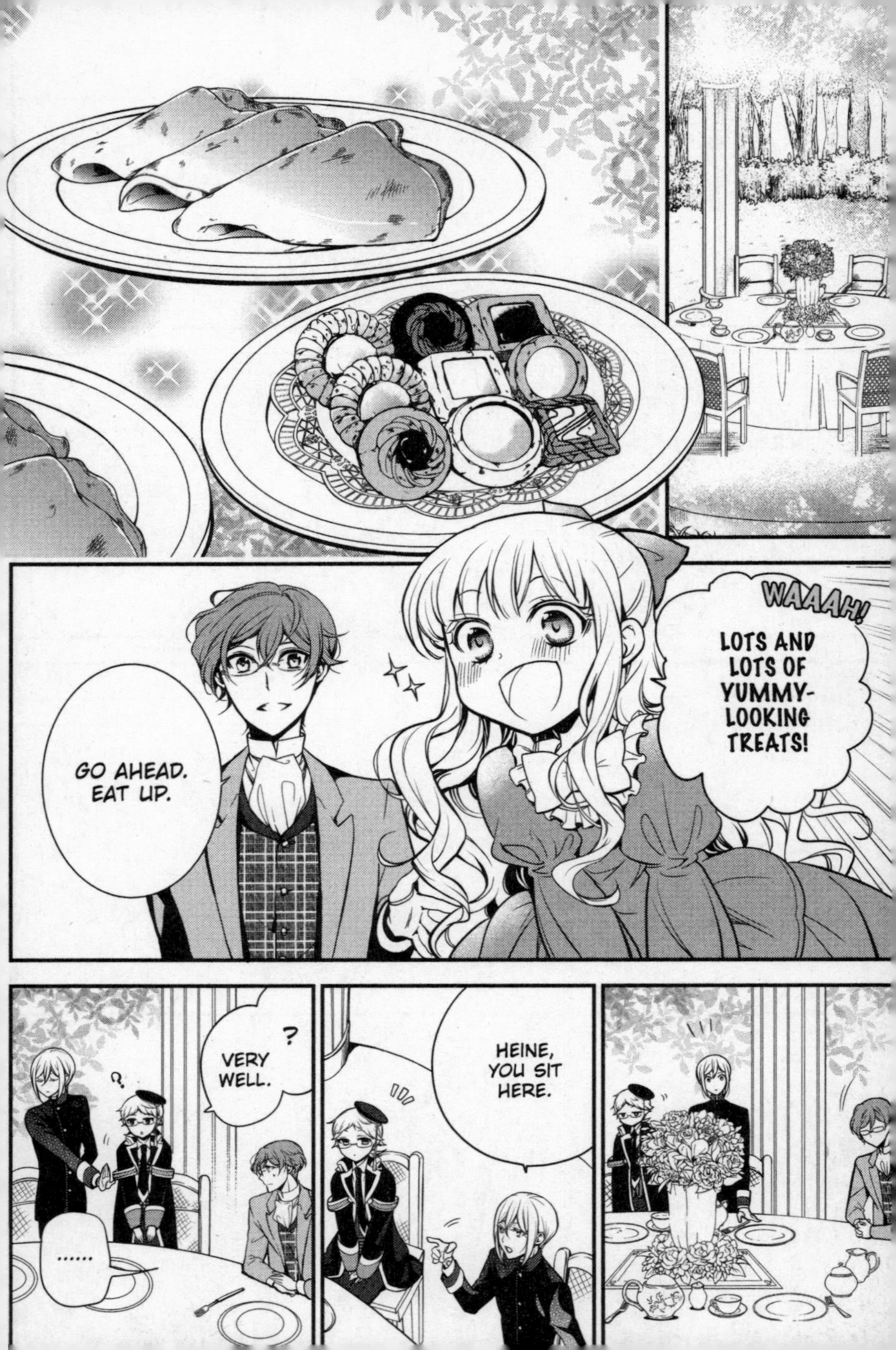
WAAAH!
LOTS AND LOTS OF YUMMY-LOOKING TREATS!
GO AHEAD. EAT UP.
HEINE, YOU SIT HERE.
?
VERY WELL.
......

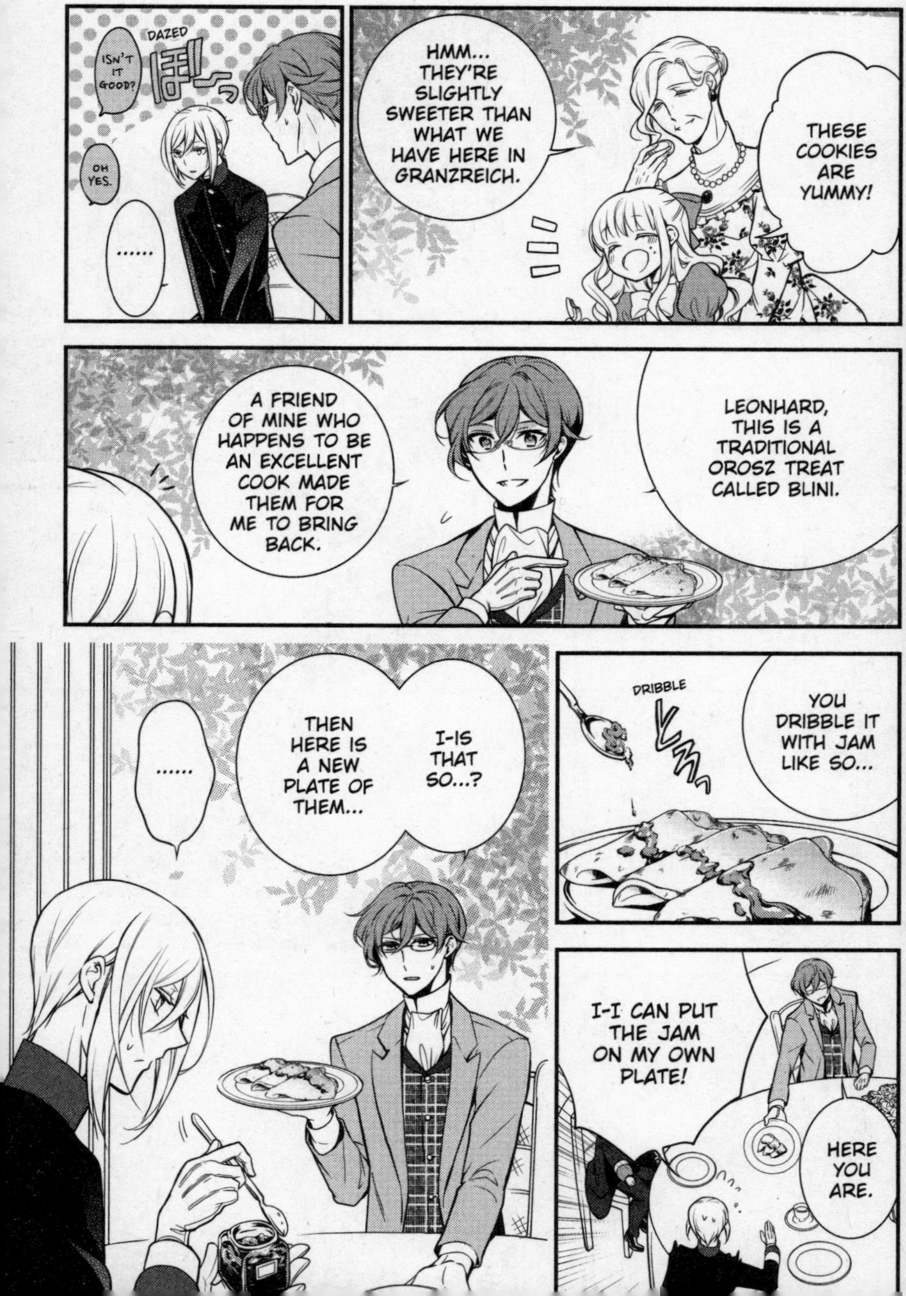
THESE COOKIES ARE YUMMY!
HMM... THEY'RE SLIGHTLY SWEETER THAN WHAT WE HAVE HERE IN GRANZREICH.
DAZED
ISN'T IT GOOD?
OH YES.
......
LEONHARD, THIS IS A TRADITIONAL OROSZ TREAT CALLED BLINI.
A FRIEND OF MINE WHO HAPPENS TO BE AN EXCELLENT COOK MADE THEM FOR ME TO BRING BACK.
YOU DRIBBLE IT WITH JAM LIKE SO...
DRIBBLE
I-I CAN PUT THE JAM ON MY OWN PLATE!
HERE YOU ARE.
I-IS THAT SO...?
THEN HERE IS A NEW PLATE OF THEM...
......

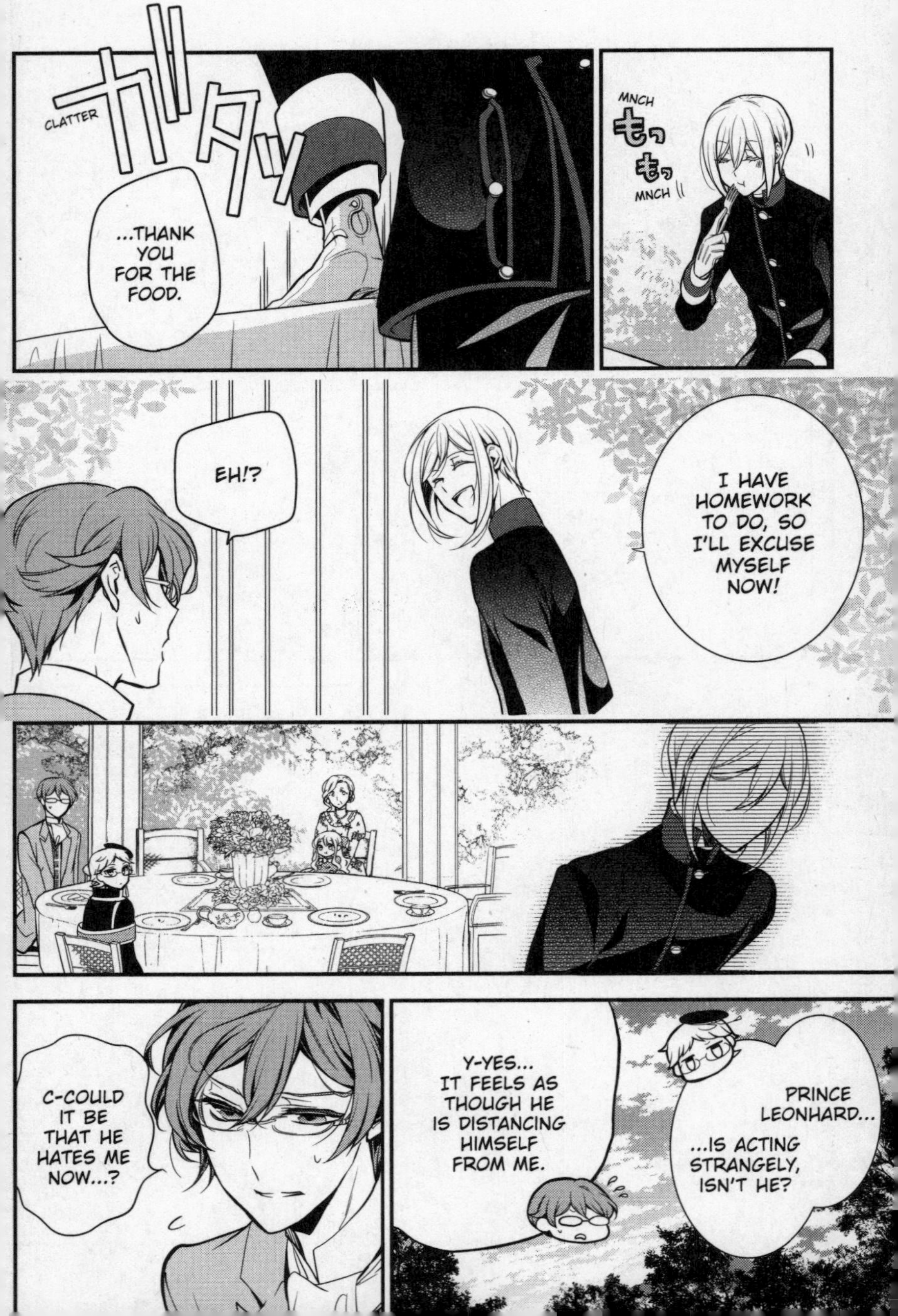
MNCH
もっ
もっ
MNCH
ガタッ
CLATTER
...THANK YOU FOR THE FOOD.
I HAVE HOMEWORK TO DO, SO I'LL EXCUSE MYSELF NOW!
EH!?
PRINCE LEONHARD...
...IS ACTING STRANGELY, ISN'T HE?
Y-YES... IT FEELS AS THOUGH HE IS DISTANCING HIMSELF FROM ME.
C-COULD IT BE THAT HE HATES ME NOW...?

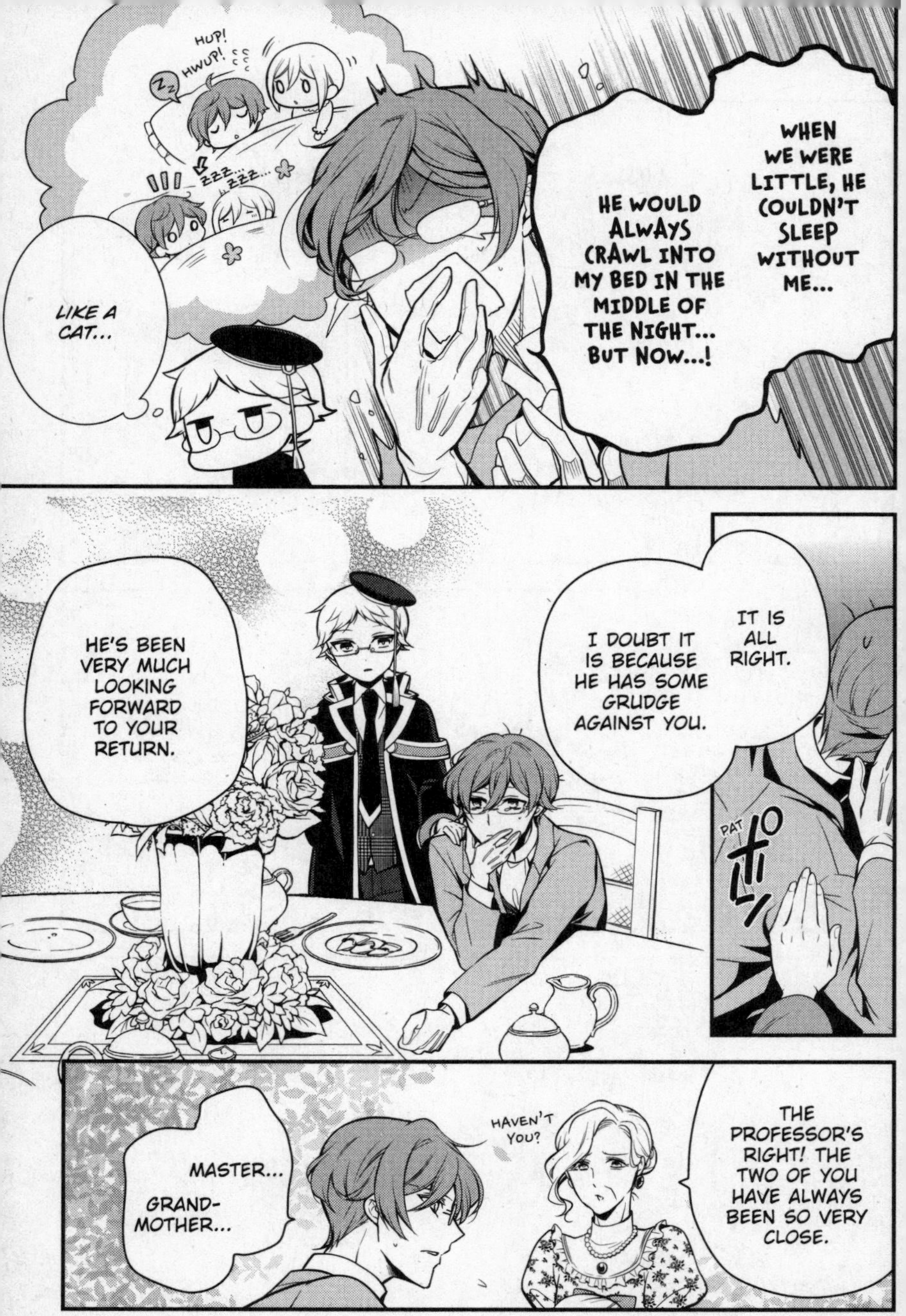
WHEN WE WERE LITTLE, HE COULDN'T SLEEP WITHOUT ME...
HE WOULD ALWAYS CRAWL INTO MY BED IN THE MIDDLE OF THE NIGHT... BUT NOW...!
HUP! HWUP!
ZZZZ... ZZZZ...
LIKE A CAT...
PAT
IT IS ALL RIGHT.
I DOUBT IT IS BECAUSE HE HAS SOME GRUDGE AGAINST YOU.
HE'S BEEN VERY MUCH LOOKING FORWARD TO YOUR RETURN.
THE PROFESSOR'S RIGHT! THE TWO OF YOU HAVE ALWAYS BEEN SO VERY CLOSE.
HAVEN'T YOU?
MASTER...
GRANDMOTHER...

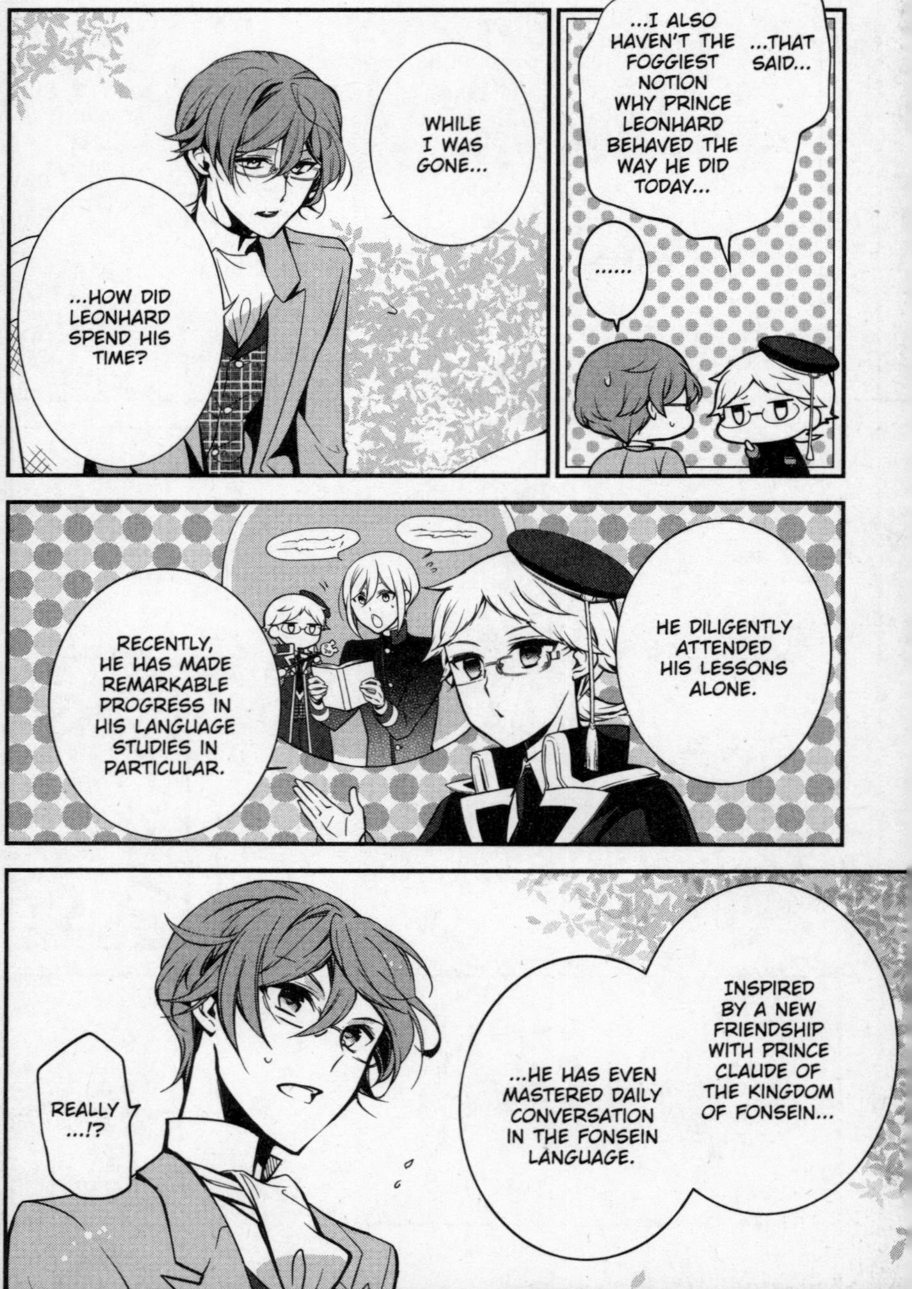
...THAT SAID...
...I ALSO HAVEN'T THE FOGGIEST NOTION WHY PRINCE LEONHARD BEHAVED THE WAY HE DID TODAY...
......
WHILE I WAS GONE...
...HOW DID LEONHARD SPEND HIS TIME?
HE DILIGENTLY ATTENDED HIS LESSONS ALONE.
RECENTLY, HE HAS MADE REMARKABLE PROGRESS IN HIS LANGUAGE STUDIES IN PARTICULAR.
INSPIRED BY A NEW FRIENDSHIP WITH PRINCE CLAUDE OF THE KINGDOM OF FONSEIN...
...HE HAS EVEN MASTERED DAILY CONVERSATION IN THE FONSEIN LANGUAGE.
REALLY ...!?

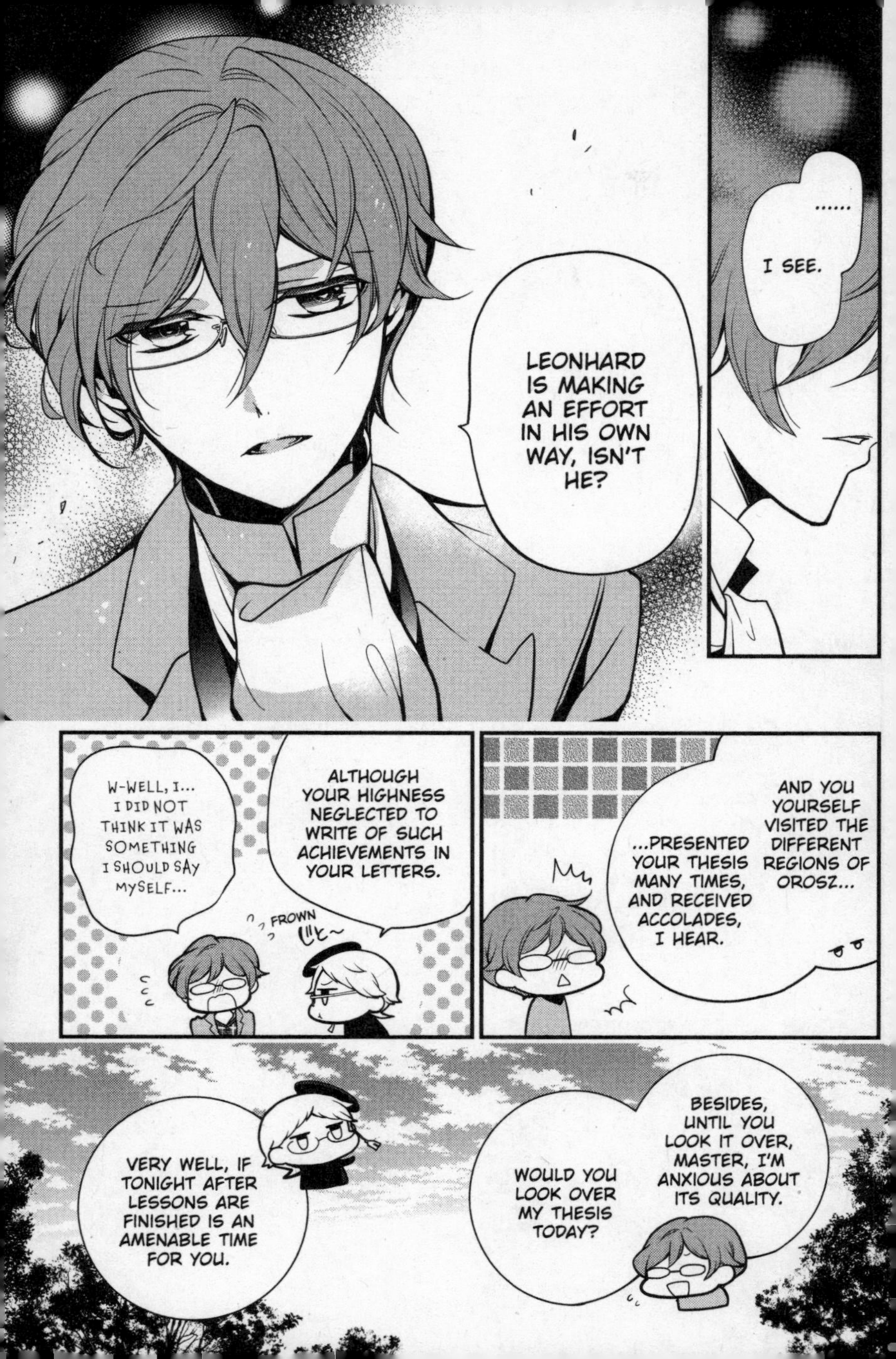
......
I SEE.
LEONHARD IS MAKING AN EFFORT IN HIS OWN WAY, ISN'T HE?
AND YOU YOURSELF VISITED THE DIFFERENT REGIONS OF OROSZ...
...PRESENTED YOUR THESIS MANY TIMES, AND RECEIVED ACCOLADES, I HEAR.
ALTHOUGH YOUR HIGHNESS NEGLECTED TO WRITE OF SUCH ACHIEVEMENTS IN YOUR LETTERS.
FROWN
じと~
W-WELL, I... I DID NOT THINK IT WAS SOMETHING I SHOULD SAY MYSELF...
BESIDES, UNTIL YOU LOOK IT OVER, MASTER, I'M ANXIOUS ABOUT ITS QUALITY.
WOULD YOU LOOK OVER MY THESIS TODAY?
VERY WELL, IF TONIGHT AFTER LESSONS ARE FINISHED IS AN AMENABLE TIME FOR YOU.

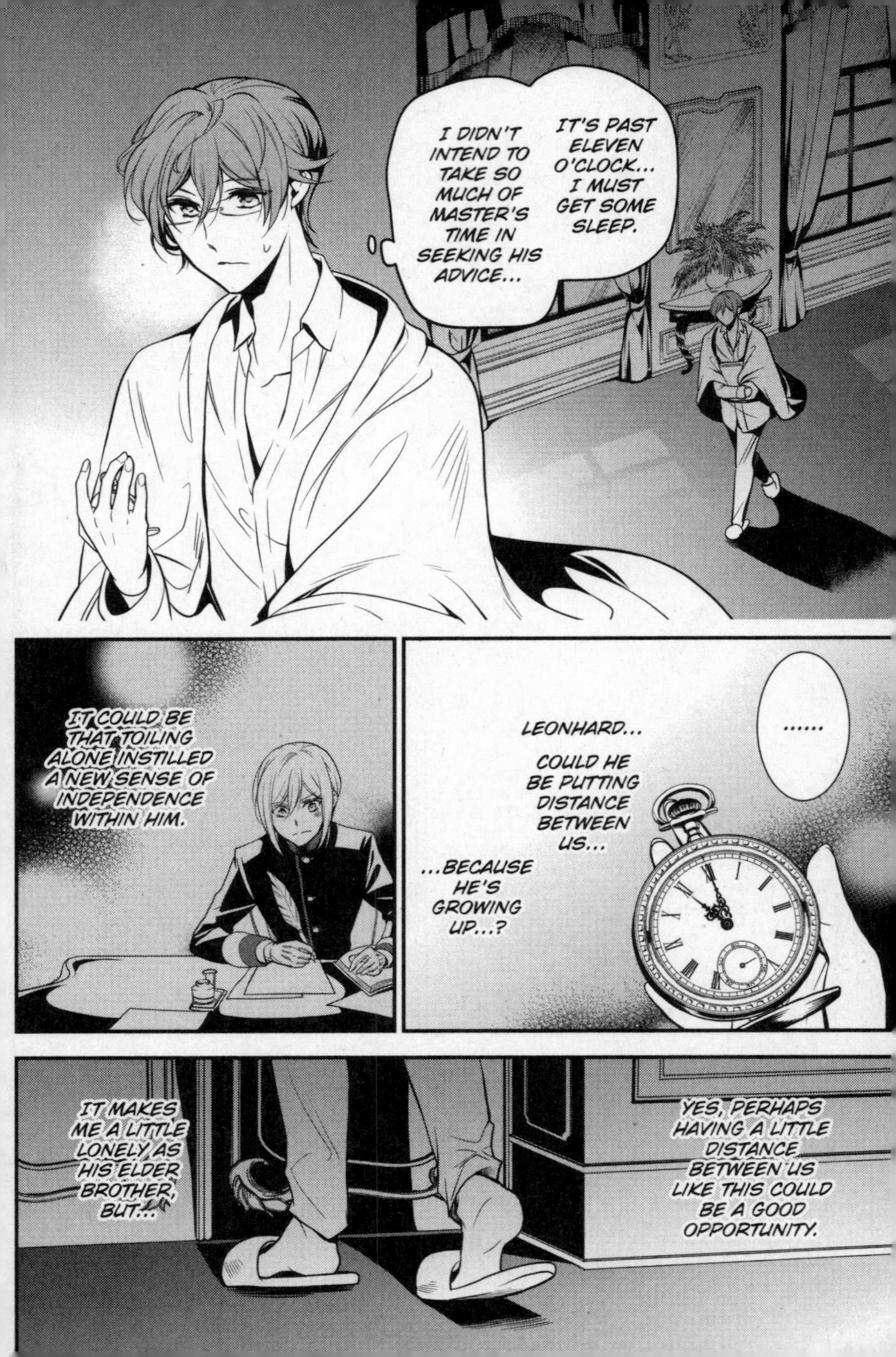
IT'S PAST ELEVEN O'CLOCK... I MUST GET SOME SLEEP.
I DIDN'T INTEND TO TAKE SO MUCH OF MASTER'S TIME IN SEEKING HIS ADVICE...
......
LEONHARD...
COULD HE BE PUTTING DISTANCE BETWEEN US...
...BECAUSE HE'S GROWING UP...?
IT COULD BE THAT TOILING ALONE INSTILLED A NEW SENSE OF INDEPENDENCE WITHIN HIM.
YES, PERHAPS HAVING A LITTLE DISTANCE BETWEEN US LIKE THIS COULD BE A GOOD OPPORTUNITY.
IT MAKES ME A LITTLE LONELY AS HIS ELDER BROTHER, BUT...

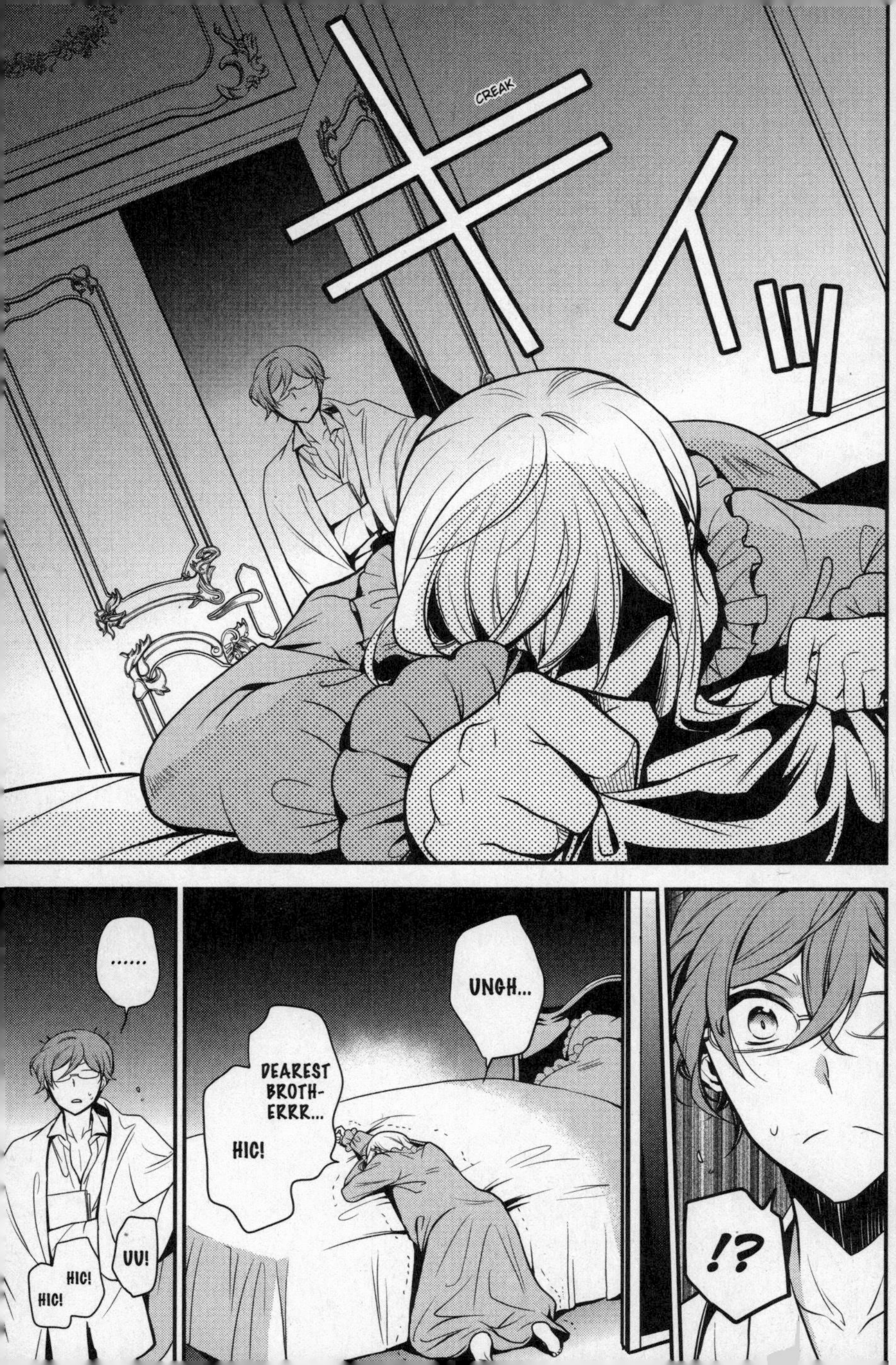
CREAK
!?
UNGH...
DEAREST BROTHER-ERRR...
HIC!
......
UU!
HIC!
HIC!

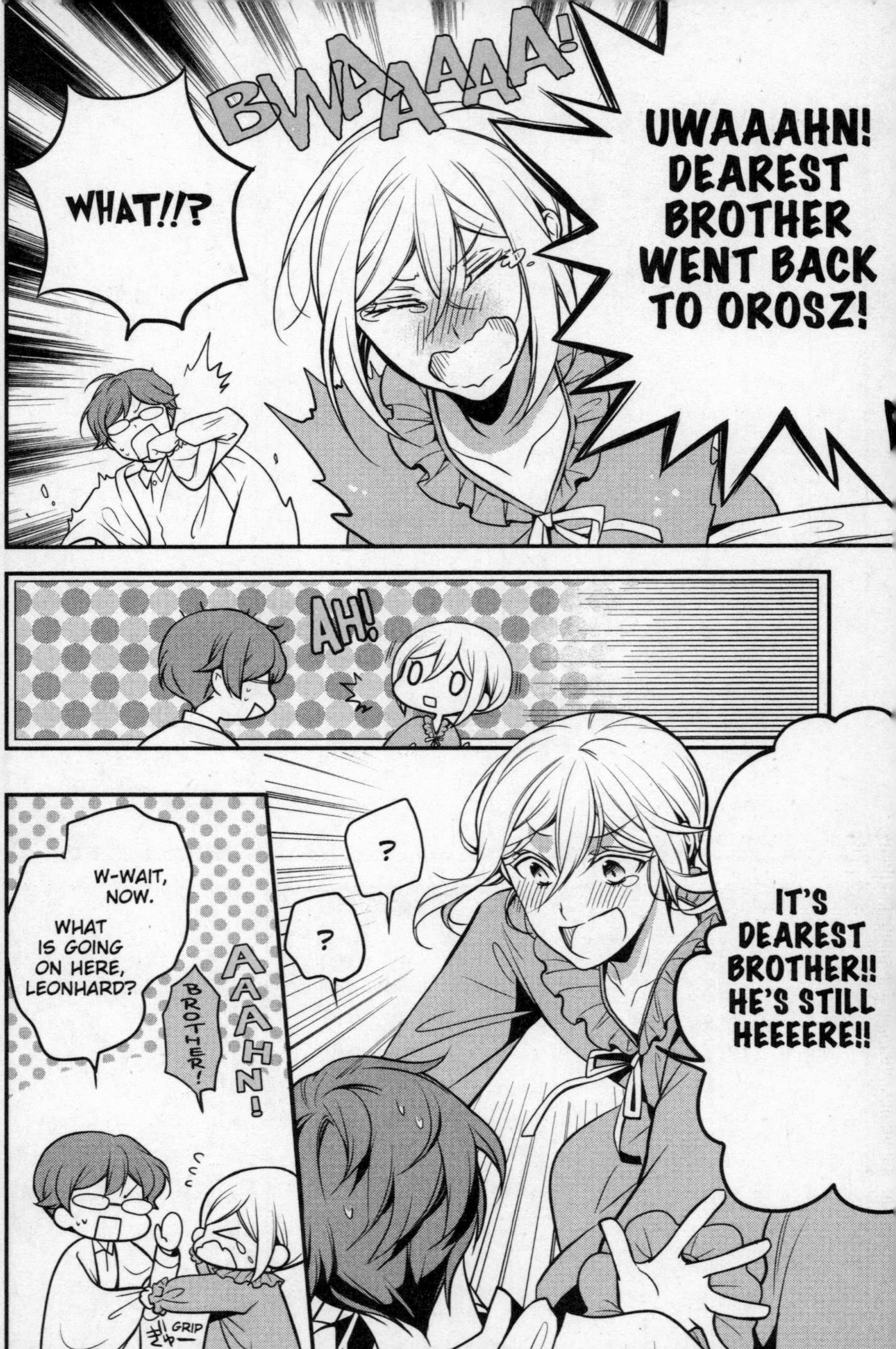
UWAAAHN! DEAREST BROTHER WENT BACK TO OROSZ!
BWAAAAA!
WHAT!!?
AH!
IT'S DEAREST BROTHER!! HE'S STILL HEEEERE!!
?
?
AAAAHN!
BROTHER!
W-WAIT, NOW. WHAT IS GOING ON HERE, LEONHARD?
GRIP

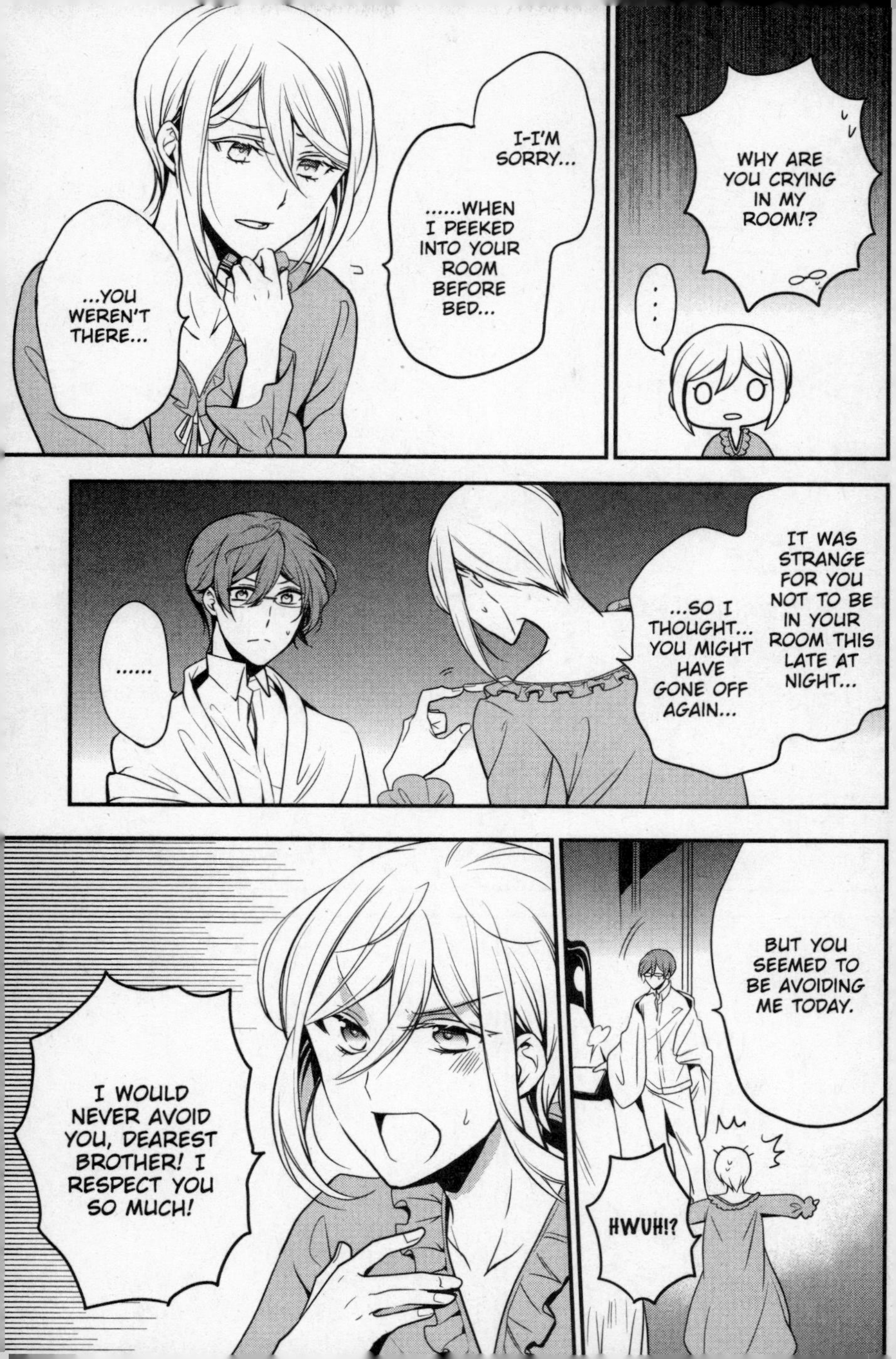
WHY ARE YOU CRYING IN MY ROOM!?
...
I-I'M SORRY...
......WHEN I PEEKED INTO YOUR ROOM BEFORE BED...
...YOU WEREN'T THERE...
IT WAS STRANGE FOR YOU NOT TO BE IN YOUR ROOM THIS LATE AT NIGHT...
...SO I THOUGHT... YOU MIGHT HAVE GONE OFF AGAIN...
......
BUT YOU SEEMED TO BE AVOIDING ME TODAY.
HWUH!?
I WOULD NEVER AVOID YOU, DEAREST BROTHER! I RESPECT YOU SO MUCH!

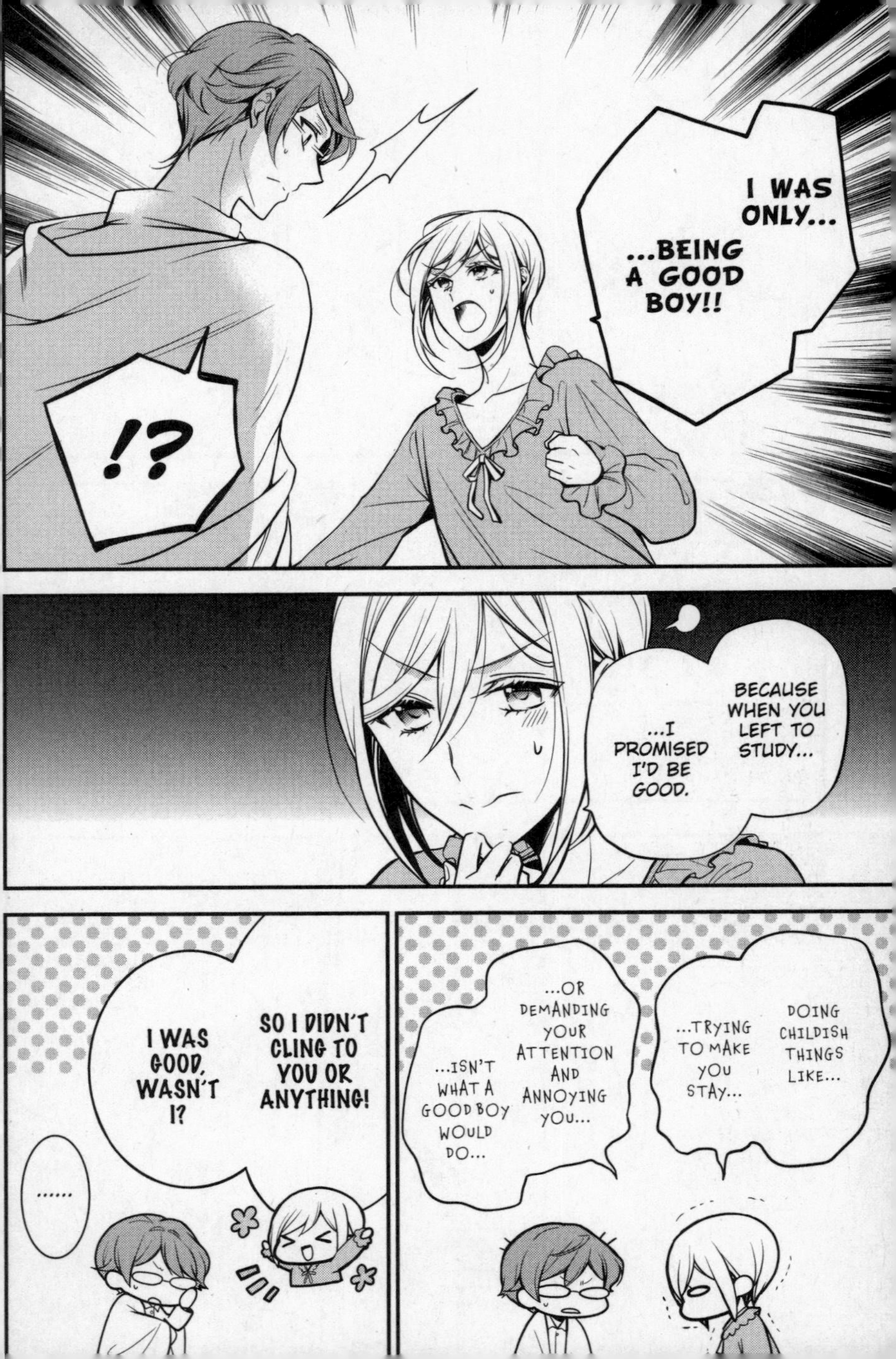
I WAS ONLY...
...BEING A GOOD BOY!!
!?
BECAUSE WHEN YOU LEFT TO STUDY...
...I PROMISED I'D BE GOOD.
DOING CHILDISH THINGS LIKE...
...TRYING TO MAKE YOU STAY...
...OR DEMANDING YOUR ATTENTION AND ANNOYING YOU...
...ISN'T WHAT A GOOD BOY WOULD DO...
SO I DIDN'T CLING TO YOU OR ANYTHING!
I WAS GOOD, WASN'T I?
......

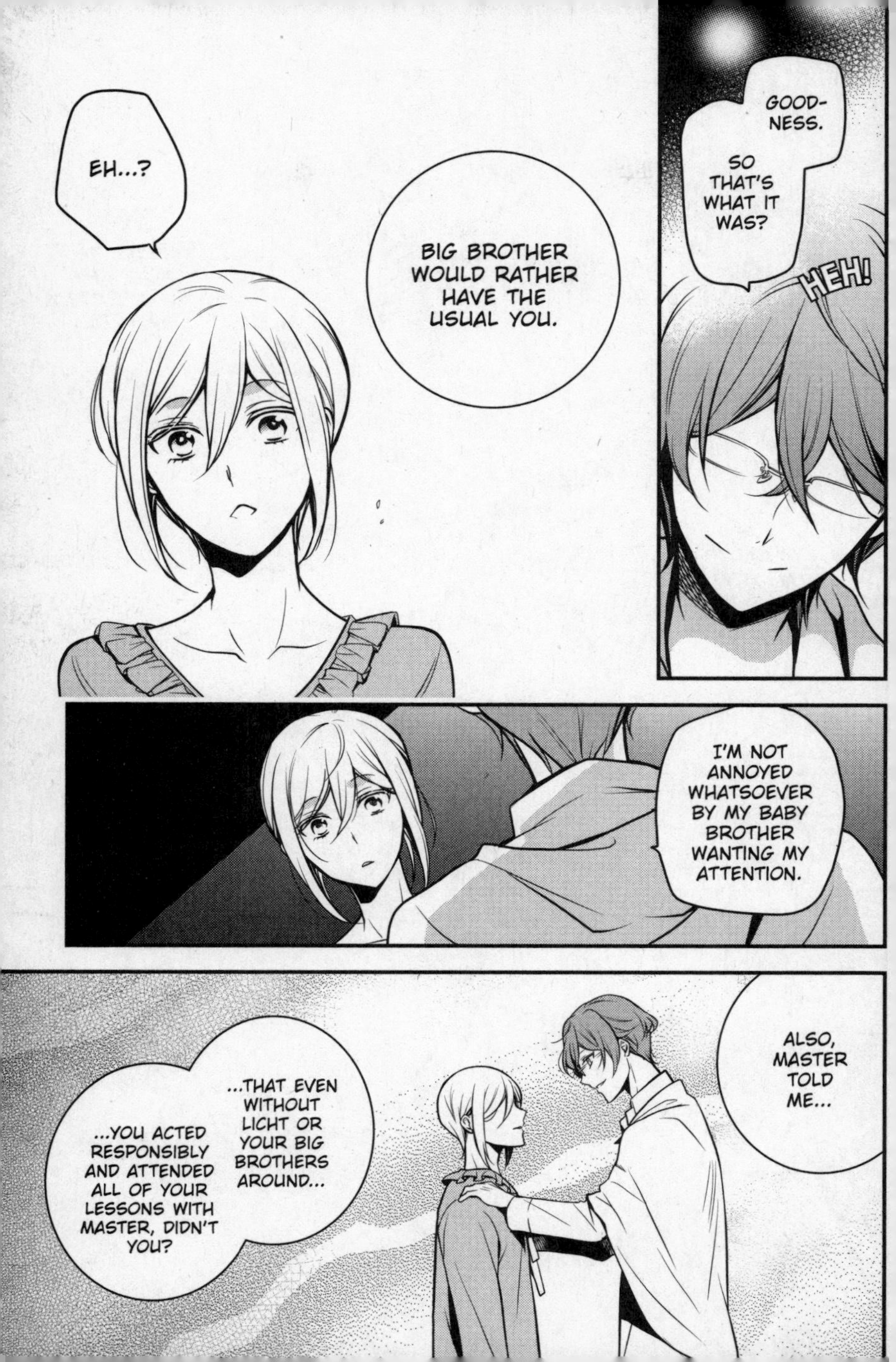
GOODNESS.
SO THAT'S WHAT IT WAS?
HEH!
BIG BROTHER WOULD RATHER HAVE THE USUAL YOU.
EH...?
I'M NOT ANNOYED WHATSOEVER BY MY BABY BROTHER WANTING MY ATTENTION.
ALSO, MASTER TOLD ME...
...THAT EVEN WITHOUT LICHT OR YOUR BIG BROTHERS AROUND...
...YOU ACTED RESPONSIBLY AND ATTENDED ALL OF YOUR LESSONS WITH MASTER, DIDN'T YOU?

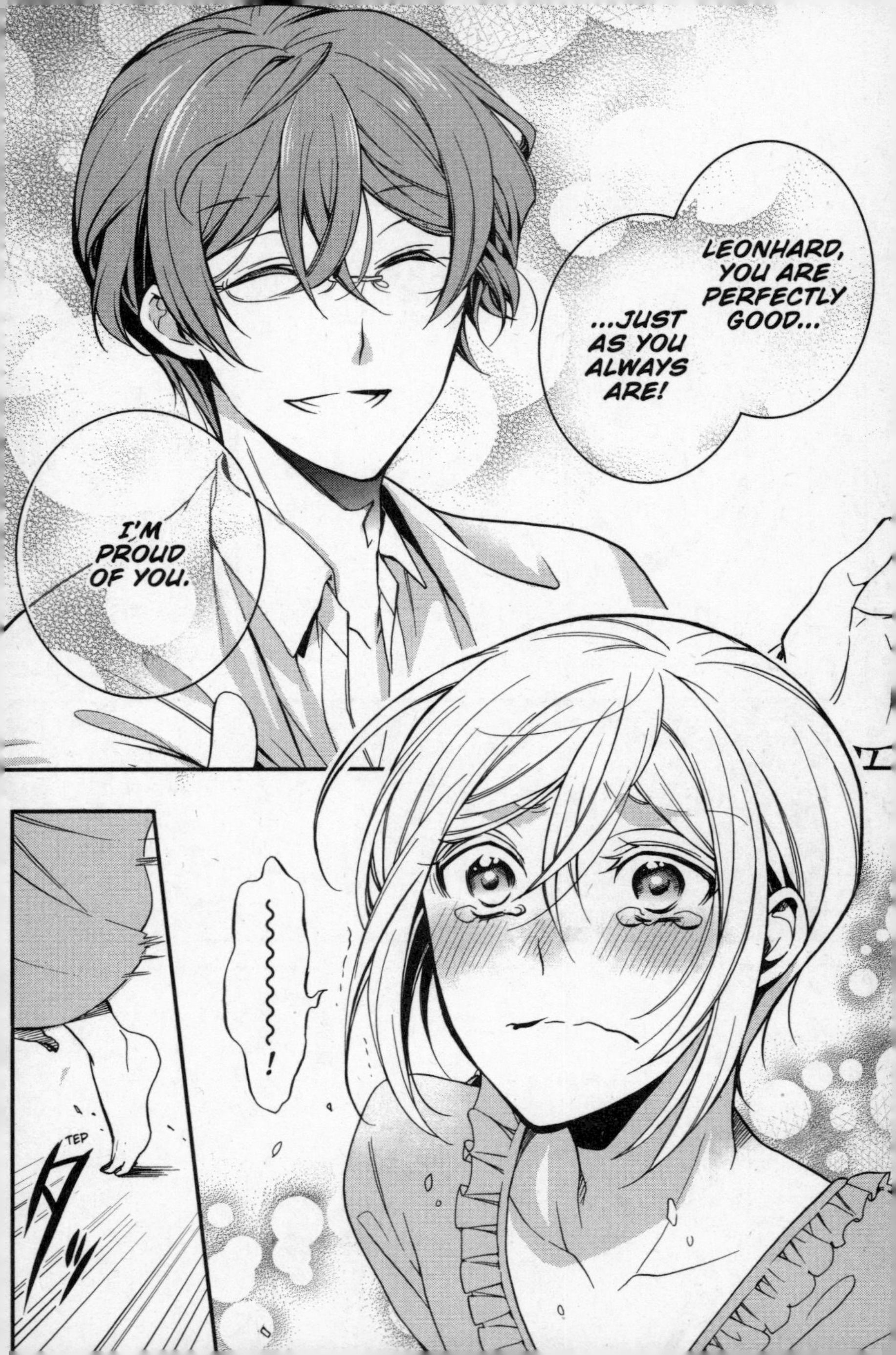
LEONHARD, YOU ARE PERFECTLY GOOD...
...JUST AS YOU ALWAYS ARE!
I'M PROUD OF YOU.
TEP

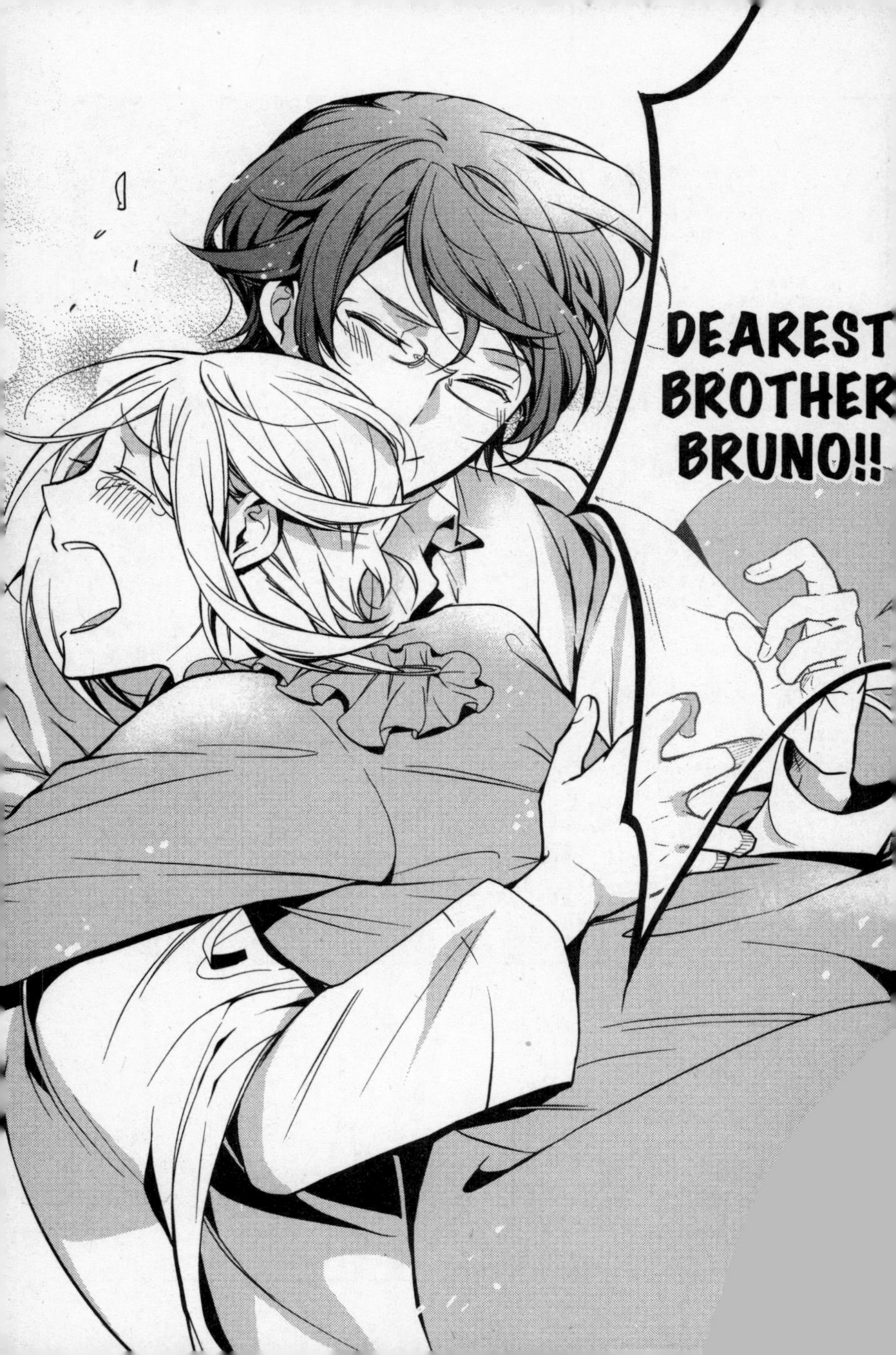
DEAREST BROTHER BRUNO!!

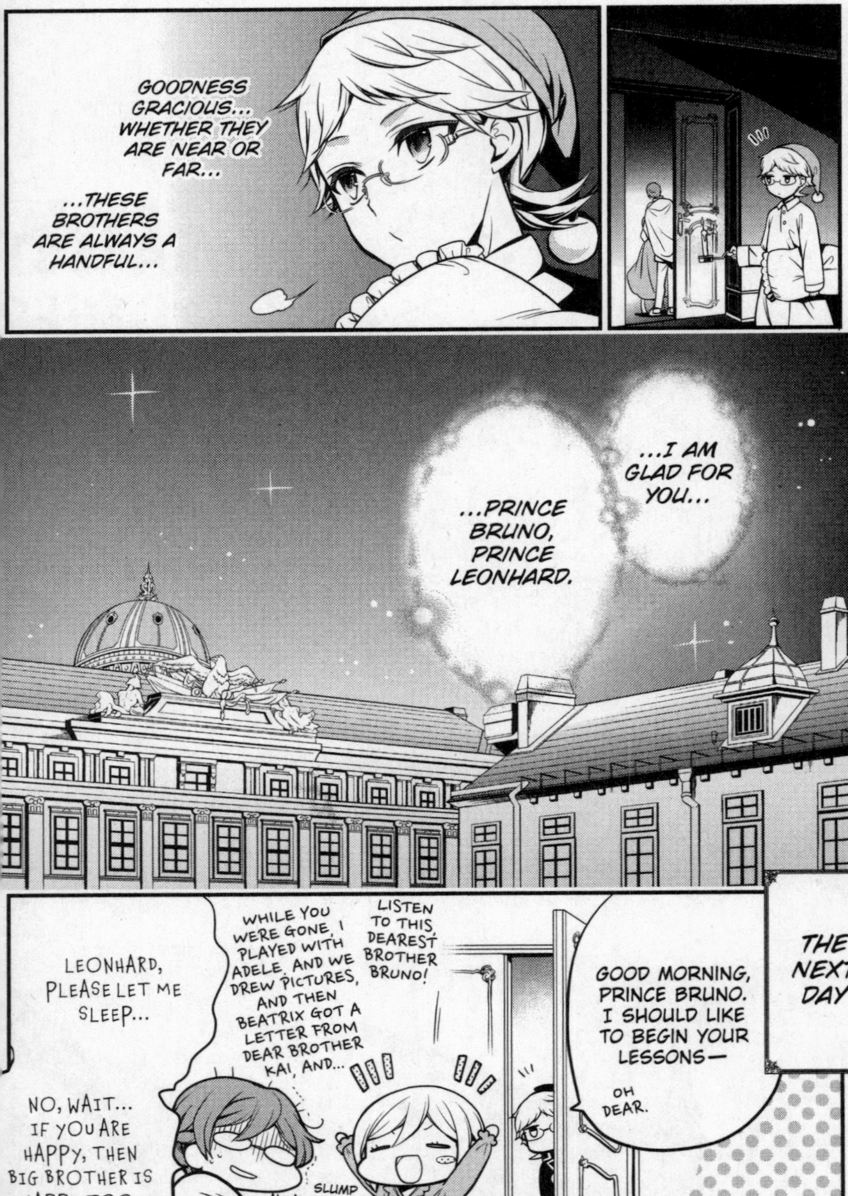
GOODNESS GRACIOUS... WHETHER THEY ARE NEAR OR FAR...
...THESE BROTHERS ARE ALWAYS A HANDFUL...
...I AM GLAD FOR YOU...
...PRINCE BRUNO, PRINCE LEONHARD.
THE NEXT DAY
GOOD MORNING, PRINCE BRUNO. I SHOULD LIKE TO BEGIN YOUR LESSONS—
OH DEAR.
LISTEN TO THIS, DEAREST BROTHER BRUNO!
WHILE YOU WERE GONE, I PLAYED WITH ADELE, AND WE DREW PICTURES, AND THEN BEATRIX GOT A LETTER FROM DEAR BROTHER KAI, AND...
SLUMP
LEONHARD, PLEASE LET ME SLEEP...
NO, WAIT... IF YOU ARE HAPPY, THEN BIG BROTHER IS HAPPY TOO.

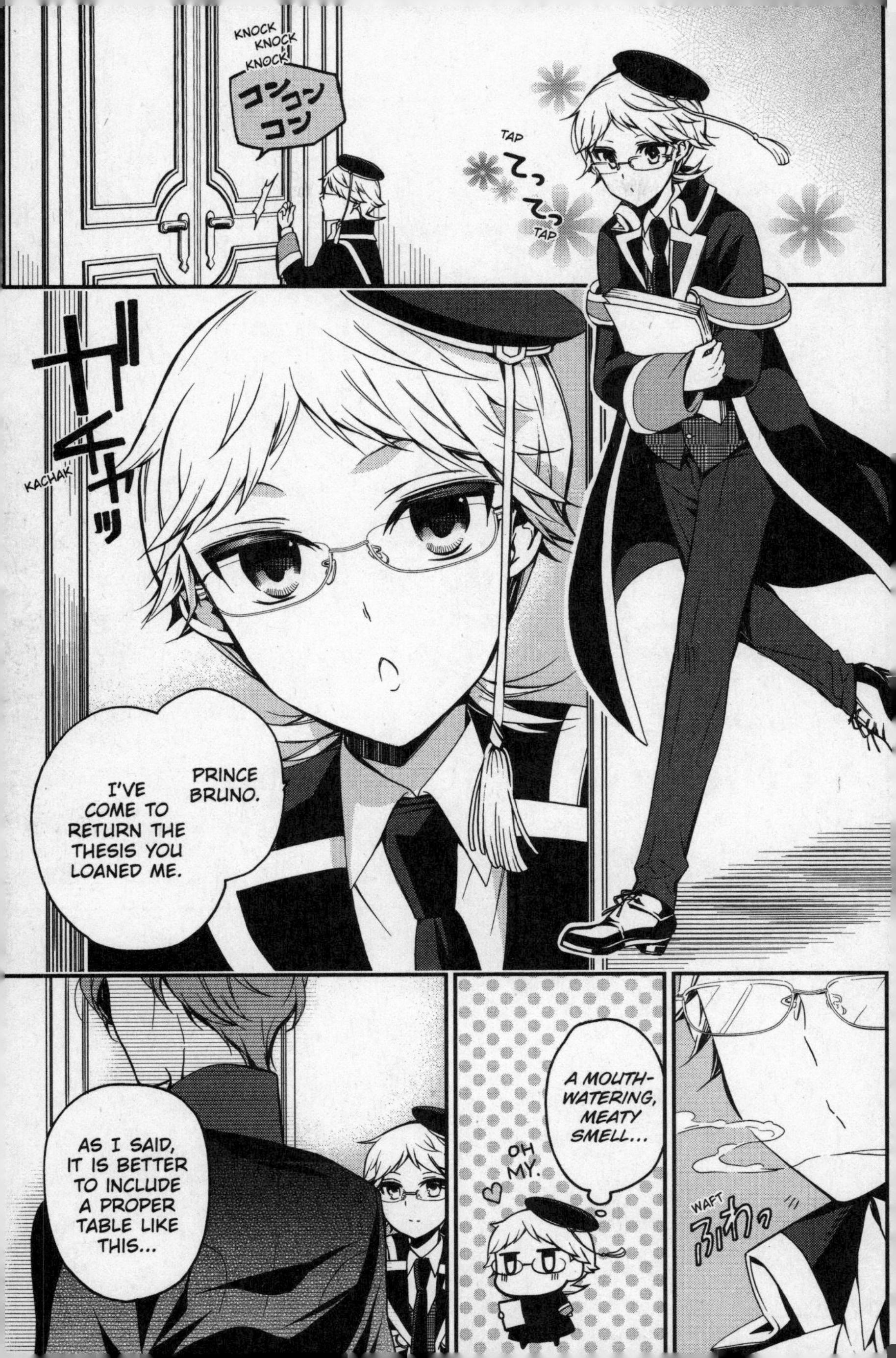
TAP
てっ
てっ
TAP
KNOCK KNOCK KNOCK
コンコンコン
ガチャッ
KACHAK
PRINCE BRUNO.
I'VE COME TO RETURN THE THESIS YOU LOANED ME.
WAFT
ふわっ
A MOUTH-WATERING, MEATY SMELL...
OH MY.
AS I SAID, IT IS BETTER TO INCLUDE A PROPER TABLE LIKE THIS...

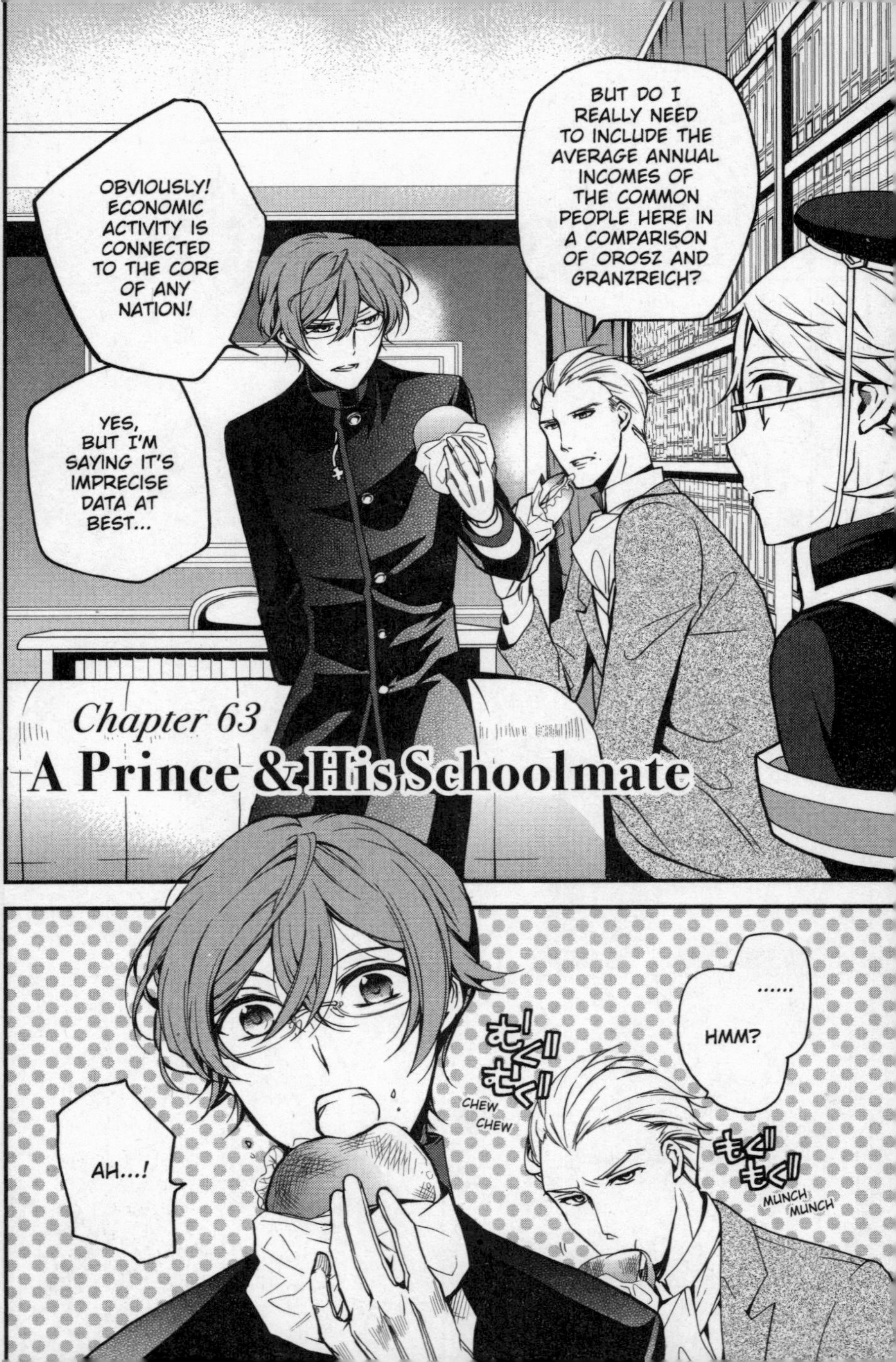

BUT DO I REALLY NEED TO INCLUDE THE AVERAGE ANNUAL INCOMES OF THE COMMON PEOPLE HERE IN A COMPARISON OF OROSZ AND GRANZREICH?
OBVIOUSLY! ECONOMIC ACTIVITY IS CONNECTED TO THE CORE OF ANY NATION!
YES, BUT I'M SAYING IT'S IMPRECISE DATA AT BEST...
Chapter 63
A Prince & His Schoolmate
......
HMM?
MUNCH MUNCH
CHEW CHEW
AH...!

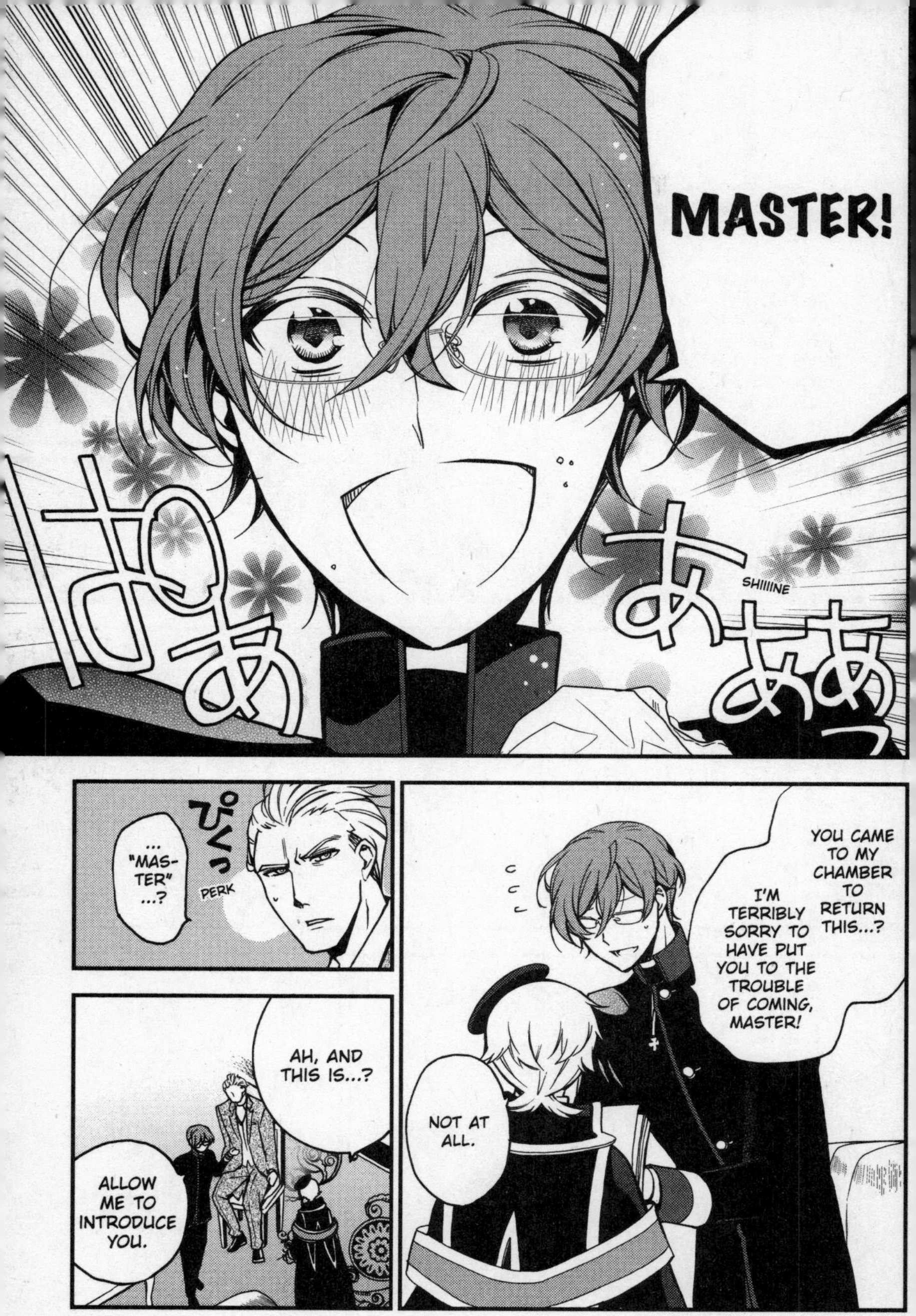
MASTER!
ぱあ
ああああっ
SHIIIINE
YOU CAME TO MY CHAMBER TO RETURN THIS...?
I'M TERRIBLY SORRY TO HAVE PUT YOU TO THE TROUBLE OF COMING, MASTER!
NOT AT ALL.
ぴくっ
PERK
... "MAS-TER" ...?
AH, AND THIS IS...?
ALLOW ME TO INTRODUCE YOU.

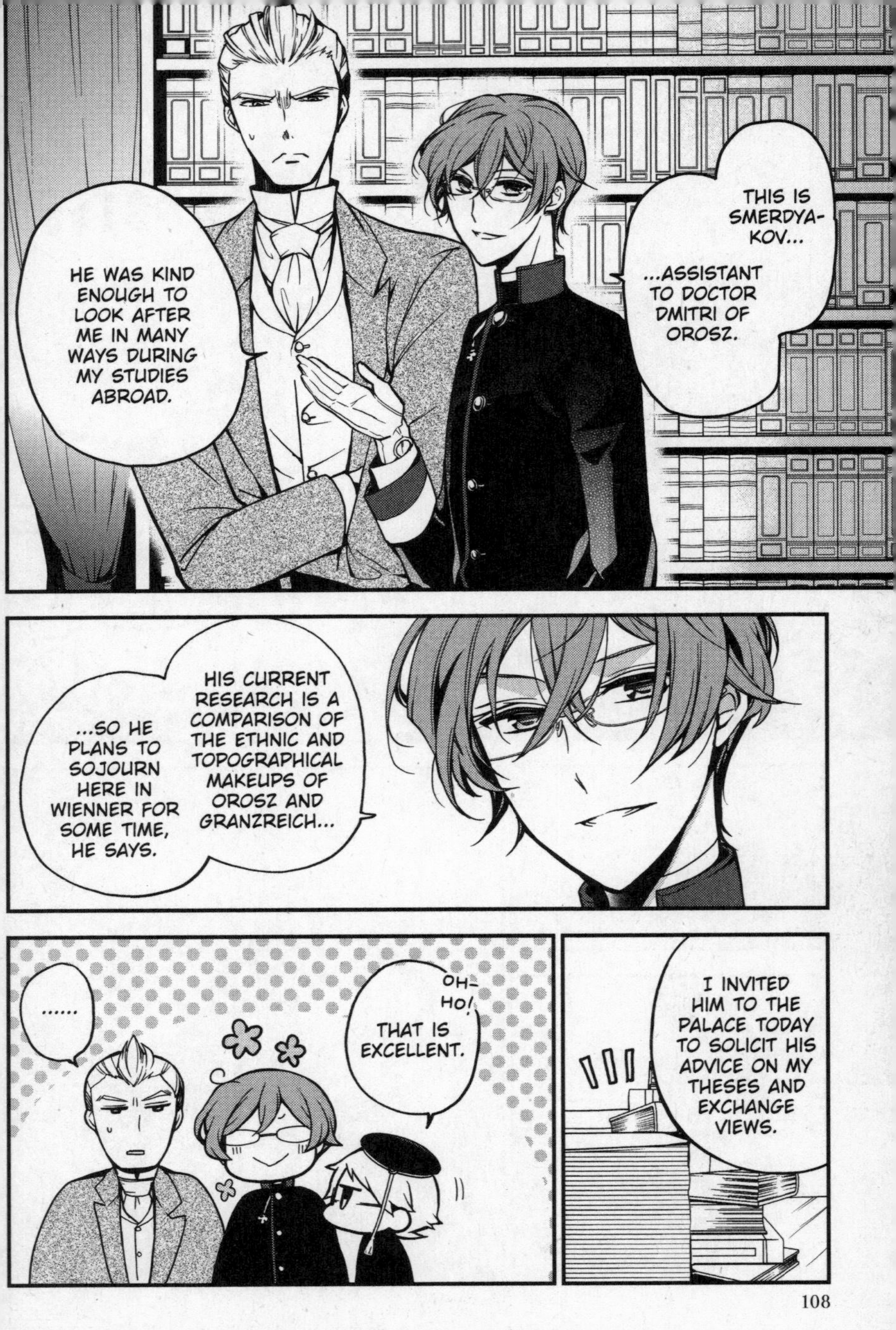
THIS IS SMERDYAKOV...
...ASSISTANT TO DOCTOR DMITRI OF OROSZ.
HE WAS KIND ENOUGH TO LOOK AFTER ME IN MANY WAYS DURING MY STUDIES ABROAD.
HIS CURRENT RESEARCH IS A COMPARISON OF THE ETHNIC AND TOPOGRAPHICAL MAKEUPS OF OROSZ AND GRANZREICH...
...SO HE PLANS TO SOJOURN HERE IN WIENNER FOR SOME TIME, HE SAYS.
I INVITED HIM TO THE PALACE TODAY TO SOLICIT HIS ADVICE ON MY THESES AND EXCHANGE VIEWS.
OH-HO!
THAT IS EXCELLENT.
......

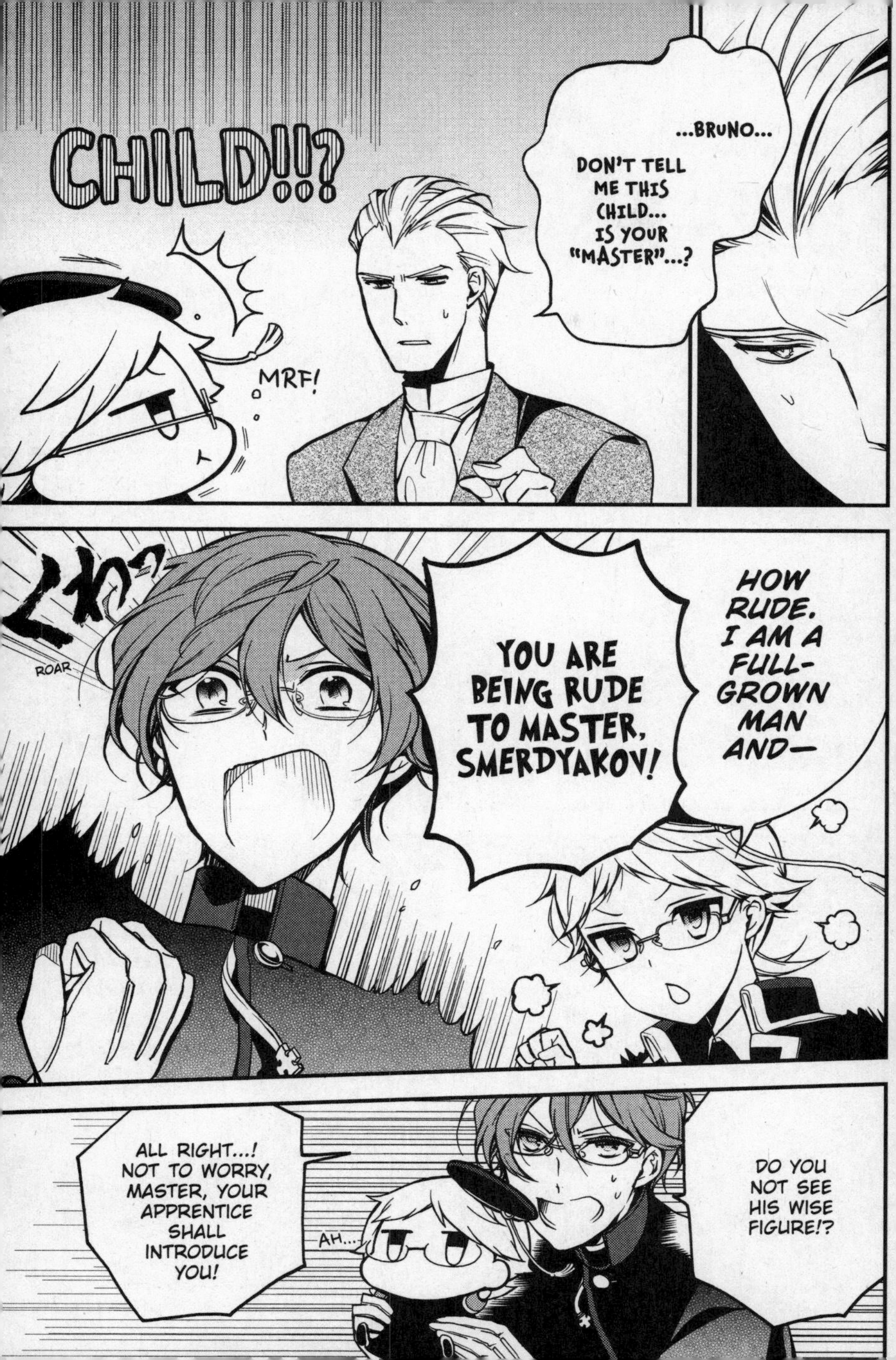
...BRUNO... DON'T TELL ME THIS CHILD... IS YOUR "MASTER"...?
CHILD!!?
MRF!
HOW RUDE. I AM A FULL-GROWN MAN AND—
YOU ARE BEING RUDE TO MASTER, SMERDYAKOV!
ROAR
DO YOU NOT SEE HIS WISE FIGURE!?
AH...
ALL RIGHT...! NOT TO WORRY, MASTER, YOUR APPRENTICE SHALL INTRODUCE YOU!

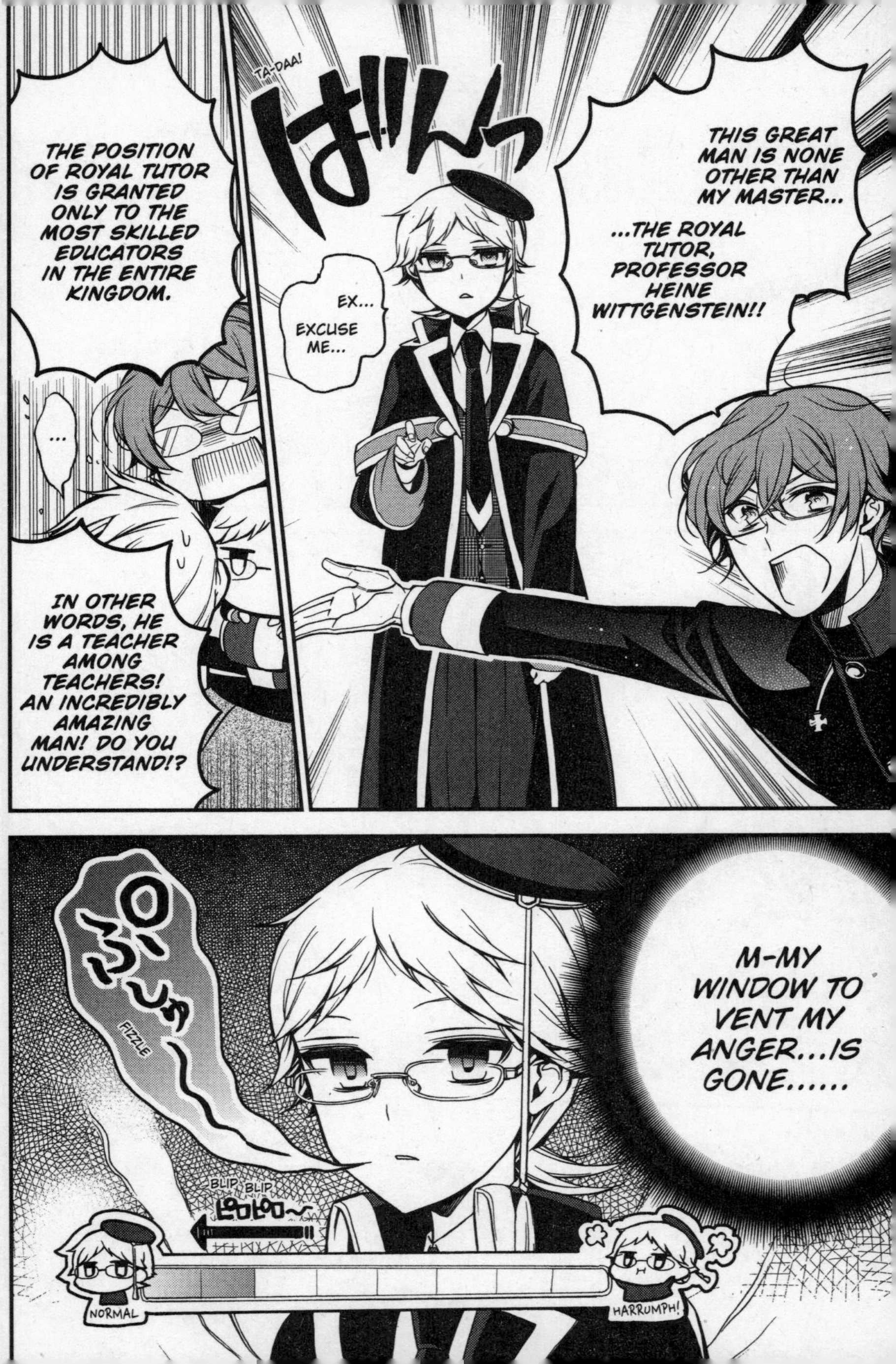
THIS GREAT MAN IS NONE OTHER THAN MY MASTER...
...THE ROYAL TUTOR, PROFESSOR HEINE WITTGENSTEIN!!
TA-DAA!
ばーんっ
EX... EXCUSE ME...
THE POSITION OF ROYAL TUTOR IS GRANTED ONLY TO THE MOST SKILLED EDUCATORS IN THE ENTIRE KINGDOM.
...
IN OTHER WORDS, HE IS A TEACHER AMONG TEACHERS! AN INCREDIBLY AMAZING MAN! DO YOU UNDERSTAND!?
M-MY WINDOW TO VENT MY ANGER...IS GONE......
ぷしゅ〜
FIZZLE
BLIP BLIP
ピロピロ〜
HARRUMPH!
NORMAL

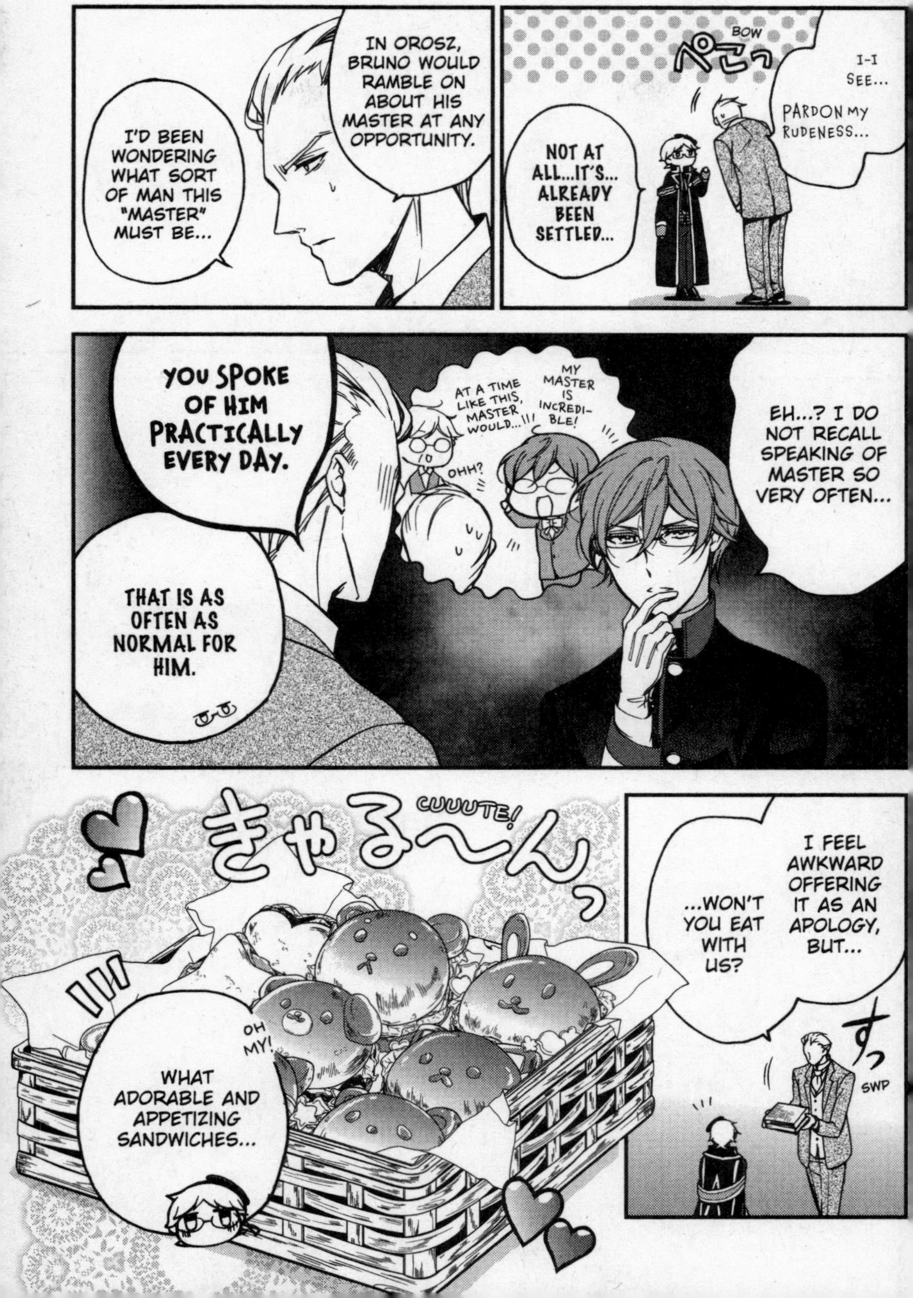
BOW
ぺこっ
I-I SEE...
PARDON MY RUDENESS...
NOT AT ALL...IT'S... ALREADY BEEN SETTLED...
IN OROSZ, BRUNO WOULD RAMBLE ON ABOUT HIS MASTER AT ANY OPPORTUNITY.
I'D BEEN WONDERING WHAT SORT OF MAN THIS "MASTER" MUST BE...
EH...? I DO NOT RECALL SPEAKING OF MASTER SO VERY OFTEN...
MY MASTER IS INCREDI-BLE!
AT A TIME LIKE THIS, MASTER WOULD...!!!
OHH?
YOU SPOKE OF HIM PRACTICALLY EVERY DAY.
THAT IS AS OFTEN AS NORMAL FOR HIM.
I FEEL AWKWARD OFFERING IT AS AN APOLOGY, BUT...
...WON'T YOU EAT WITH US?
すっ
SWP
CUUUTE!
きゃる〜んっ
OH MY!
WHAT ADORABLE AND APPETIZING SANDWICHES...

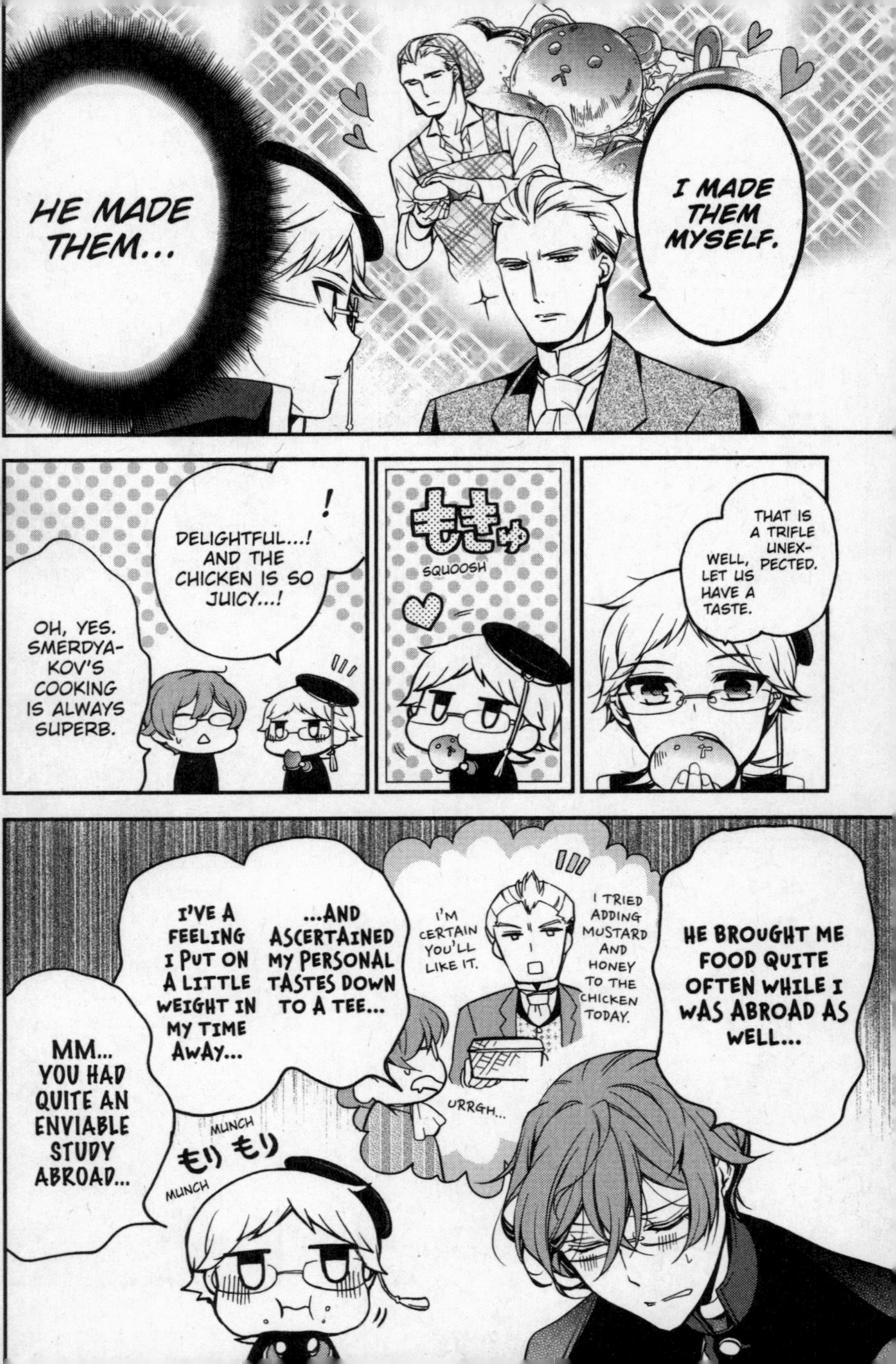
I MADE THEM MYSELF.
HE MADE THEM...
THAT IS A TRIFLE UNEXPECTED.
WELL, LET US HAVE A TASTE.
もきゅ
SQUOOSH
!
DELIGHTFUL...! AND THE CHICKEN IS SO JUICY...!
OH, YES. SMERDYAKOV'S COOKING IS ALWAYS SUPERB.
HE BROUGHT ME FOOD QUITE OFTEN WHILE I WAS ABROAD AS WELL...
I TRIED ADDING MUSTARD AND HONEY TO THE CHICKEN TODAY.
I'M CERTAIN YOU'LL LIKE IT.
...AND ASCERTAINED MY PERSONAL TASTES DOWN TO A TEE...
I'VE A FEELING I PUT ON A LITTLE WEIGHT IN MY TIME AWAY...
URRGH...
MM... YOU HAD QUITE AN ENVIABLE STUDY ABROAD...
もり もり
MUNCH
MUNCH

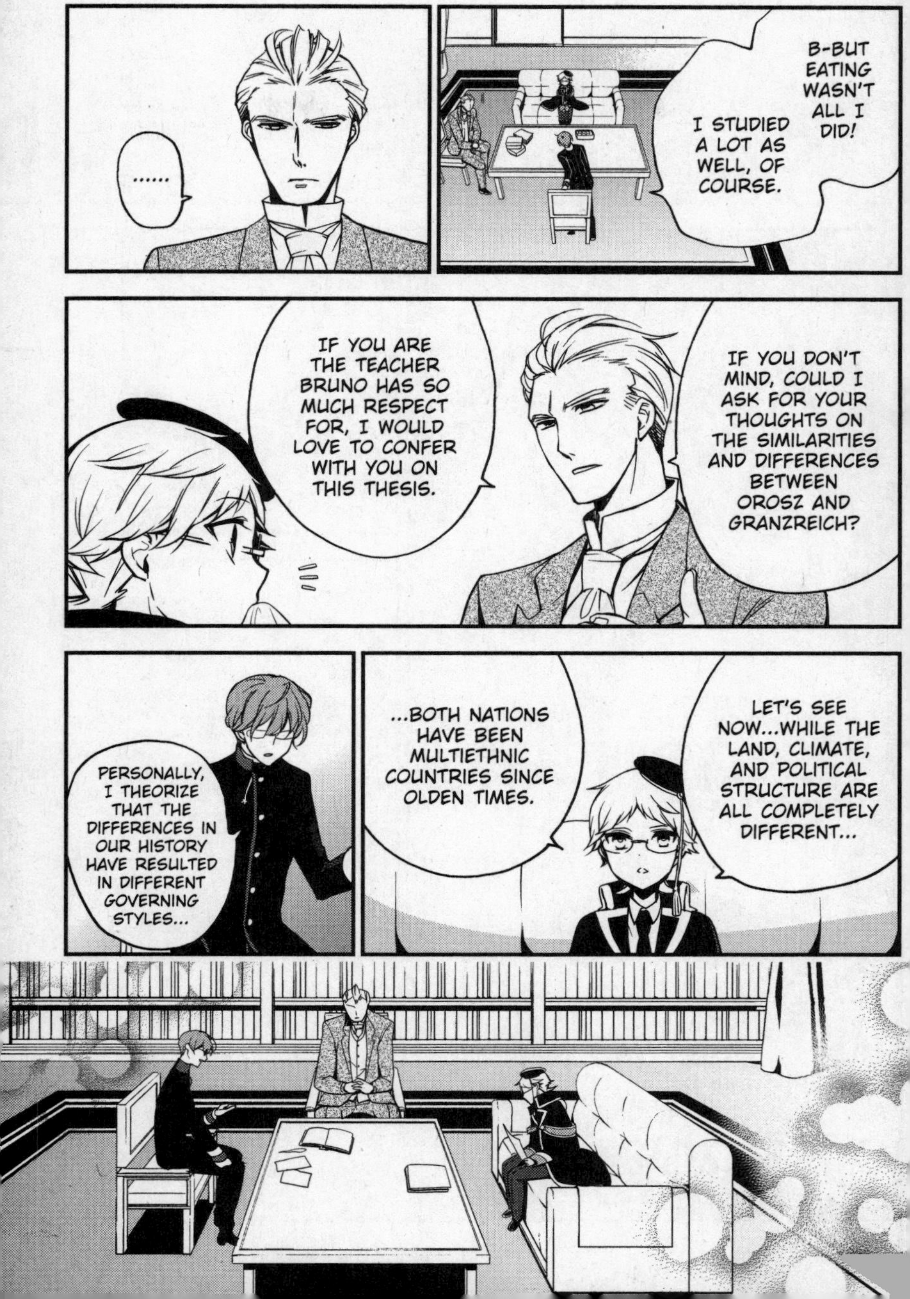
B-BUT EATING WASN'T ALL I DID!
I STUDIED A LOT AS WELL, OF COURSE.
......
IF YOU DON'T MIND, COULD I ASK FOR YOUR THOUGHTS ON THE SIMILARITIES AND DIFFERENCES BETWEEN OROSZ AND GRANZREICH?
IF YOU ARE THE TEACHER BRUNO HAS SO MUCH RESPECT FOR, I WOULD LOVE TO CONFER WITH YOU ON THIS THESIS.
LET'S SEE NOW...WHILE THE LAND, CLIMATE, AND POLITICAL STRUCTURE ARE ALL COMPLETELY DIFFERENT...
...BOTH NATIONS HAVE BEEN MULTIETHNIC COUNTRIES SINCE OLDEN TIMES.
PERSONALLY, I THEORIZE THAT THE DIFFERENCES IN OUR HISTORY HAVE RESULTED IN DIFFERENT GOVERNING STYLES...

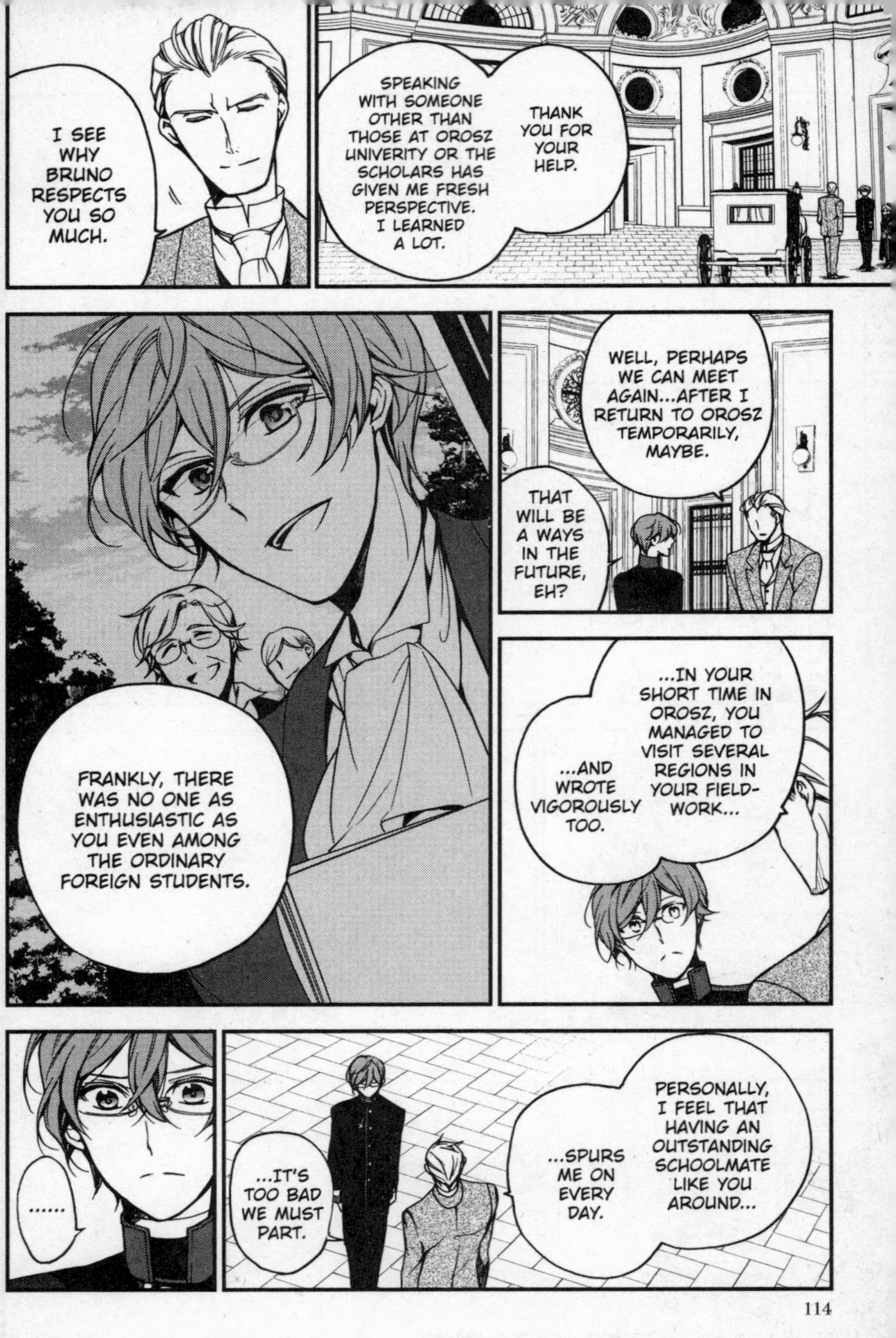
THANK YOU FOR YOUR HELP.
SPEAKING WITH SOMEONE OTHER THAN THOSE AT OROSZ UNIVERITY OR THE SCHOLARS HAS GIVEN ME FRESH PERSPECTIVE. I LEARNED A LOT.
I SEE WHY BRUNO RESPECTS YOU SO MUCH.
WELL, PERHAPS WE CAN MEET AGAIN...AFTER I RETURN TO OROSZ TEMPORARILY, MAYBE.
THAT WILL BE A WAYS IN THE FUTURE, EH?
...IN YOUR SHORT TIME IN OROSZ, YOU MANAGED TO VISIT SEVERAL REGIONS IN YOUR FIELD-WORK...
...AND WROTE VIGOROUSLY TOO.
FRANKLY, THERE WAS NO ONE AS ENTHUSIASTIC AS YOU EVEN AMONG THE ORDINARY FOREIGN STUDENTS.
PERSONALLY, I FEEL THAT HAVING AN OUTSTANDING SCHOOLMATE LIKE YOU AROUND...
...SPURS ME ON EVERY DAY.
...IT'S TOO BAD WE MUST PART.
......

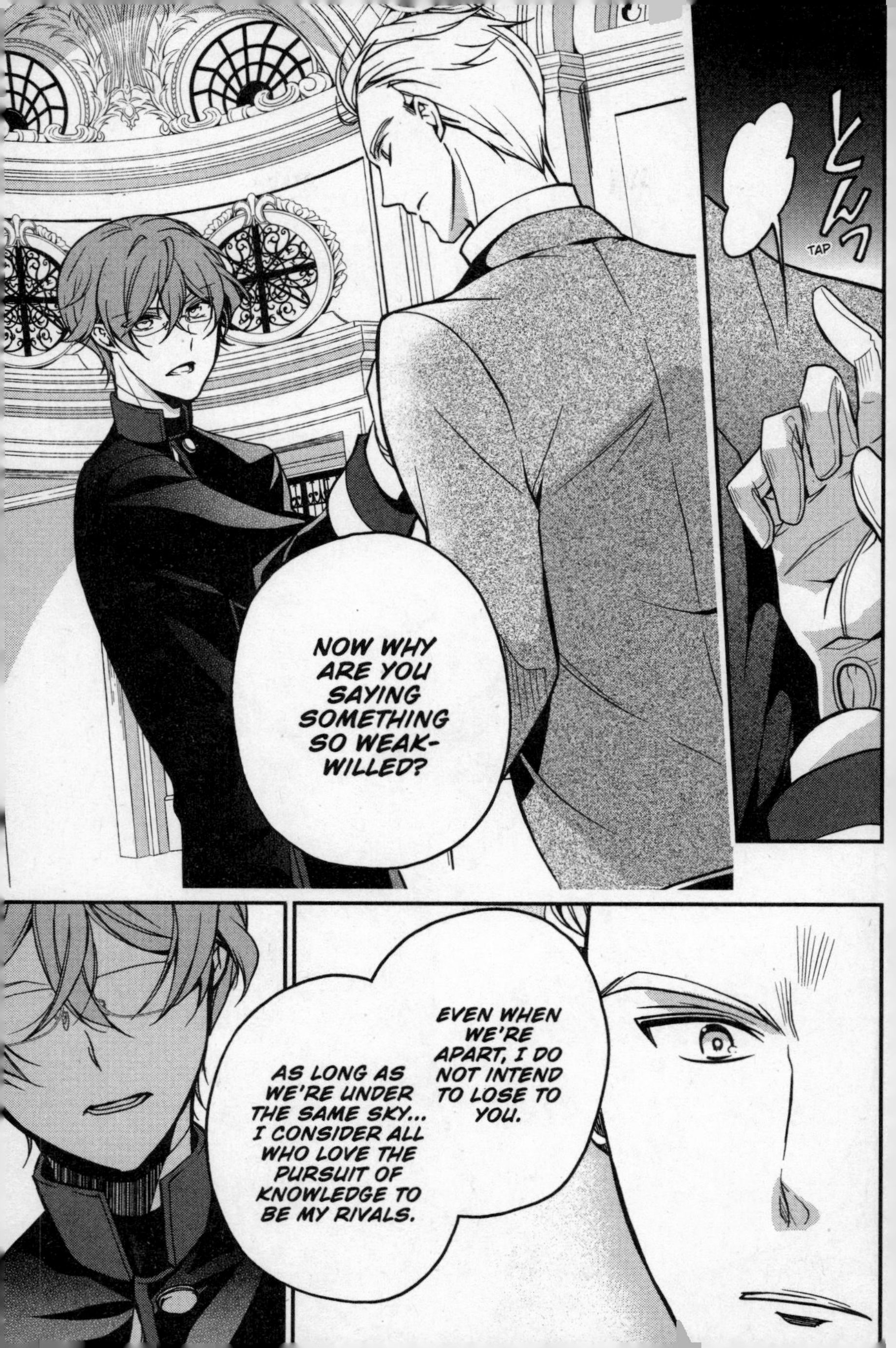
とんっ
TAP
NOW WHY ARE YOU SAYING SOMETHING SO WEAK-WILLED?
EVEN WHEN WE'RE APART, I DO NOT INTEND TO LOSE TO YOU.
AS LONG AS WE'RE UNDER THE SAME SKY... I CONSIDER ALL WHO LOVE THE PURSUIT OF KNOWLEDGE TO BE MY RIVALS.

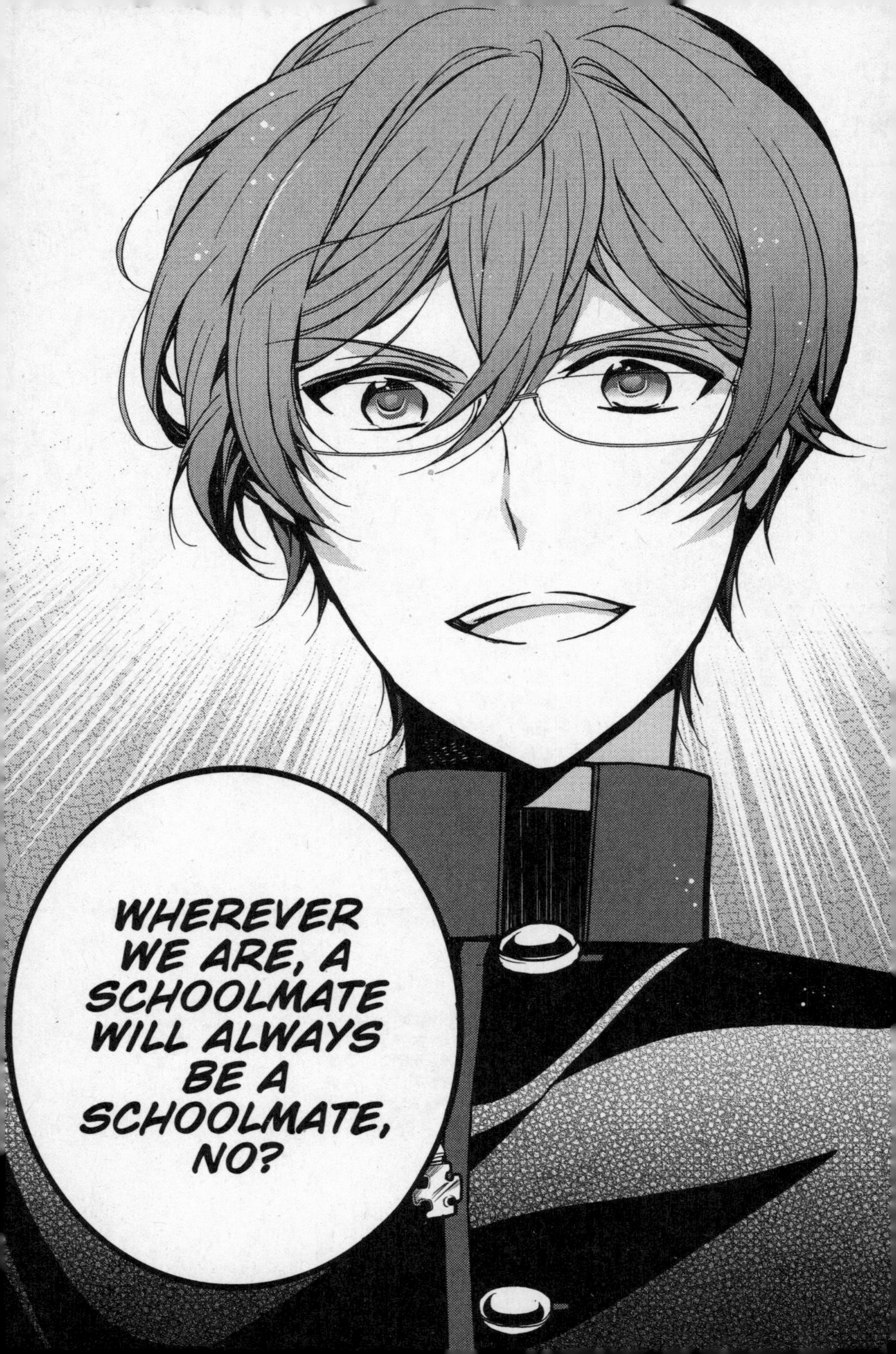
WHEREVER WE ARE, A SCHOOLMATE WILL ALWAYS BE A SCHOOLMATE, NO?

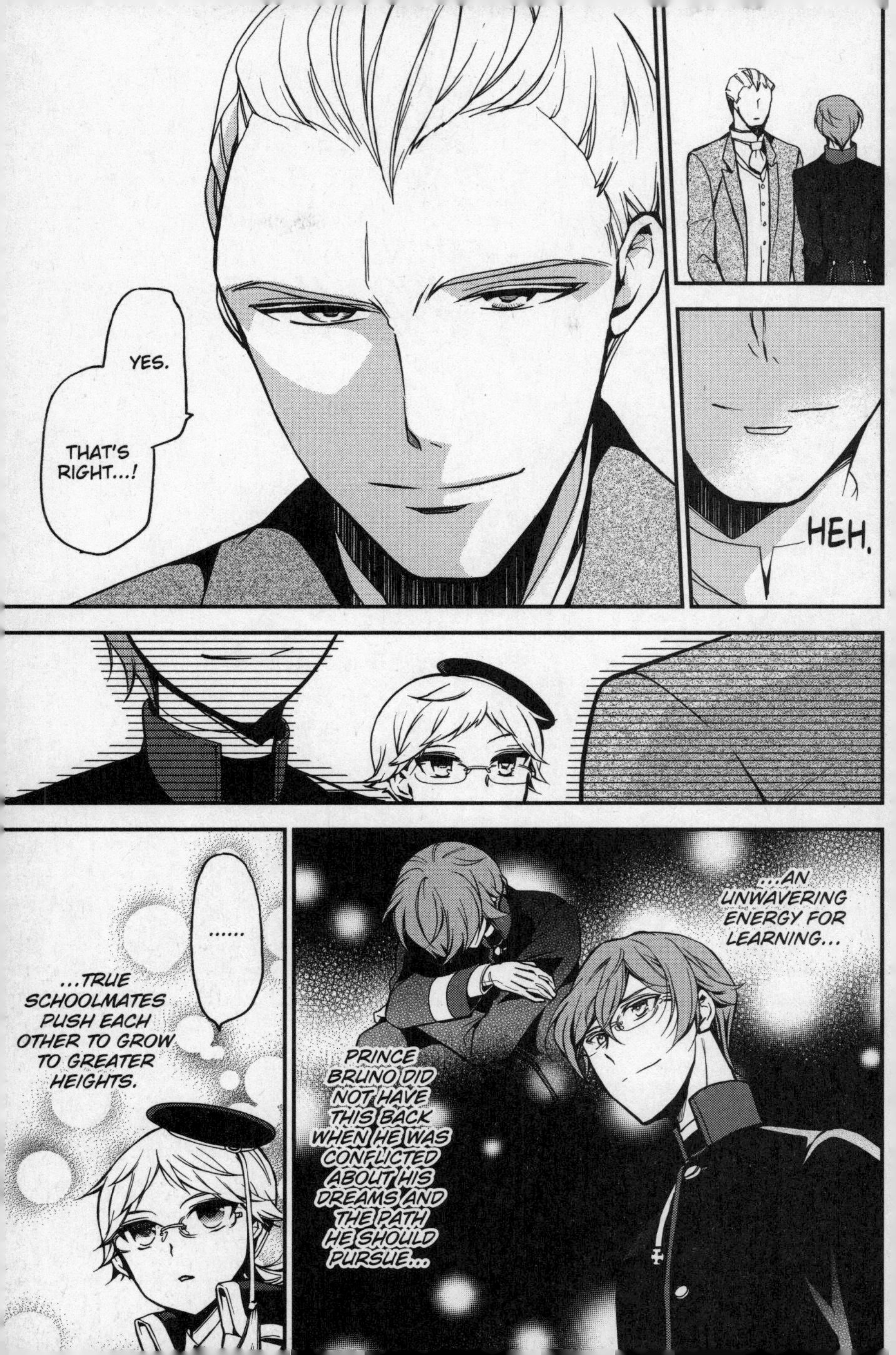
HEH.
YES.
THAT'S RIGHT...!
...AN UNWAVERING ENERGY FOR LEARNING...
PRINCE BRUNO DID NOT HAVE THIS BACK WHEN HE WAS CONFLICTED ABOUT HIS DREAMS AND THE PATH HE SHOULD PURSUE...
......
...TRUE SCHOOLMATES PUSH EACH OTHER TO GROW TO GREATER HEIGHTS.

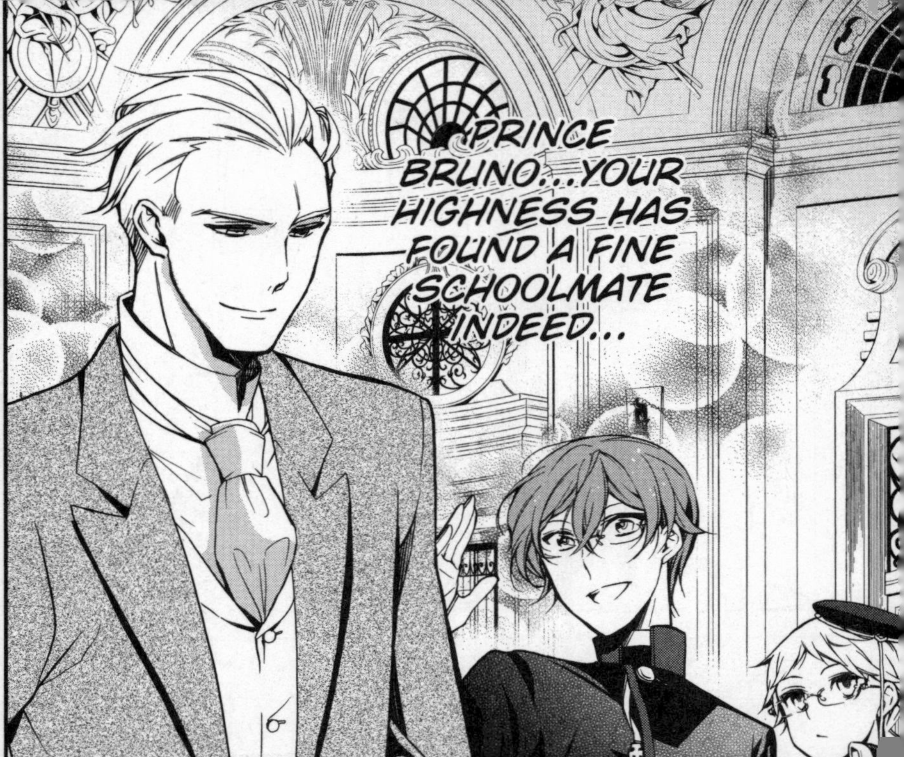
PRINCE BRUNO...YOUR HIGHNESS HAS FOUND A FINE SCHOOLMATE INDEED...
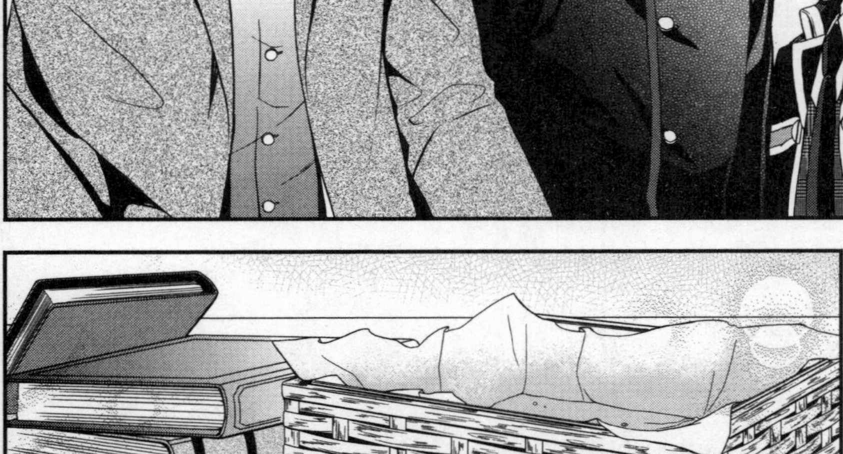

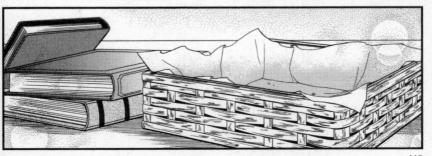

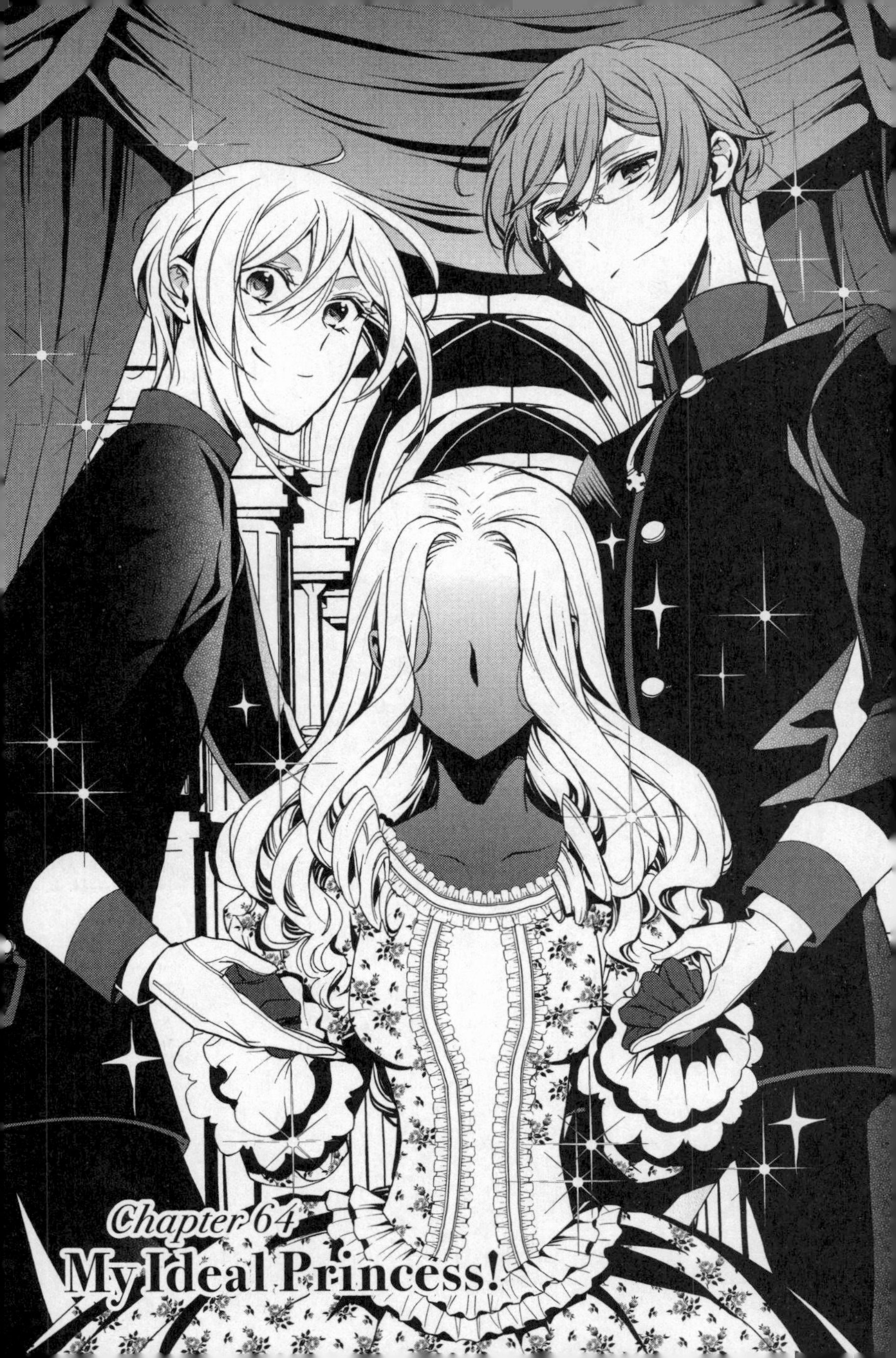
Chapter 64
My Ideal Princess!

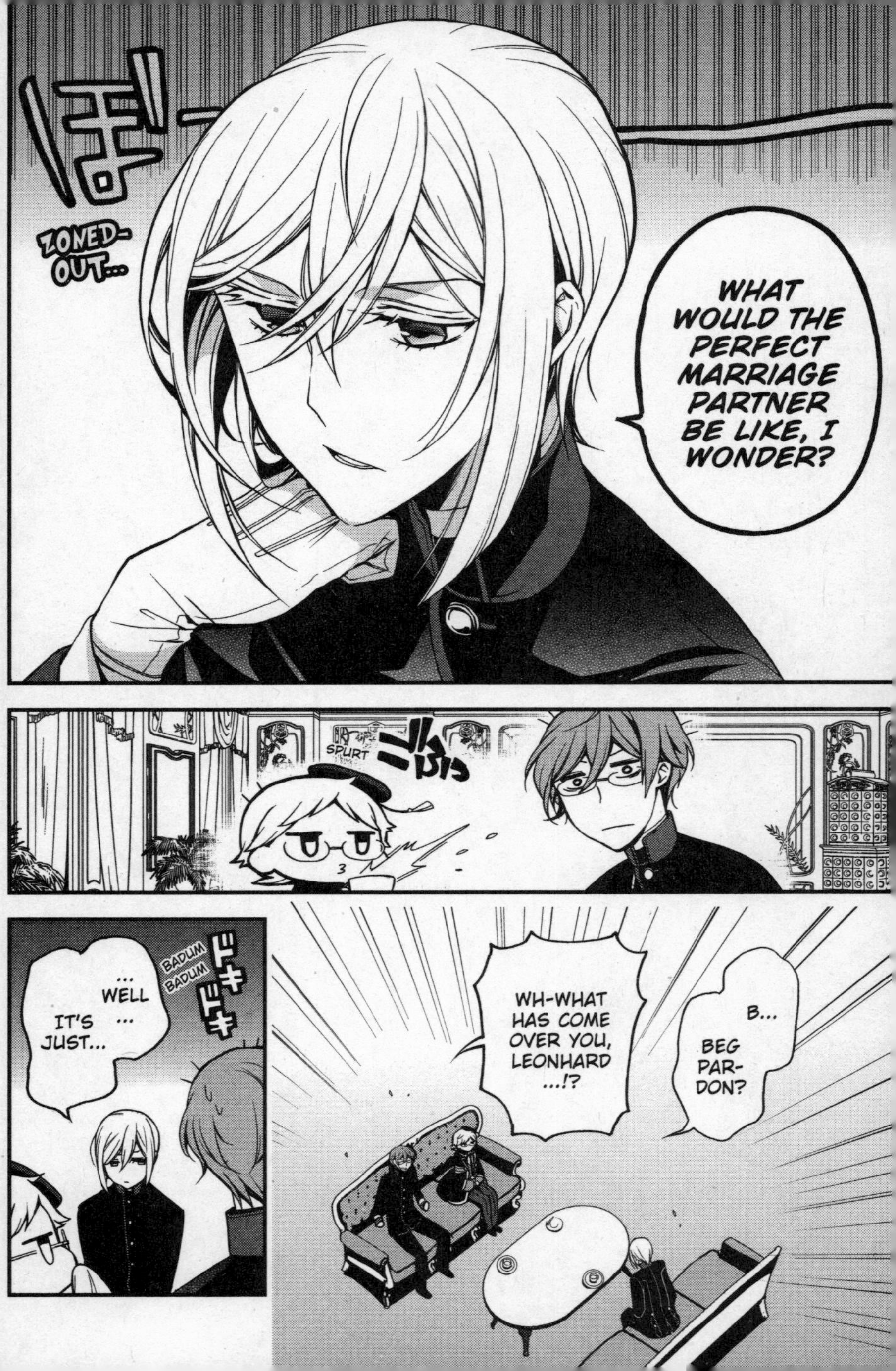
ぼー
ZONED-OUT...
WHAT WOULD THE PERFECT MARRIAGE PARTNER BE LIKE, I WONDER?
SPURT
B... BEG PARDON?
WH-WHAT HAS COME OVER YOU, LEONHARD ...!?
BADUM BADUM
ドキドキ
... WELL ... IT'S JUST...

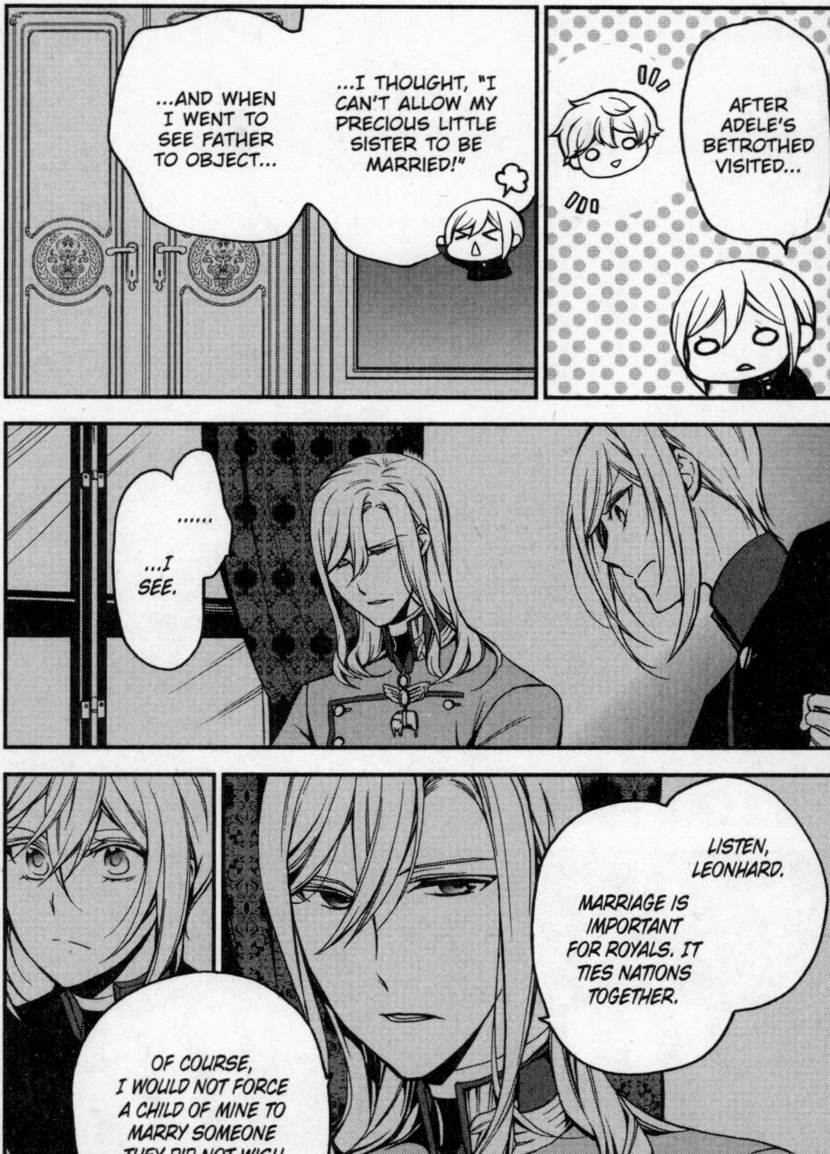
AFTER ADELE'S BETROTHED VISITED...
...AND WHEN I WENT TO SEE FATHER TO OBJECT...
...I THOUGHT, "I CAN'T ALLOW MY PRECIOUS LITTLE SISTER TO BE MARRIED!"
......
...I SEE.
LISTEN, LEONHARD.
MARRIAGE IS IMPORTANT FOR ROYALS. IT TIES NATIONS TOGETHER.
OF COURSE, I WOULD NOT FORCE A CHILD OF MINE TO MARRY SOMEONE THEY DID NOT WISH TO WED...

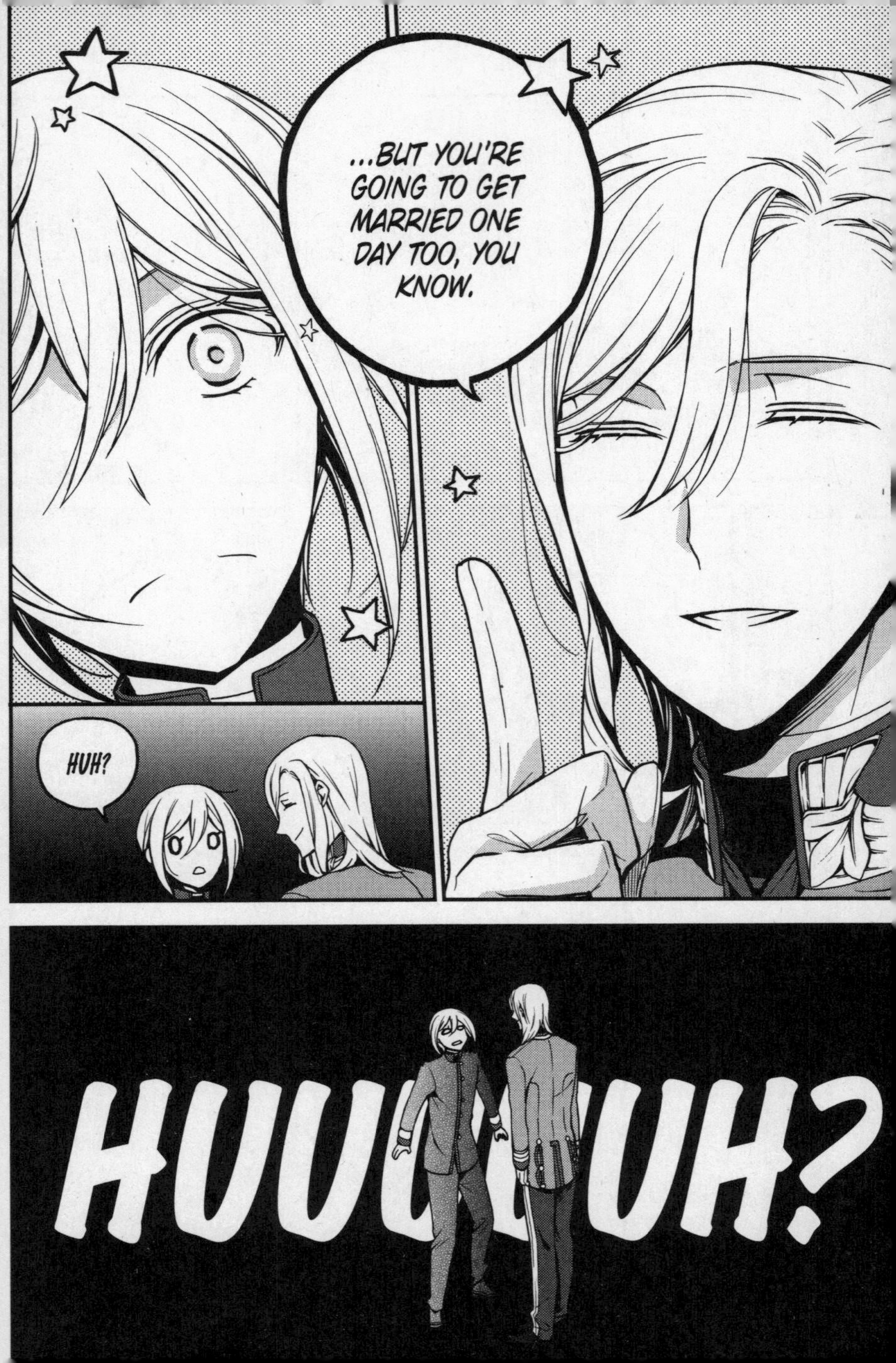
...BUT YOU'RE GOING TO GET MARRIED ONE DAY TOO, YOU KNOW.
HUH?
HUU UH?

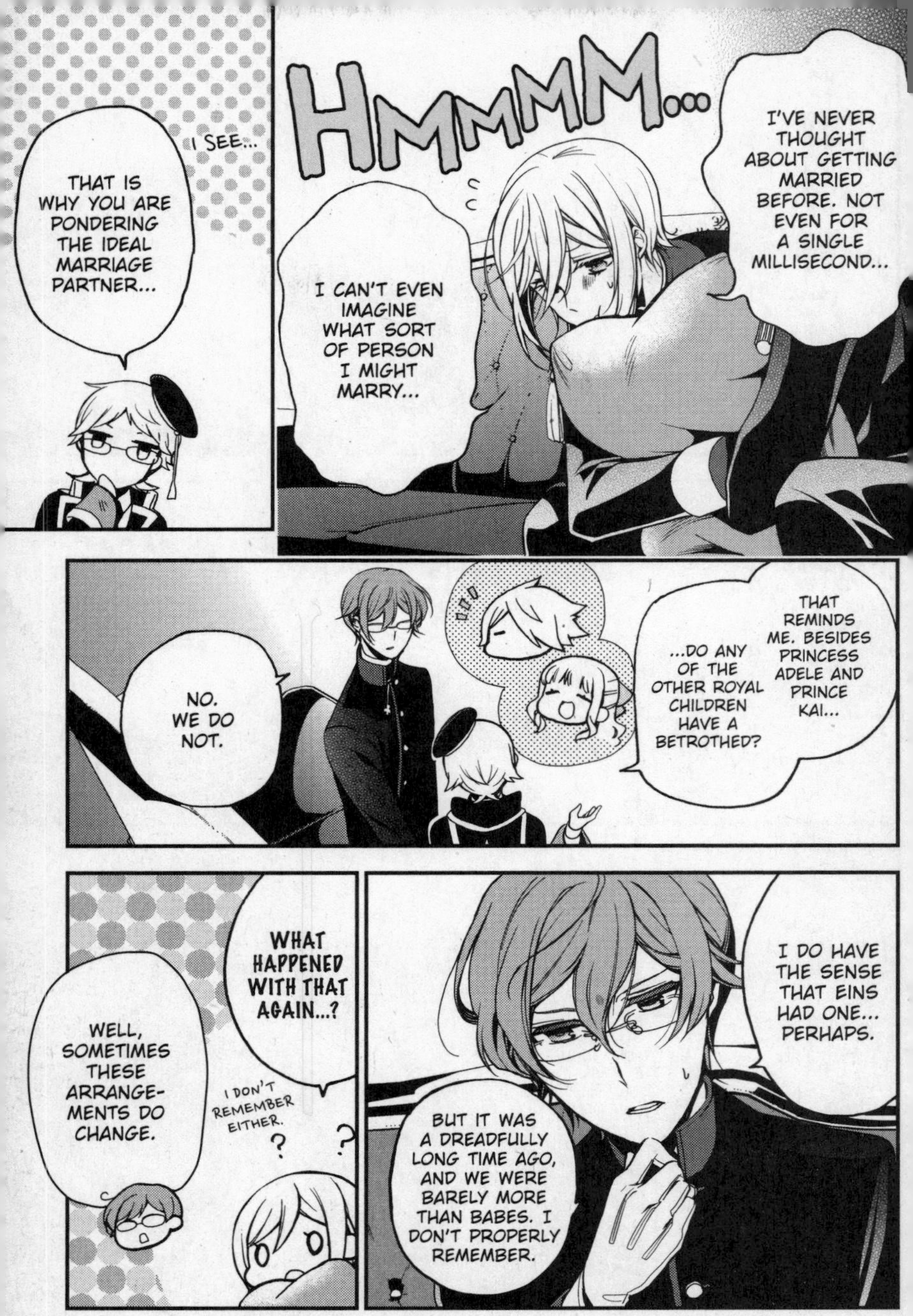
I'VE NEVER THOUGHT ABOUT GETTING MARRIED BEFORE. NOT EVEN FOR A SINGLE MILLISECOND...
HMMMM...
I CAN'T EVEN IMAGINE WHAT SORT OF PERSON I MIGHT MARRY...
I SEE...
THAT IS WHY YOU ARE PONDERING THE IDEAL MARRIAGE PARTNER...
THAT REMINDS ME. BESIDES PRINCESS ADELE AND PRINCE KAI...
...DO ANY OF THE OTHER ROYAL CHILDREN HAVE A BETROTHED?
NO. WE DO NOT.
I DO HAVE THE SENSE THAT EINS HAD ONE... PERHAPS.
BUT IT WAS A DREADFULLY LONG TIME AGO, AND WE WERE BARELY MORE THAN BABES. I DON'T PROPERLY REMEMBER.
WHAT HAPPENED WITH THAT AGAIN...?
I DON'T REMEMBER EITHER.
WELL, SOMETIMES THESE ARRANGE-MENTS DO CHANGE.

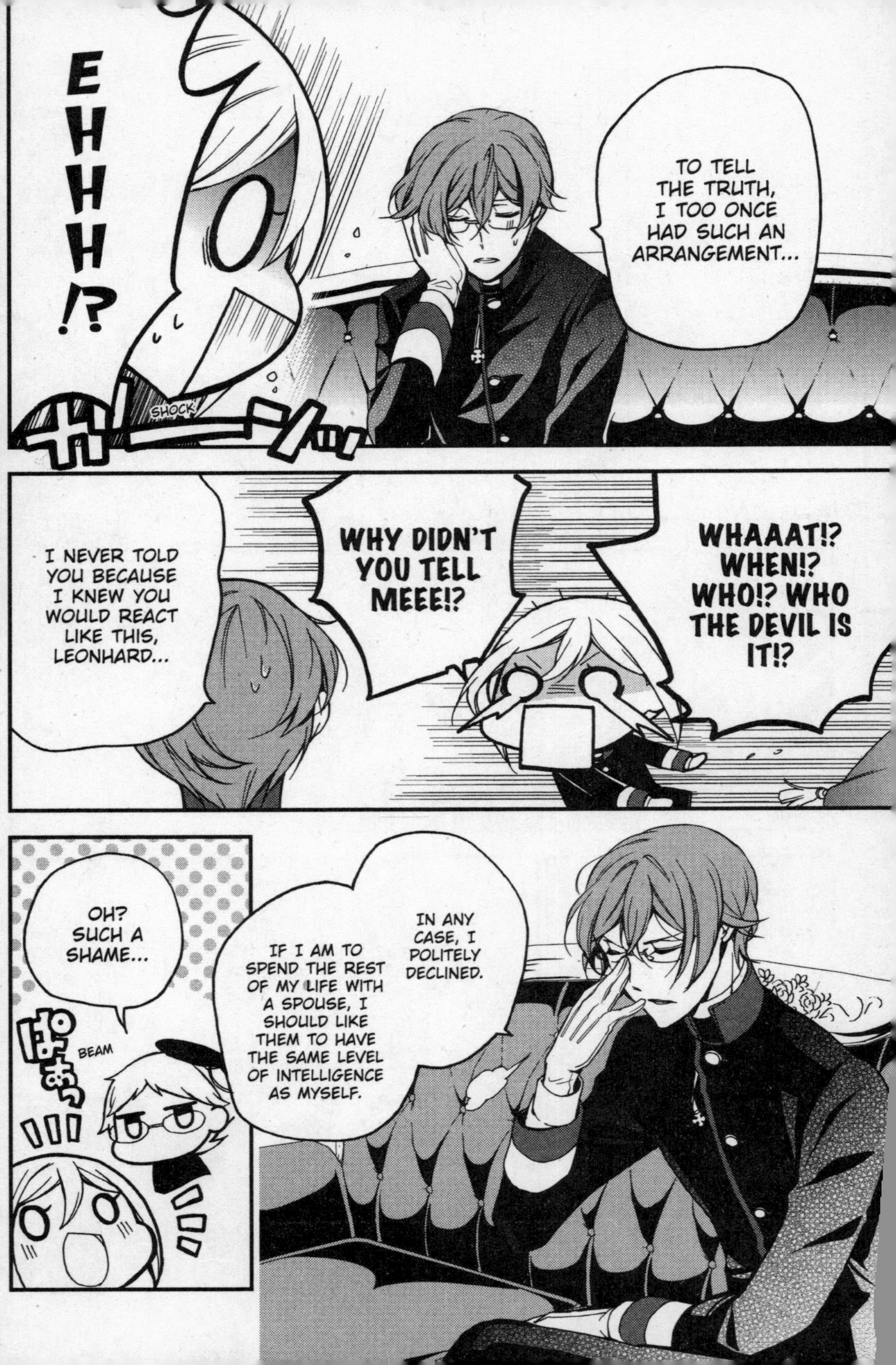
TO TELL THE TRUTH, I TOO ONCE HAD SUCH AN ARRANGEMENT...
EHHH!?
SHOCK
WHAAAT!? WHEN!? WHO!? WHO THE DEVIL IS IT!?
WHY DIDN'T YOU TELL MEEE!?
I NEVER TOLD YOU BECAUSE I KNEW YOU WOULD REACT LIKE THIS, LEONHARD...
IN ANY CASE, I POLITELY DECLINED.
IF I AM TO SPEND THE REST OF MY LIFE WITH A SPOUSE, I SHOULD LIKE THEM TO HAVE THE SAME LEVEL OF INTELLIGENCE AS MYSELF.
OH? SUCH A SHAME...
BEAM

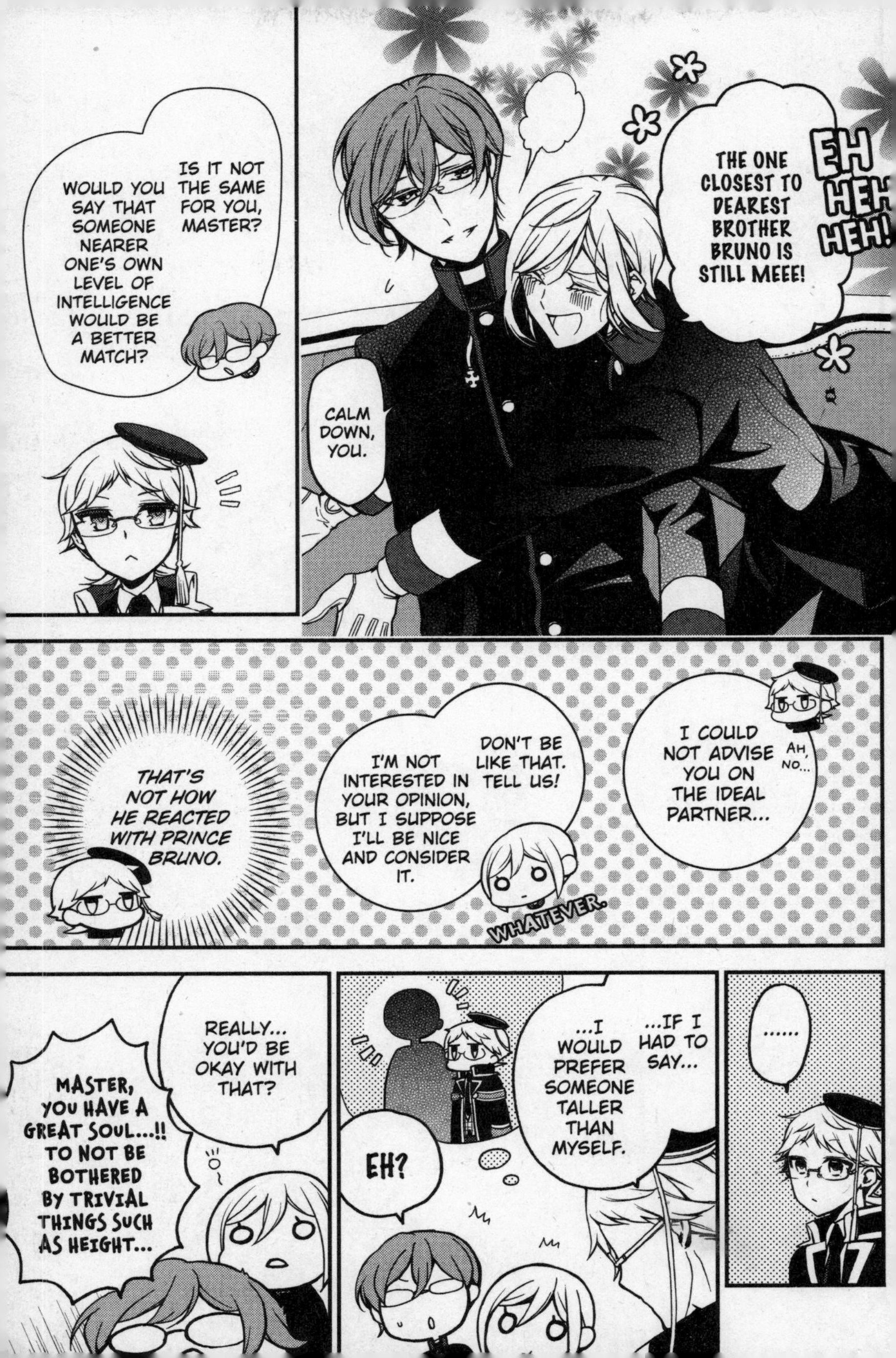
THE ONE CLOSEST TO DEAREST BROTHER BRUNO IS STILL MEEE!
EH HEH HEH!
CALM DOWN, YOU.
IS IT NOT THE SAME FOR YOU, MASTER?
WOULD YOU SAY THAT SOMEONE NEARER ONE'S OWN LEVEL OF INTELLIGENCE WOULD BE A BETTER MATCH?
I COULD NOT ADVISE YOU ON THE IDEAL PARTNER...
AH, NO...
DON'T BE LIKE THAT. TELL US!
I'M NOT INTERESTED IN YOUR OPINION, BUT I SUPPOSE I'LL BE NICE AND CONSIDER IT.
WHATEVER.
THAT'S NOT HOW HE REACTED WITH PRINCE BRUNO.
......
...IF I HAD TO SAY...
...I WOULD PREFER SOMEONE TALLER THAN MYSELF.
EH?
REALLY... YOU'D BE OKAY WITH THAT?
MASTER, YOU HAVE A GREAT SOUL...!! TO NOT BE BOTHERED BY TRIVIAL THINGS SUCH AS HEIGHT...

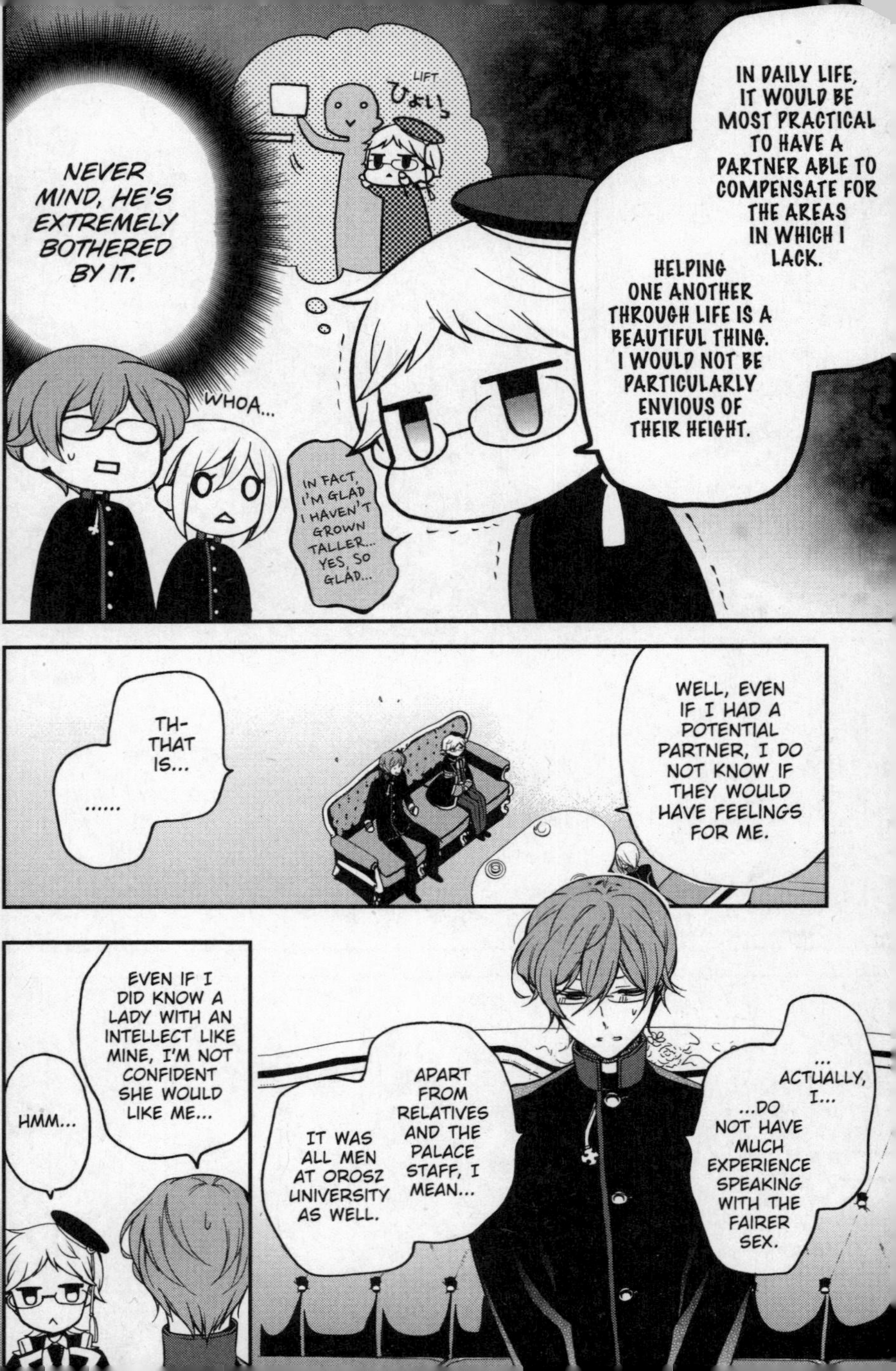
IN DAILY LIFE, IT WOULD BE MOST PRACTICAL TO HAVE A PARTNER ABLE TO COMPENSATE FOR THE AREAS IN WHICH I LACK.
HELPING ONE ANOTHER THROUGH LIFE IS A BEAUTIFUL THING. I WOULD NOT BE PARTICULARLY ENVIOUS OF THEIR HEIGHT.
ひょい
LIFT
IN FACT, I'M GLAD I HAVEN'T GROWN TALLER... YES, SO GLAD...
WHOA...
NEVER MIND, HE'S EXTREMELY BOTHERED BY IT.
WELL, EVEN IF I HAD A POTENTIAL PARTNER, I DO NOT KNOW IF THEY WOULD HAVE FEELINGS FOR ME.
TH-THAT IS...
......
...ACTUALLY, I...
...DO NOT HAVE MUCH EXPERIENCE SPEAKING WITH THE FAIRER SEX.
APART FROM RELATIVES AND THE PALACE STAFF, I MEAN...
IT WAS ALL MEN AT OROSZ UNIVERSITY AS WELL.
EVEN IF I DID KNOW A LADY WITH AN INTELLECT LIKE MINE, I'M NOT CONFIDENT SHE WOULD LIKE ME...
HMM...

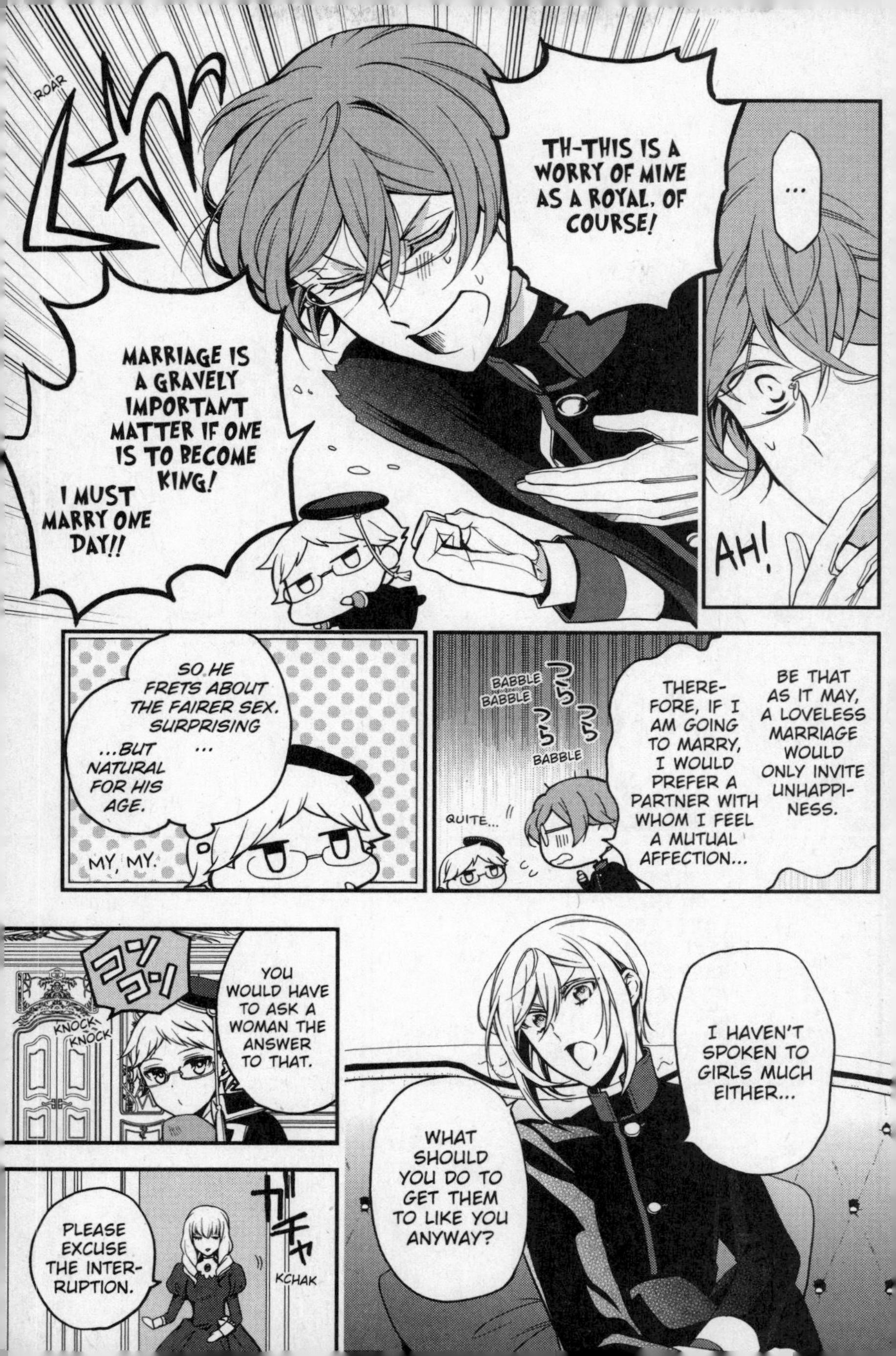
...
AH!
TH-THIS IS A WORRY OF MINE AS A ROYAL, OF COURSE!
ROAR
MARRIAGE IS A GRAVELY IMPORTANT MATTER IF ONE IS TO BECOME KING!
I MUST MARRY ONE DAY!!
BE THAT AS IT MAY, A LOVELESS MARRIAGE WOULD ONLY INVITE UNHAPPINESS.
THEREFORE, IF I AM GOING TO MARRY, I WOULD PREFER A PARTNER WITH WHOM I FEEL A MUTUAL AFFECTION...
BABBLE BABBLE
BABBLE
QUITE...
SO HE FRETS ABOUT THE FAIRER SEX. SURPRISING ...
...BUT NATURAL FOR HIS AGE.
MY, MY.
I HAVEN'T SPOKEN TO GIRLS MUCH EITHER...
WHAT SHOULD YOU DO TO GET THEM TO LIKE YOU ANYWAY?
YOU WOULD HAVE TO ASK A WOMAN THE ANSWER TO THAT.
KNOCK KNOCK
KCHAK
PLEASE EXCUSE THE INTERRUPTION.

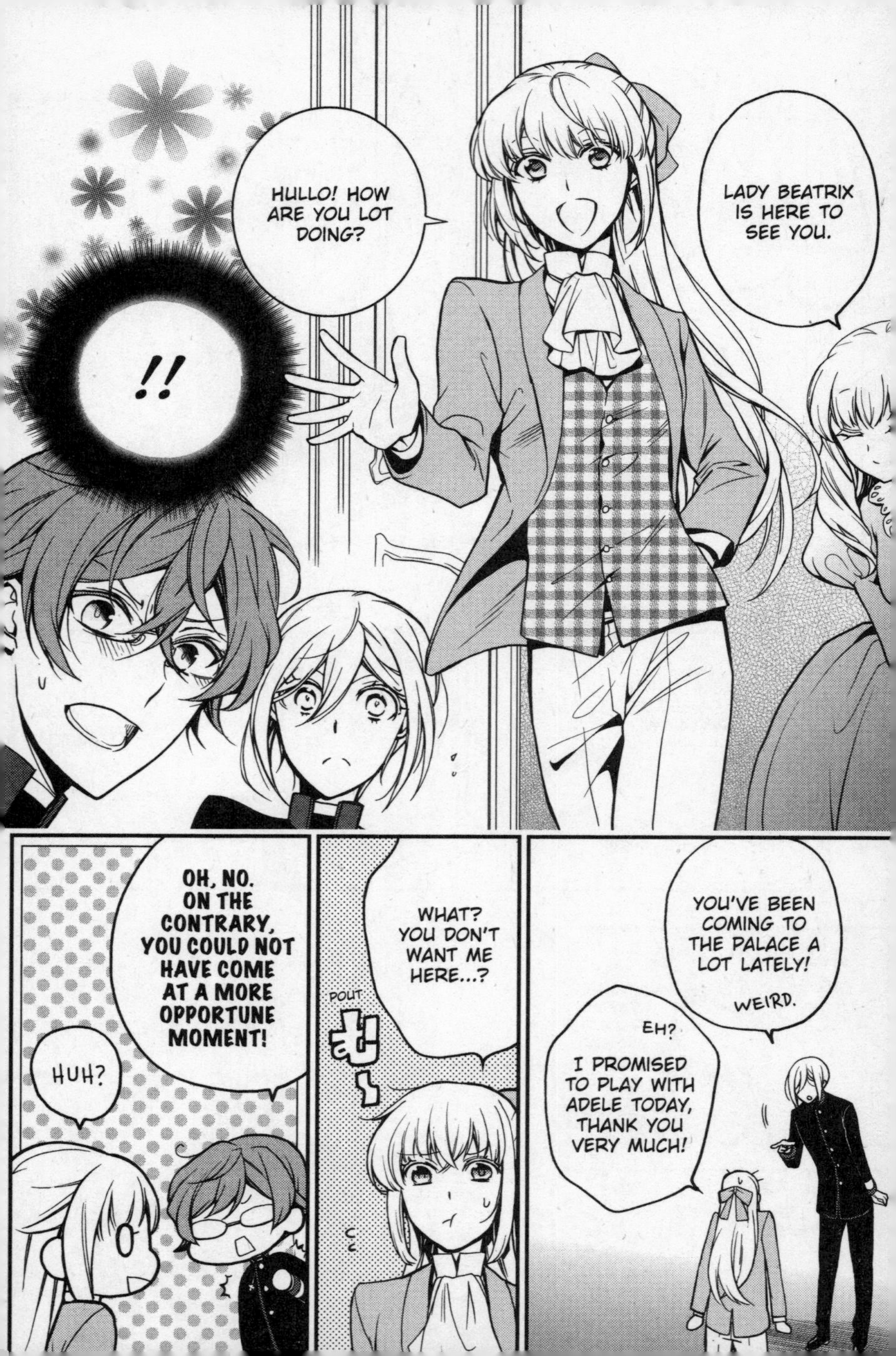
LADY BEATRIX IS HERE TO SEE YOU.
HULLO! HOW ARE YOU LOT DOING?
!!
YOU'VE BEEN COMING TO THE PALACE A LOT LATELY!
WEIRD.
EH?
I PROMISED TO PLAY WITH ADELE TODAY, THANK YOU VERY MUCH!
WHAT? YOU DON'T WANT ME HERE...?
POUT
OH, NO. ON THE CONTRARY, YOU COULD NOT HAVE COME AT A MORE OPPORTUNE MOMENT!
HUH?

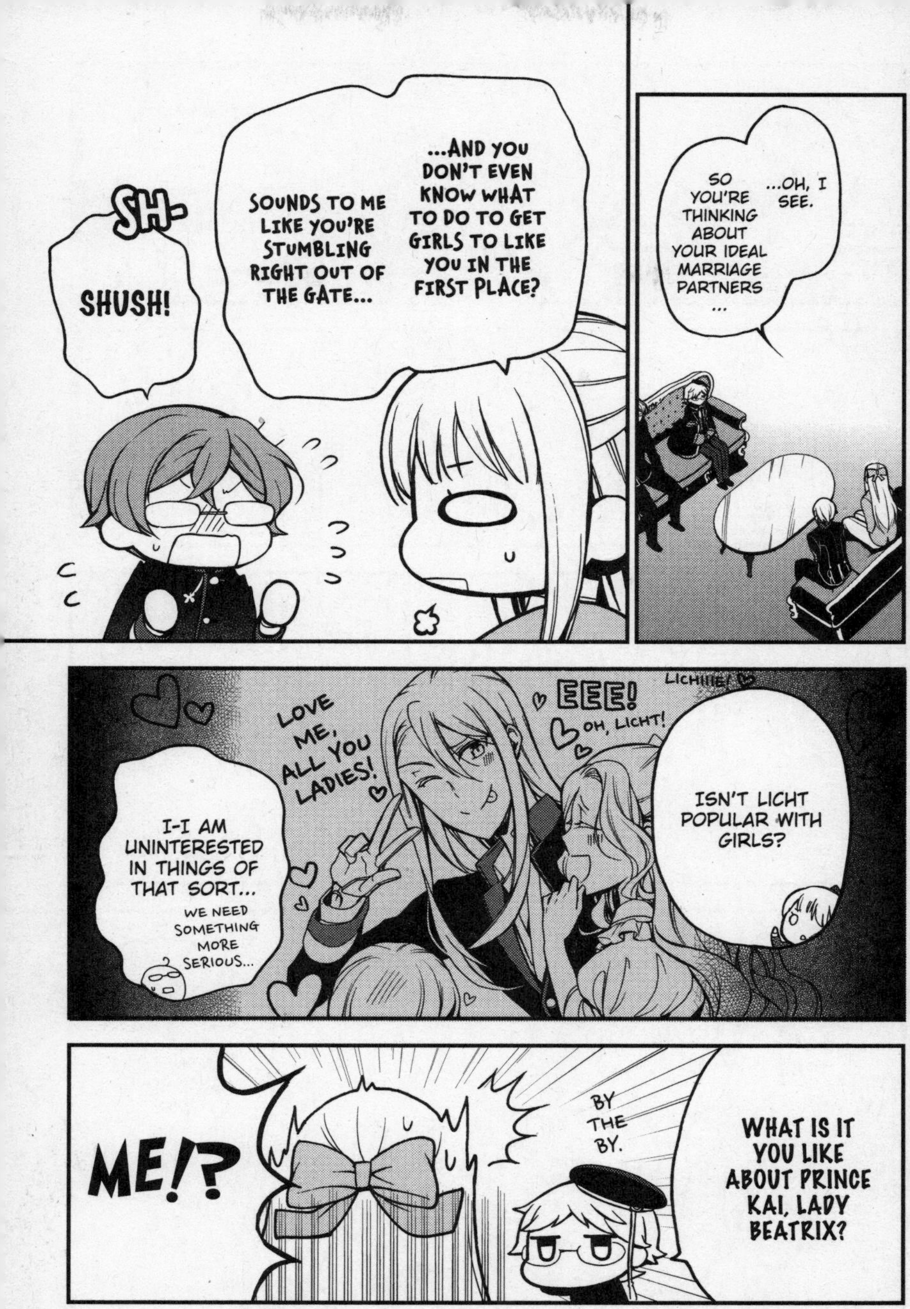
...OH, I SEE.
SO YOU'RE THINKING ABOUT YOUR IDEAL MARRIAGE PARTNERS...
SOUNDS TO ME LIKE YOU'RE STUMBLING RIGHT OUT OF THE GATE... ...AND YOU DON'T EVEN KNOW WHAT TO DO TO GET GIRLS TO LIKE YOU IN THE FIRST PLACE?
SH-
SHUSH!
ISN'T LICHT POPULAR WITH GIRLS?
LICHIIIE!
EEE!
OH, LICHT!
LOVE ME, ALL YOU LADIES!
I-I AM UNINTERESTED IN THINGS OF THAT SORT...
WE NEED SOMETHING MORE SERIOUS...
BY THE BY.
WHAT IS IT YOU LIKE ABOUT PRINCE KAI, LADY BEATRIX?
ME!?

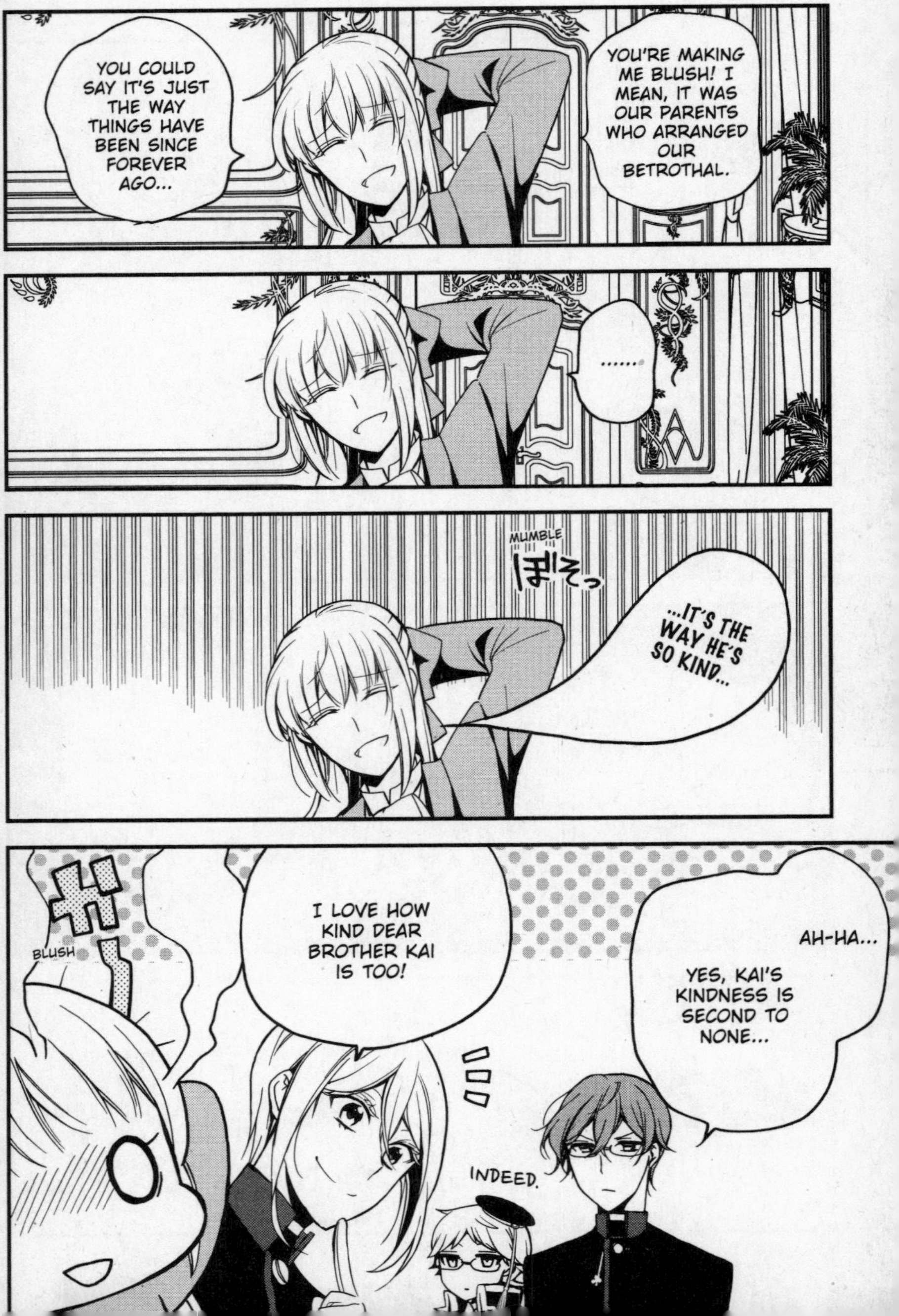
YOU'RE MAKING ME BLUSH! I MEAN, IT WAS OUR PARENTS WHO ARRANGED OUR BETROTHAL.
YOU COULD SAY IT'S JUST THE WAY THINGS HAVE BEEN SINCE FOREVER AGO...
......
MUMBLE
ぼそっ
...IT'S THE WAY HE'S SO KIND...
AH-HA...
YES, KAI'S KINDNESS IS SECOND TO NONE...
I LOVE HOW KIND DEAR BROTHER KAI IS TOO!
BLUSH
INDEED.

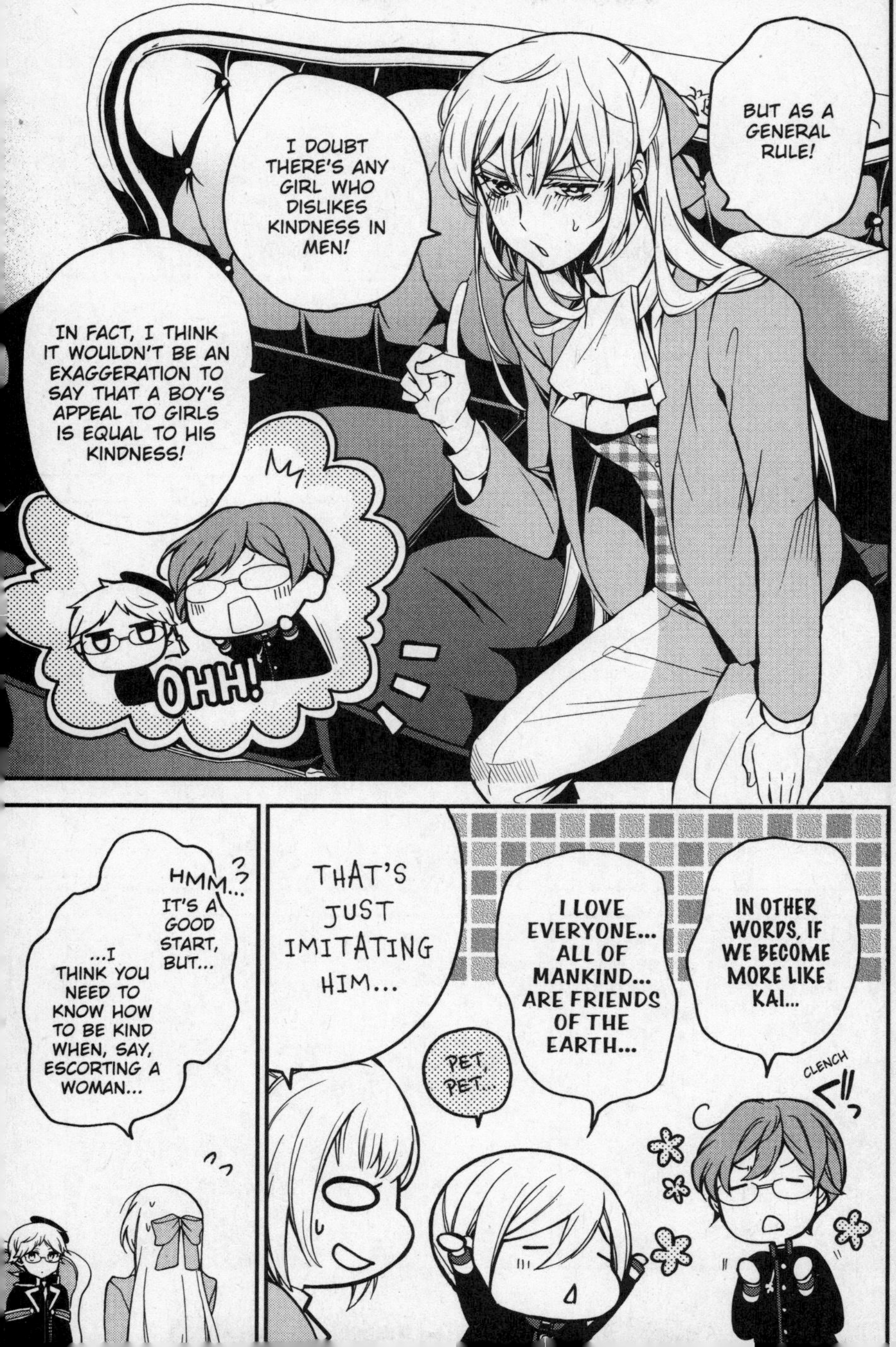
BUT AS A GENERAL RULE!
I DOUBT THERE'S ANY GIRL WHO DISLIKES KINDNESS IN MEN!
IN FACT, I THINK IT WOULDN'T BE AN EXAGGERATION TO SAY THAT A BOY'S APPEAL TO GIRLS IS EQUAL TO HIS KINDNESS!
OHH!
IN OTHER WORDS, IF WE BECOME MORE LIKE KAI...
CLENCH
I LOVE EVERYONE... ALL OF MANKIND... ARE FRIENDS OF THE EARTH...
PET, PET...
THAT'S JUST IMITATING HIM...
HMM...?
IT'S A GOOD START, BUT...
...I THINK YOU NEED TO KNOW HOW TO BE KIND WHEN, SAY, ESCORTING A WOMAN...

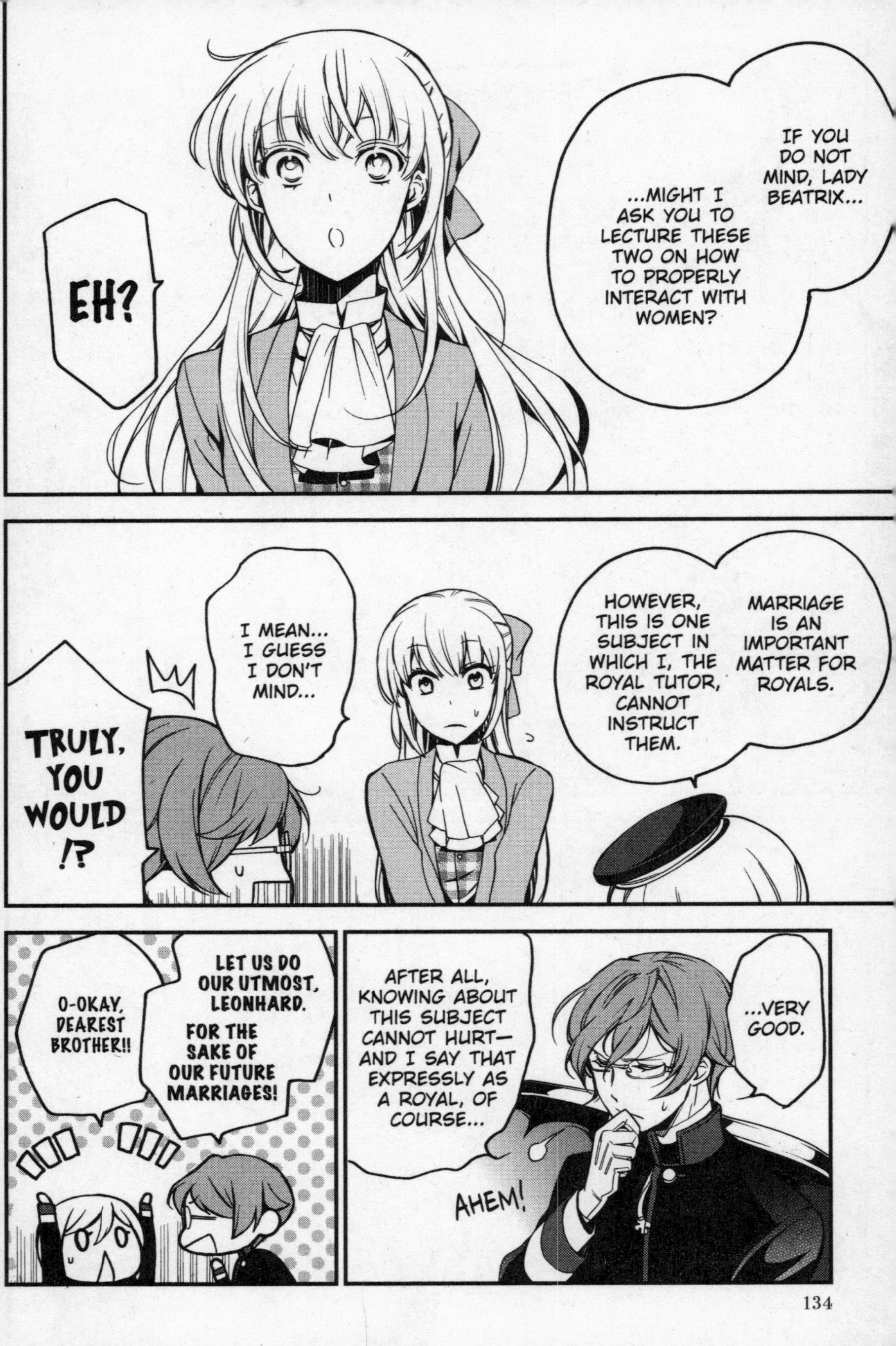
IF YOU DO NOT MIND, LADY BEATRIX...
...MIGHT I ASK YOU TO LECTURE THESE TWO ON HOW TO PROPERLY INTERACT WITH WOMEN?
EH?
MARRIAGE IS AN IMPORTANT MATTER FOR ROYALS.
HOWEVER, THIS IS ONE SUBJECT IN WHICH I, THE ROYAL TUTOR, CANNOT INSTRUCT THEM.
I MEAN... I GUESS I DON'T MIND...
TRULY, YOU WOULD!?
...VERY GOOD.
AFTER ALL, KNOWING ABOUT THIS SUBJECT CANNOT HURT—AND I SAY THAT EXPRESSLY AS A ROYAL, OF COURSE...
AHEM!
LET US DO OUR UTMOST, LEONHARD.
FOR THE SAKE OF OUR FUTURE MARRIAGES!
O-OKAY, DEAREST BROTHER!!

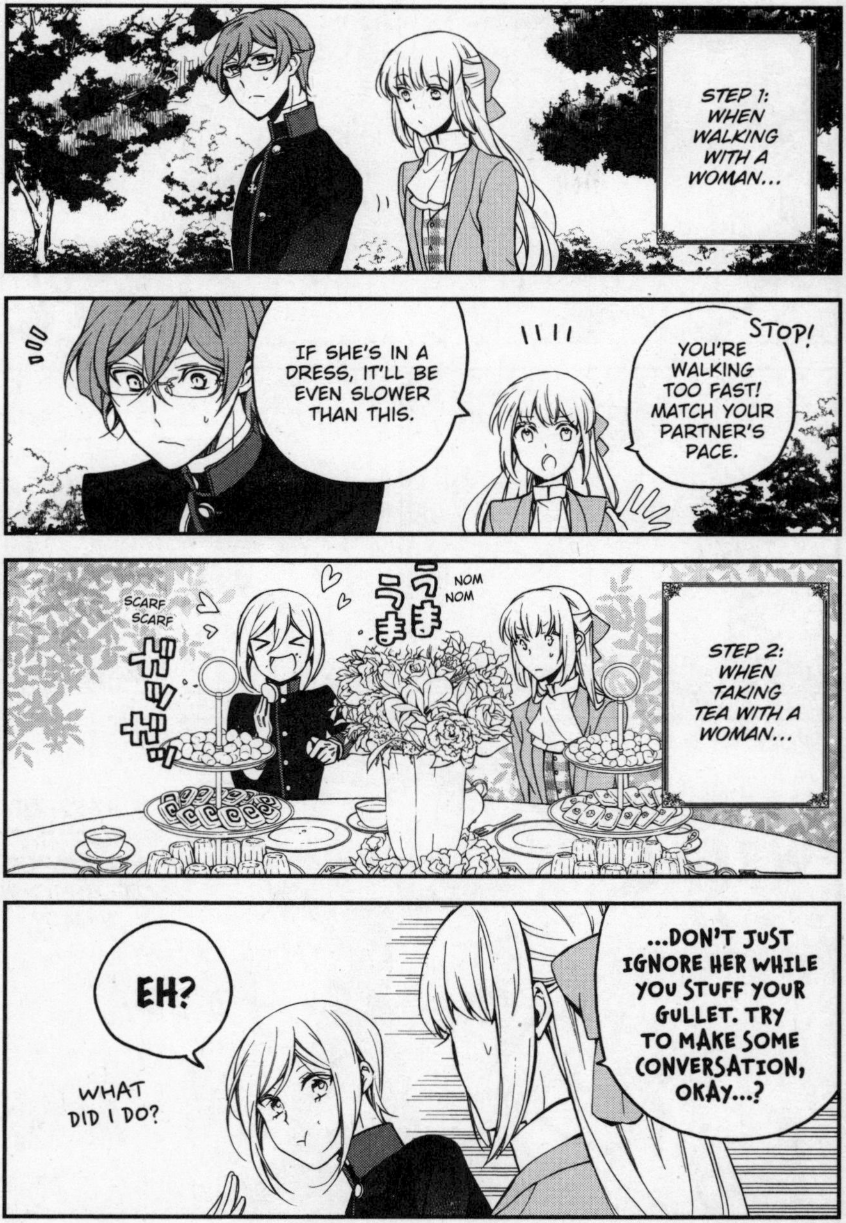

STEP 1: WHEN WALKING WITH A WOMAN…
STOP!
YOU'RE WALKING TOO FAST! MATCH YOUR PARTNER'S PACE.
IF SHE'S IN A DRESS, IT'LL BE EVEN SLOWER THAN THIS.
STEP 2: WHEN TAKING TEA WITH A WOMAN…
NOM NOM
うまうま
SCARF SCARF
…DON'T JUST IGNORE HER WHILE YOU STUFF YOUR GULLET. TRY TO MAKE SOME CONVERSATION, OKAY…?
EH?
WHAT DID I DO?

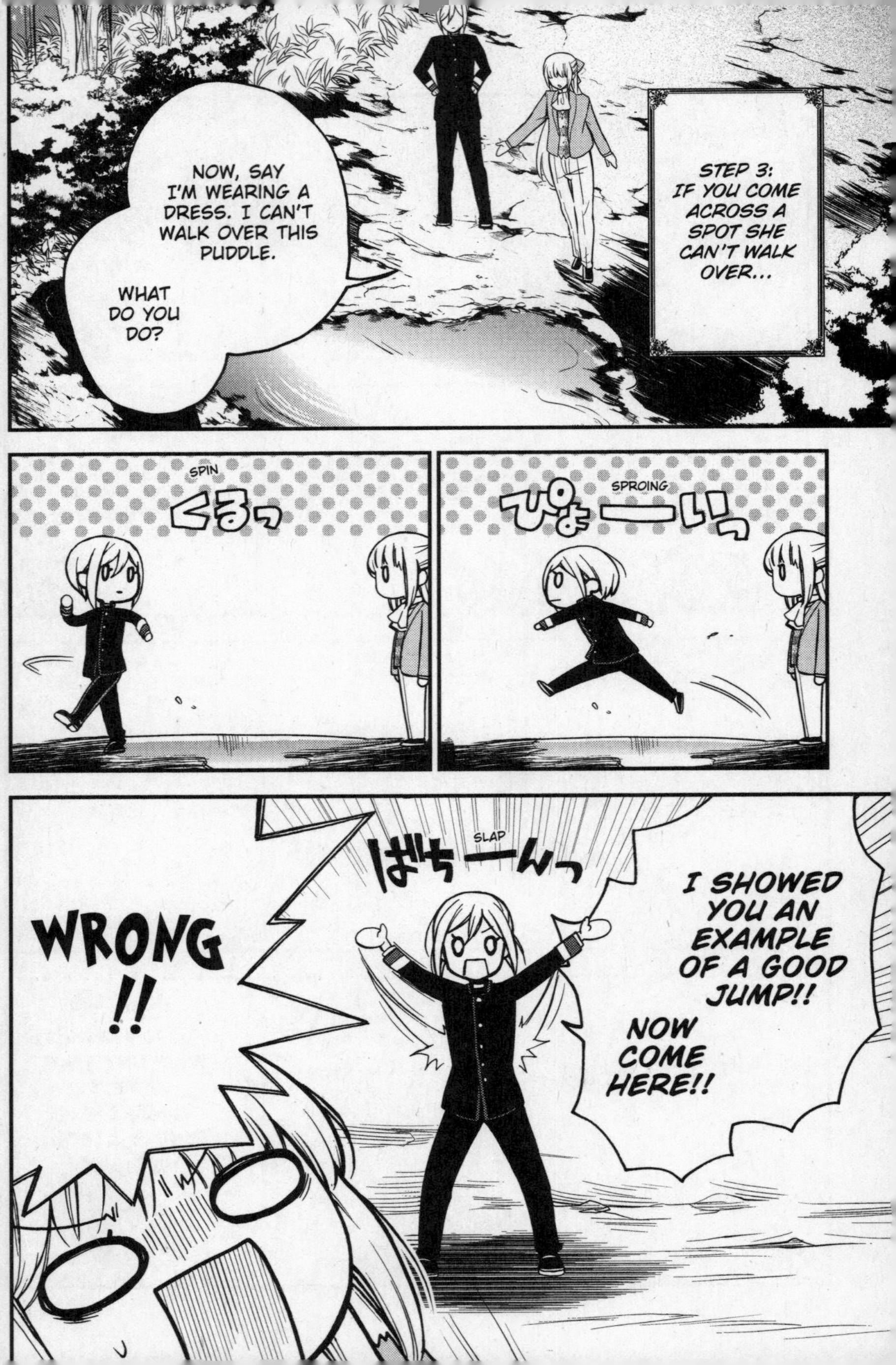
STEP 3: IF YOU COME ACROSS A SPOT SHE CAN'T WALK OVER...
NOW, SAY I'M WEARING A DRESS. I CAN'T WALK OVER THIS PUDDLE.
WHAT DO YOU DO?
SPROING
ぴょーいっ
SPIN
くるっ
SLAP
ぱちーんっ
I SHOWED YOU AN EXAMPLE OF A GOOD JUMP!!
NOW COME HERE!!
WRONG!!

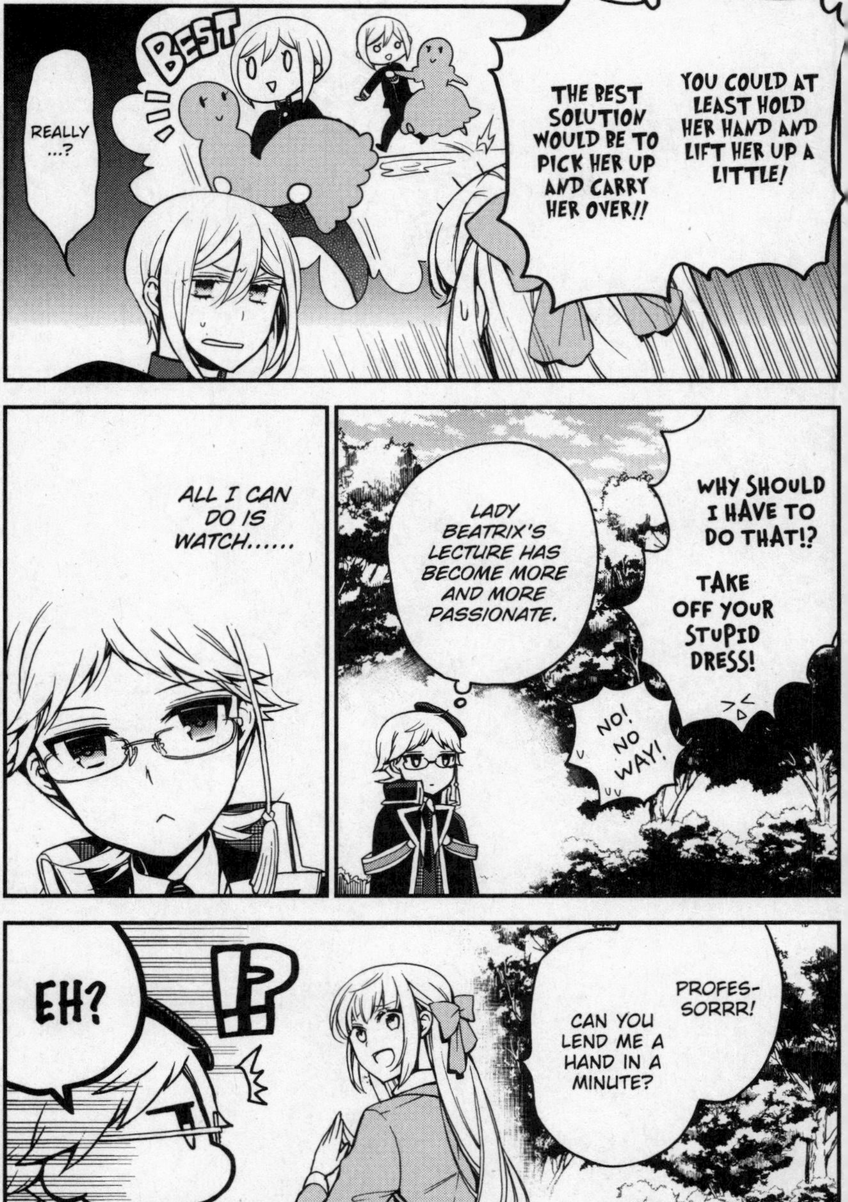
YOU COULD AT LEAST HOLD HER HAND AND LIFT HER UP A LITTLE!
THE BEST SOLUTION WOULD BE TO PICK HER UP AND CARRY HER OVER!!
BEST
REALLY ...?
WHY SHOULD I HAVE TO DO THAT!?
TAKE OFF YOUR STUPID DRESS!
NO! NO WAY!
LADY BEATRIX'S LECTURE HAS BECOME MORE AND MORE PASSIONATE.
ALL I CAN DO IS WATCH......
PROFES-SORRR!
CAN YOU LEND ME A HAND IN A MINUTE?
!?
EH?

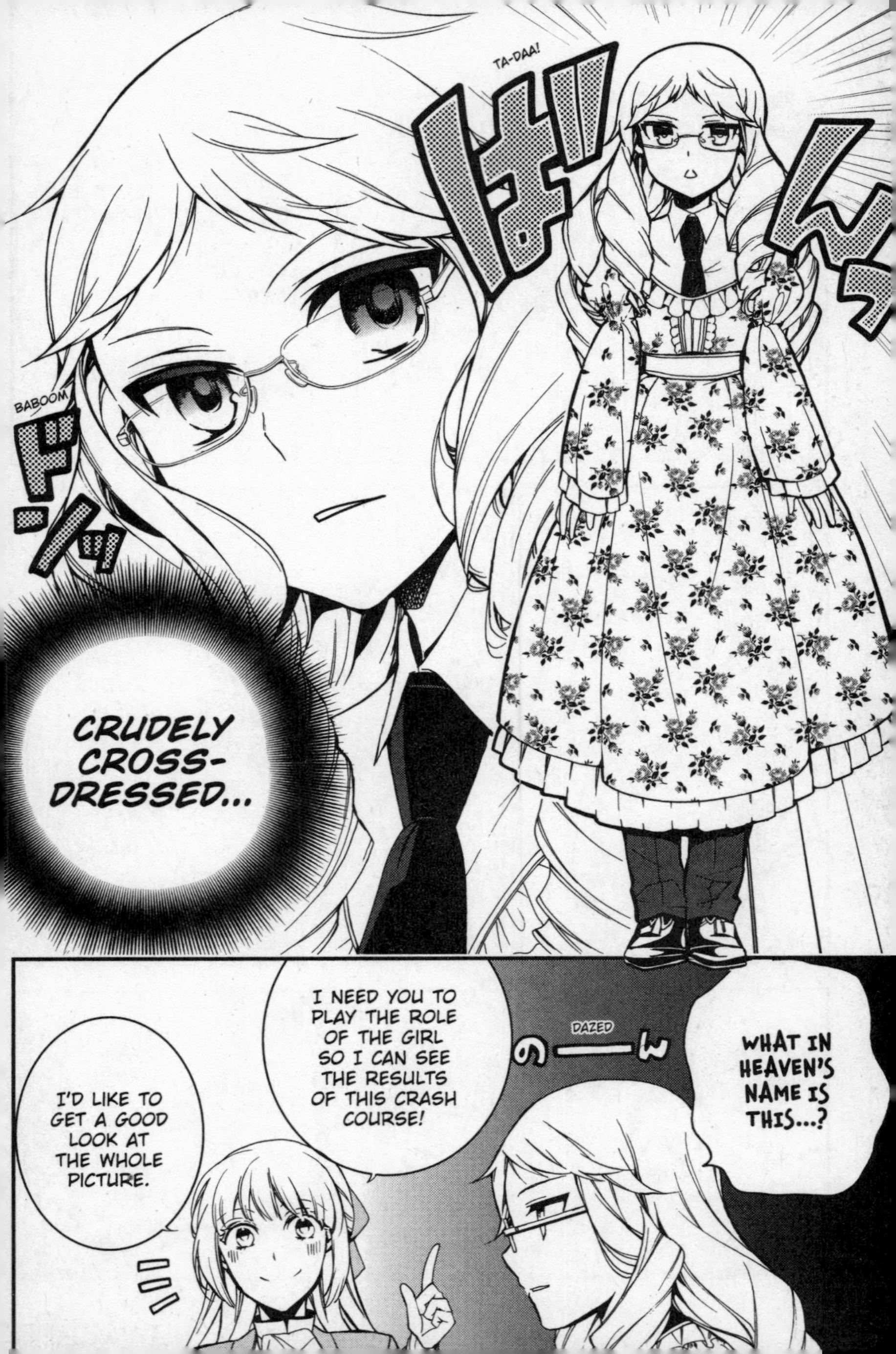
TA-DAA!
BABOOM
CRUDELY CROSS-DRESSED...
WHAT IN HEAVEN'S NAME IS THIS...?
DAZED
I NEED YOU TO PLAY THE ROLE OF THE GIRL SO I CAN SEE THE RESULTS OF THIS CRASH COURSE!
I'D LIKE TO GET A GOOD LOOK AT THE WHOLE PICTURE.

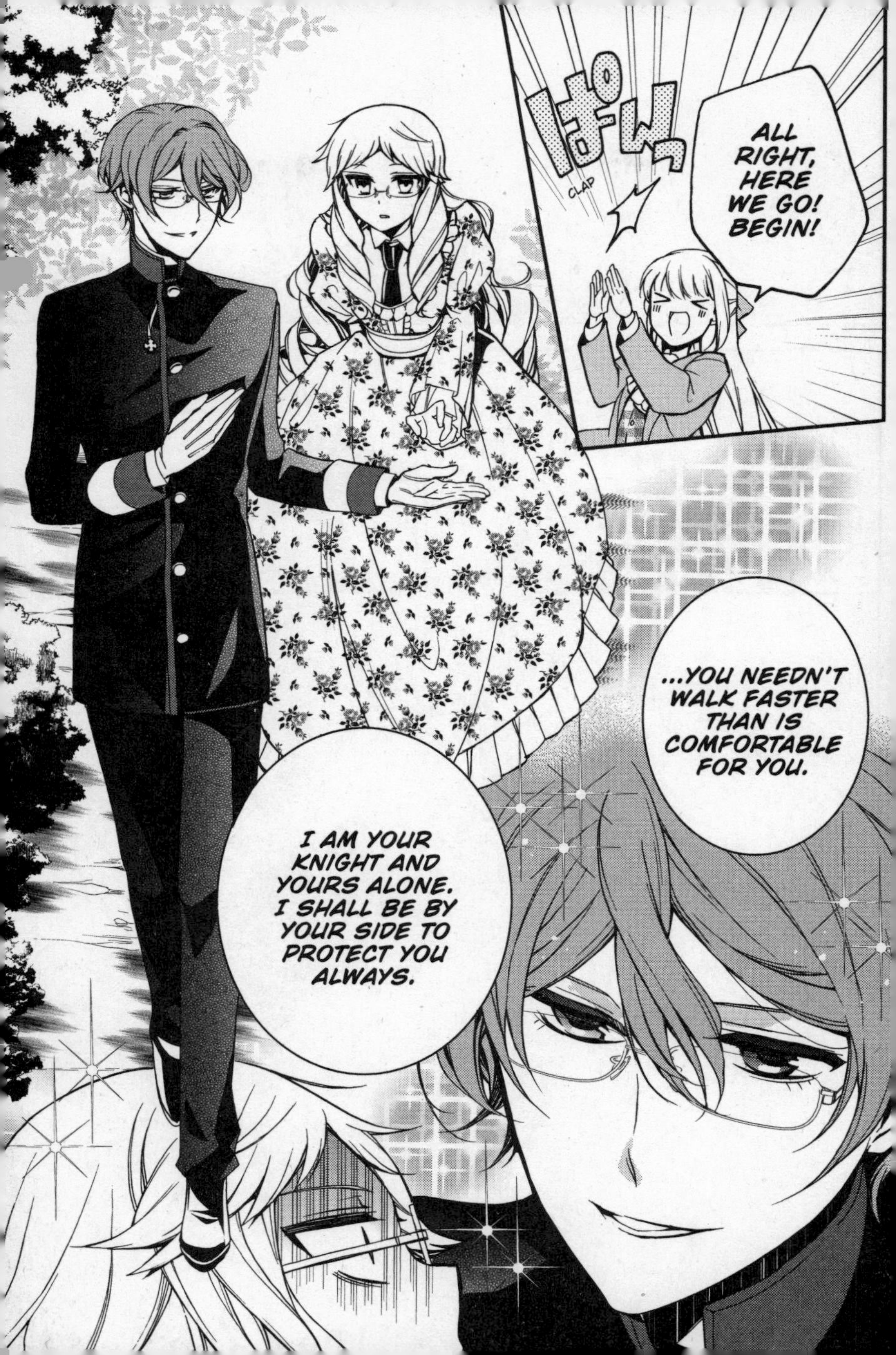
ぱんっ
CLAP
ALL RIGHT, HERE WE GO! BEGIN!
...YOU NEEDN'T WALK FASTER THAN IS COMFORTABLE FOR YOU.
I AM YOUR KNIGHT AND YOURS ALONE. I SHALL BE BY YOUR SIDE TO PROTECT YOU ALWAYS.

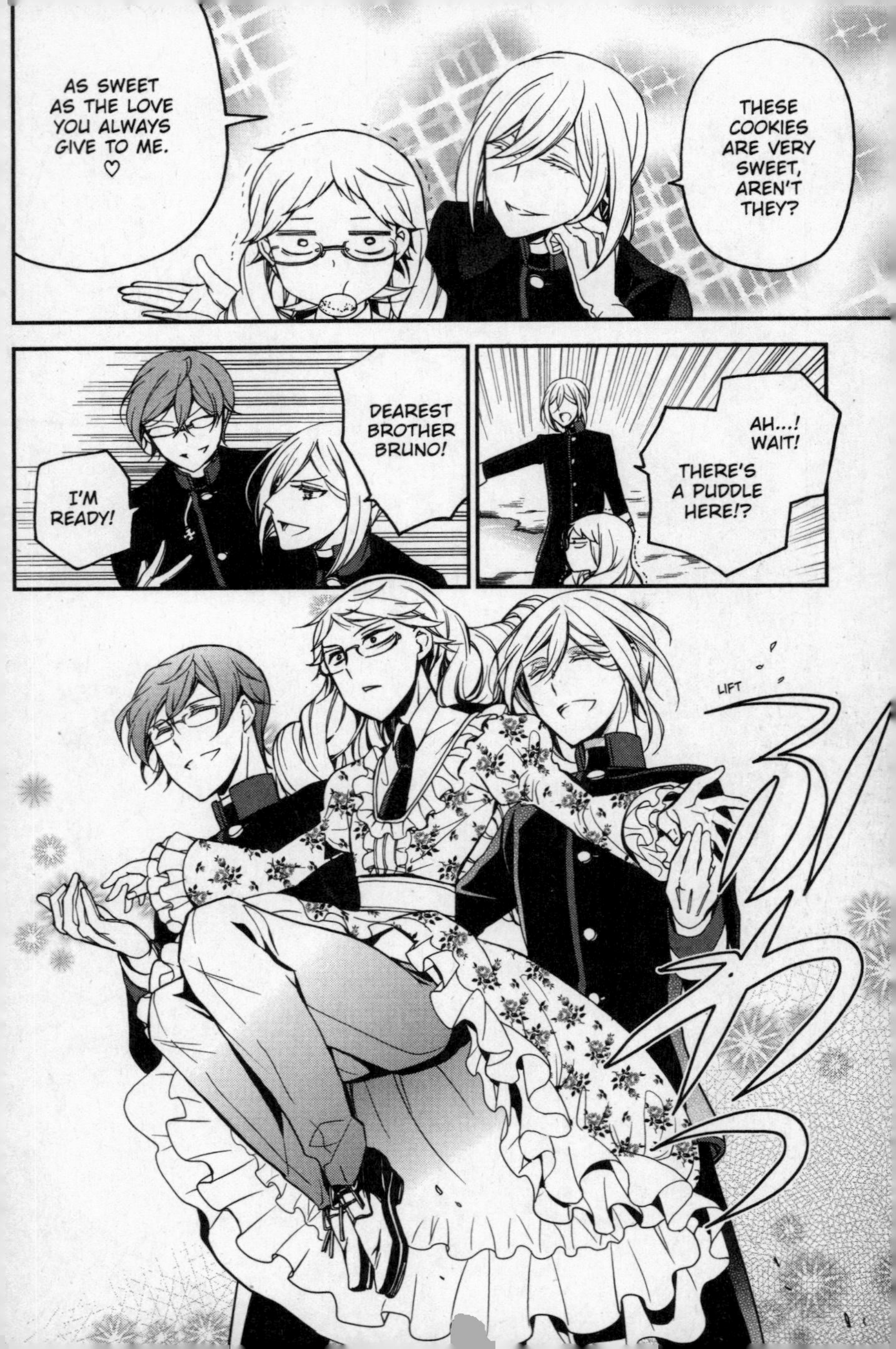
THESE COOKIES ARE VERY SWEET, AREN'T THEY?
AS SWEET AS THE LOVE YOU ALWAYS GIVE TO ME. ♡
AH...! WAIT!
THERE'S A PUDDLE HERE!?
DEAREST BROTHER BRUNO!
I'M READY!
LIFT

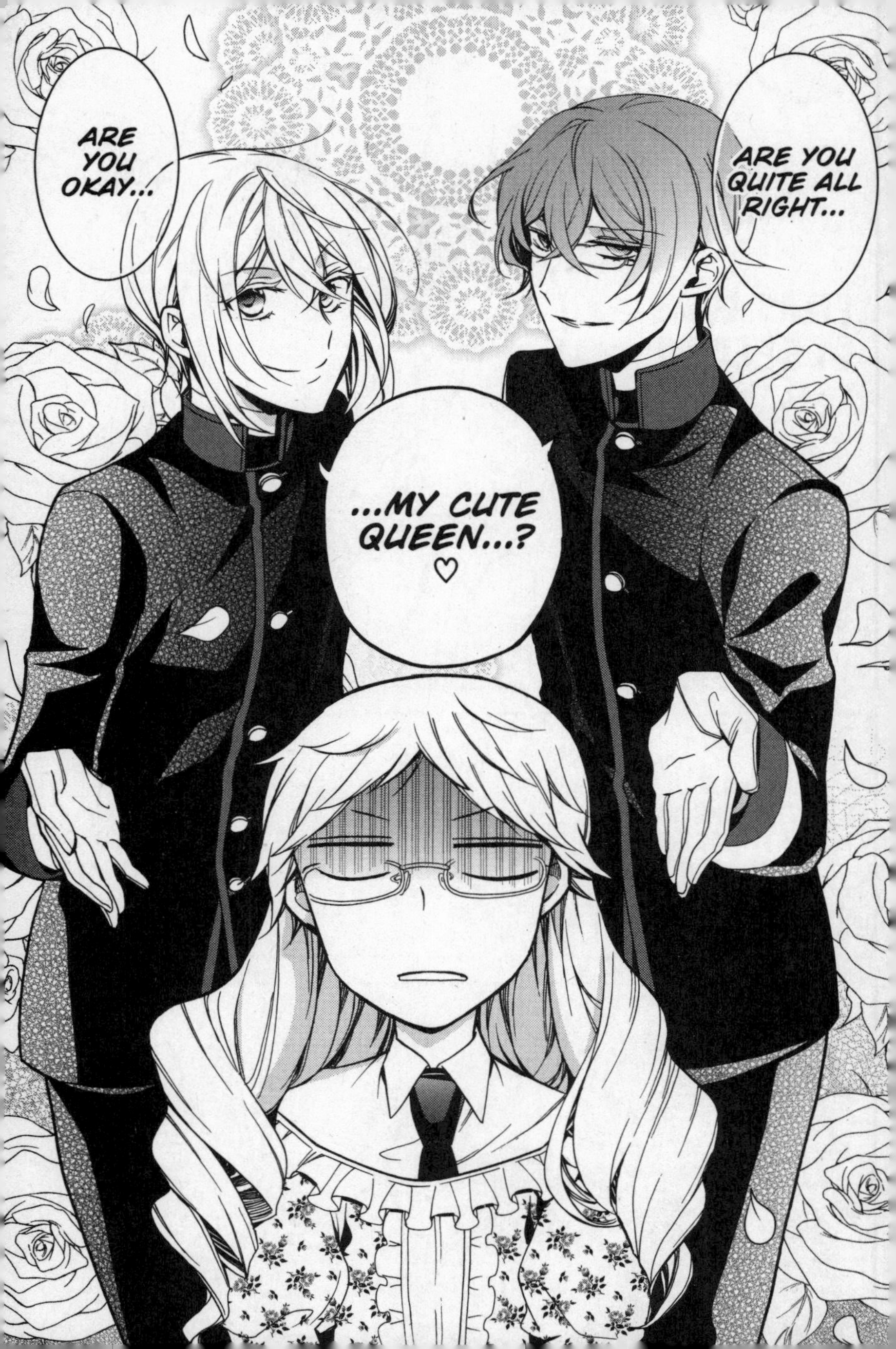
ARE YOU QUITE ALL RIGHT...
ARE YOU OKAY...
...MY CUTE QUEEN...? ♡

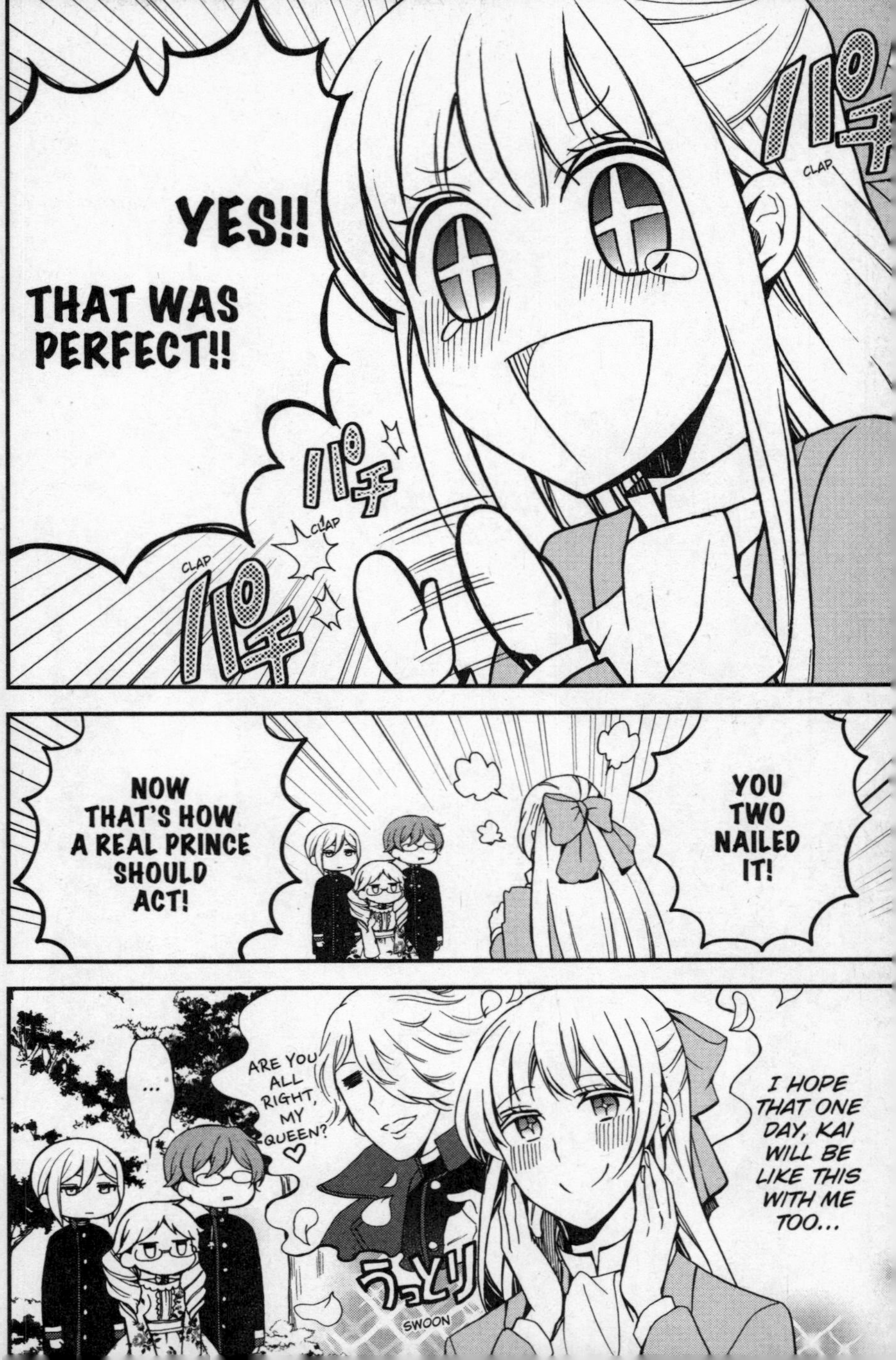
パチ
CLAP
YES!!
THAT WAS PERFECT!!
パチ
CLAP
パチ
CLAP
YOU TWO NAILED IT!
NOW THAT'S HOW A REAL PRINCE SHOULD ACT!
I HOPE THAT ONE DAY, KAI WILL BE LIKE THIS WITH ME TOO...
うっとり
SWOON
ARE YOU ALL RIGHT, MY QUEEN? ♥
...

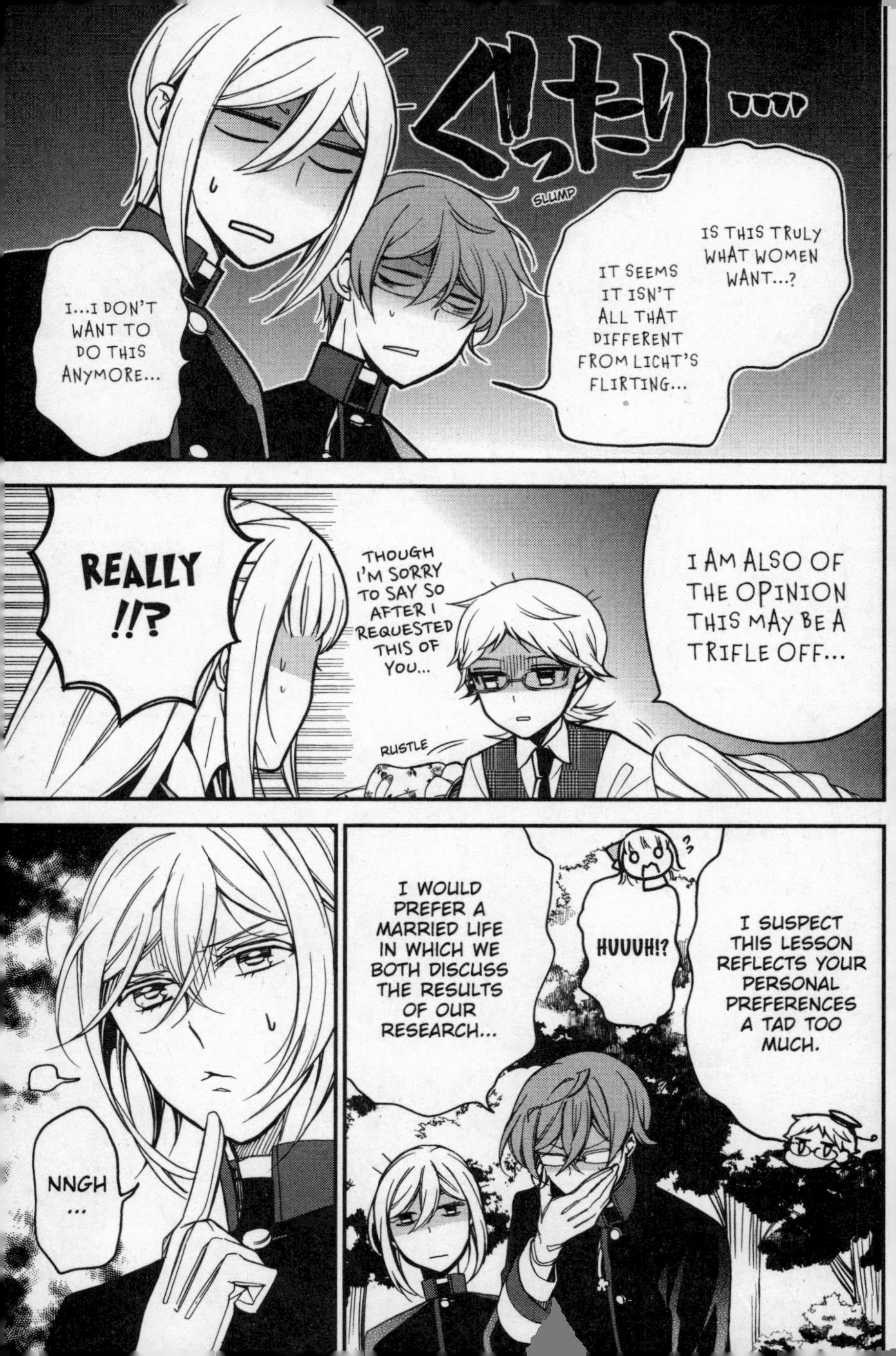
くったり…
SLUMP
IS THIS TRULY WHAT WOMEN WANT...?
IT SEEMS IT ISN'T ALL THAT DIFFERENT FROM LICHT'S FLIRTING...
I...I DON'T WANT TO DO THIS ANYMORE...
I AM ALSO OF THE OPINION THIS MAY BE A TRIFLE OFF...
THOUGH I'M SORRY TO SAY SO AFTER I REQUESTED THIS OF YOU...
RUSTLE
REALLY!!?
I SUSPECT THIS LESSON REFLECTS YOUR PERSONAL PREFERENCES A TAD TOO MUCH.
HUUUH!?
I WOULD PREFER A MARRIED LIFE IN WHICH WE BOTH DISCUSS THE RESULTS OF OUR RESEARCH...
NNGH...

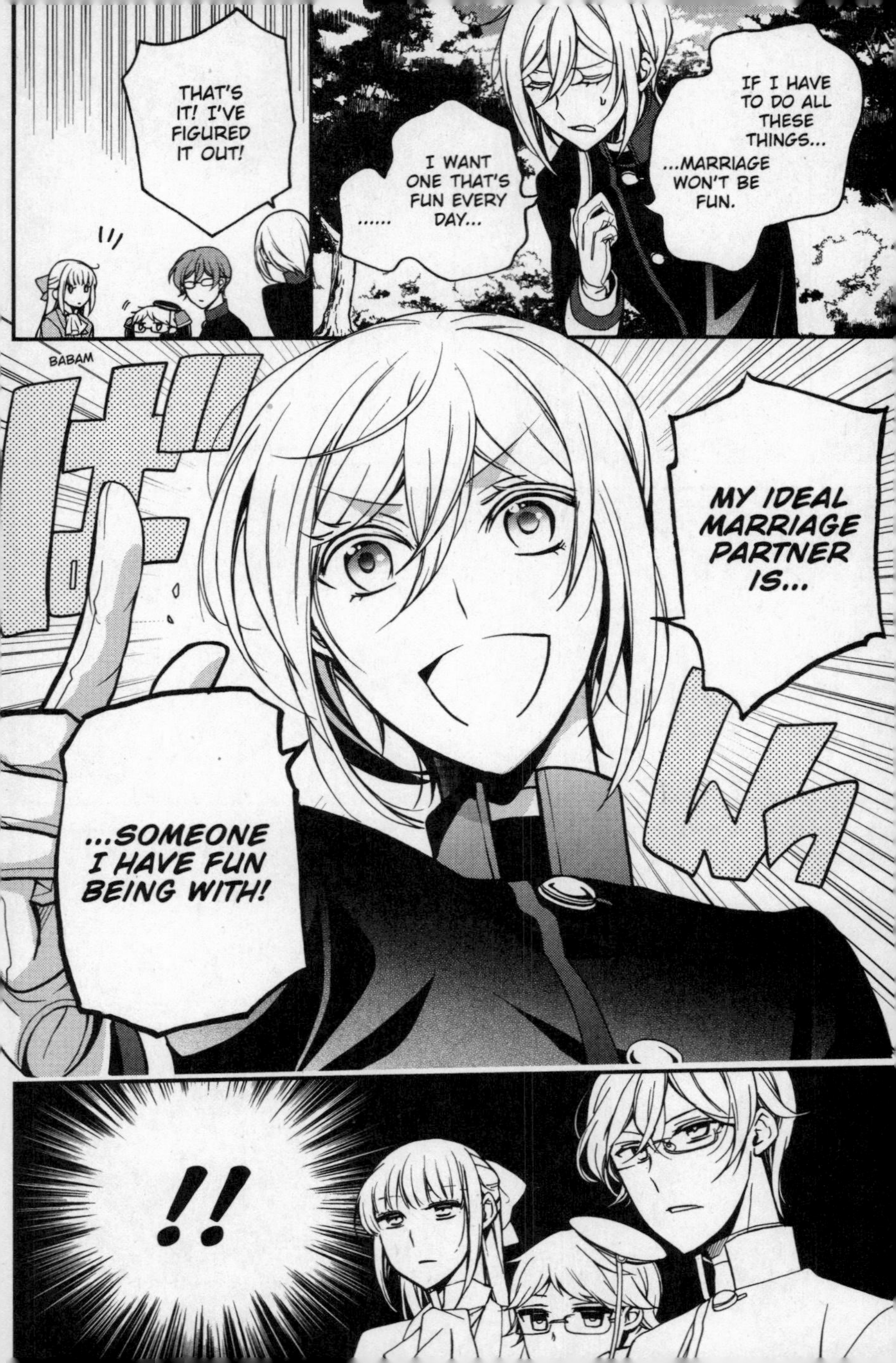
IF I HAVE TO DO ALL THESE THINGS...
...MARRIAGE WON'T BE FUN.
I WANT ONE THAT'S FUN EVERY DAY...
......
THAT'S IT! I'VE FIGURED IT OUT!
BABAM
MY IDEAL MARRIAGE PARTNER IS...
...SOMEONE I HAVE FUN BEING WITH!
!!

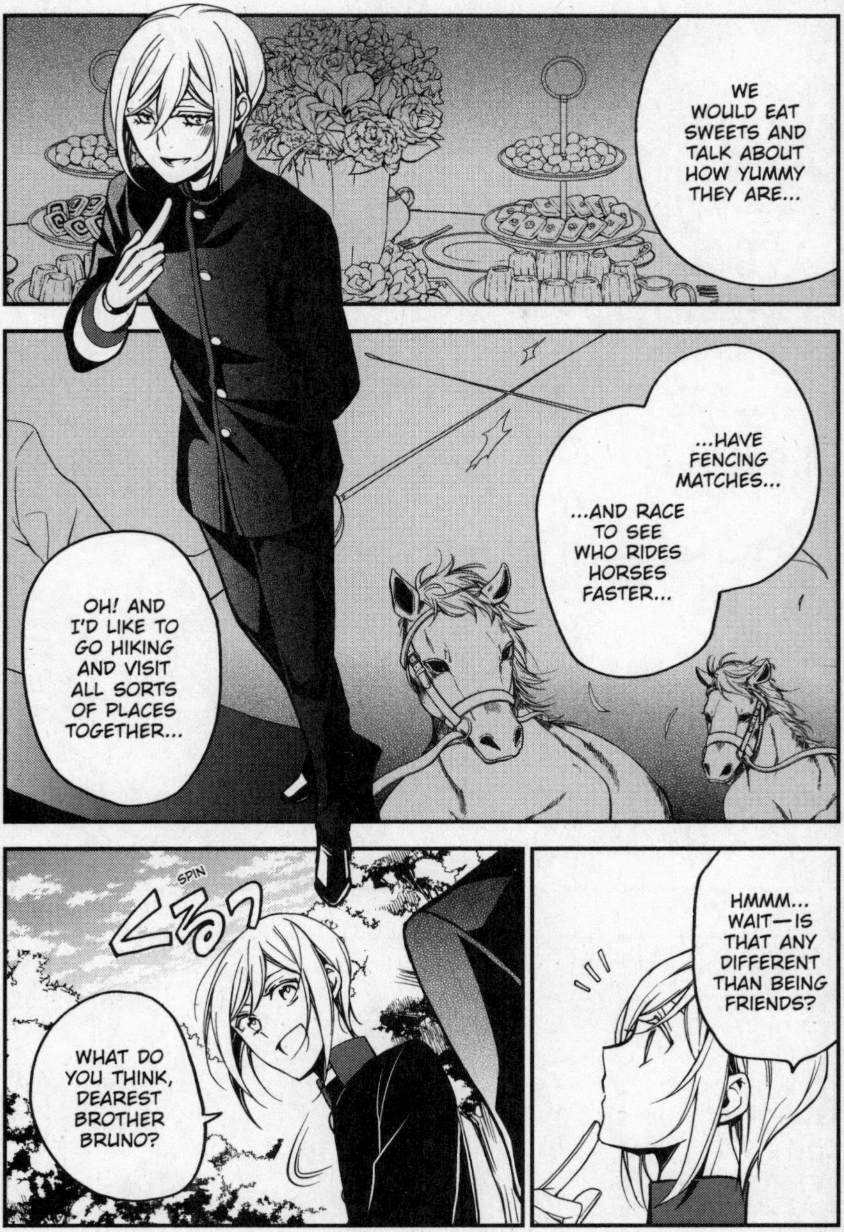
WE WOULD EAT SWEETS AND TALK ABOUT HOW YUMMY THEY ARE...
...HAVE FENCING MATCHES...
...AND RACE TO SEE WHO RIDES HORSES FASTER...
OH! AND I'D LIKE TO GO HIKING AND VISIT ALL SORTS OF PLACES TOGETHER...
HMMM... WAIT—IS THAT ANY DIFFERENT THAN BEING FRIENDS?
SPIN
WHAT DO YOU THINK, DEAREST BROTHER BRUNO?

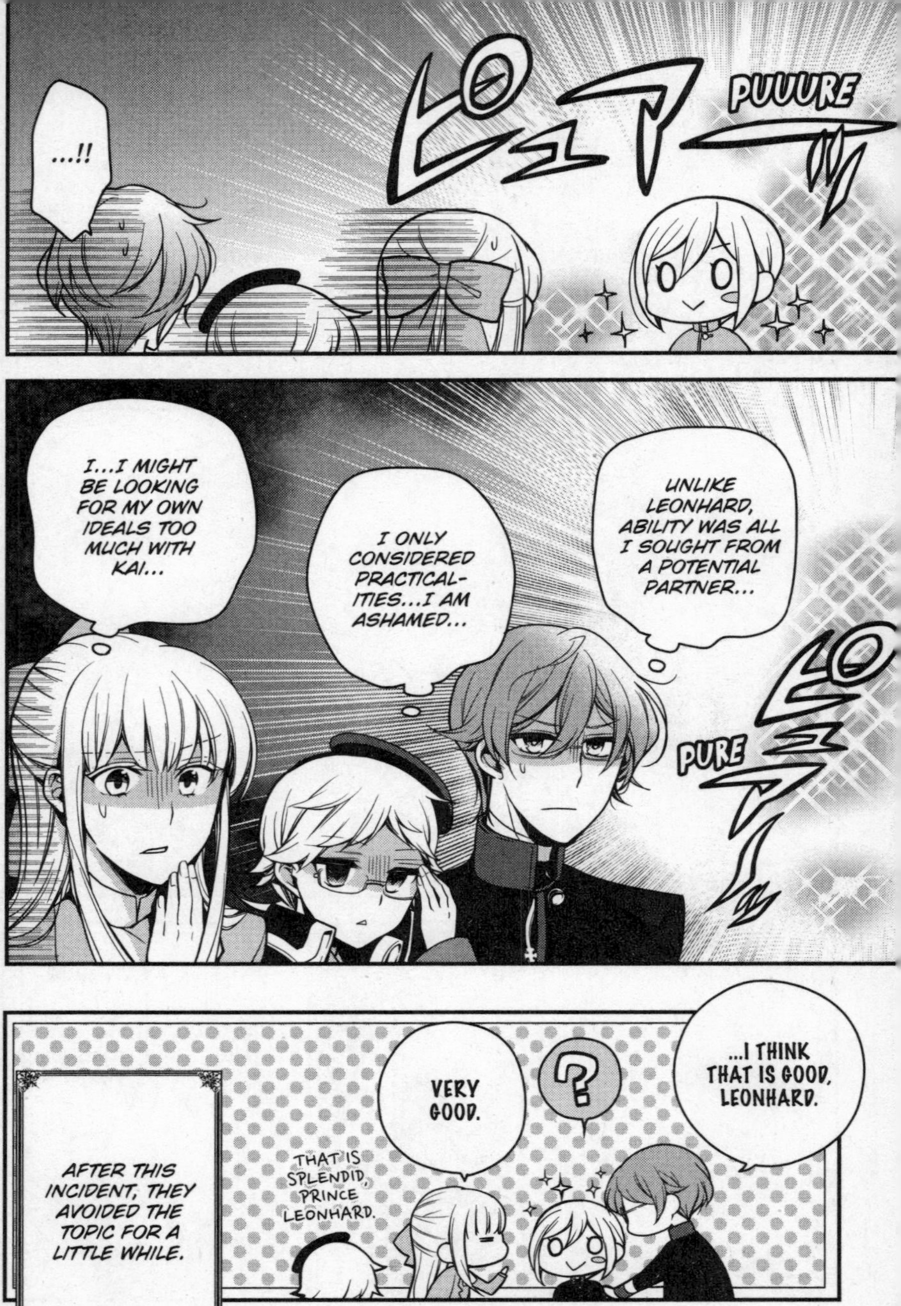
PUUURE
...!!
UNLIKE LEONHARD, ABILITY WAS ALL I SOUGHT FROM A POTENTIAL PARTNER...
PURE
I ONLY CONSIDERED PRACTICAL-ITIES...I AM ASHAMED...
I...I MIGHT BE LOOKING FOR MY OWN IDEALS TOO MUCH WITH KAI...
...I THINK THAT IS GOOD, LEONHARD.
?
VERY GOOD.
THAT IS SPLENDID, PRINCE LEONHARD.
AFTER THIS INCIDENT, THEY AVOIDED THE TOPIC FOR A LITTLE WHILE.

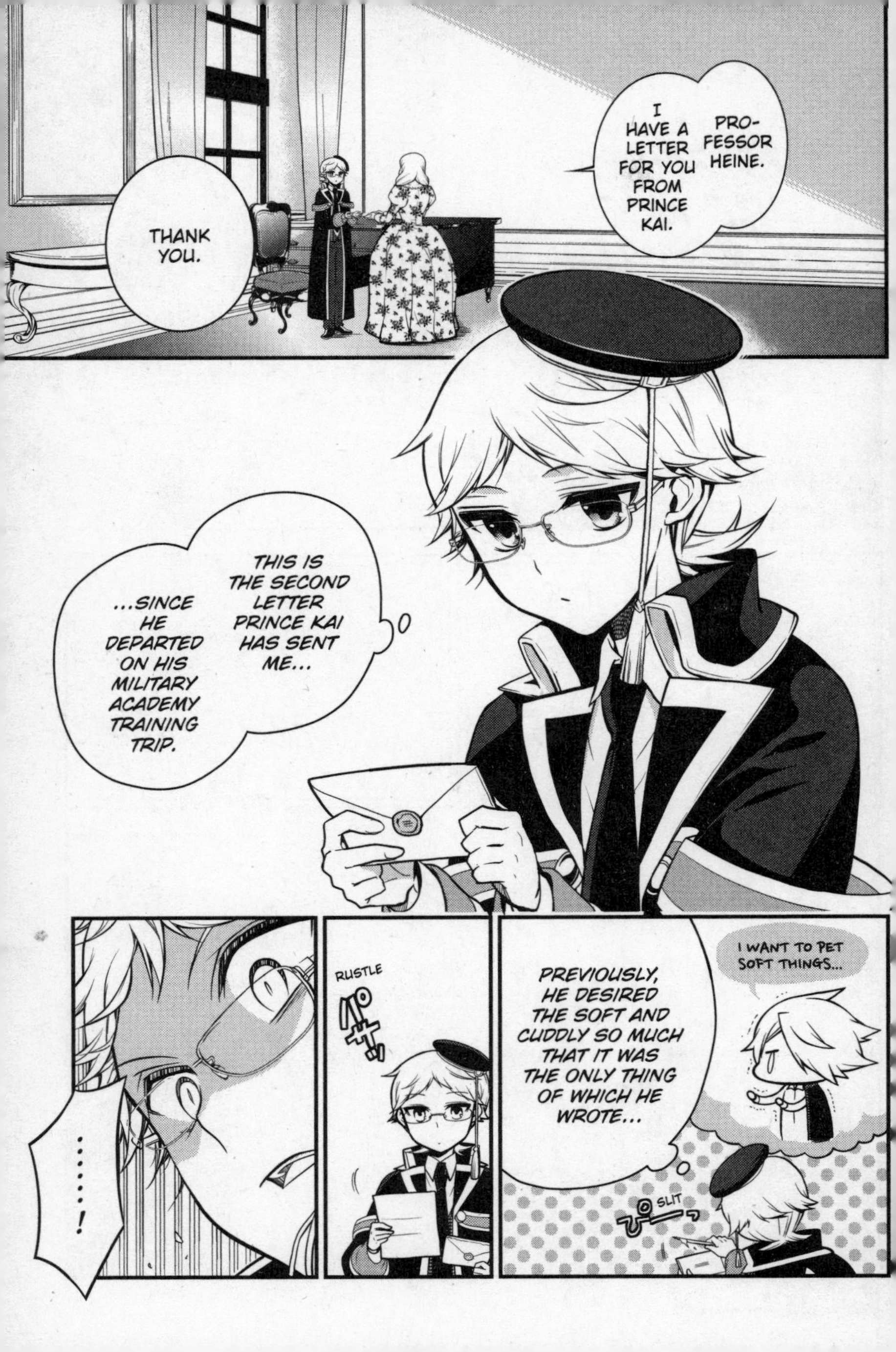
PROFESSOR HEINE.
I HAVE A LETTER FOR YOU FROM PRINCE KAI.
THANK YOU.
THIS IS THE SECOND LETTER PRINCE KAI HAS SENT ME...
...SINCE HE DEPARTED ON HIS MILITARY ACADEMY TRAINING TRIP.
I WANT TO PET SOFT THINGS...
PREVIOUSLY, HE DESIRED THE SOFT AND CUDDLY SO MUCH THAT IT WAS THE ONLY THING OF WHICH HE WROTE...
SLIT
RUSTLE
......!

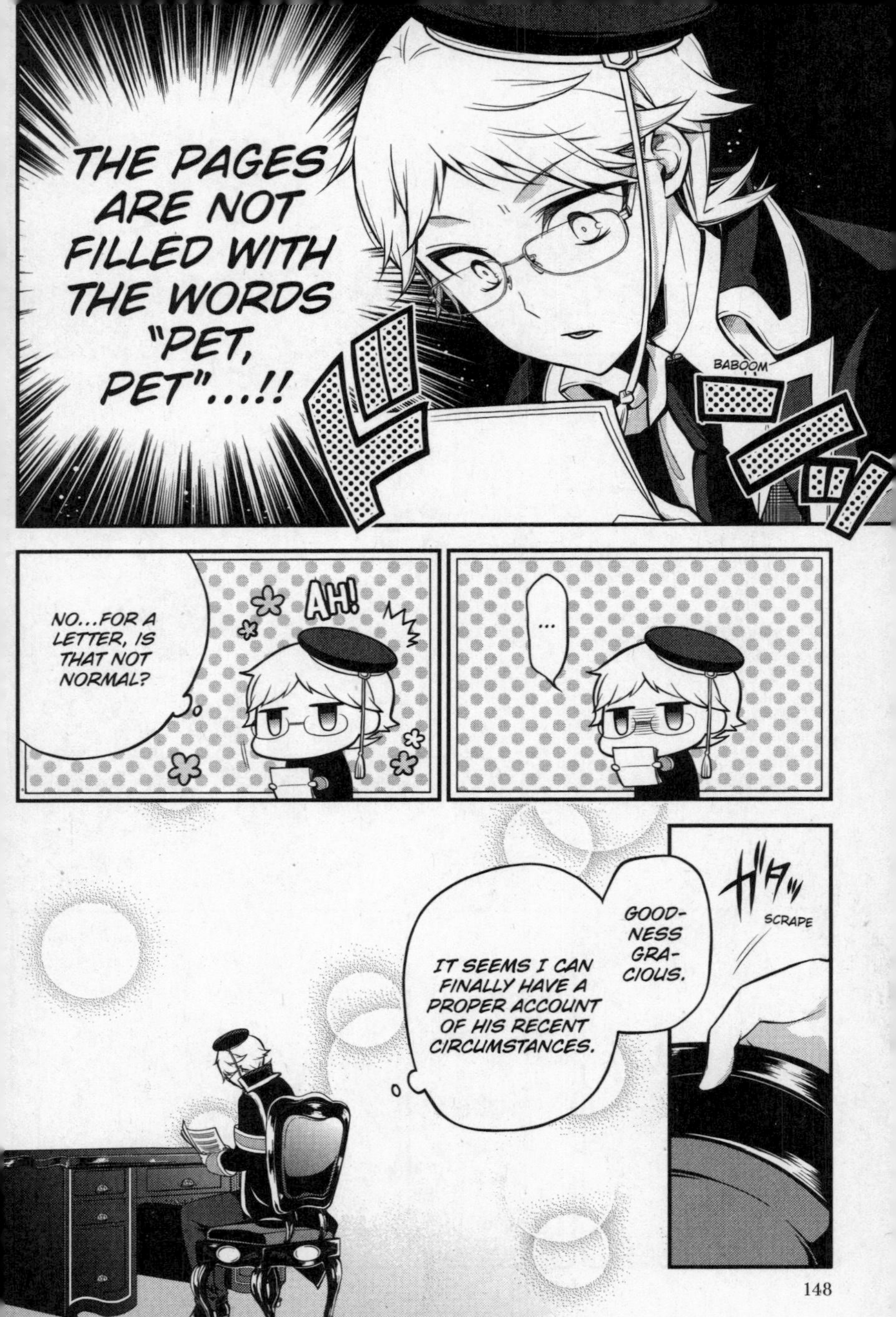
THE PAGES ARE NOT FILLED WITH THE WORDS "PET, PET"...!!
BABOOM
...
AH!
NO...FOR A LETTER, IS THAT NOT NORMAL?
SCRAPE
GOODNESS GRACIOUS.
IT SEEMS I CAN FINALLY HAVE A PROPER ACCOUNT OF HIS RECENT CIRCUMSTANCES.

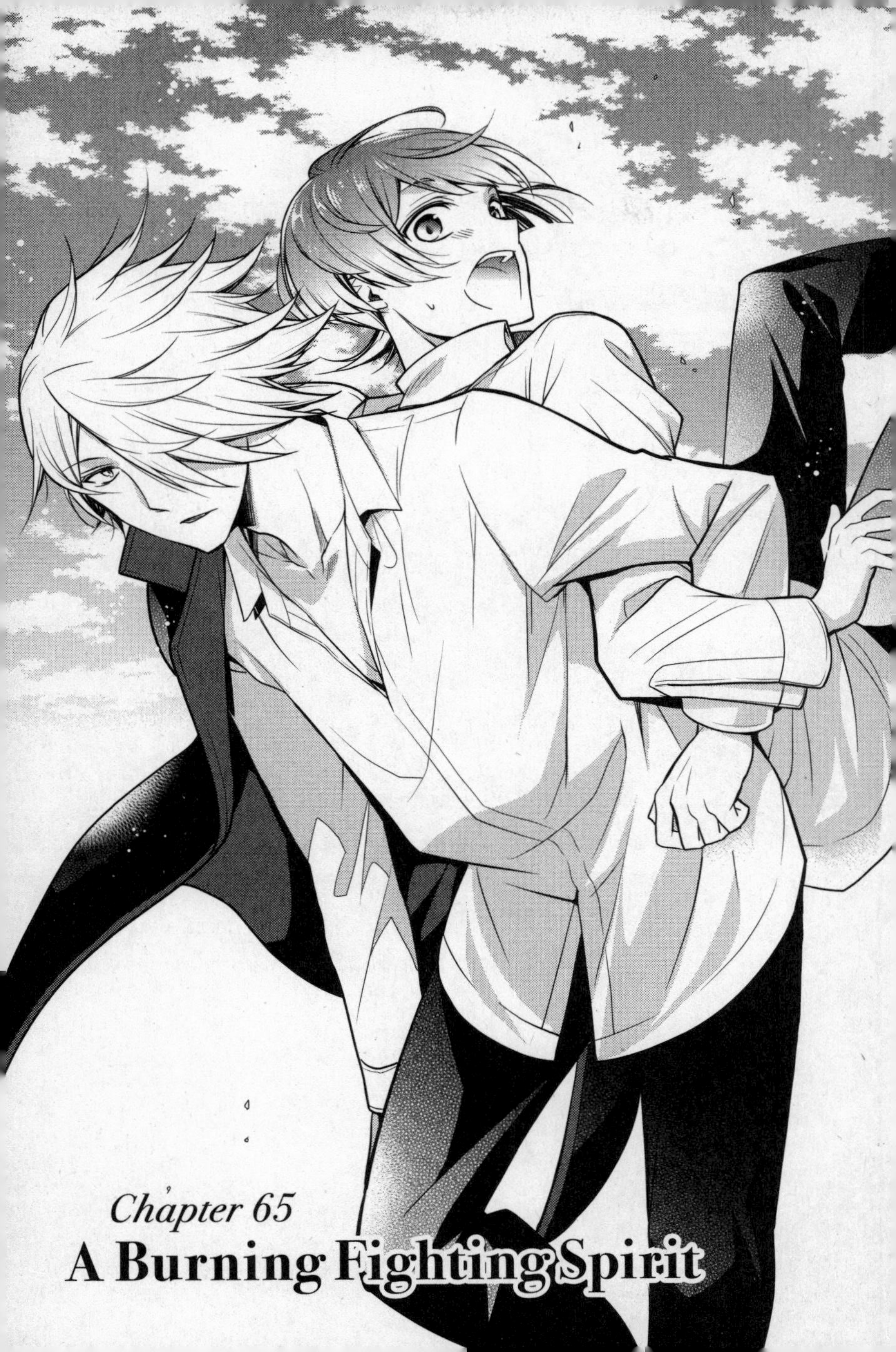

Chapter 65

A Burning Fighting Spirit

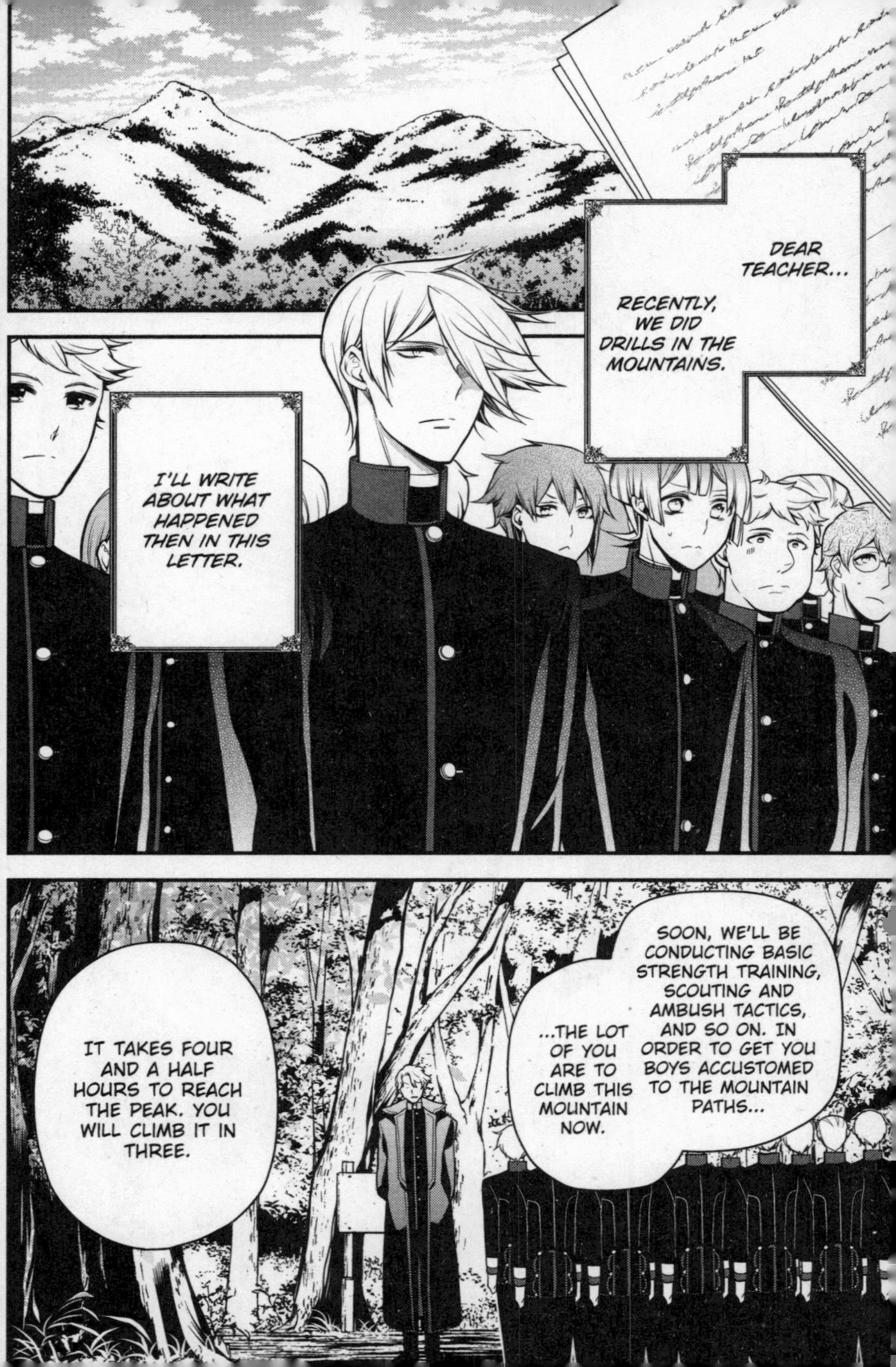
DEAR TEACHER...
RECENTLY, WE DID DRILLS IN THE MOUNTAINS.
I'LL WRITE ABOUT WHAT HAPPENED THEN IN THIS LETTER.
SOON, WE'LL BE CONDUCTING BASIC STRENGTH TRAINING, SCOUTING AND AMBUSH TACTICS, AND SO ON. IN ORDER TO GET YOU BOYS ACCUSTOMED TO THE MOUNTAIN PATHS...
...THE LOT OF YOU ARE TO CLIMB THIS MOUNTAIN NOW.
IT TAKES FOUR AND A HALF HOURS TO REACH THE PEAK. YOU WILL CLIMB IT IN THREE.

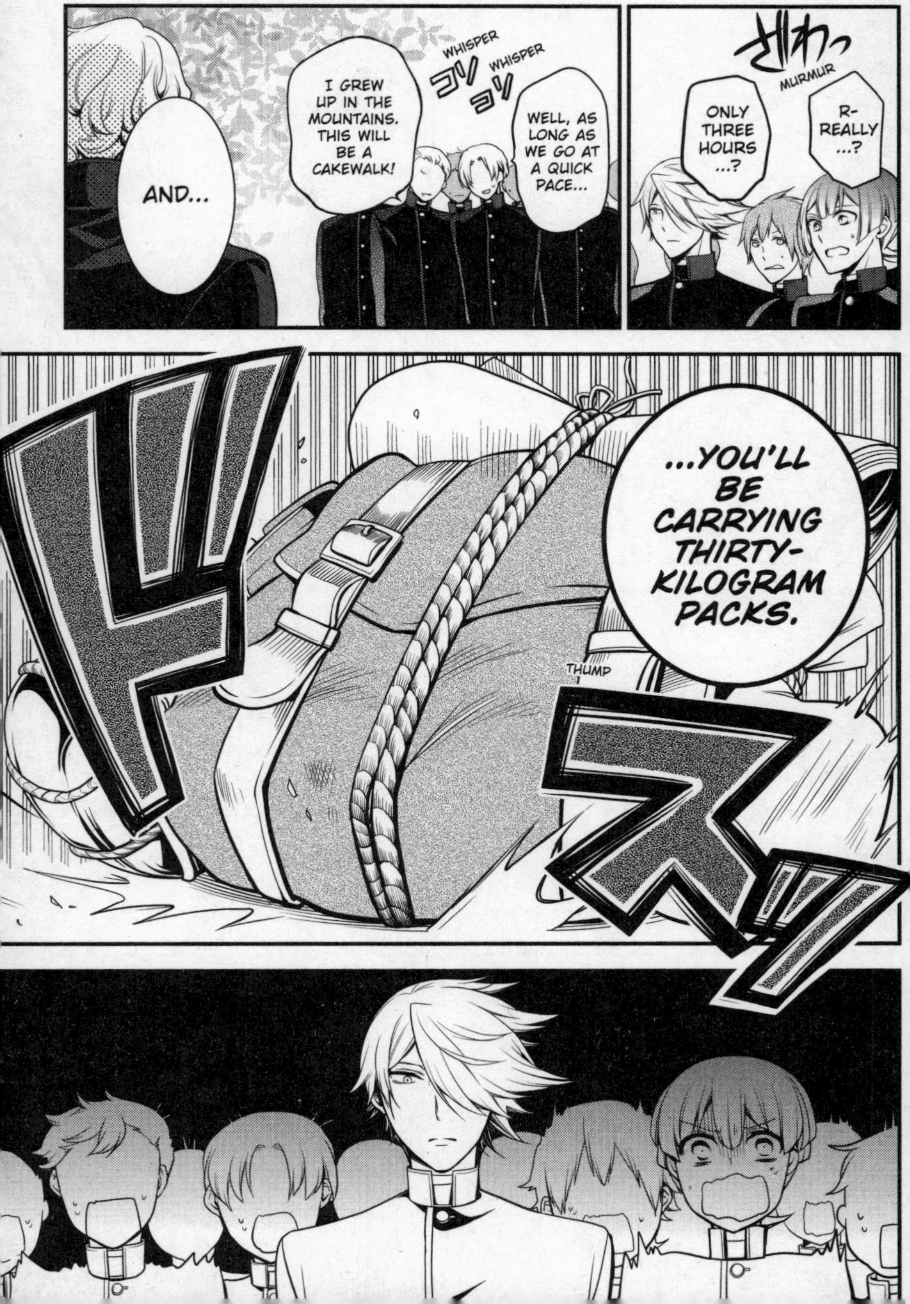
ざわっ
MURMUR
R-REALLY...?
ONLY THREE HOURS...?
WHISPER
WHISPER
コソコソ
WELL, AS LONG AS WE GO AT A QUICK PACE...
I GREW UP IN THE MOUNTAINS. THIS WILL BE A CAKEWALK!
AND...
...YOU'LL BE CARRYING THIRTY-KILOGRAM PACKS.
THUMP
ドスッ

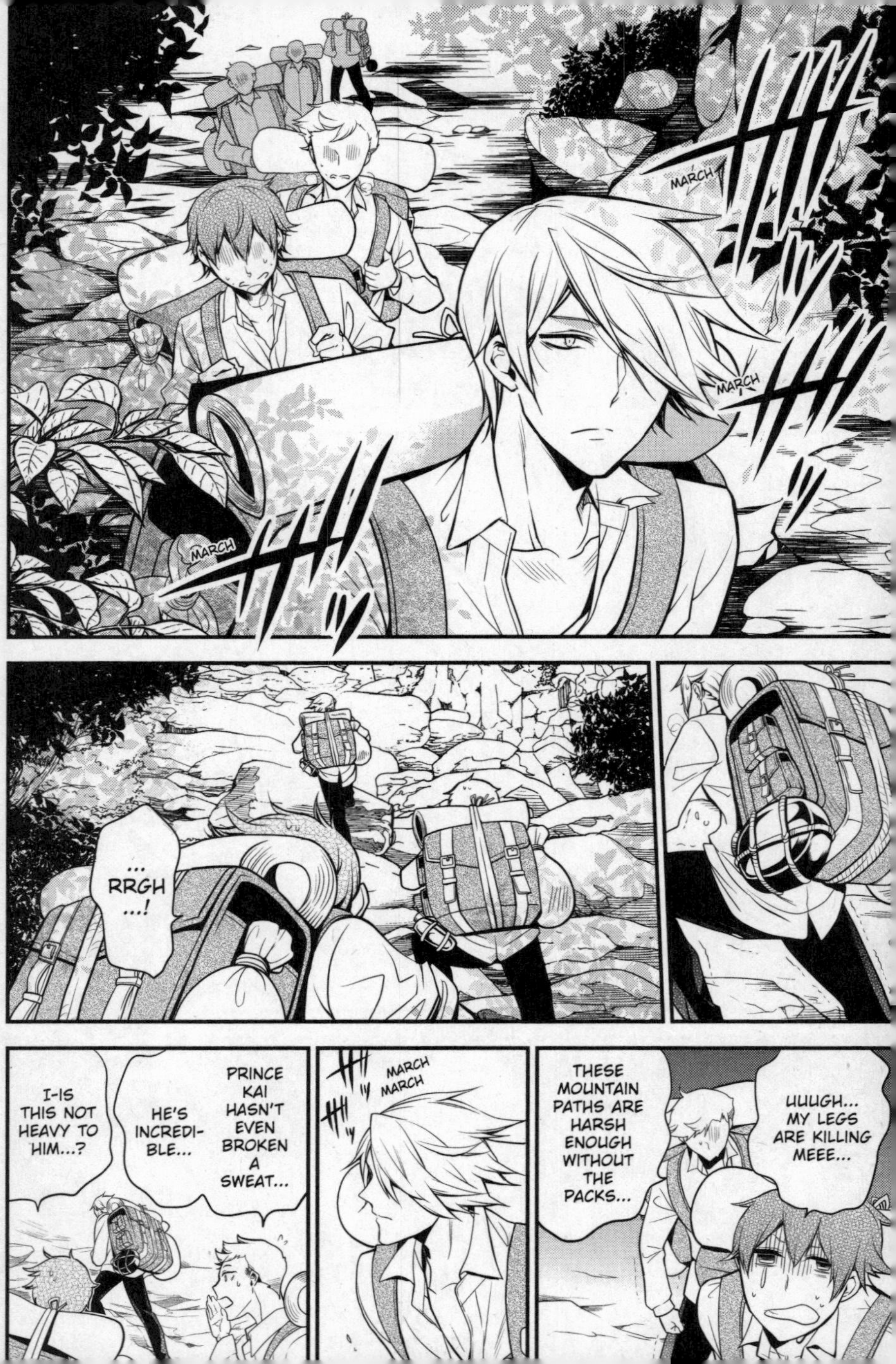
MARCH
MARCH
MARCH
...RRGH...!
UUUGH... MY LEGS ARE KILLING MEEE...
THESE MOUNTAIN PATHS ARE HARSH ENOUGH WITHOUT THE PACKS...
MARCH MARCH
PRINCE KAI HASN'T EVEN BROKEN A SWEAT...
HE'S INCREDIBLE...
I-IS THIS NOT HEAVY TO HIM...?

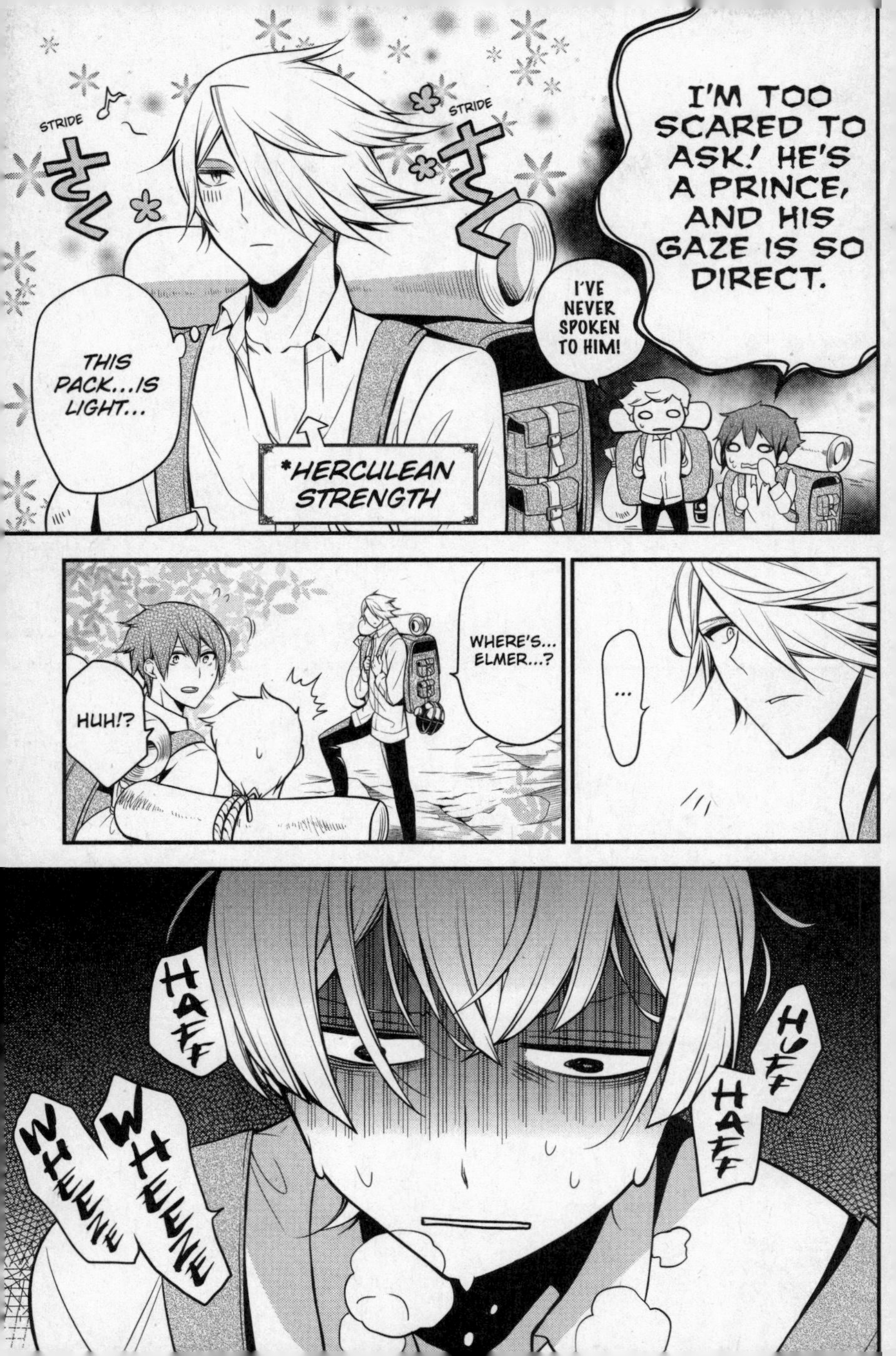
I'M TOO SCARED TO ASK! HE'S A PRINCE, AND HIS GAZE IS SO DIRECT.
I'VE NEVER SPOKEN TO HIM!
STRIDE
STRIDE
*HERCULEAN STRENGTH
THIS PACK...IS LIGHT...
...
WHERE'S... ELMER...?
HUH!?
HUFF
HAFF
HAFF
WHEEZE
WHEEZE

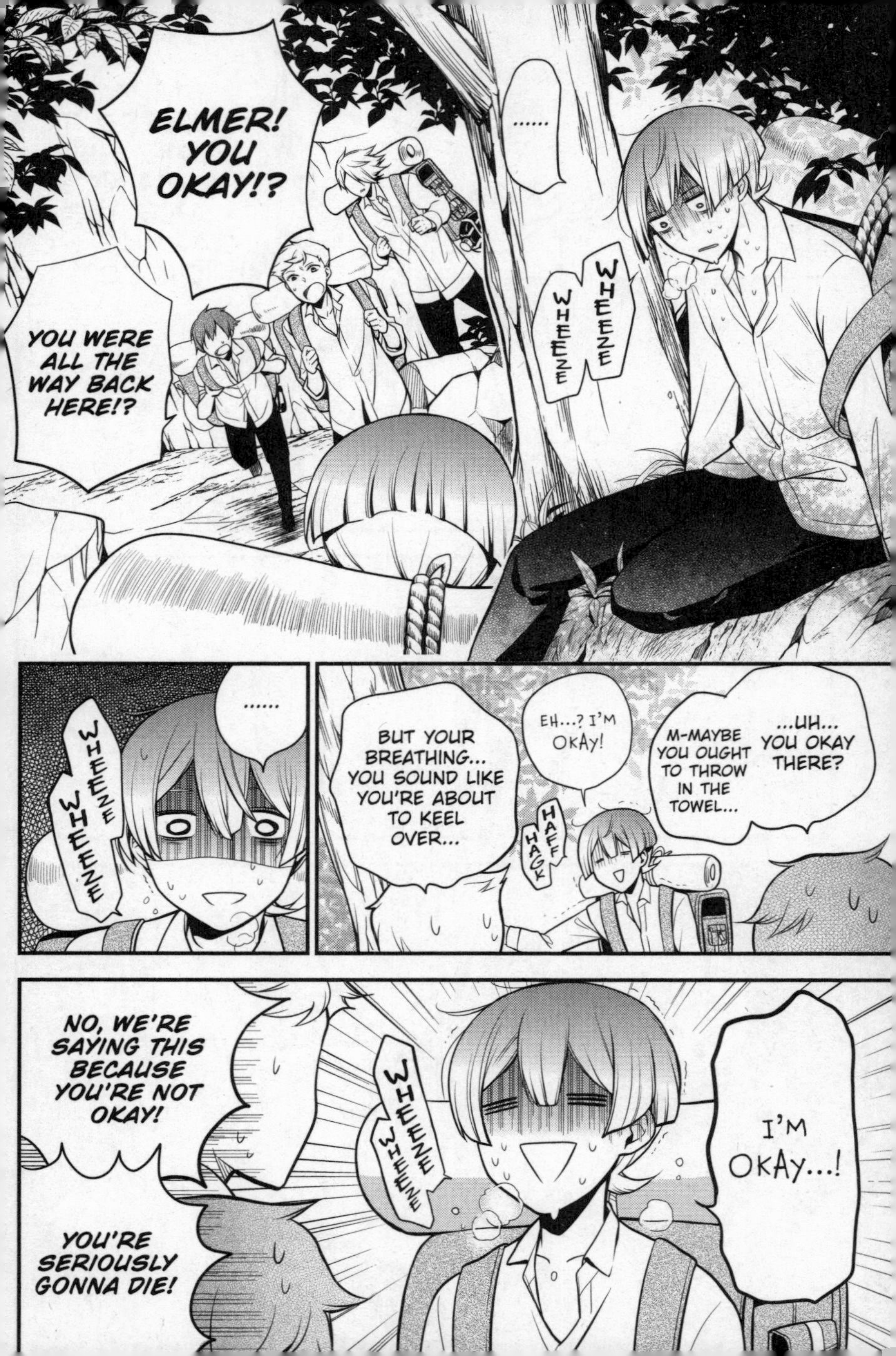
......
WHEEZE WHEEZE
ELMER! YOU OKAY!?
YOU WERE ALL THE WAY BACK HERE!?
...UH... YOU OKAY THERE?
M-MAYBE YOU OUGHT TO THROW IN THE TOWEL...
EH...? I'M OKAY!
HAFF HAGK
BUT YOUR BREATHING... YOU SOUND LIKE YOU'RE ABOUT TO KEEL OVER...
......
WHEEZE WHEEZE
I'M OKAY...!
WHEEZE WHEEZE
NO, WE'RE SAYING THIS BECAUSE YOU'RE NOT OKAY!
YOU'RE SERIOUSLY GONNA DIE!

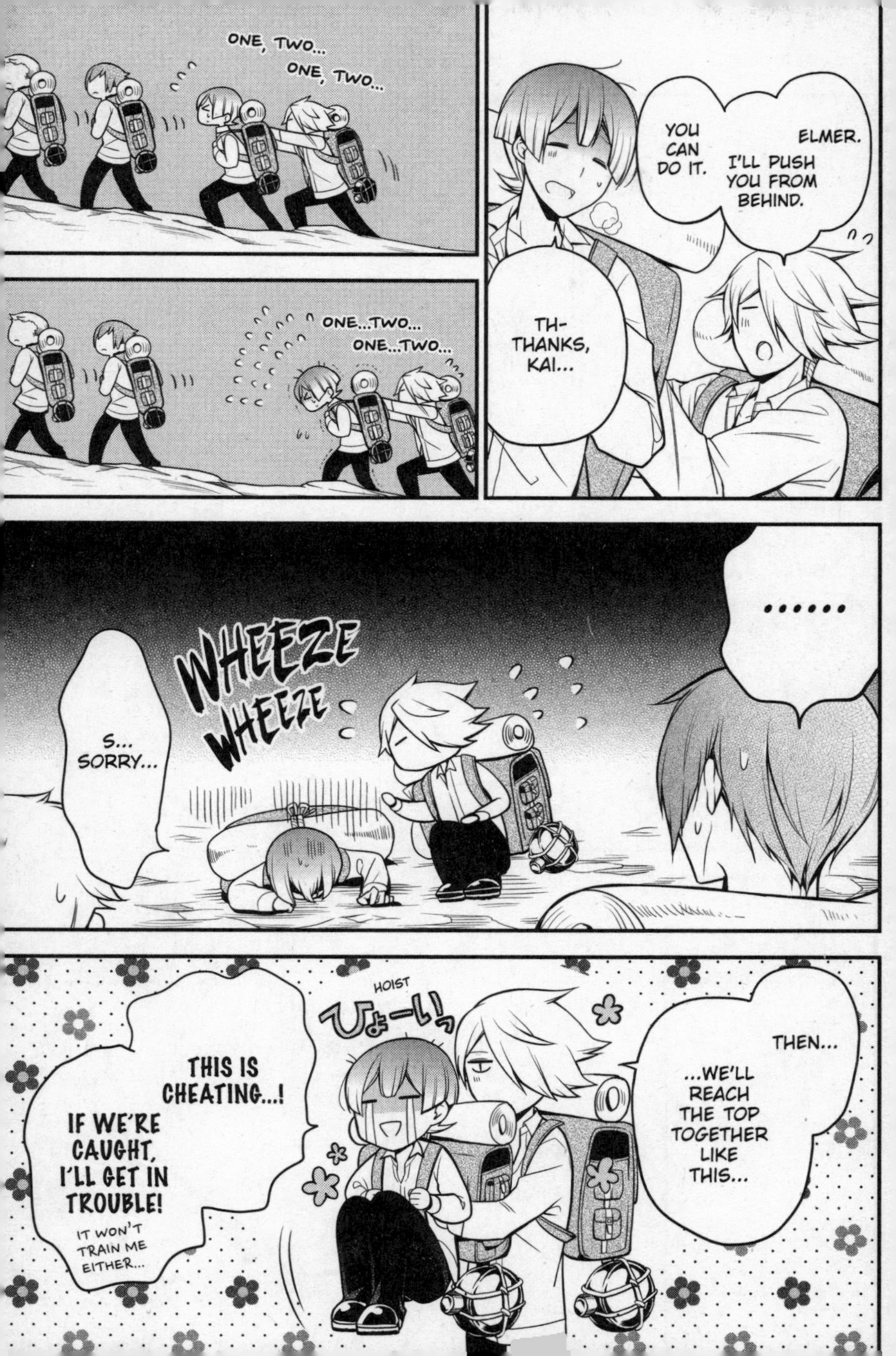

YOU CAN DO IT. ELMER. I'LL PUSH YOU FROM BEHIND.
TH- THANKS, KAI...
ONE, TWO...
ONE, TWO...
ONE...TWO...
ONE...TWO...
......
WHEEZE WHEEZE
S... SORRY...
THEN...
...WE'LL REACH THE TOP TOGETHER LIKE THIS...
HOIST
ひょーいっ
THIS IS CHEATING...!
IF WE'RE CAUGHT, I'LL GET IN TROUBLE!
IT WON'T TRAIN ME EITHER...

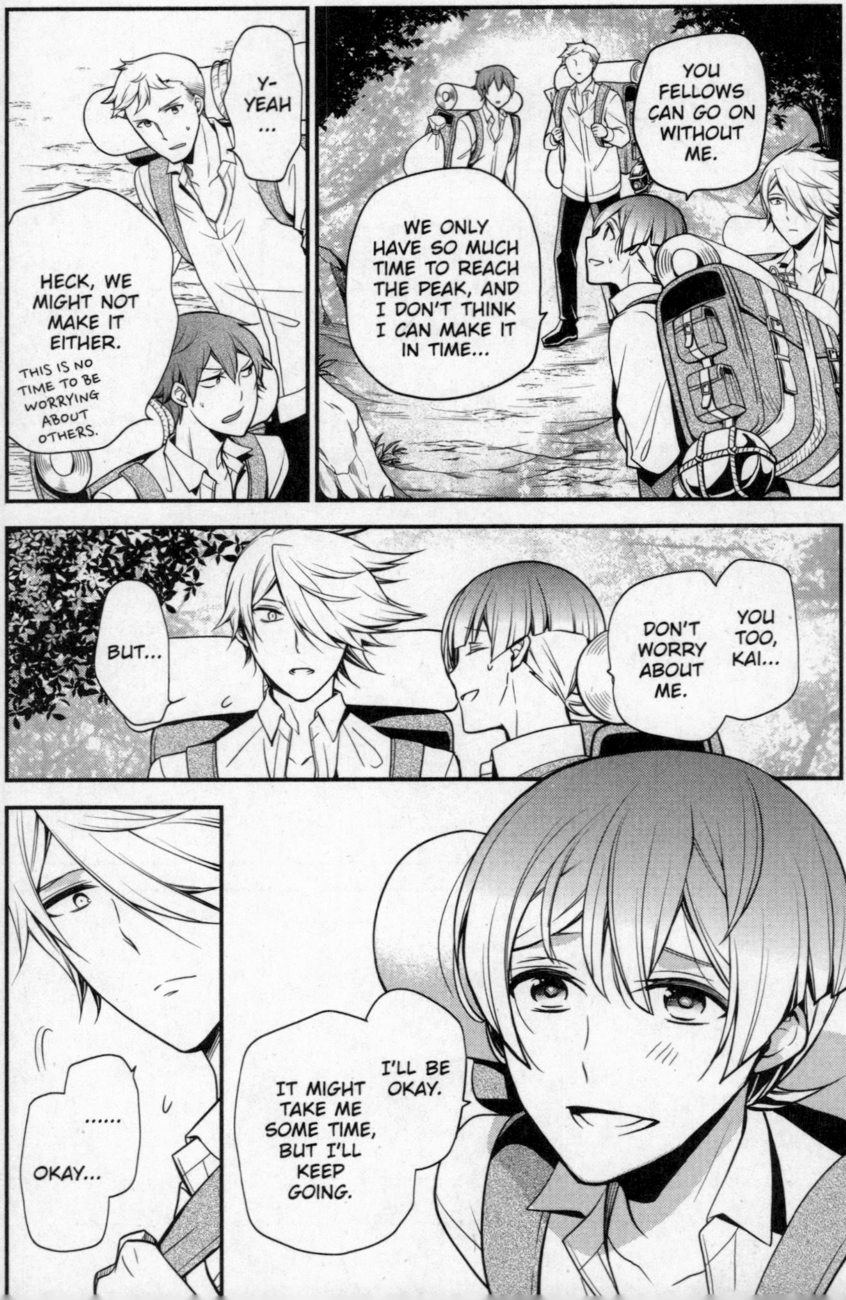
YOU FELLOWS CAN GO ON WITHOUT ME.
WE ONLY HAVE SO MUCH TIME TO REACH THE PEAK, AND I DON'T THINK I CAN MAKE IT IN TIME...
Y-YEAH ...
HECK, WE MIGHT NOT MAKE IT EITHER.
THIS IS NO TIME TO BE WORRYING ABOUT OTHERS.
YOU TOO, KAI...
DON'T WORRY ABOUT ME.
BUT...
I'LL BE OKAY.
IT MIGHT TAKE ME SOME TIME, BUT I'LL KEEP GOING.
......
OKAY...

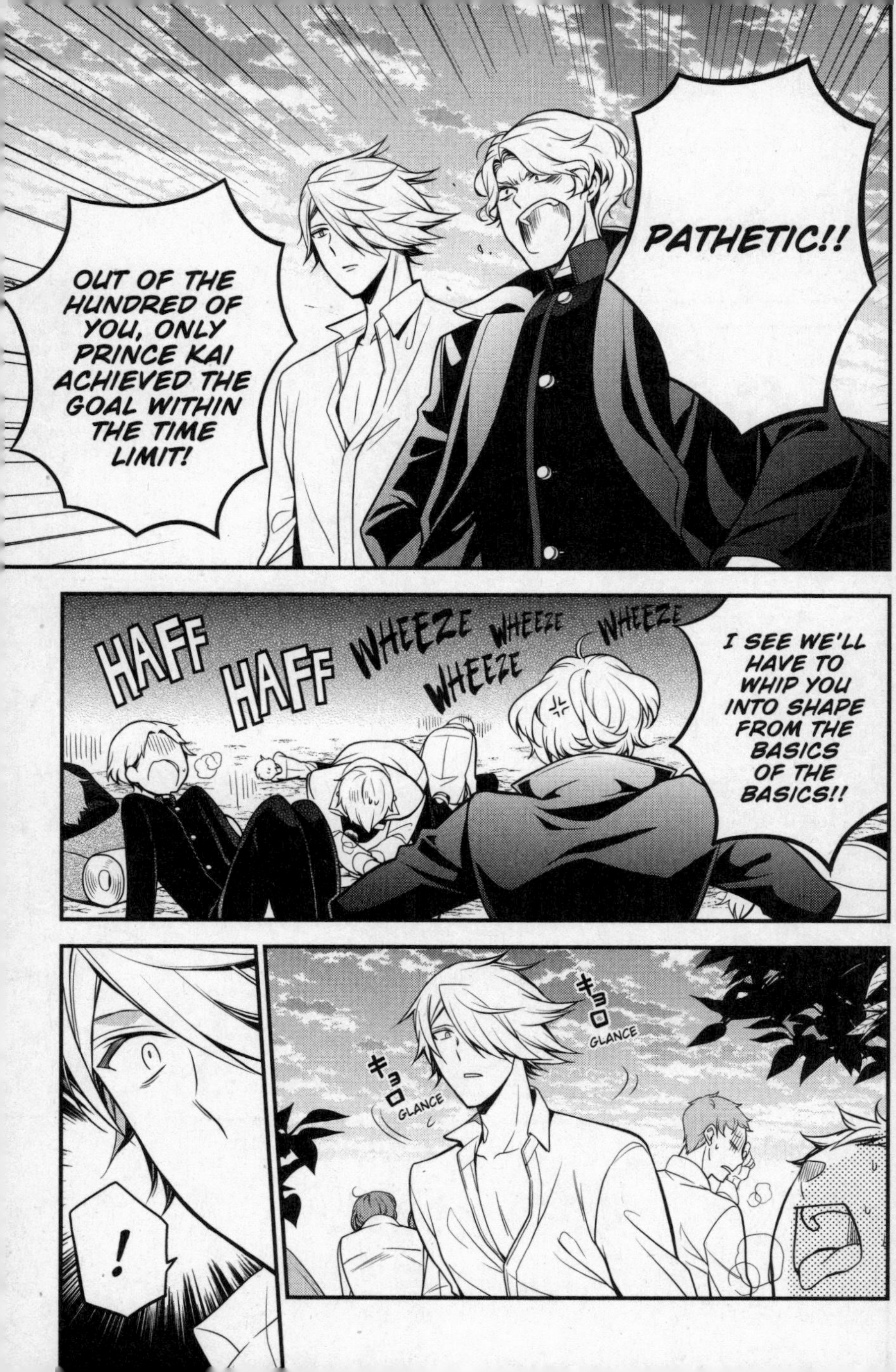
PATHETIC!!
OUT OF THE HUNDRED OF YOU, ONLY PRINCE KAI ACHIEVED THE GOAL WITHIN THE TIME LIMIT!
I SEE WE'LL HAVE TO WHIP YOU INTO SHAPE FROM THE BASICS OF THE BASICS!!
WHEEZE
WHEEZE WHEEZE
WHEEZE
HAFF HAFF
キョロ GLANCE
キョロ GLANCE
!

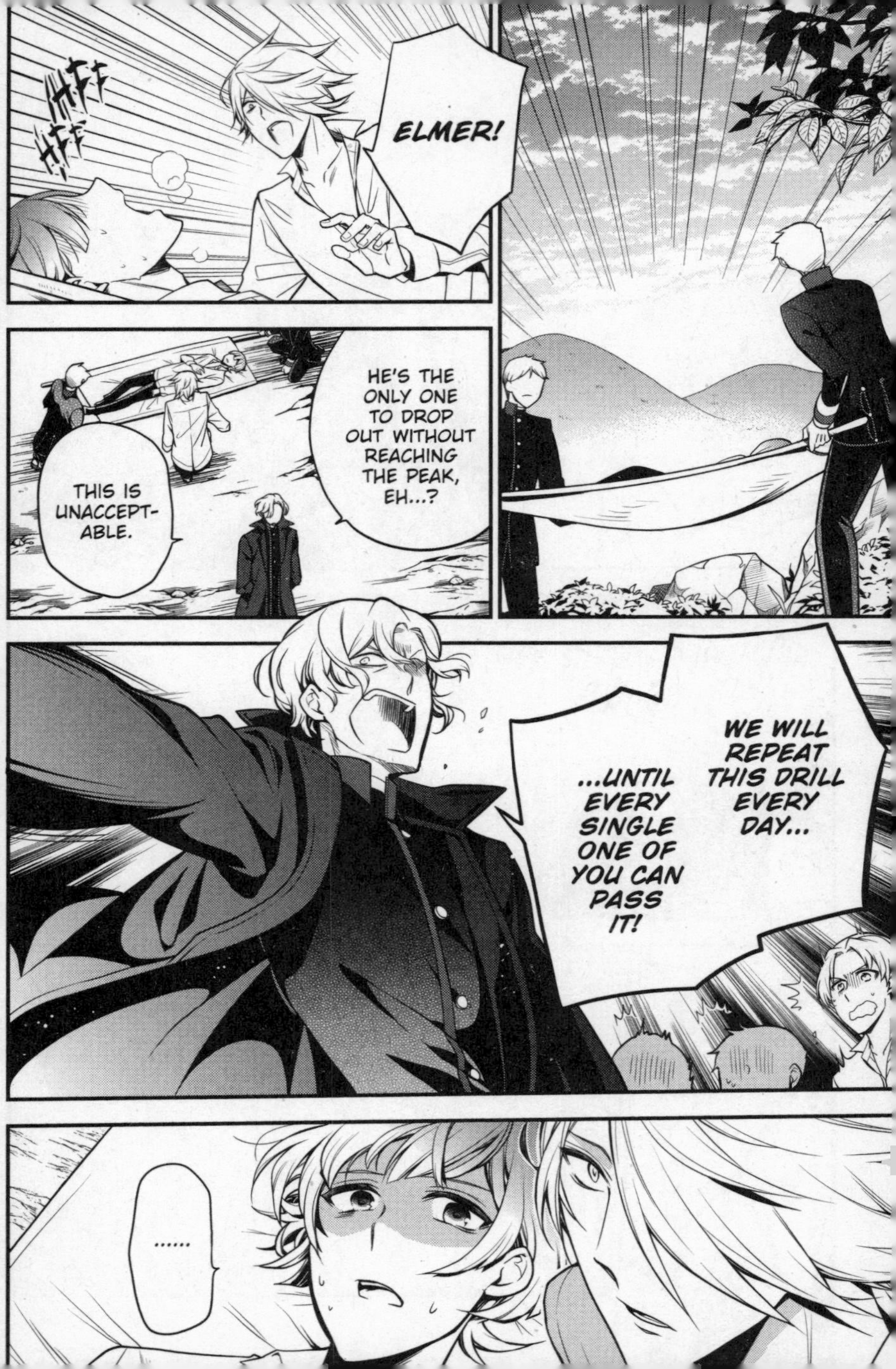
ELMER!
HFF HFF
HE'S THE ONLY ONE TO DROP OUT WITHOUT REACHING THE PEAK, EH...?
THIS IS UNACCEPT-ABLE.
WE WILL REPEAT THIS DRILL EVERY DAY...
...UNTIL EVERY SINGLE ONE OF YOU CAN PASS IT!
......

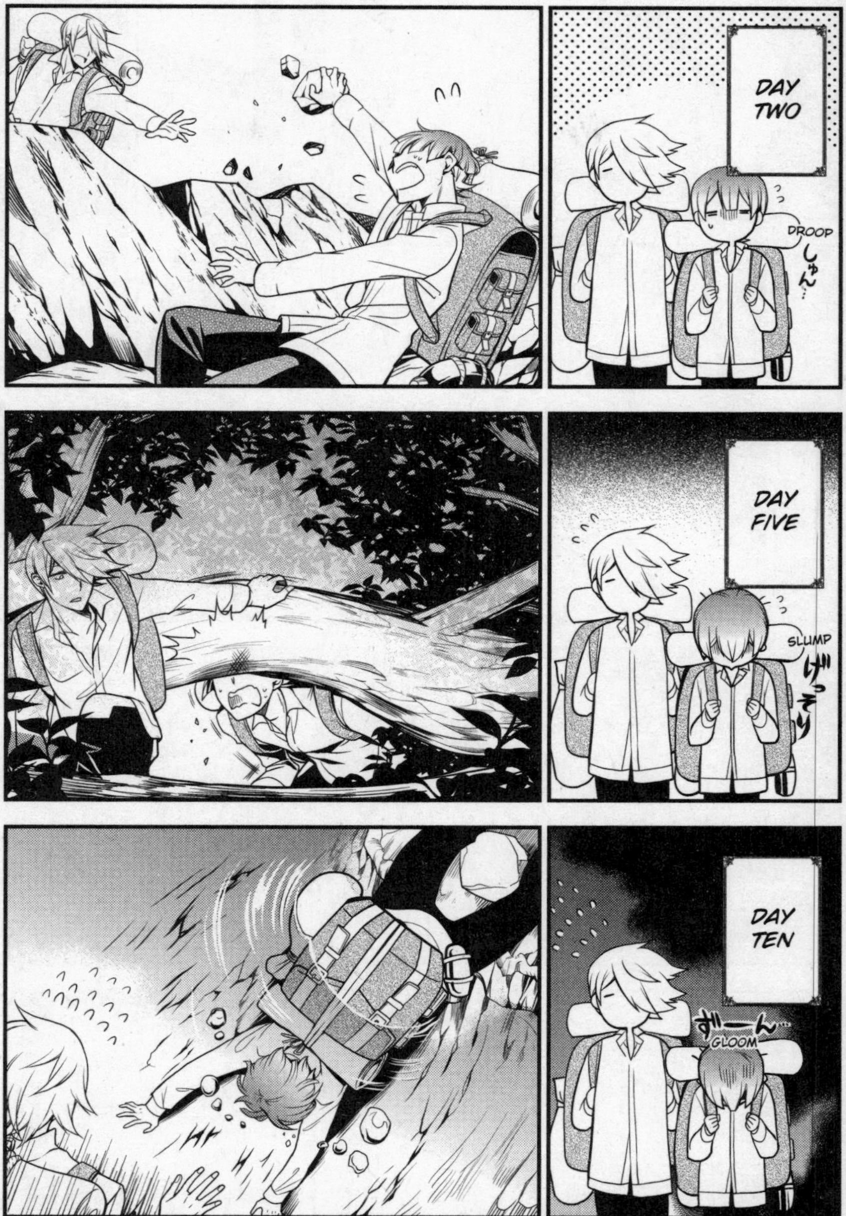
DAY TWO
DROOP
しゅん…
DAY FIVE
SLUMP
げっそり
DAY TEN
ずーん…
GLOOM

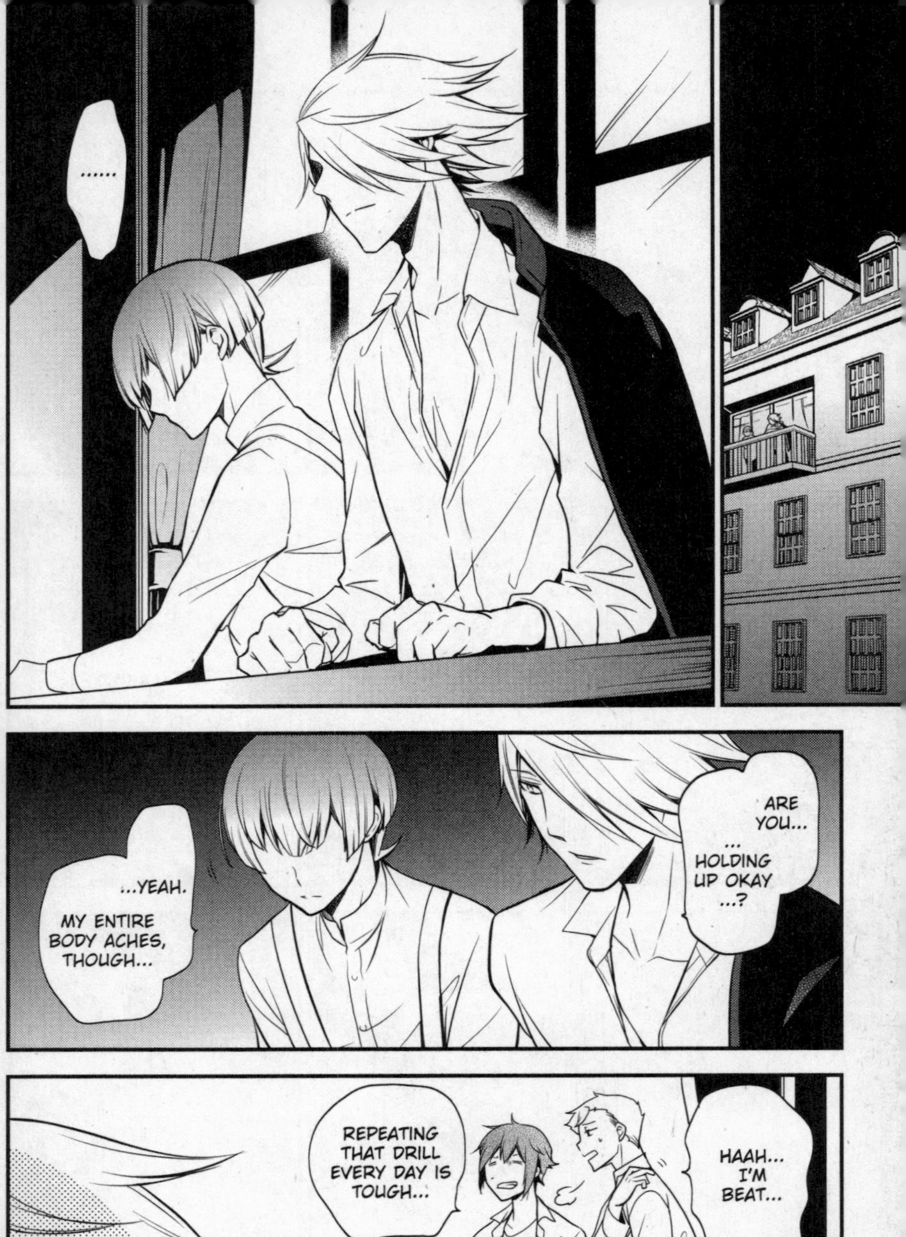
......
ARE YOU... ... HOLDING UP OKAY ...?
...YEAH.
MY ENTIRE BODY ACHES, THOUGH...
HAAH... I'M BEAT...
REPEATING THAT DRILL EVERY DAY IS TOUGH...

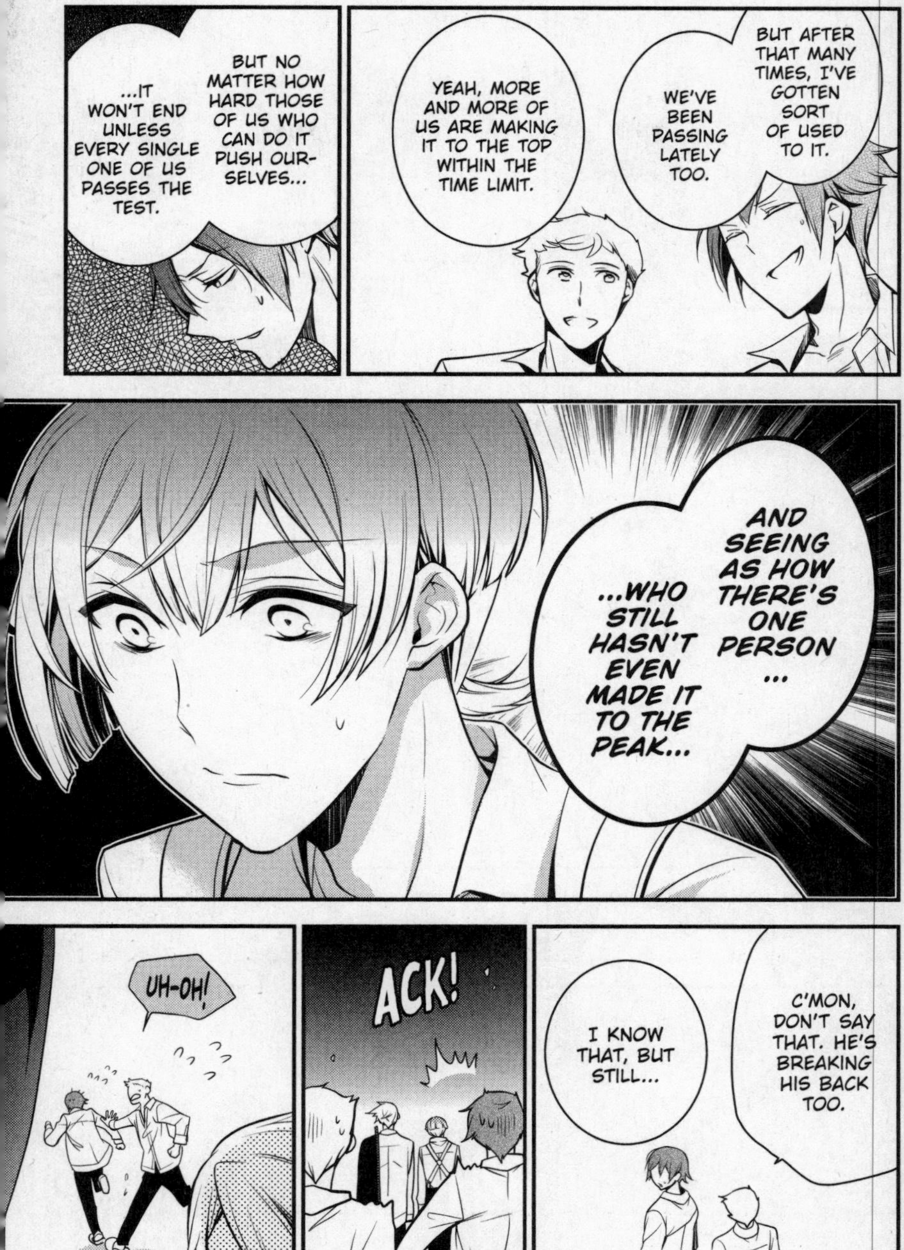

BUT AFTER THAT MANY TIMES, I'VE GOTTEN SORT OF USED TO IT.
WE'VE BEEN PASSING LATELY TOO.
YEAH, MORE AND MORE OF US ARE MAKING IT TO THE TOP WITHIN THE TIME LIMIT.
BUT NO MATTER HOW HARD THOSE OF US WHO CAN DO IT PUSH OURSELVES...
...IT WON'T END UNLESS EVERY SINGLE ONE OF US PASSES THE TEST.
AND SEEING AS HOW THERE'S ONE PERSON...
...WHO STILL HASN'T EVEN MADE IT TO THE PEAK...
C'MON, DON'T SAY THAT. HE'S BREAKING HIS BACK TOO.
I KNOW THAT, BUT STILL...
ACK!
UH-OH!

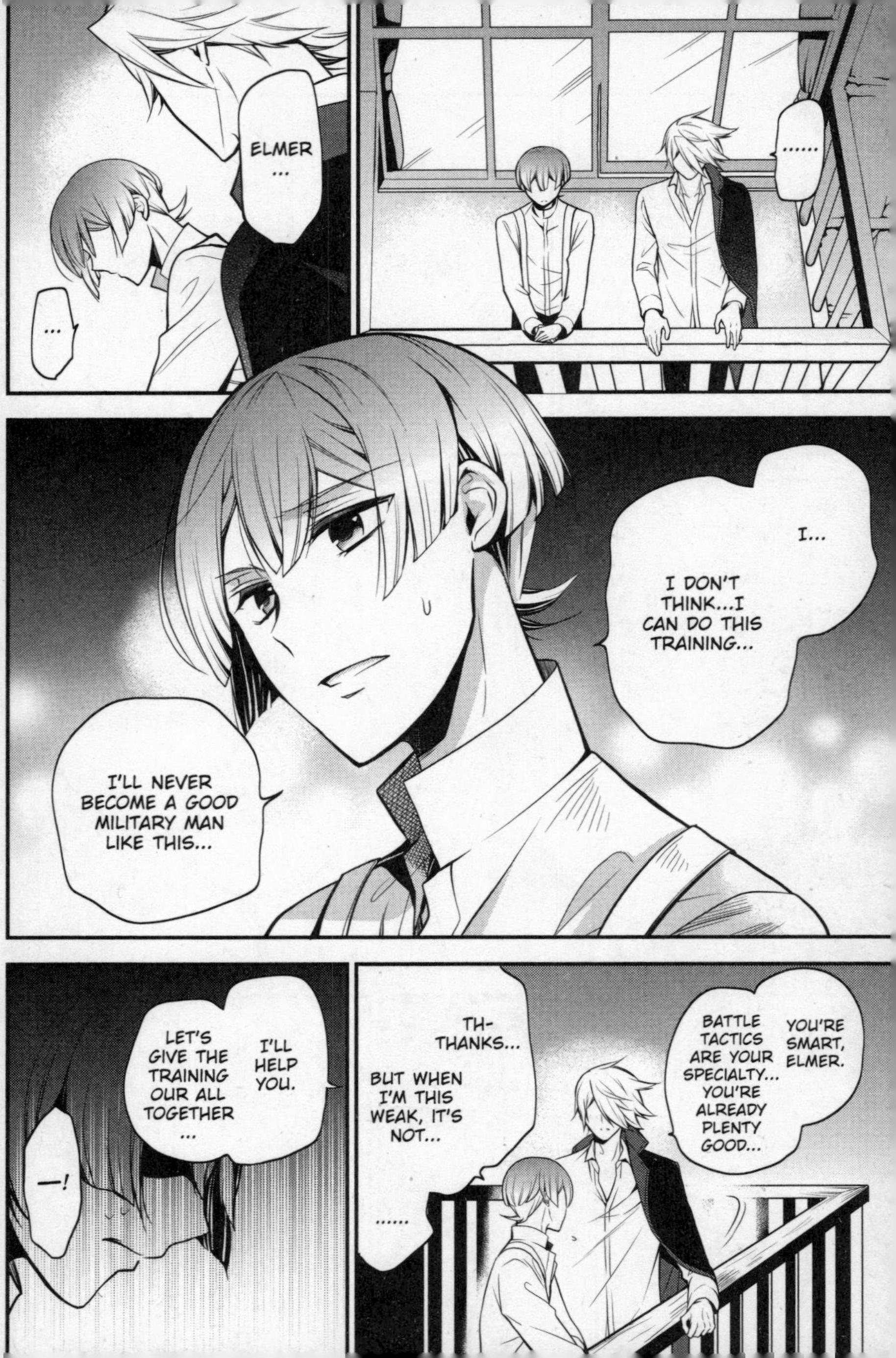
......
ELMER ...
...
I...
I DON'T THINK...I CAN DO THIS TRAINING...
I'LL NEVER BECOME A GOOD MILITARY MAN LIKE THIS...
YOU'RE SMART, ELMER.
BATTLE TACTICS ARE YOUR SPECIALTY... YOU'RE ALREADY PLENTY GOOD...
TH-THANKS...
BUT WHEN I'M THIS WEAK, IT'S NOT...
......
I'LL HELP YOU.
LET'S GIVE THE TRAINING OUR ALL TOGETHER ...
—!

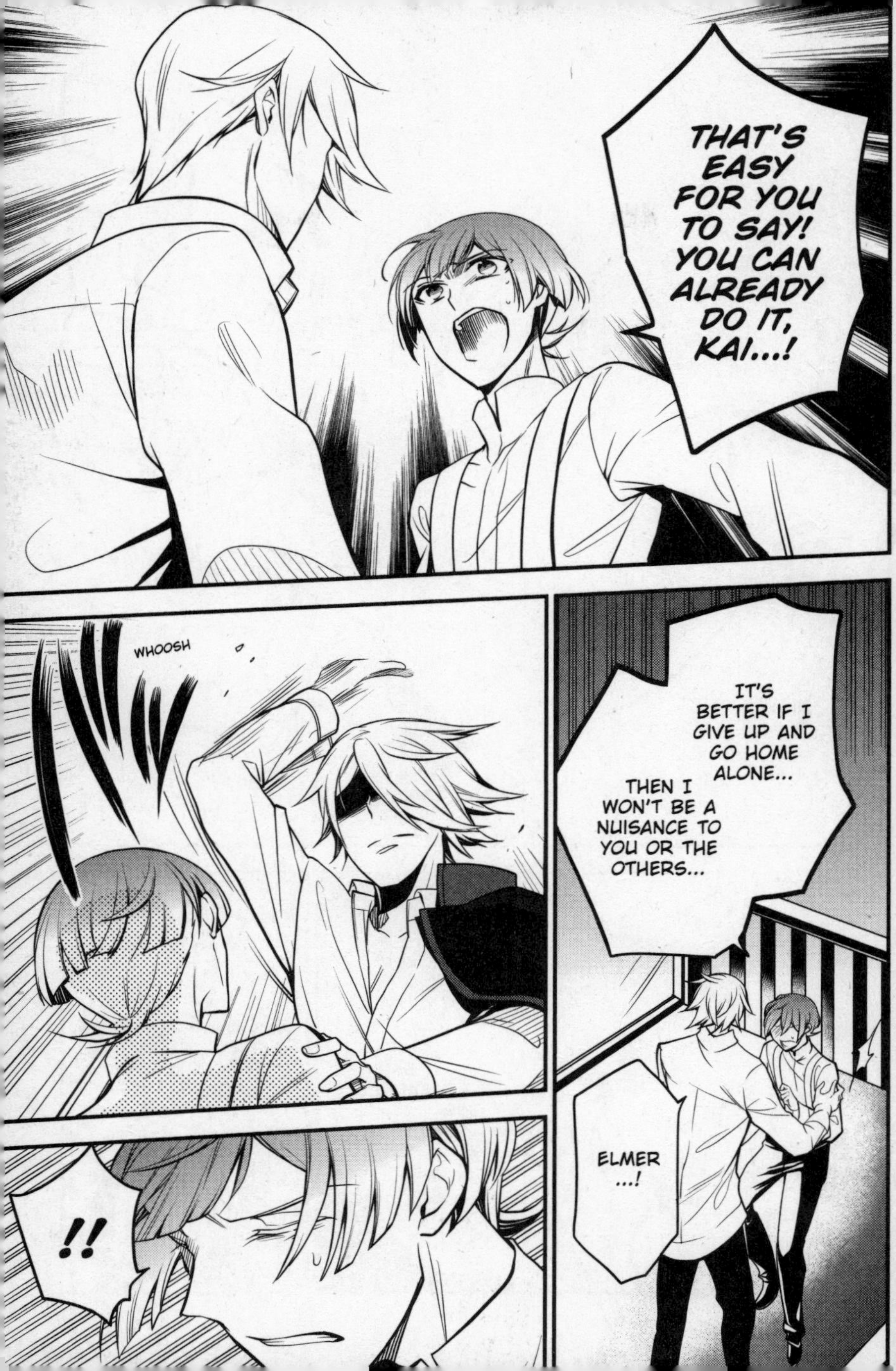
THAT'S EASY FOR YOU TO SAY! YOU CAN ALREADY DO IT, KAI...!
IT'S BETTER IF I GIVE UP AND GO HOME ALONE...
THEN I WON'T BE A NUISANCE TO YOU OR THE OTHERS...
ELMER ...!
WHOOSH
!!

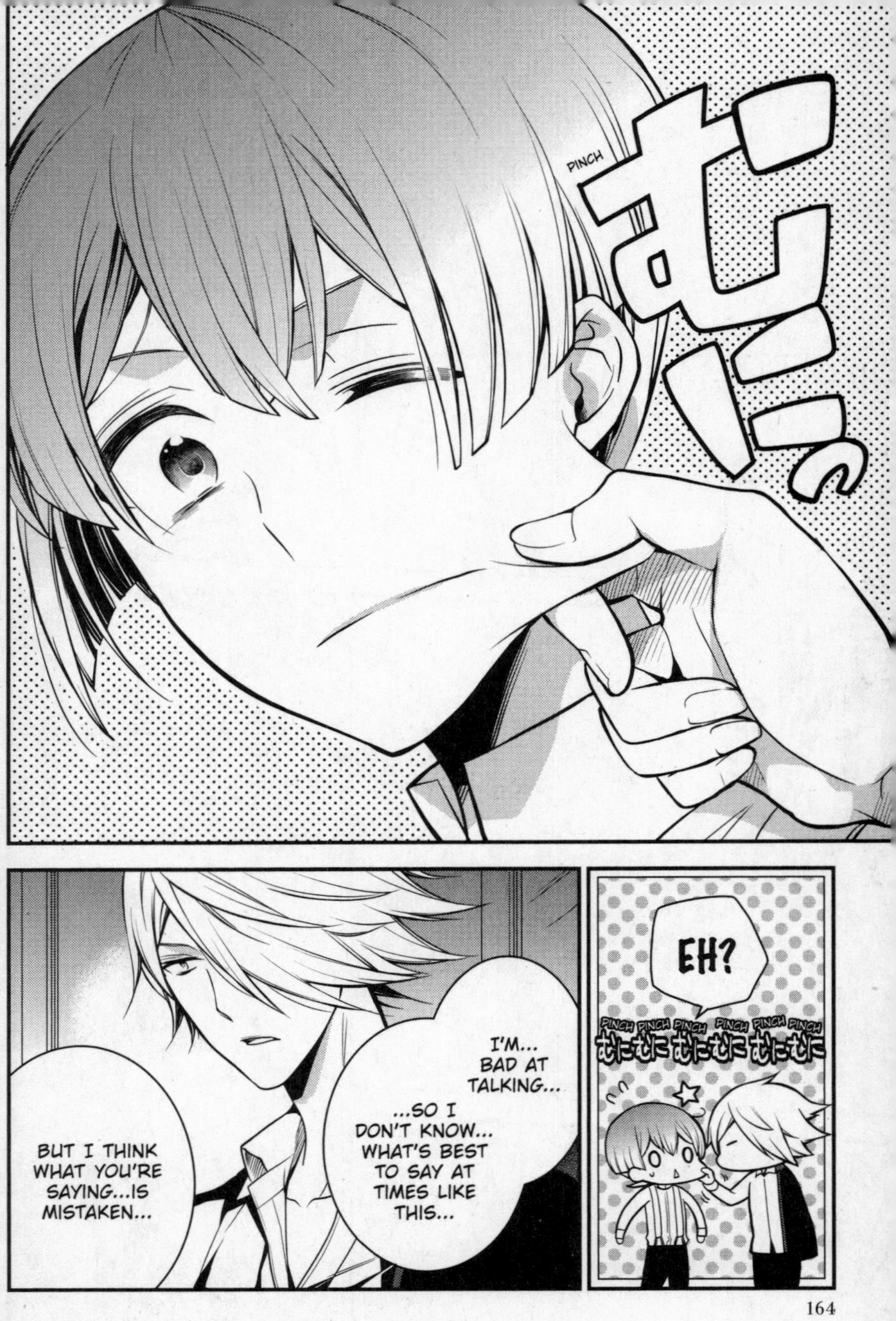
PINCH
むにっ
EH?
PINCH PINCH PINCH PINCH PINCH PINCH
むにむにむにむにむにむに
I'M... BAD AT TALKING...
...SO I DON'T KNOW... WHAT'S BEST TO SAY AT TIMES LIKE THIS...
BUT I THINK WHAT YOU'RE SAYING...IS MISTAKEN...

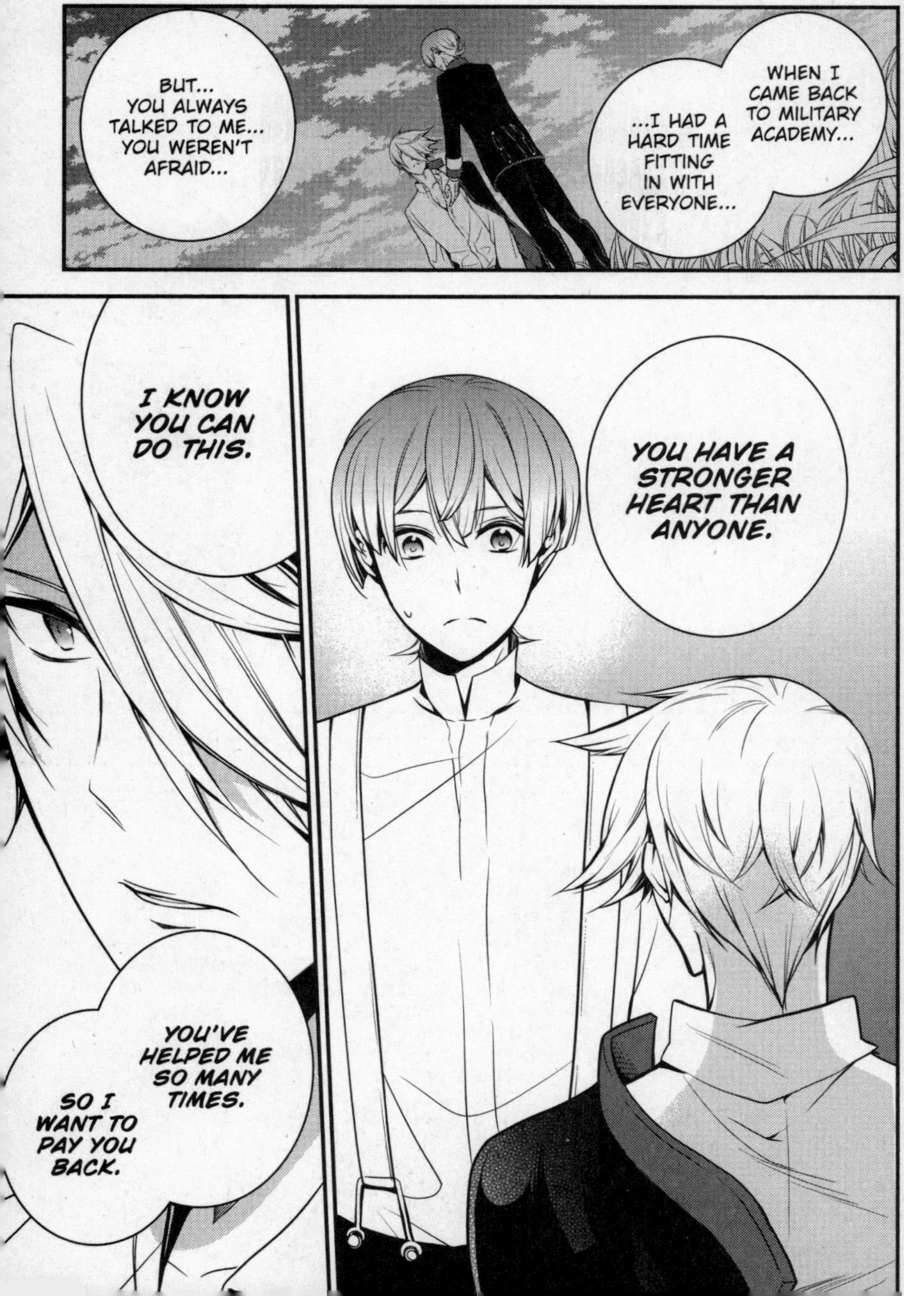
WHEN I CAME BACK TO MILITARY ACADEMY...
...I HAD A HARD TIME FITTING IN WITH EVERYONE...
BUT... YOU ALWAYS TALKED TO ME... YOU WEREN'T AFRAID...
YOU HAVE A STRONGER HEART THAN ANYONE.
I KNOW YOU CAN DO THIS.
YOU'VE HELPED ME SO MANY TIMES.
SO I WANT TO PAY YOU BACK.

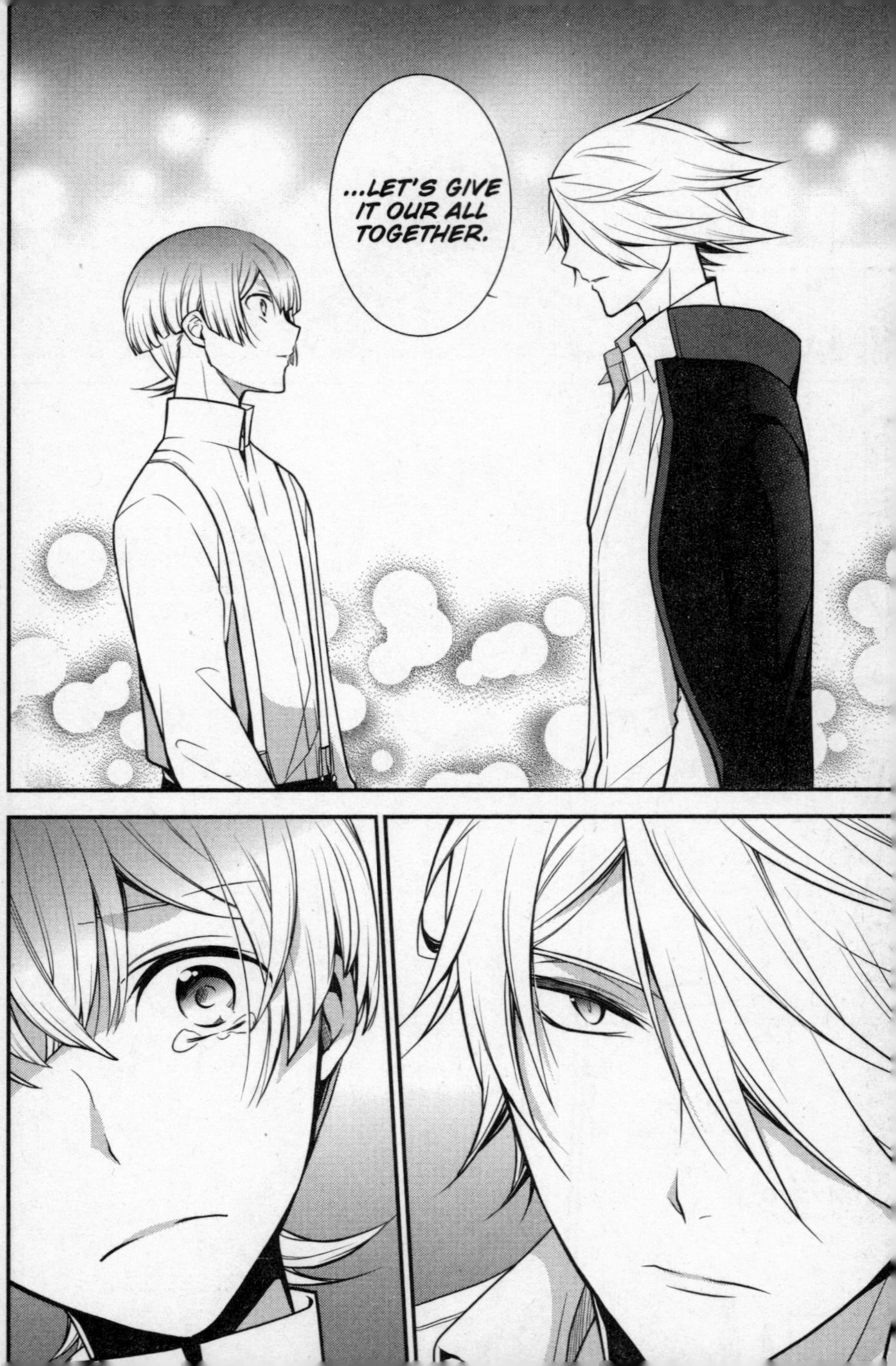
...LET'S GIVE IT OUR ALL TOGETHER.

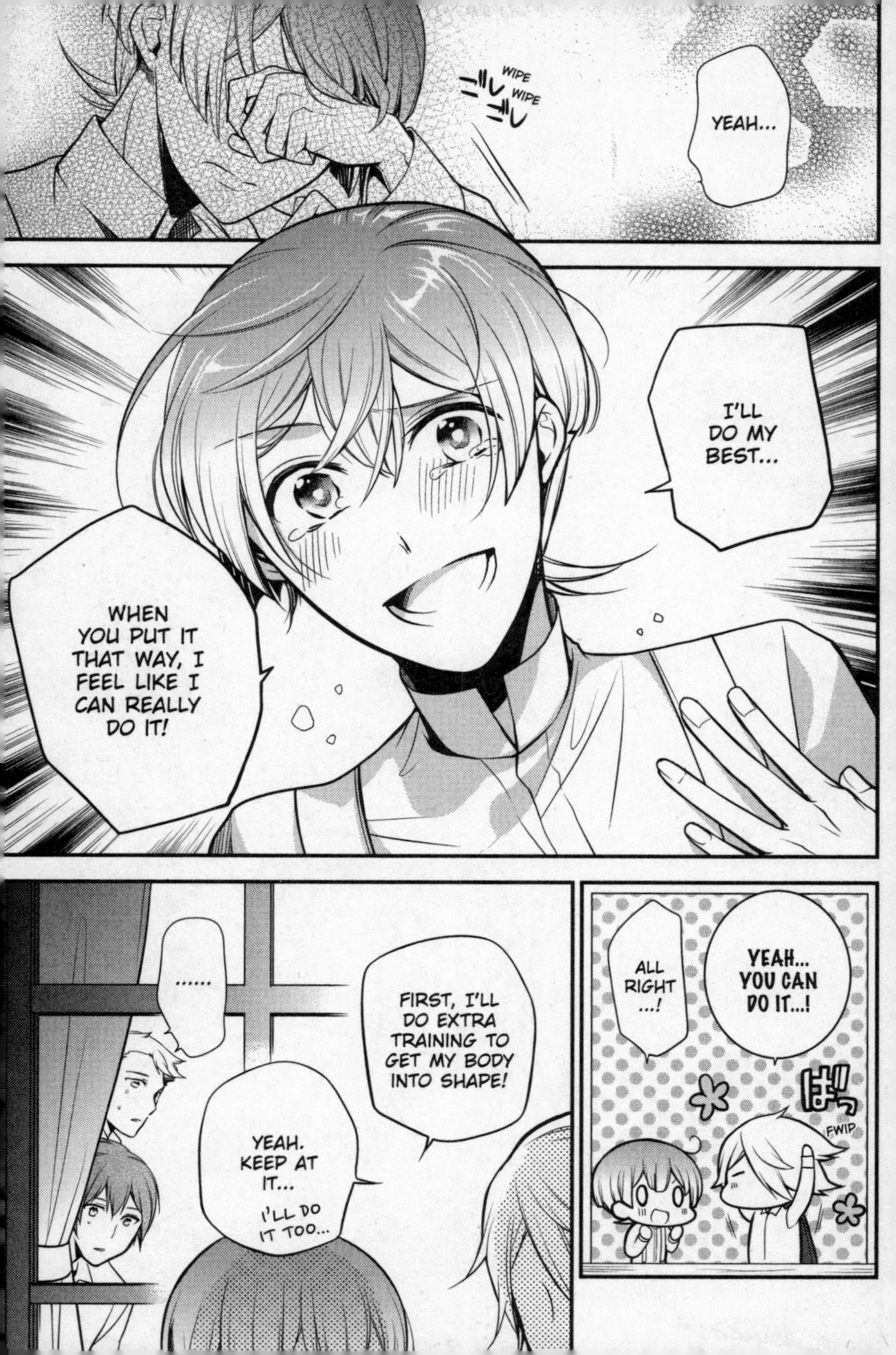
YEAH...
WIPE WIPE
I'LL DO MY BEST...
WHEN YOU PUT IT THAT WAY, I FEEL LIKE I CAN REALLY DO IT!
YEAH... YOU CAN DO IT...!
ALL RIGHT ...!
ぱっ
FWIP
FIRST, I'LL DO EXTRA TRAINING TO GET MY BODY INTO SHAPE!
......
YEAH. KEEP AT IT...
I'LL DO IT TOO...

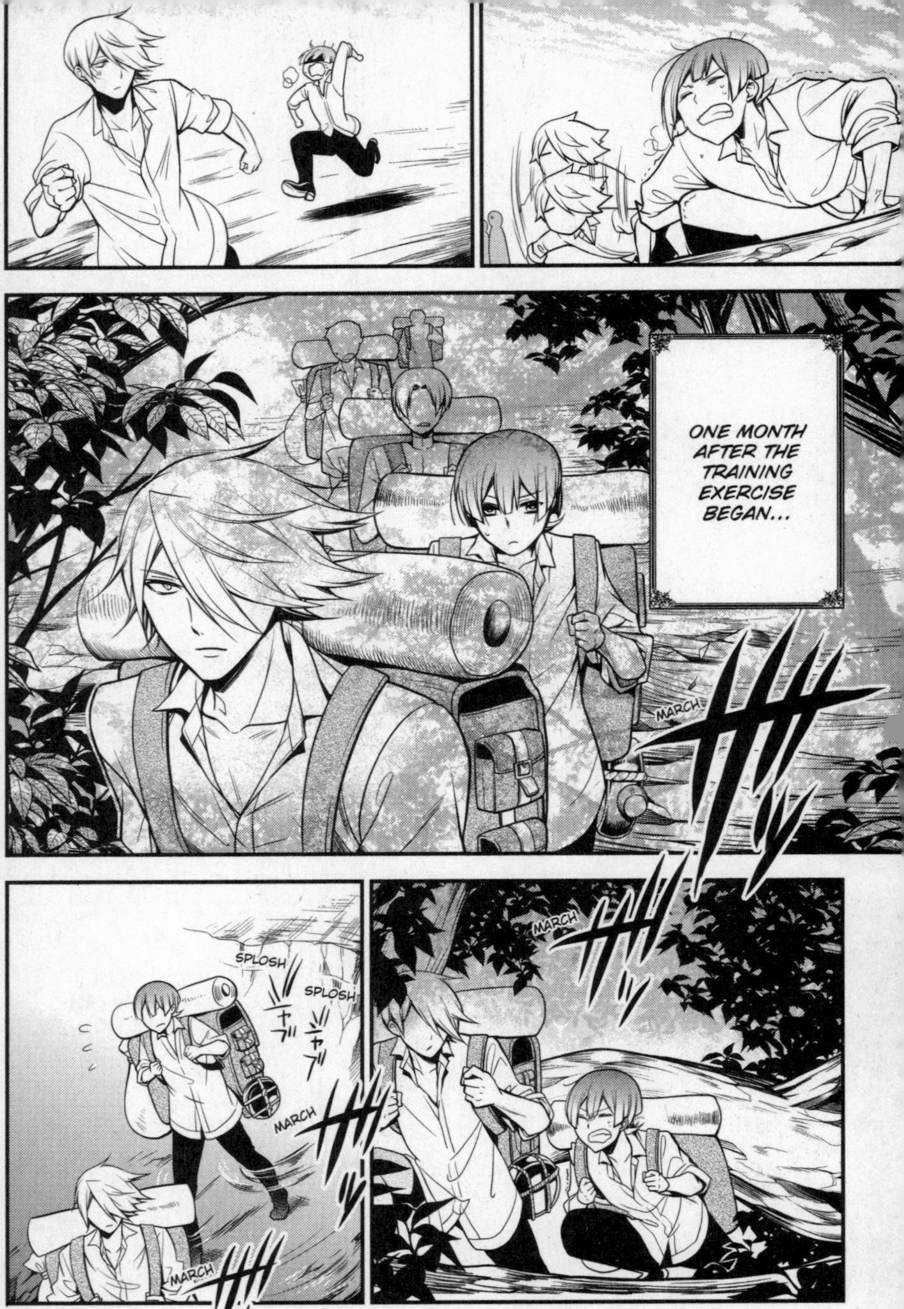
ONE MONTH AFTER THE TRAINING EXERCISE BEGAN...
MARCH
MARCH
SPLOSH
ジャブ
SPLOSH
ジャブ
MARCH
MARCH

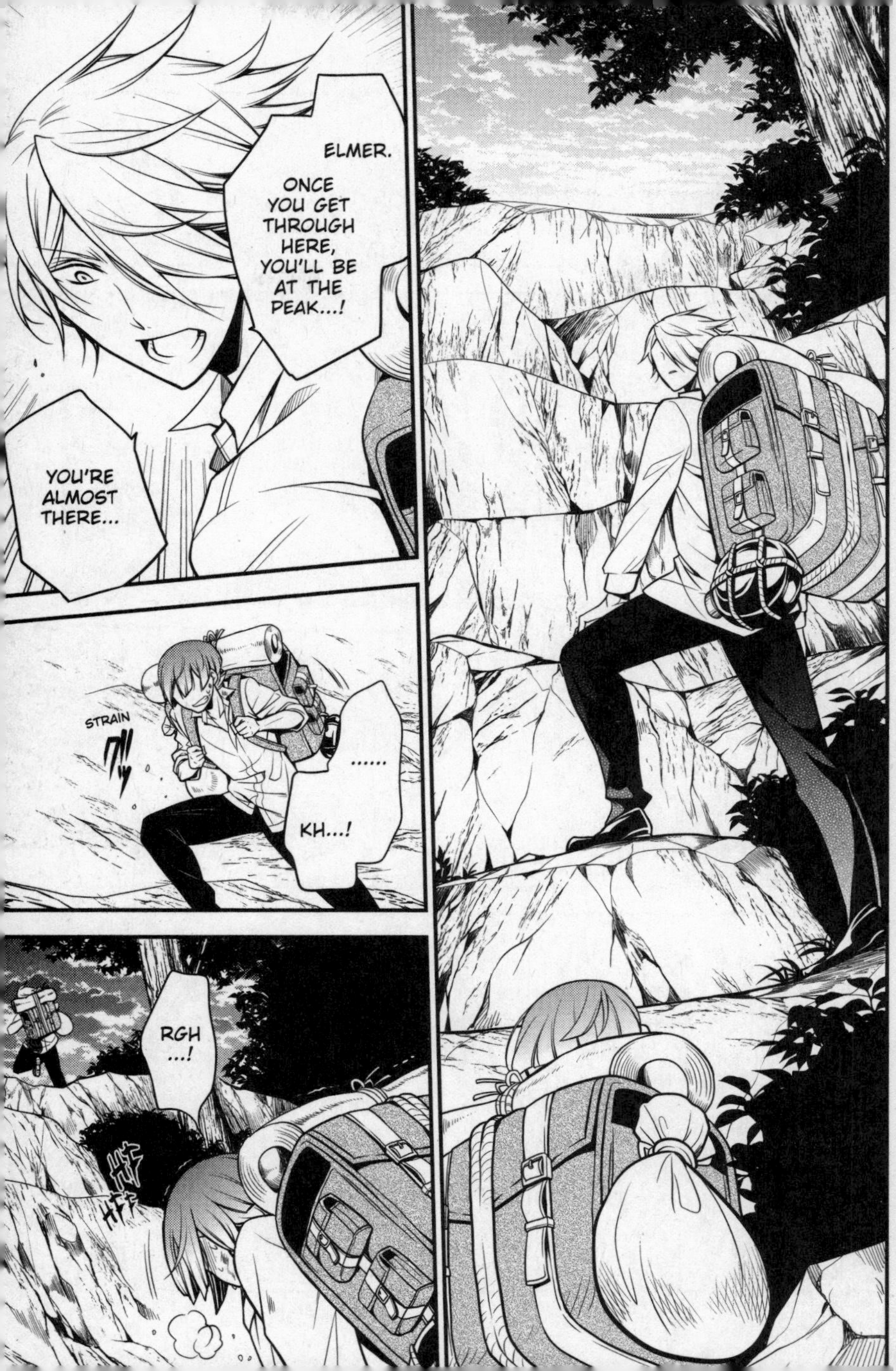
ELMER.
ONCE YOU GET THROUGH HERE, YOU'LL BE AT THE PEAK...!
YOU'RE ALMOST THERE...
......
KH...!
STRAIN
RGH ...!

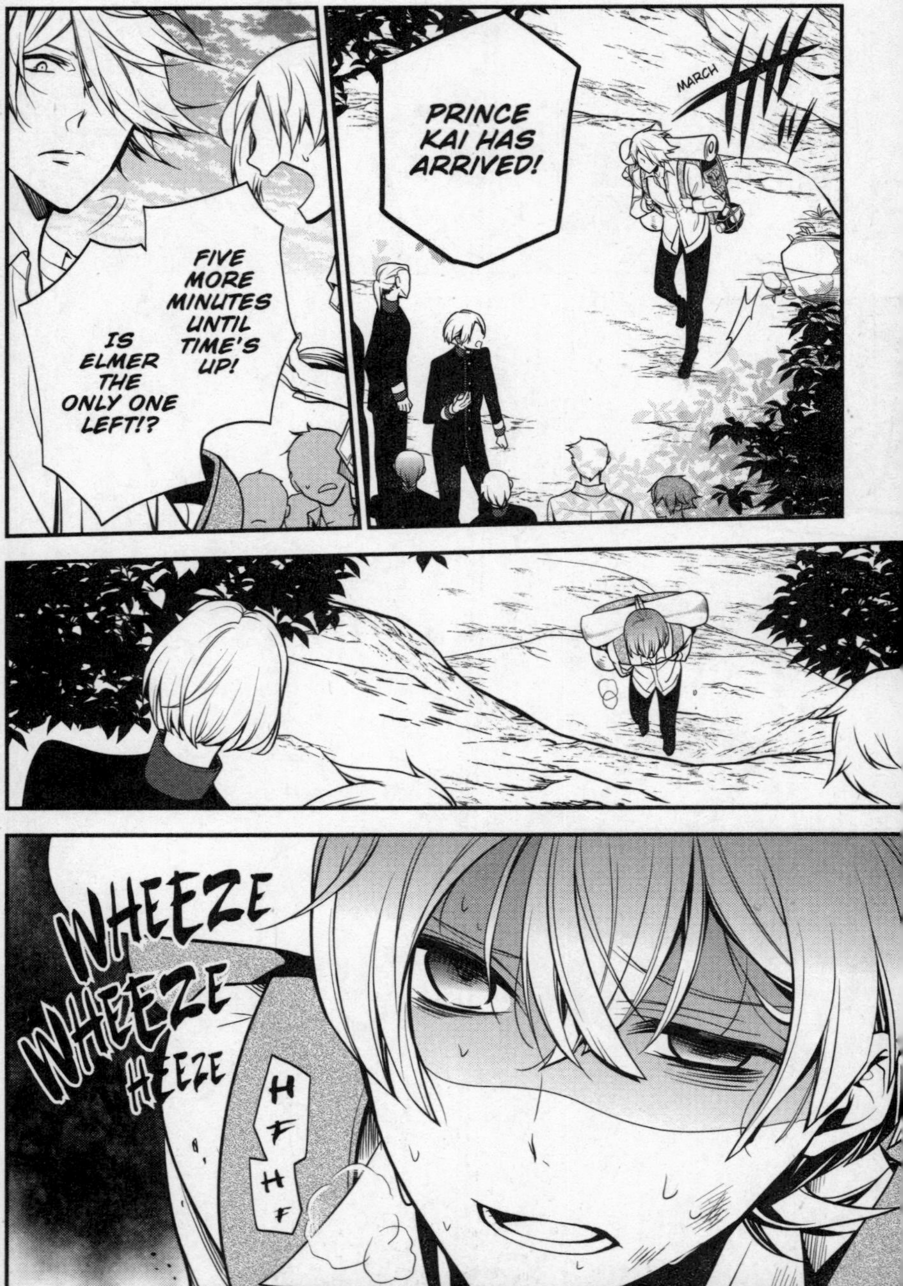
PRINCE KAI HAS ARRIVED!
MARCH
FIVE MORE MINUTES UNTIL TIME'S UP!
IS ELMER THE ONLY ONE LEFT!?
WHEEZE
WHEEZE
HEEZE
HFHF
HF

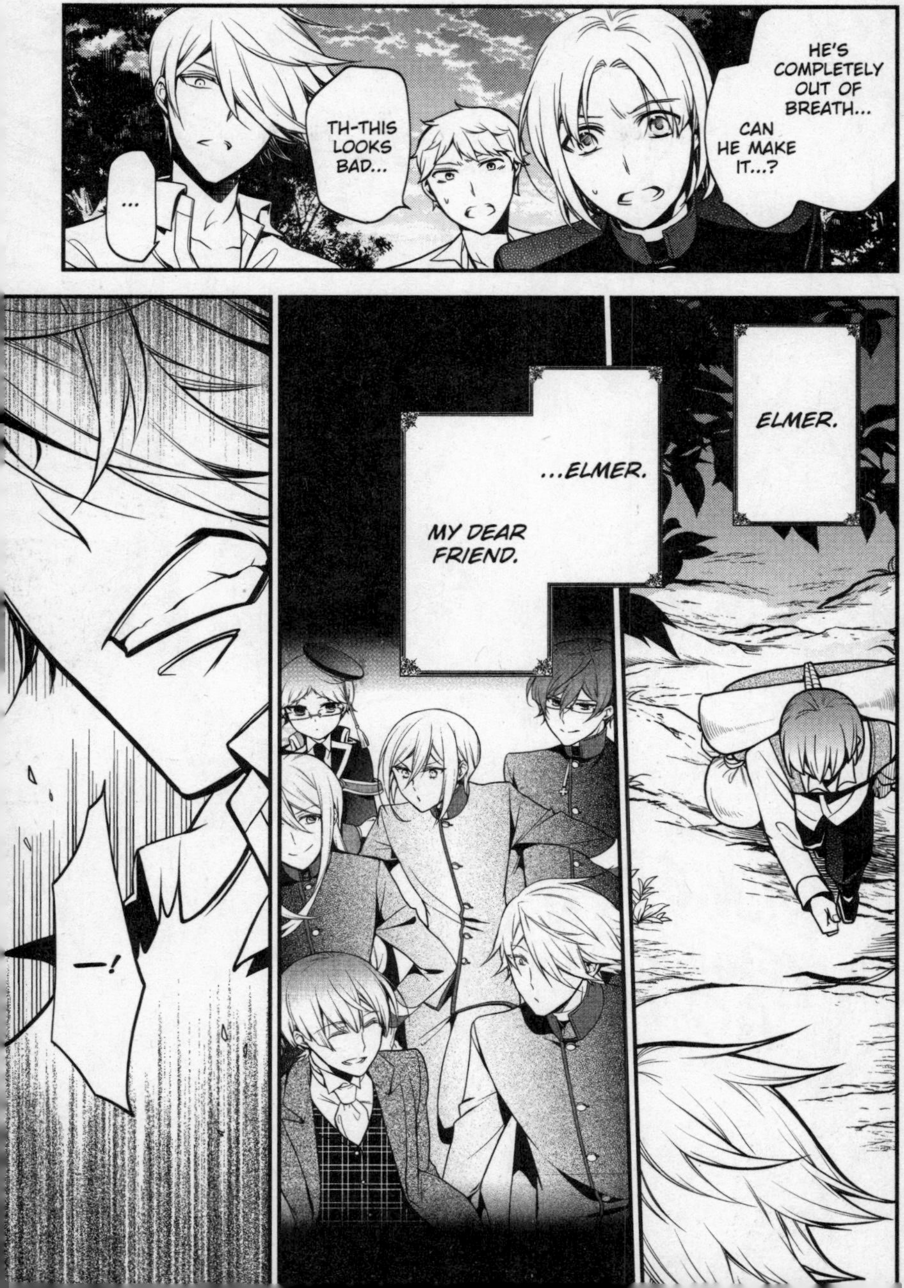
HE'S COMPLETELY OUT OF BREATH...
CAN HE MAKE IT...?
TH-THIS LOOKS BAD...
...
ELMER.
...ELMER.
MY DEAR FRIEND.
—!

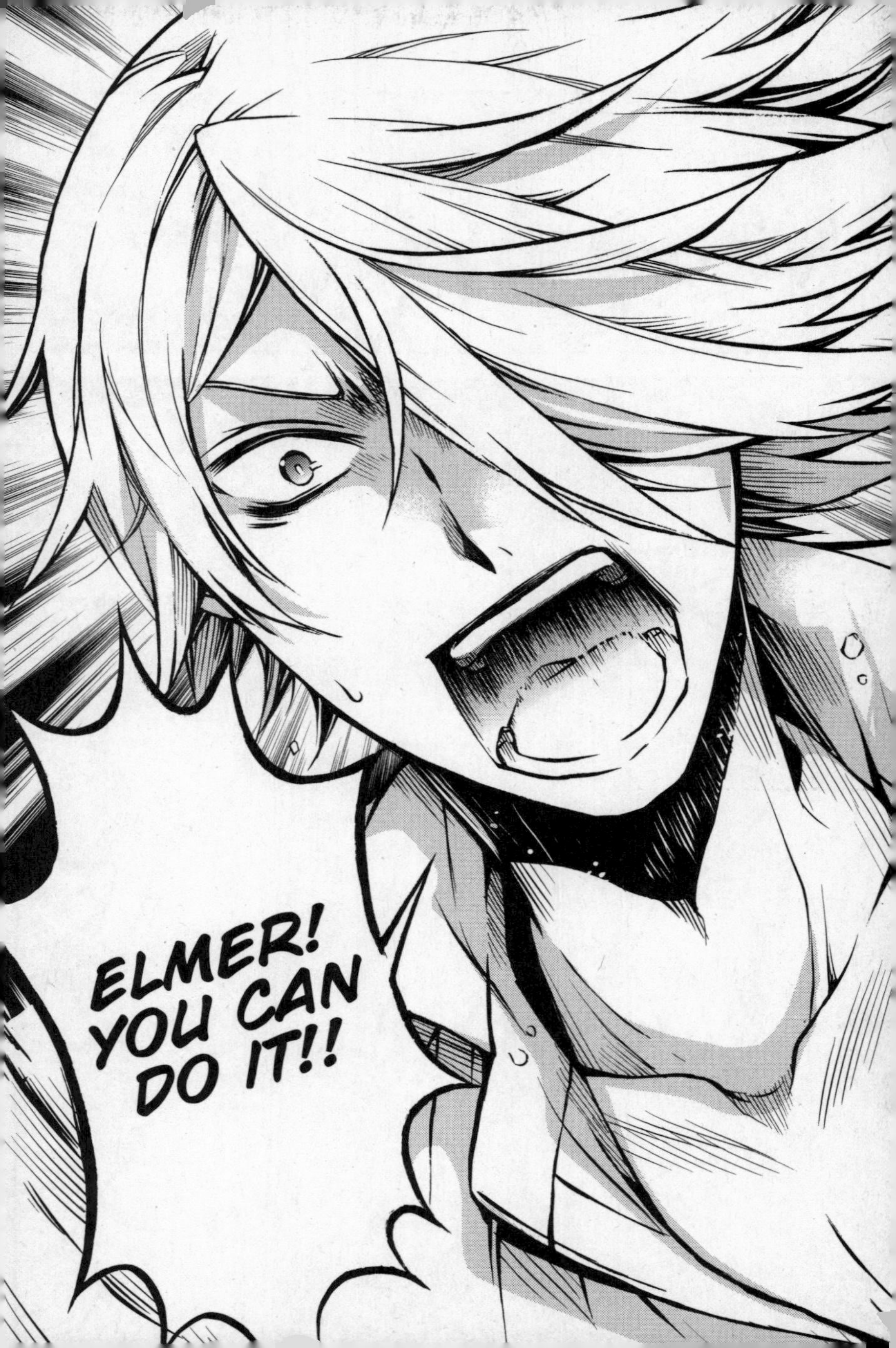
ELMER! YOU CAN DO IT!!

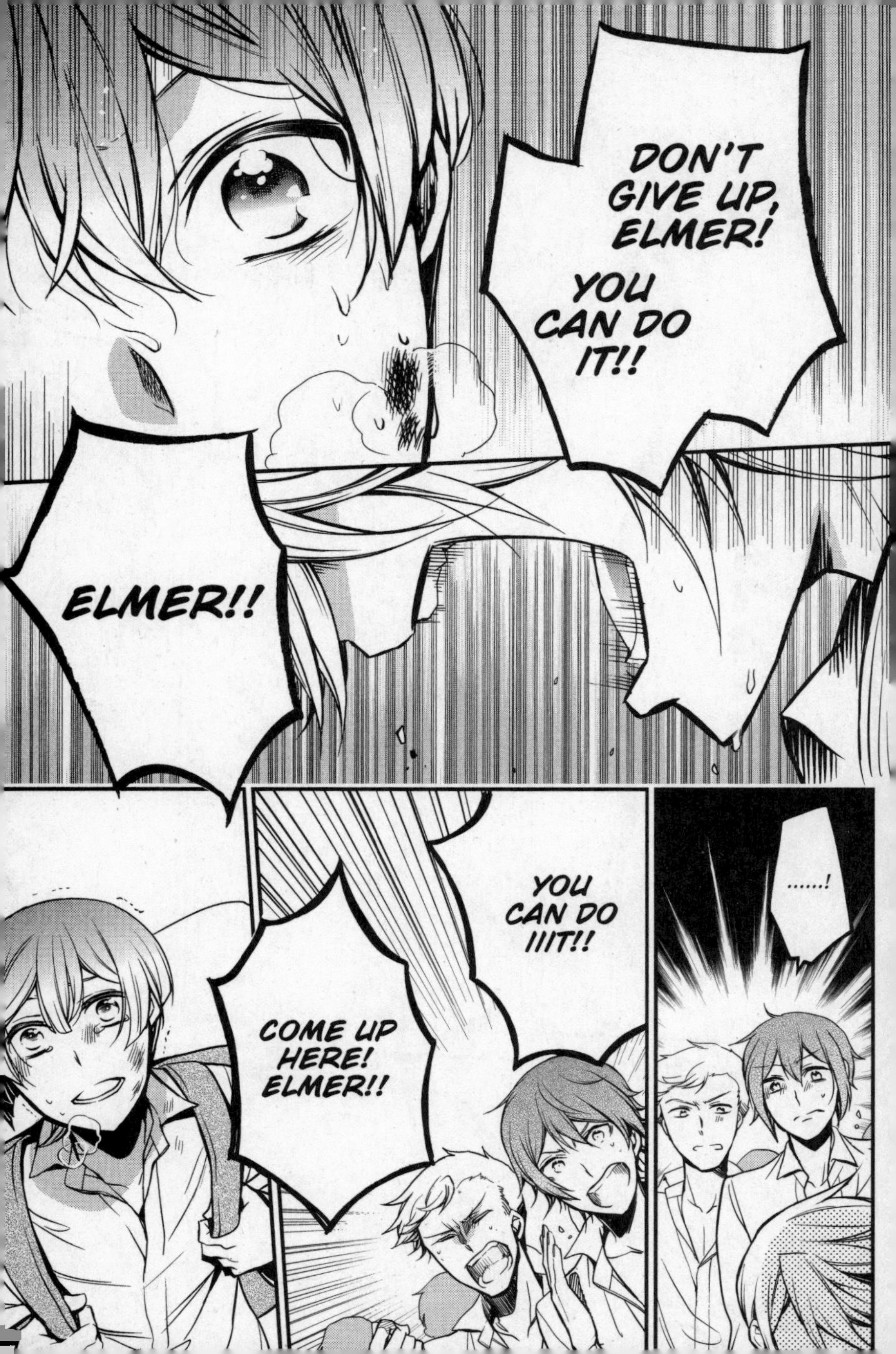
DON'T GIVE UP, ELMER!
YOU CAN DO IT!!
ELMER!!
......!
YOU CAN DO IIIT!!
COME UP HERE! ELMER!!

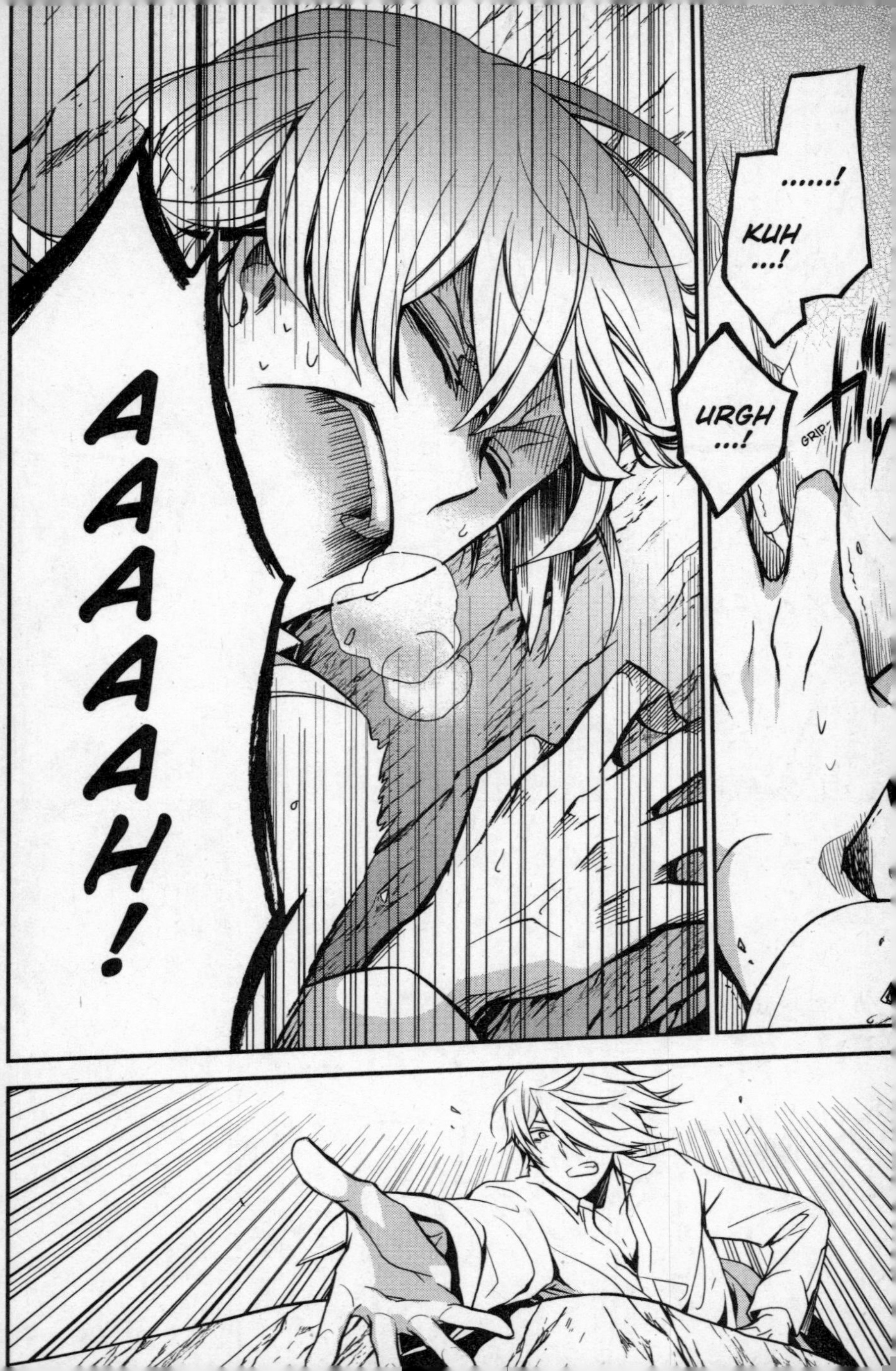
......!
KUH ...!
URGH ...!
GRIP-
AAAAAH!

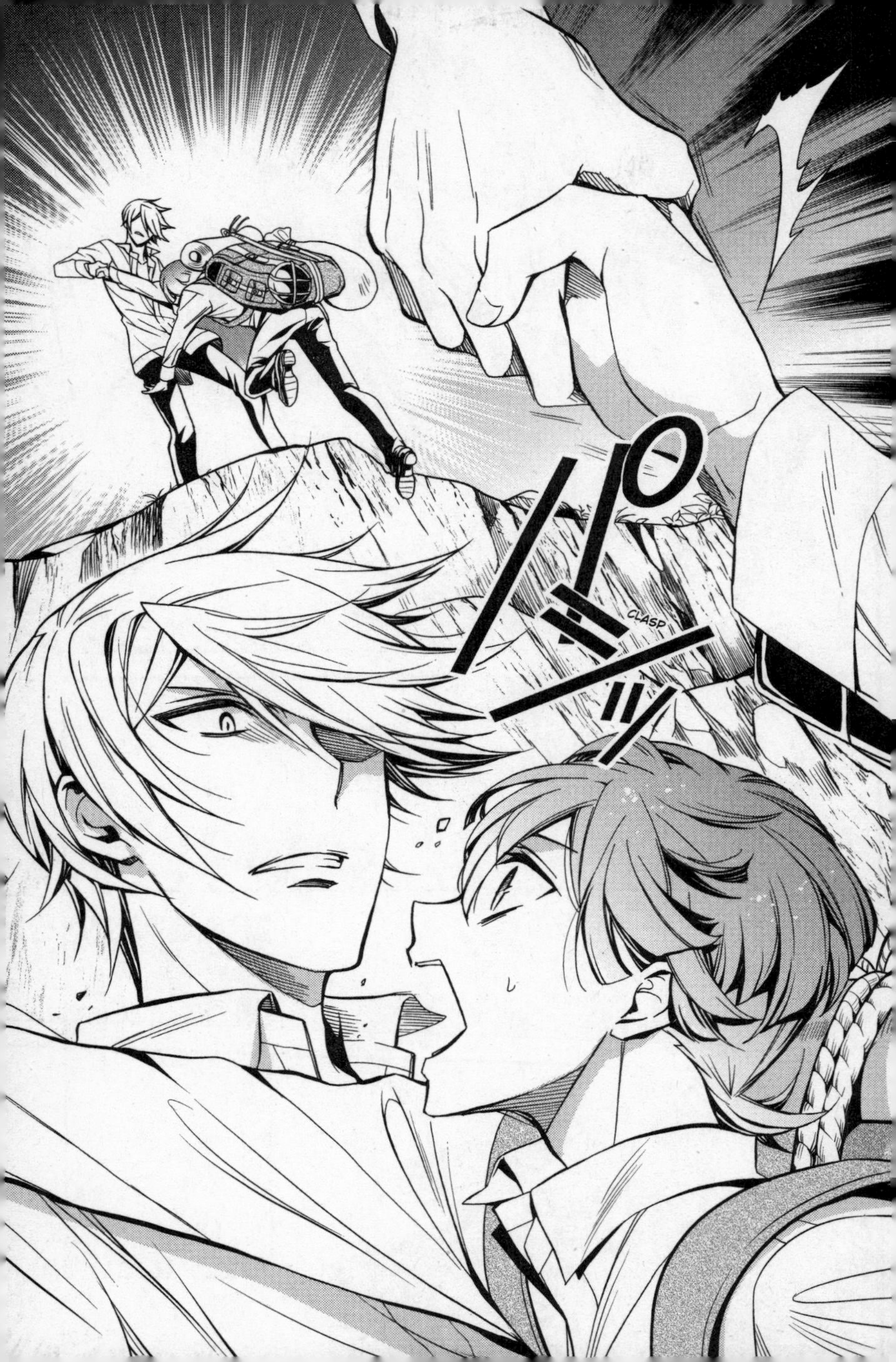
CLASP

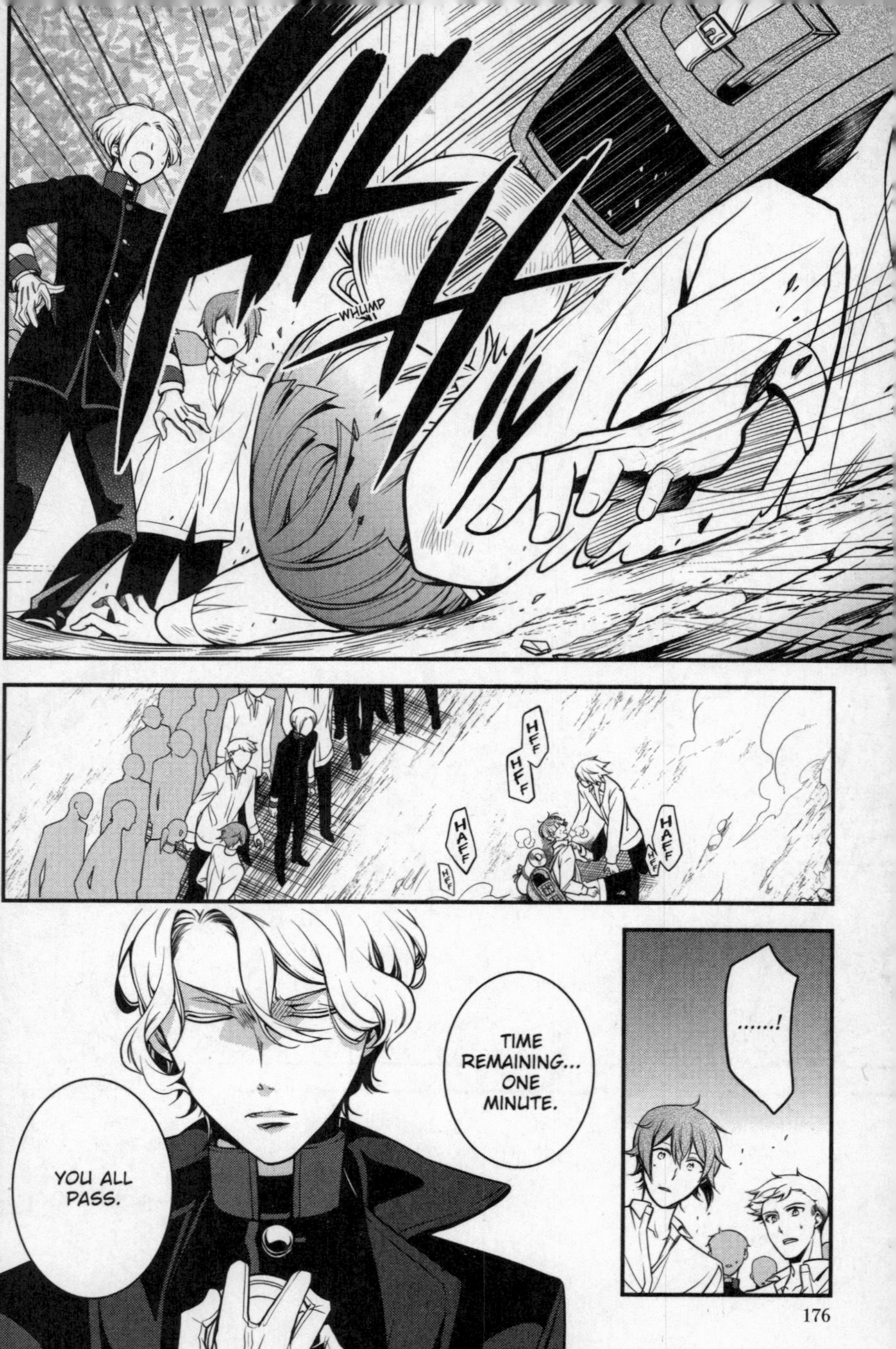
WHUMP
HAFF
HEFF
HFF
HFF
HAFF
HEFF
......!
TIME REMAINING... ONE MINUTE.
YOU ALL PASS.

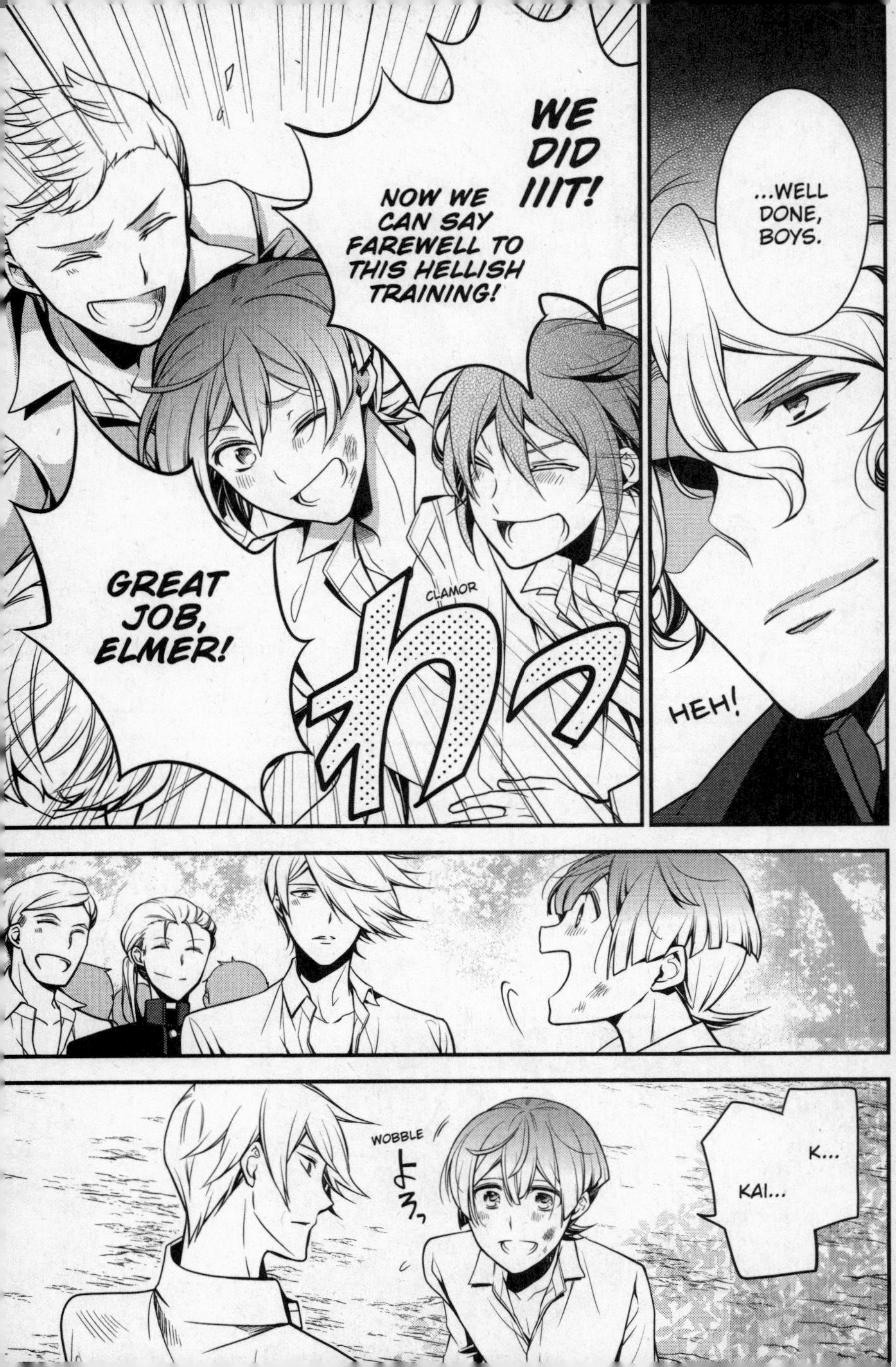
...WELL DONE, BOYS.
HEH!
WE DID IIIT!
NOW WE CAN SAY FAREWELL TO THIS HELLISH TRAINING!
CLAMOR
わっ
GREAT JOB, ELMER!
K... KAI...
WOBBLE
よろっ

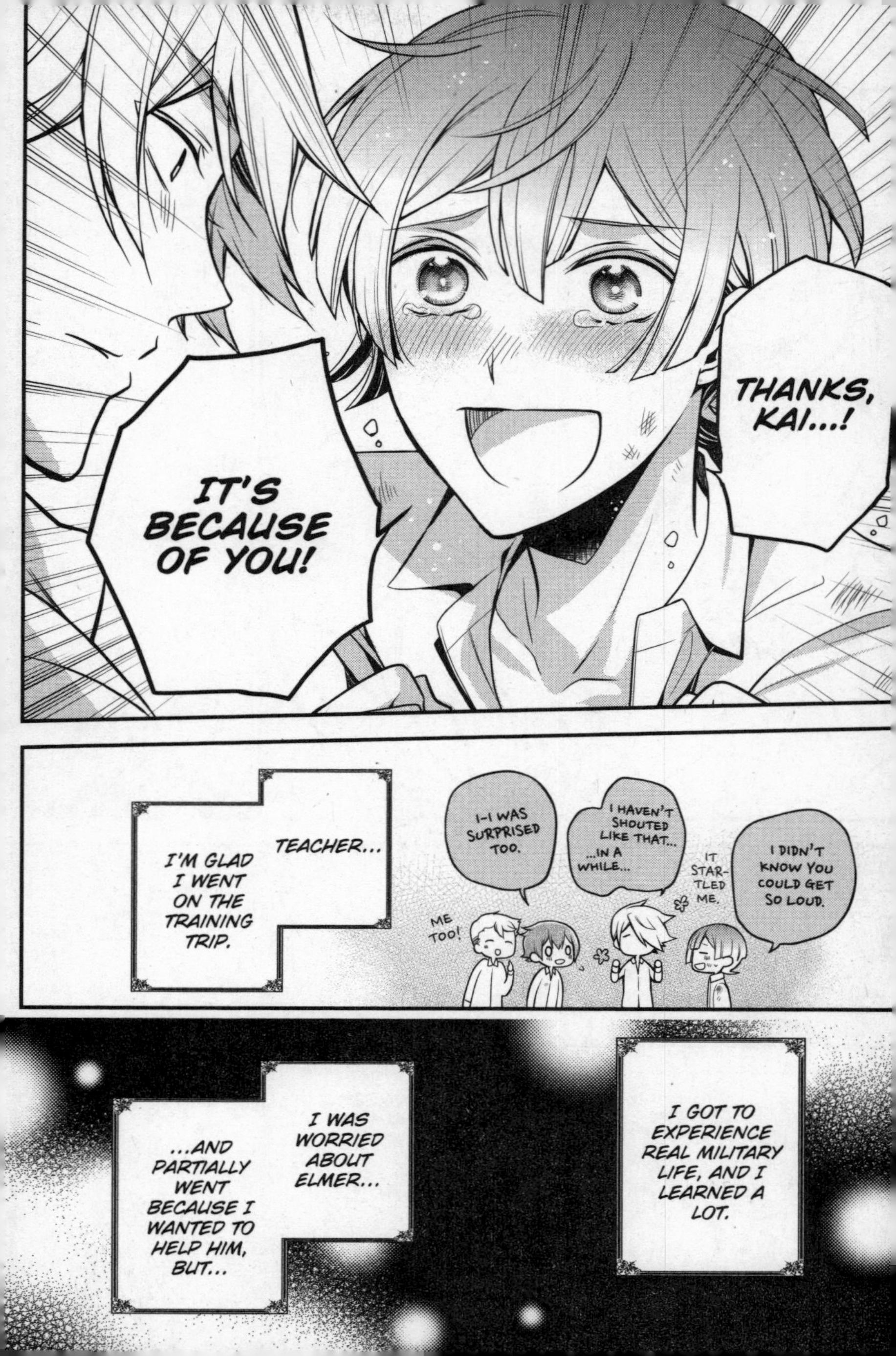
THANKS, KAI...!
IT'S BECAUSE OF YOU!
I DIDN'T KNOW YOU COULD GET SO LOUD.
IT STAR-TLED ME.
I HAVEN'T SHOUTED LIKE THAT... ...IN A WHILE...
I-I WAS SURPRISED TOO.
ME TOO!
TEACHER...
I'M GLAD I WENT ON THE TRAINING TRIP.
I GOT TO EXPERIENCE REAL MILITARY LIFE, AND I LEARNED A LOT.
I WAS WORRIED ABOUT ELMER...
...AND PARTIALLY WENT BECAUSE I WANTED TO HELP HIM, BUT...

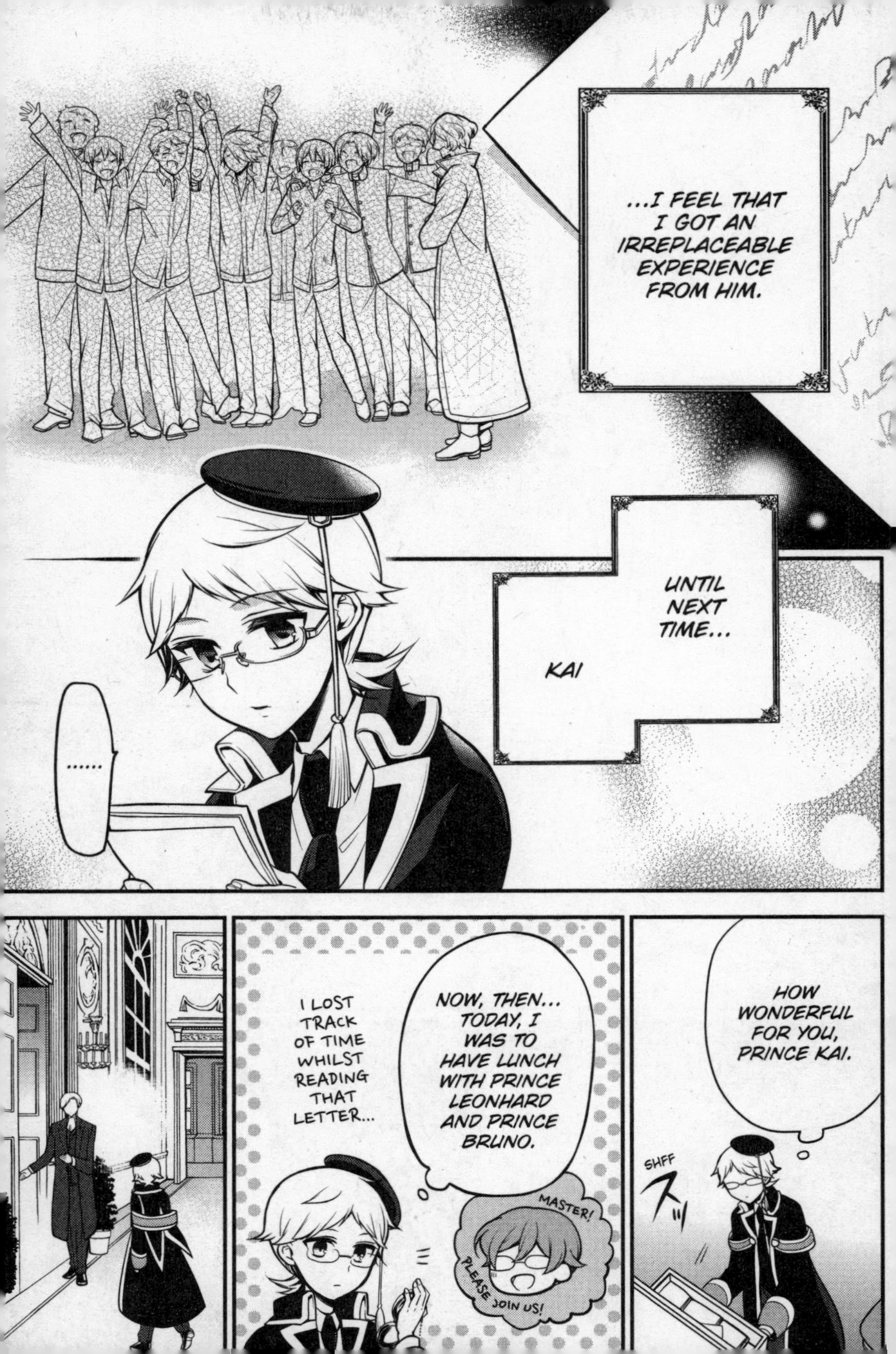
...I FEEL THAT I GOT AN IRREPLACEABLE EXPERIENCE FROM HIM.
UNTIL NEXT TIME...
KAI
......
HOW WONDERFUL FOR YOU, PRINCE KAI.
SHFF
NOW, THEN... TODAY, I WAS TO HAVE LUNCH WITH PRINCE LEONHARD AND PRINCE BRUNO.
I LOST TRACK OF TIME WHILST READING THAT LETTER...
MASTER!
PLEASE JOIN US!

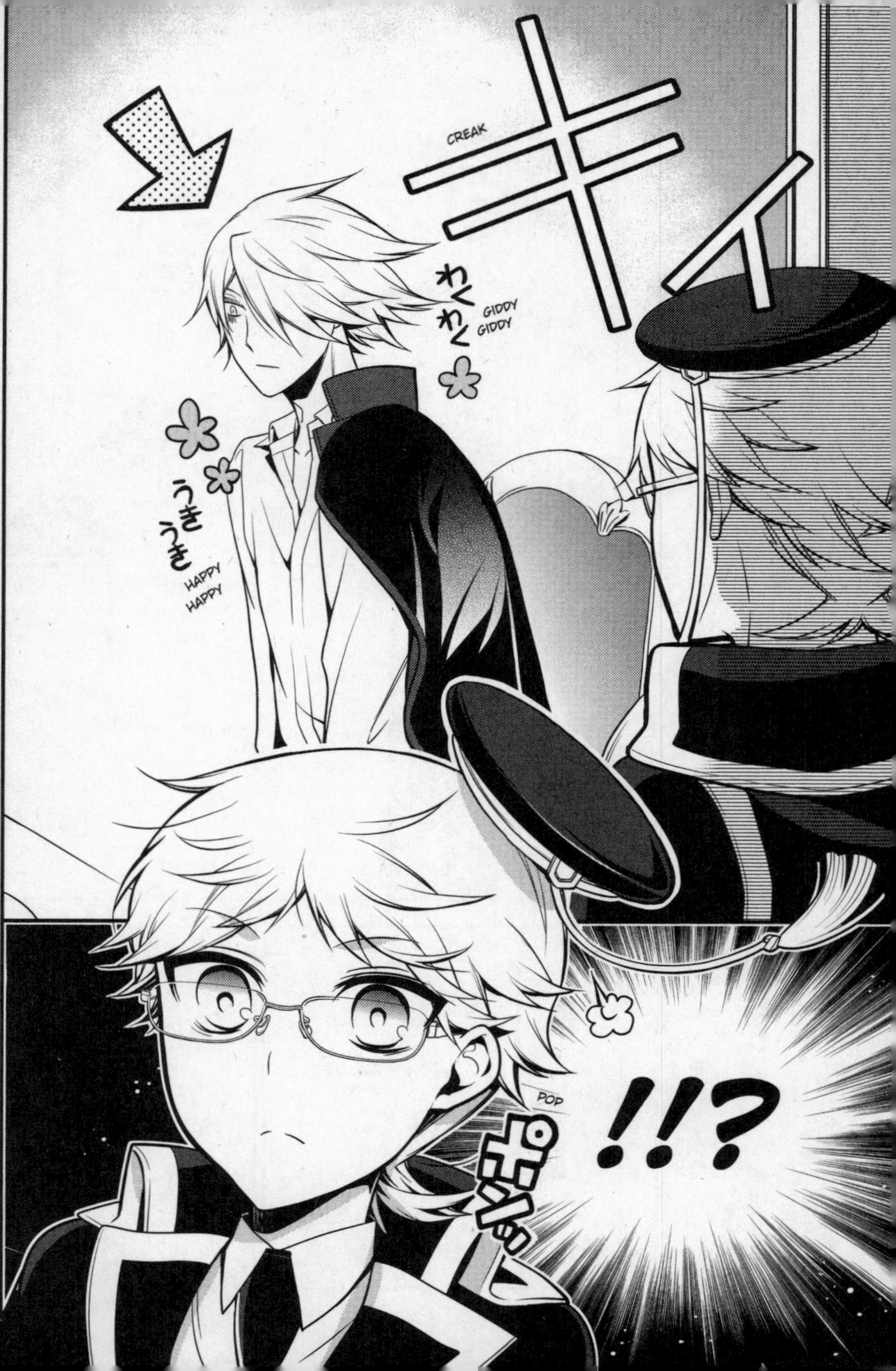
キィ
CREAK
わくわく
GIDDY GIDDY
うきうき
HAPPY HAPPY
ポン
POP
!!?

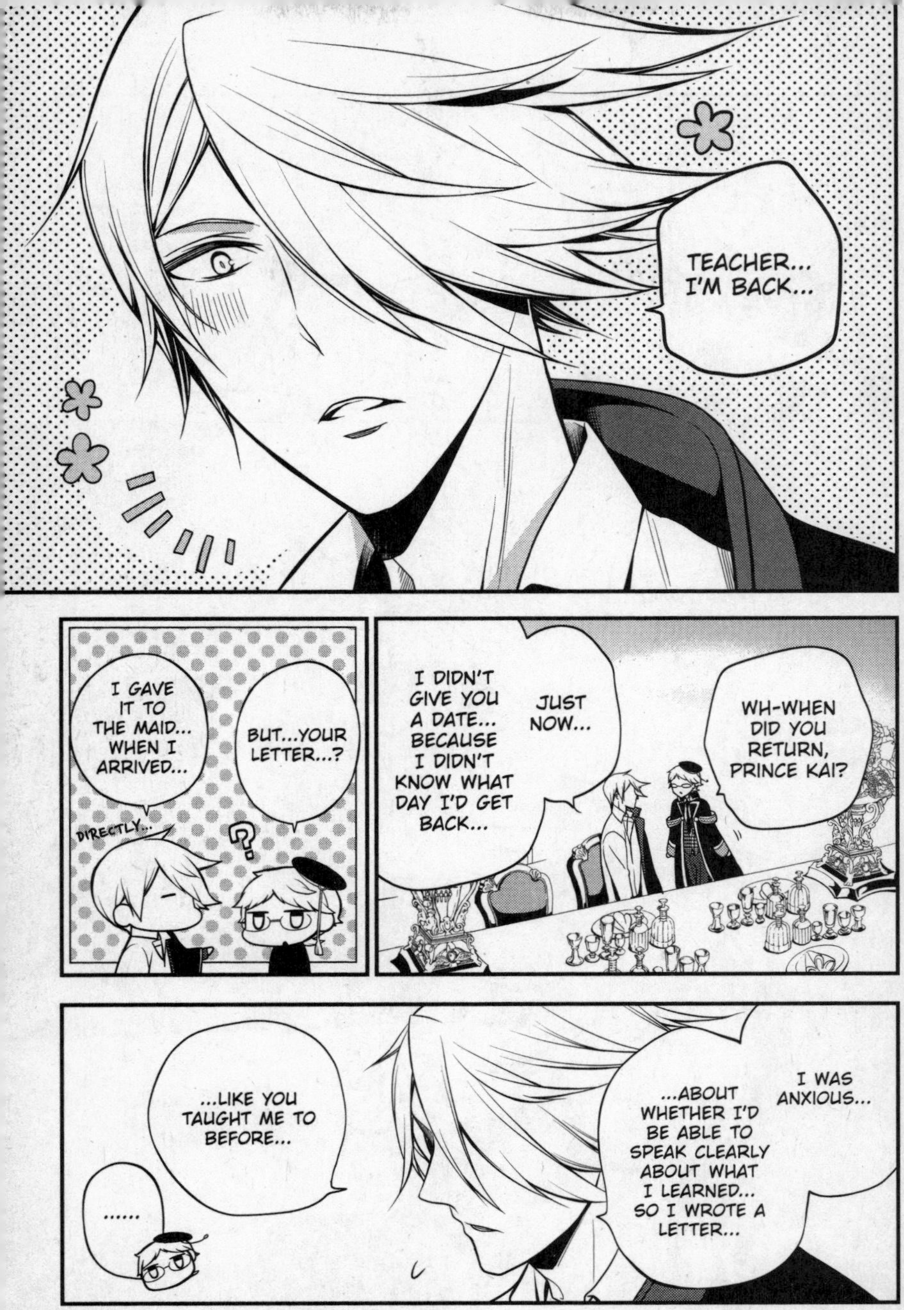
TEACHER... I'M BACK...
WH-WHEN DID YOU RETURN, PRINCE KAI?
JUST NOW...
I DIDN'T GIVE YOU A DATE... BECAUSE I DIDN'T KNOW WHAT DAY I'D GET BACK...
BUT...YOUR LETTER...?
I GAVE IT TO THE MAID... WHEN I ARRIVED...
DIRECTLY...
I WAS ANXIOUS...
...ABOUT WHETHER I'D BE ABLE TO SPEAK CLEARLY ABOUT WHAT I LEARNED... SO I WROTE A LETTER...
...LIKE YOU TAUGHT ME TO BEFORE...
......

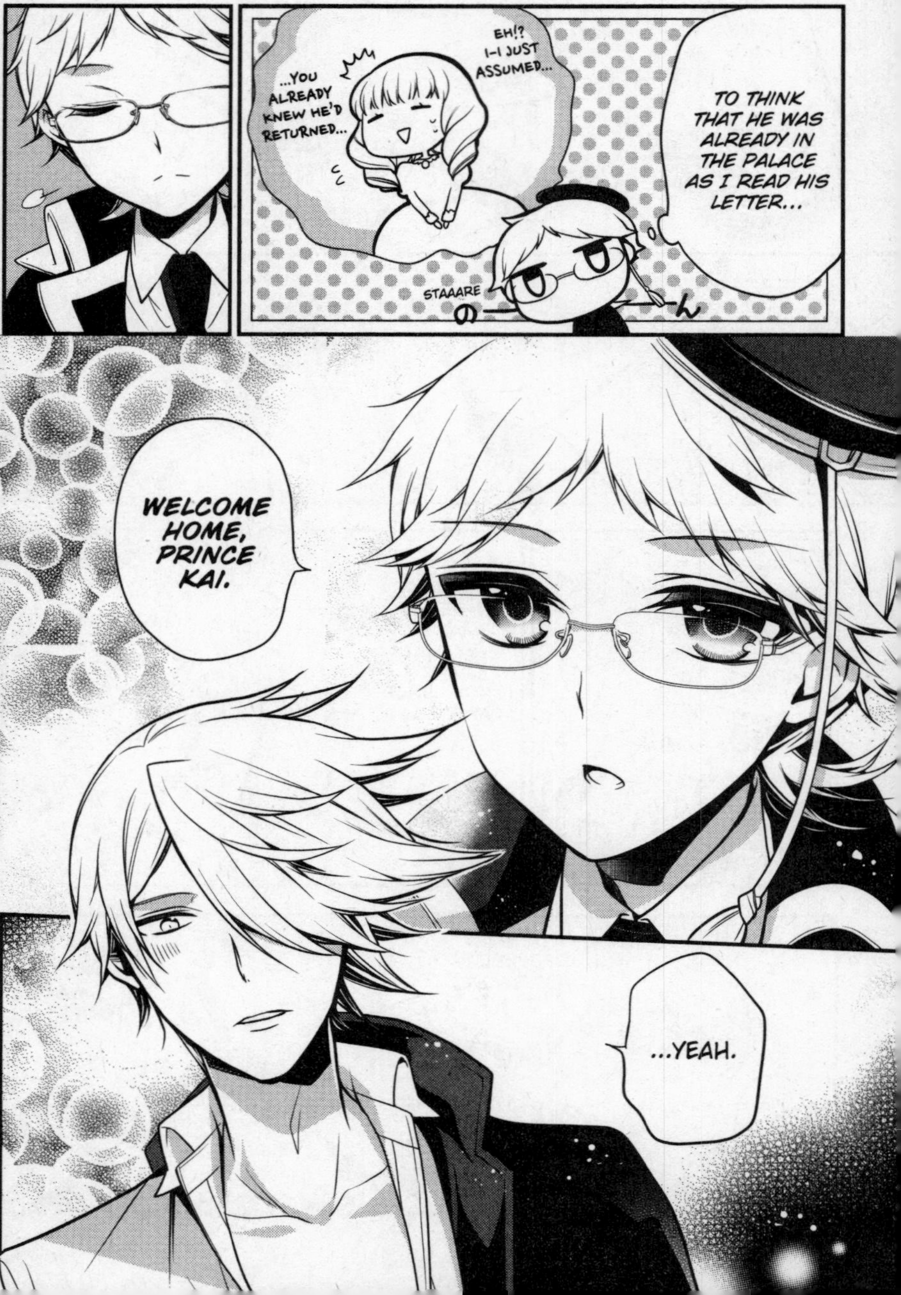
TO THINK THAT HE WAS ALREADY IN THE PALACE AS I READ HIS LETTER...
EH!? I-I JUST ASSUMED...
...YOU ALREADY KNEW HE'D RETURNED...
STAAARE
WELCOME HOME, PRINCE KAI.
...YEAH.

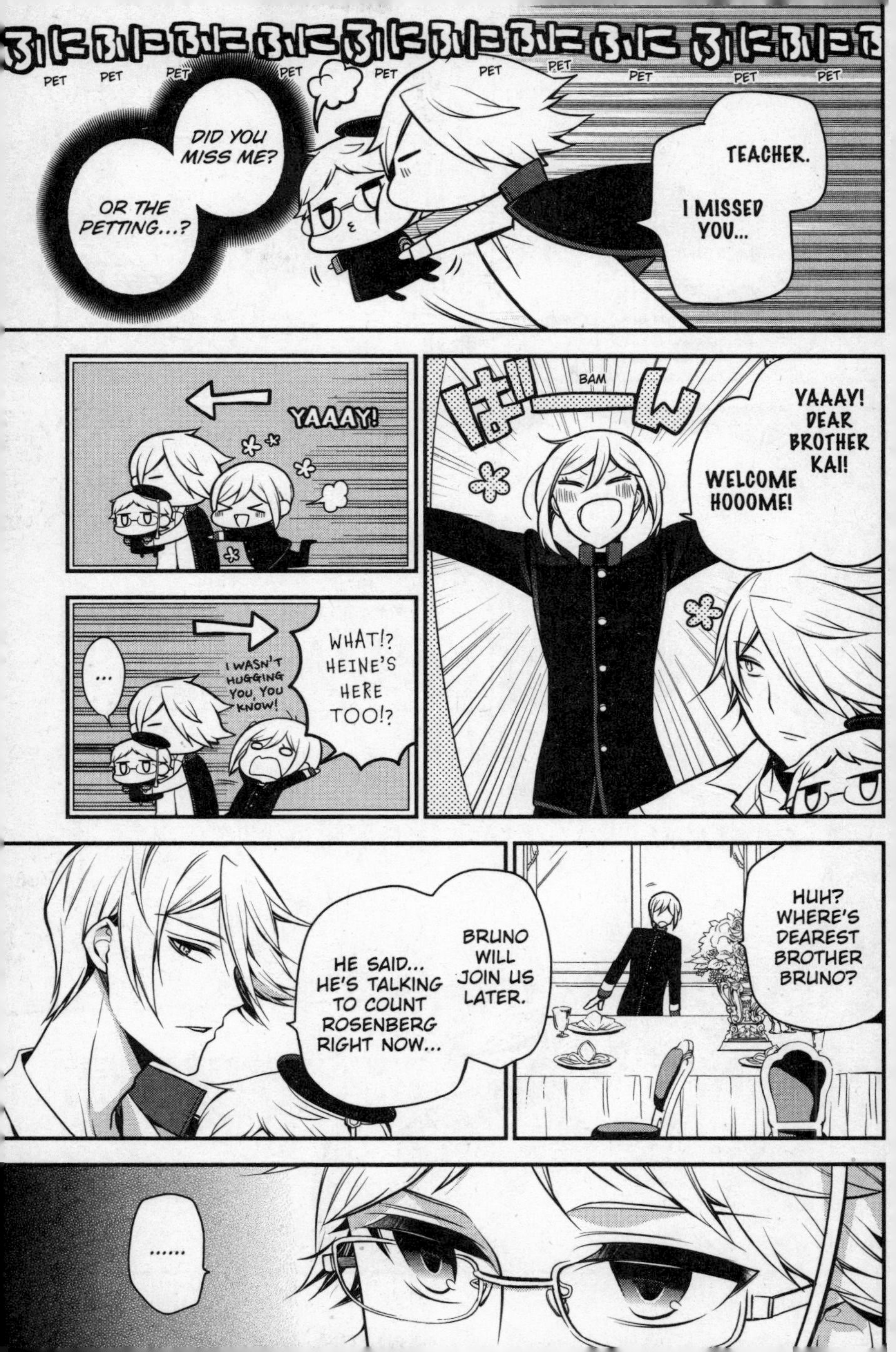
ふにふにふにふにふにふにふにふに ふにふにふ
PET PET PET PET PET PET PET PET PET PET
TEACHER.
I MISSED YOU...
DID YOU MISS ME?
OR THE PETTING...?
ばーーん
BAM
YAAAY! DEAR BROTHER KAI!
WELCOME HOOOME!
YAAAY!
WHAT!? HEINE'S HERE TOO!?
I WASN'T HUGGING YOU, YOU KNOW!
...
HUH? WHERE'S DEAREST BROTHER BRUNO?
BRUNO WILL JOIN US LATER.
HE SAID... HE'S TALKING TO COUNT ROSENBERG RIGHT NOW...
......

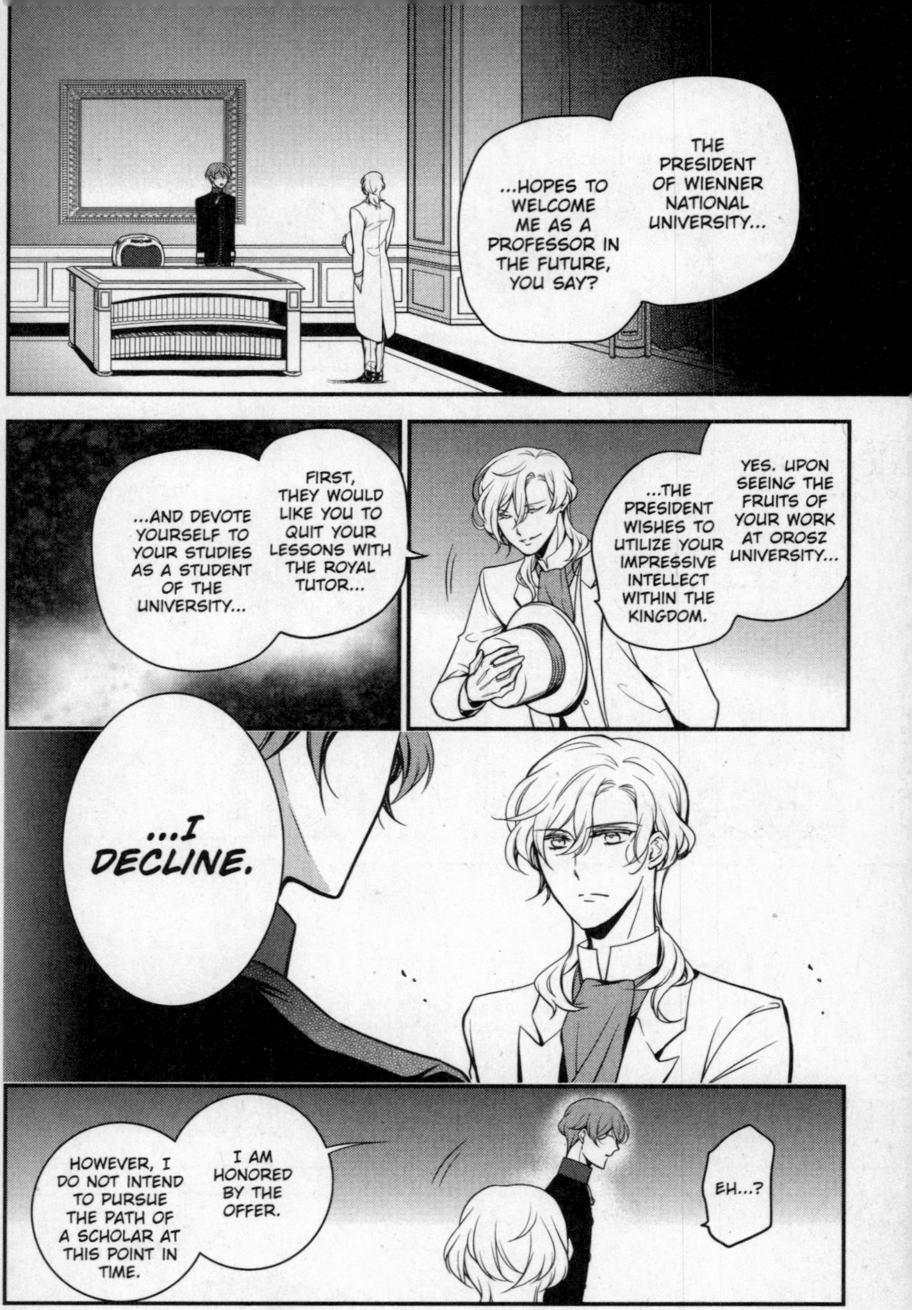
THE PRESIDENT OF WIENNER NATIONAL UNIVERSITY...
...HOPES TO WELCOME ME AS A PROFESSOR IN THE FUTURE, YOU SAY?
YES. UPON SEEING THE FRUITS OF YOUR WORK AT OROSZ UNIVERSITY...
...THE PRESIDENT WISHES TO UTILIZE YOUR IMPRESSIVE INTELLECT WITHIN THE KINGDOM.
FIRST, THEY WOULD LIKE YOU TO QUIT YOUR LESSONS WITH THE ROYAL TUTOR...
...AND DEVOTE YOURSELF TO YOUR STUDIES AS A STUDENT OF THE UNIVERSITY...
...I DECLINE.
EH...?
I AM HONORED BY THE OFFER.
HOWEVER, I DO NOT INTEND TO PURSUE THE PATH OF A SCHOLAR AT THIS POINT IN TIME.

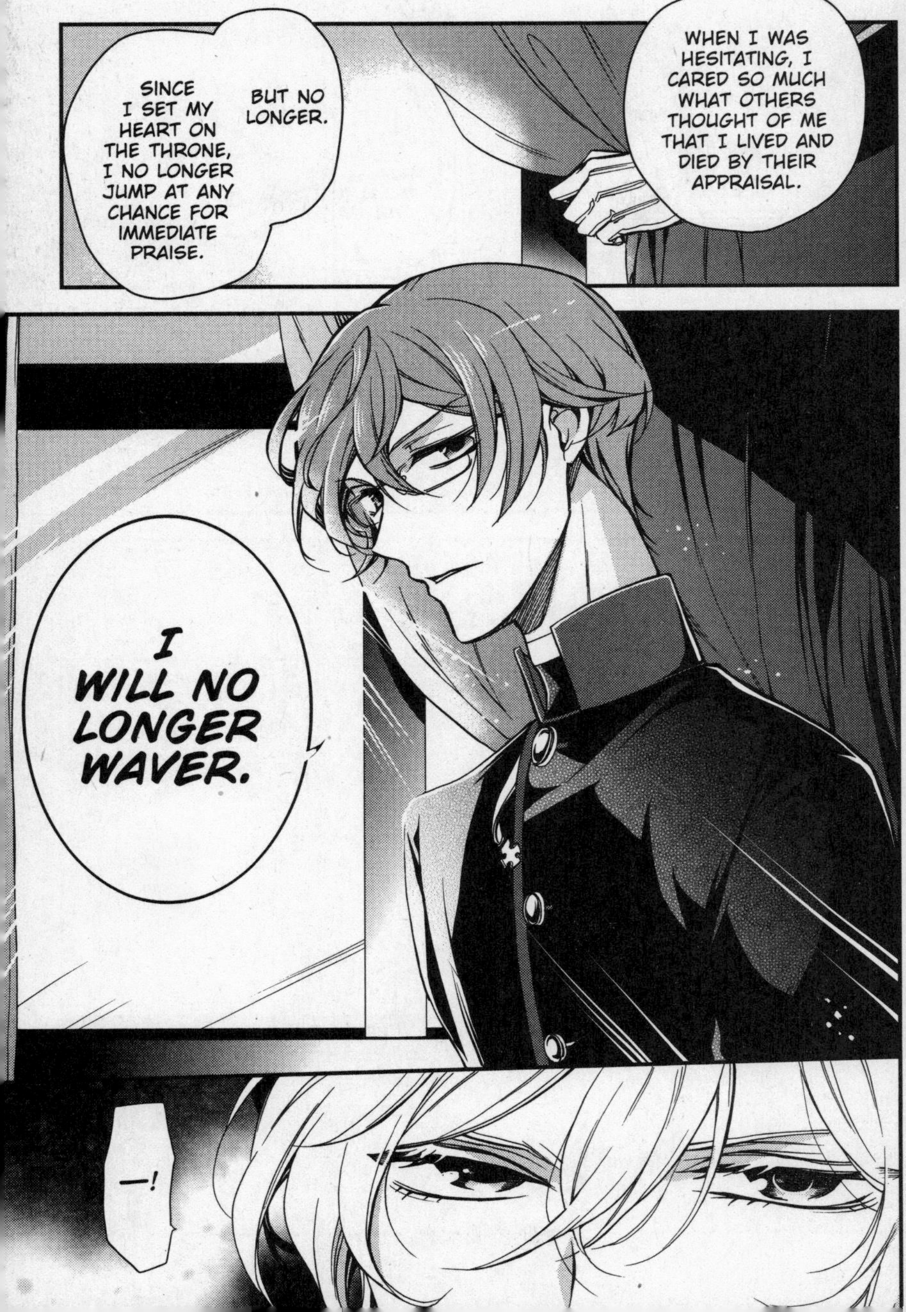
WHEN I WAS HESITATING, I CARED SO MUCH WHAT OTHERS THOUGHT OF ME THAT I LIVED AND DIED BY THEIR APPRAISAL.
BUT NO LONGER.
SINCE I SET MY HEART ON THE THRONE, I NO LONGER JUMP AT ANY CHANCE FOR IMMEDIATE PRAISE.
I WILL NO LONGER WAVER.
—!

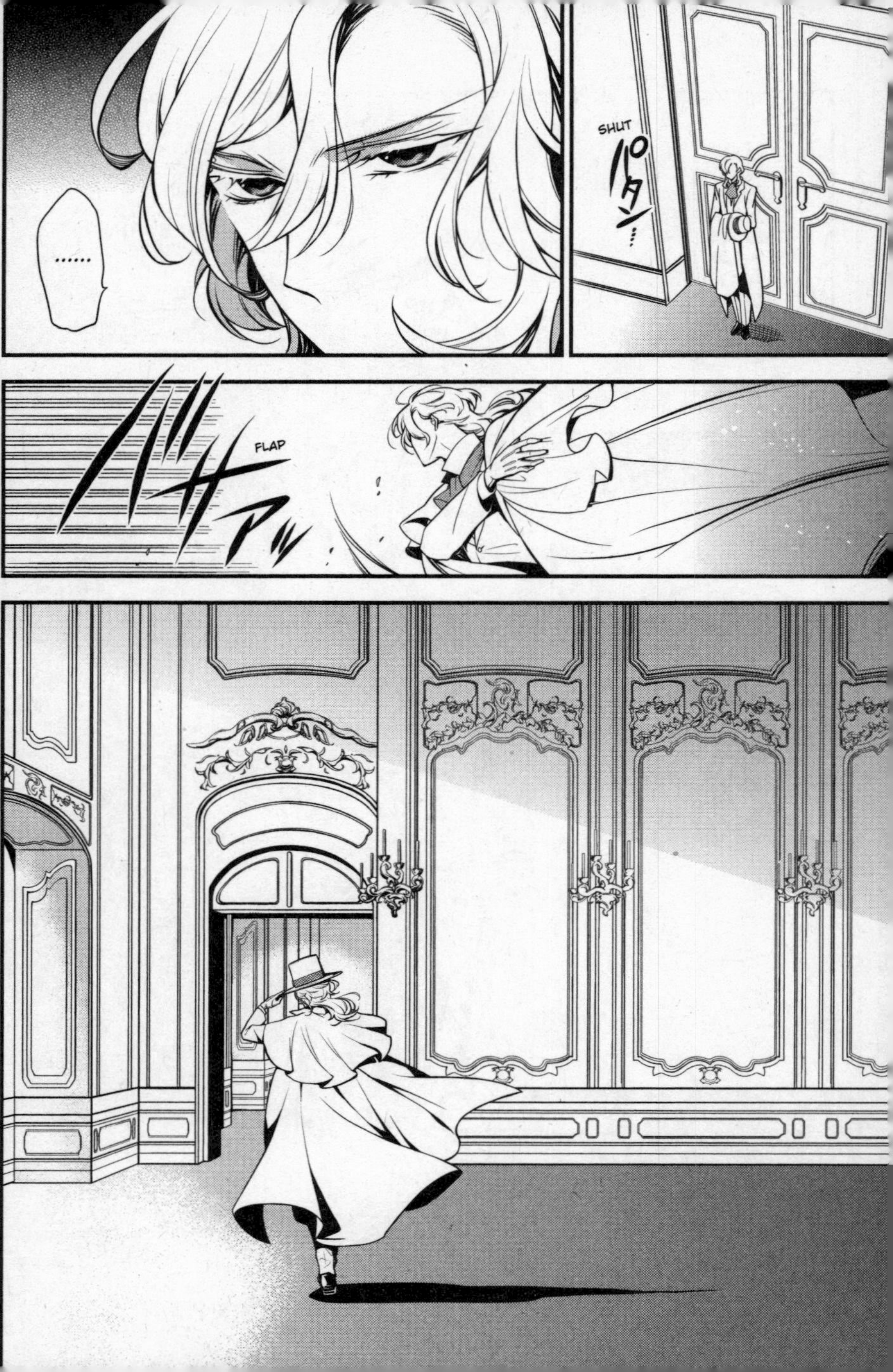
SHUT
パタン…
……
FLAP
バサアッ

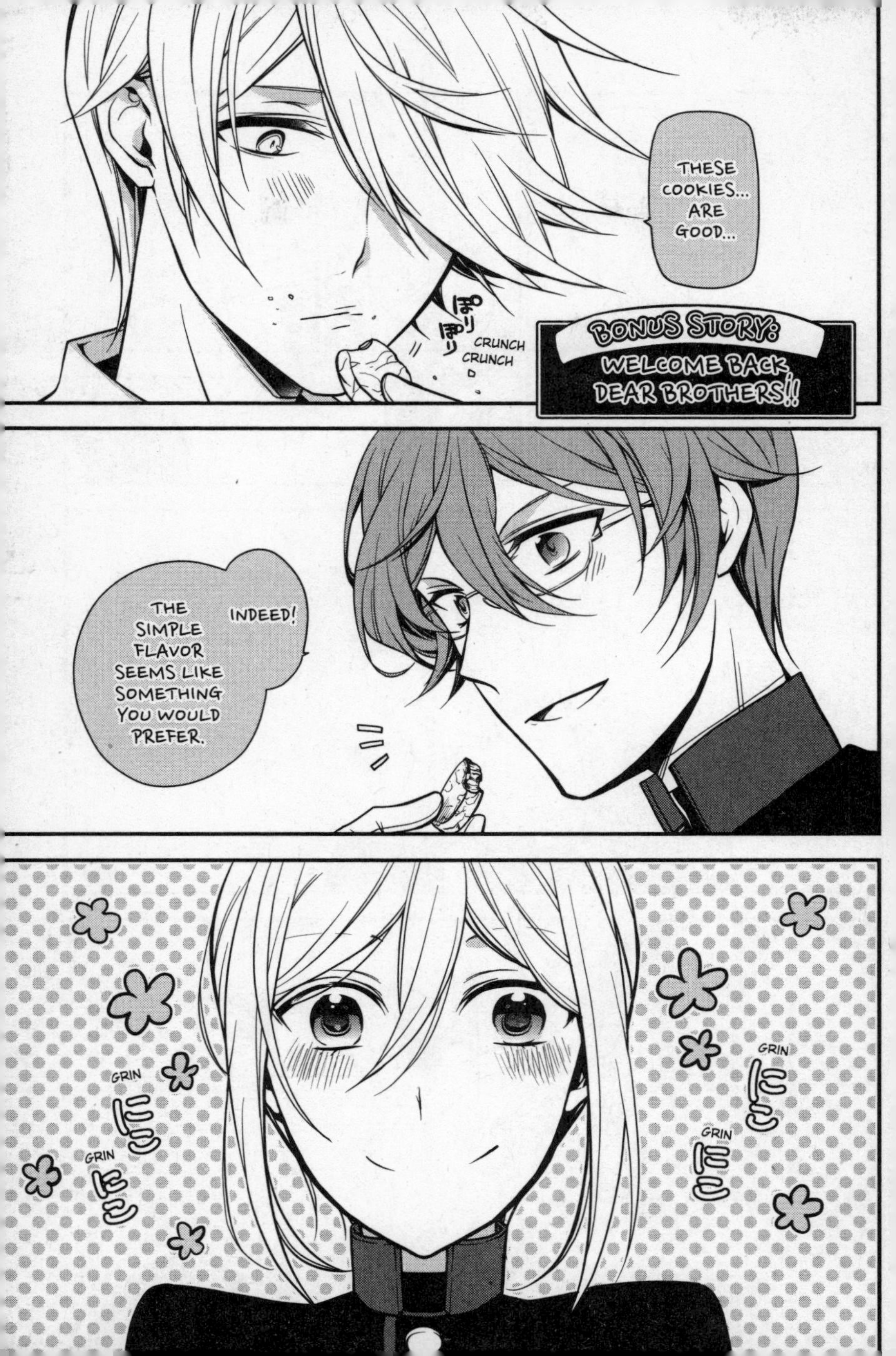
THESE COOKIES... ARE GOOD...
BONUS STORY:
WELCOME BACK DEAR BROTHERS!!
ぽりぽり
CRUNCH CRUNCH
INDEED!
THE SIMPLE FLAVOR SEEMS LIKE SOMETHING YOU WOULD PREFER.
GRIN
にこ
GRIN
にこ
GRIN
にこ
GRIN
にこ

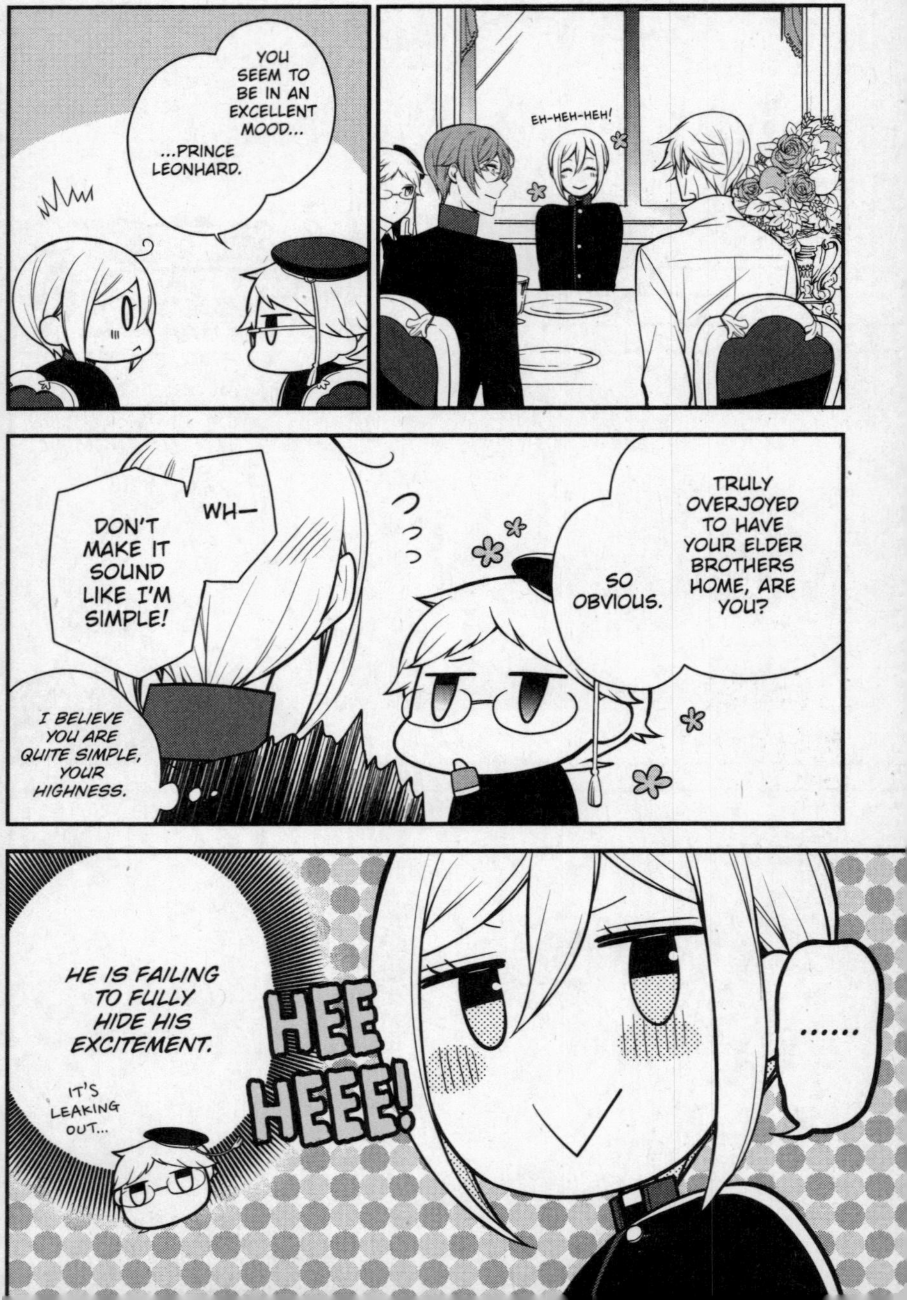
EH-HEH-HEH!
YOU SEEM TO BE IN AN EXCELLENT MOOD...
...PRINCE LEONHARD.
TRULY OVERJOYED TO HAVE YOUR ELDER BROTHERS HOME, ARE YOU?
SO OBVIOUS.
WH—
DON'T MAKE IT SOUND LIKE I'M SIMPLE!
I BELIEVE YOU ARE QUITE SIMPLE, YOUR HIGHNESS.
......
HEE HEEE!
HE IS FAILING TO FULLY HIDE HIS EXCITEMENT.
IT'S LEAKING OUT...

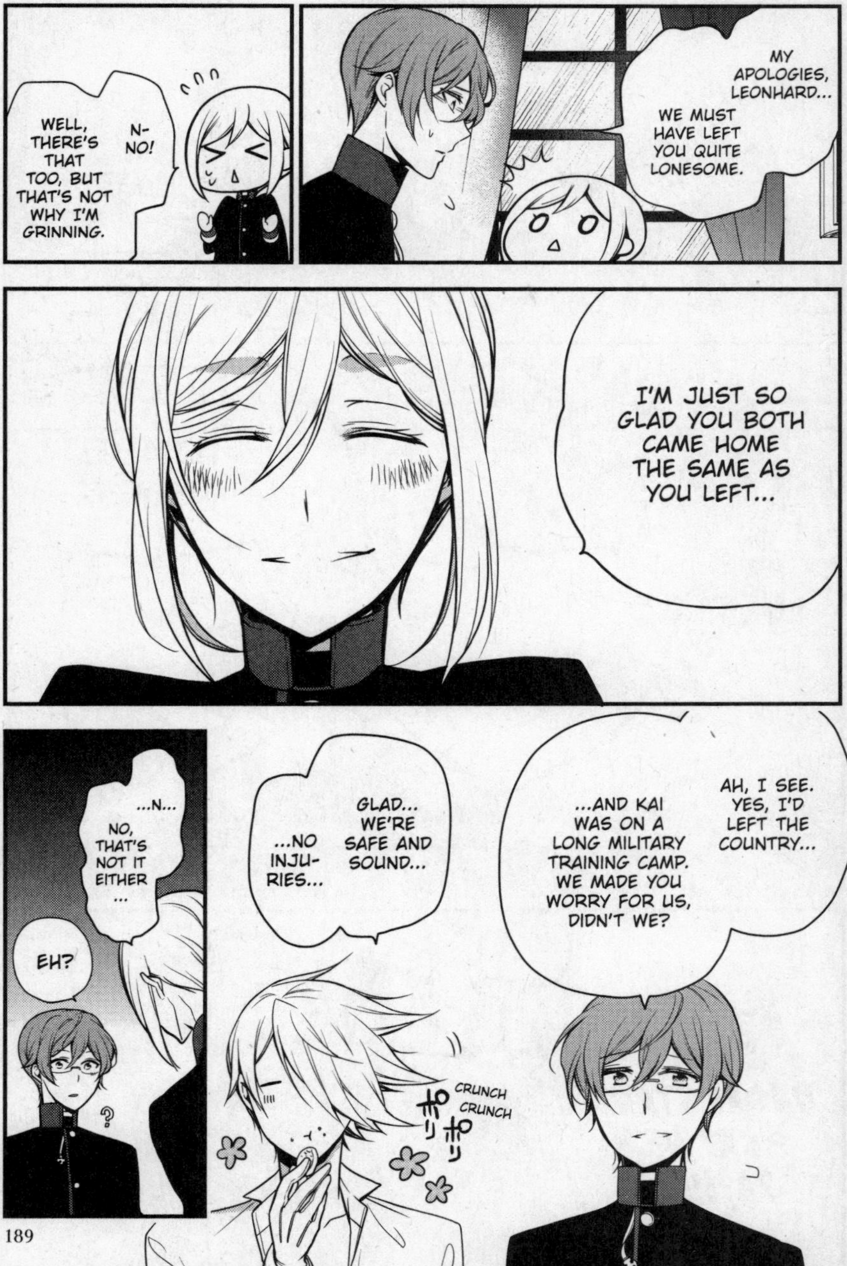
MY APOLOGIES, LEONHARD...
WE MUST HAVE LEFT YOU QUITE LONESOME.
N-NO!
WELL, THERE'S THAT TOO, BUT THAT'S NOT WHY I'M GRINNING.
I'M JUST SO GLAD YOU BOTH CAME HOME THE SAME AS YOU LEFT...
AH, I SEE. YES, I'D LEFT THE COUNTRY...
...AND KAI WAS ON A LONG MILITARY TRAINING CAMP. WE MADE YOU WORRY FOR US, DIDN'T WE?
GLAD... WE'RE SAFE AND SOUND...
...NO INJURIES...
CRUNCH CRUNCH
...N...
NO, THAT'S NOT IT EITHER...
EH?

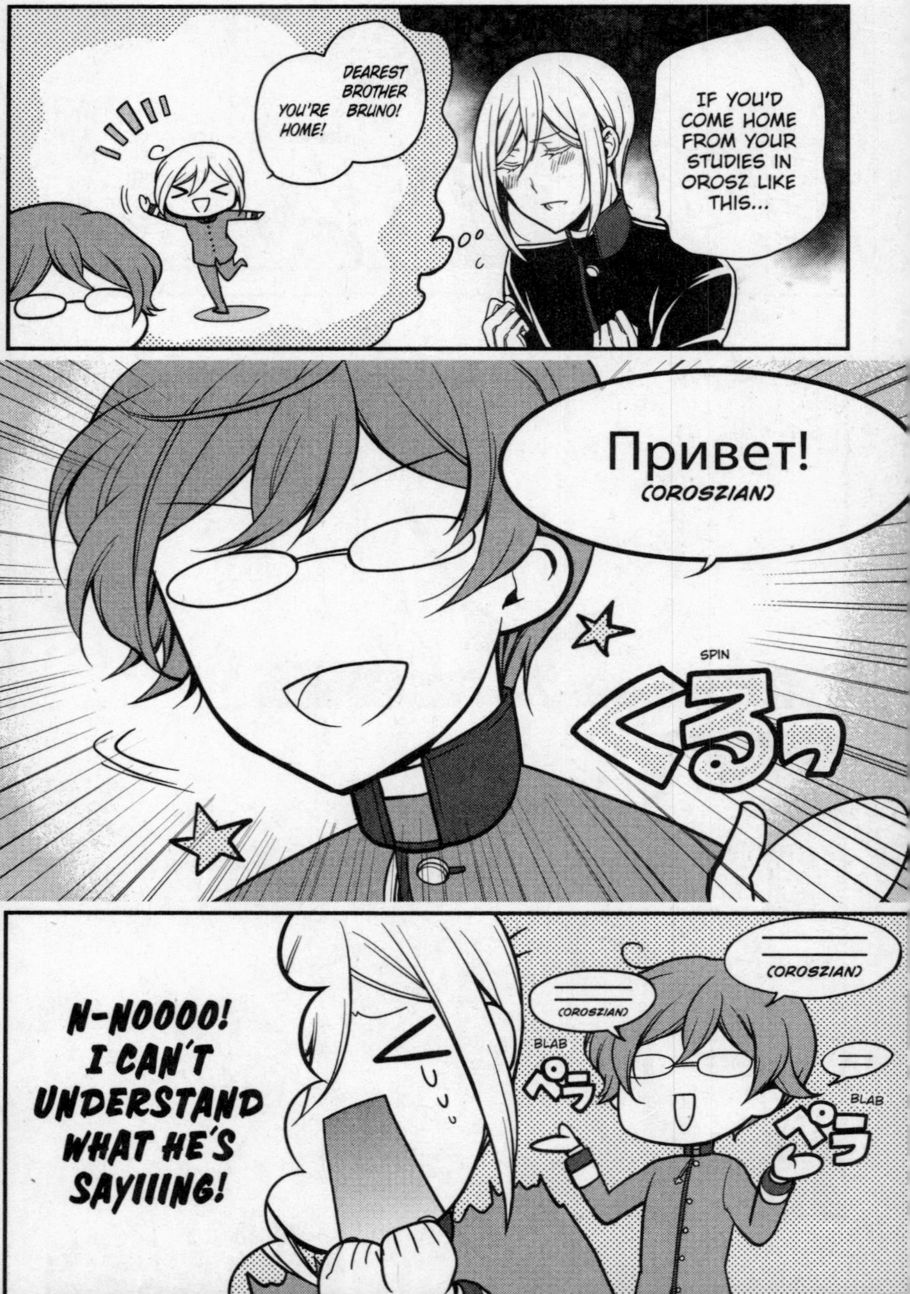
IF YOU'D COME HOME FROM YOUR STUDIES IN OROSZ LIKE THIS...
DEAREST BROTHER BRUNO!
YOU'RE HOME!
Привет!
(OROSZIAN)
SPIN
くるっ
(OROSZIAN)
(OROSZIAN)
BLAB
ぺら
BLAB
ぺら
N-NOOOO! I CAN'T UNDERSTAND WHAT HE'S SAYIIIING!

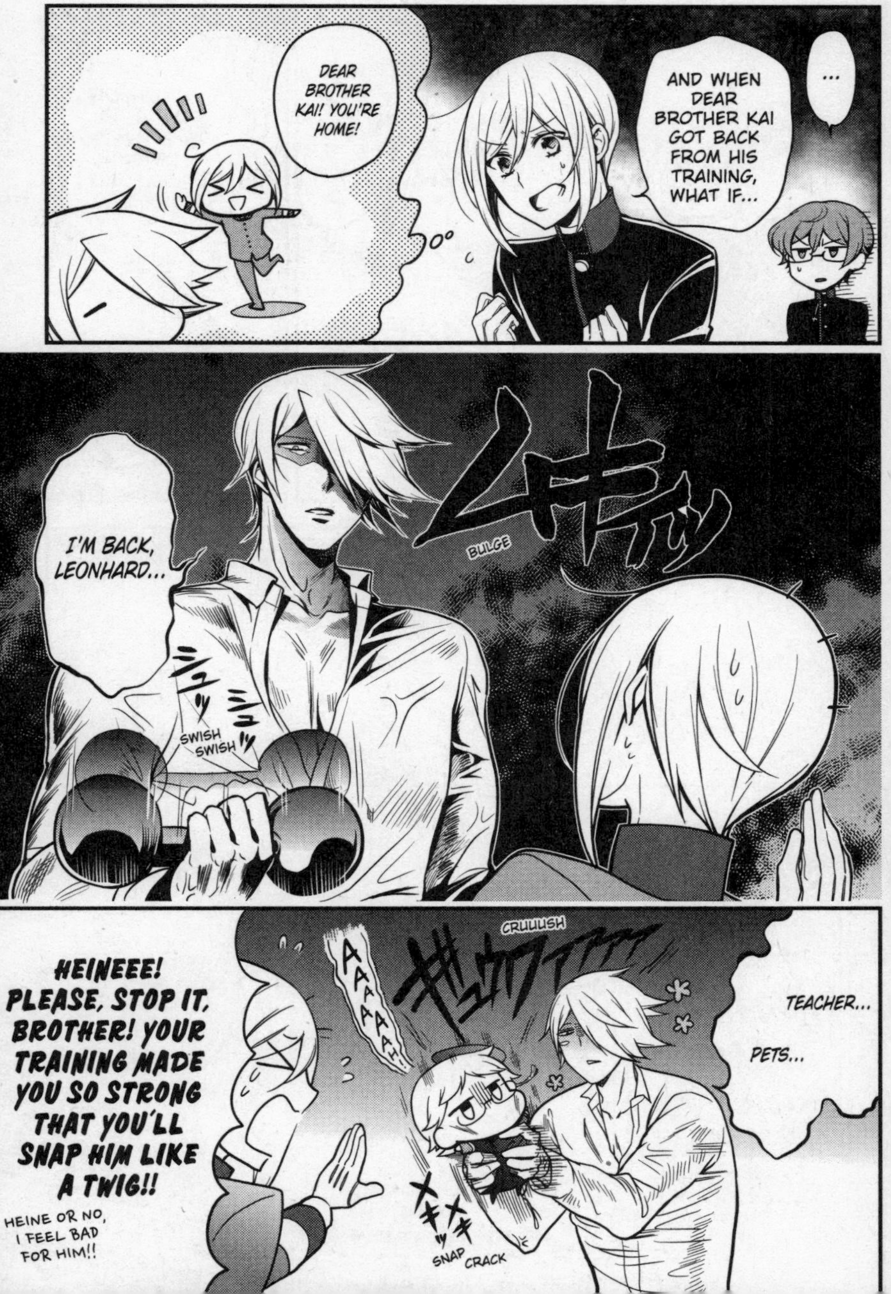
...
AND WHEN DEAR BROTHER KAI GOT BACK FROM HIS TRAINING, WHAT IF...
DEAR BROTHER KAI! YOU'RE HOME!
BULGE
SWISH SWISH
I'M BACK, LEONHARD...
TEACHER...
PETS...
CRUUUSH
SNAP CRACK
HEINEEE! PLEASE, STOP IT, BROTHER! YOUR TRAINING MADE YOU SO STRONG THAT YOU'LL SNAP HIM LIKE A TWIG!!
HEINE OR NO, I FEEL BAD FOR HIM!!

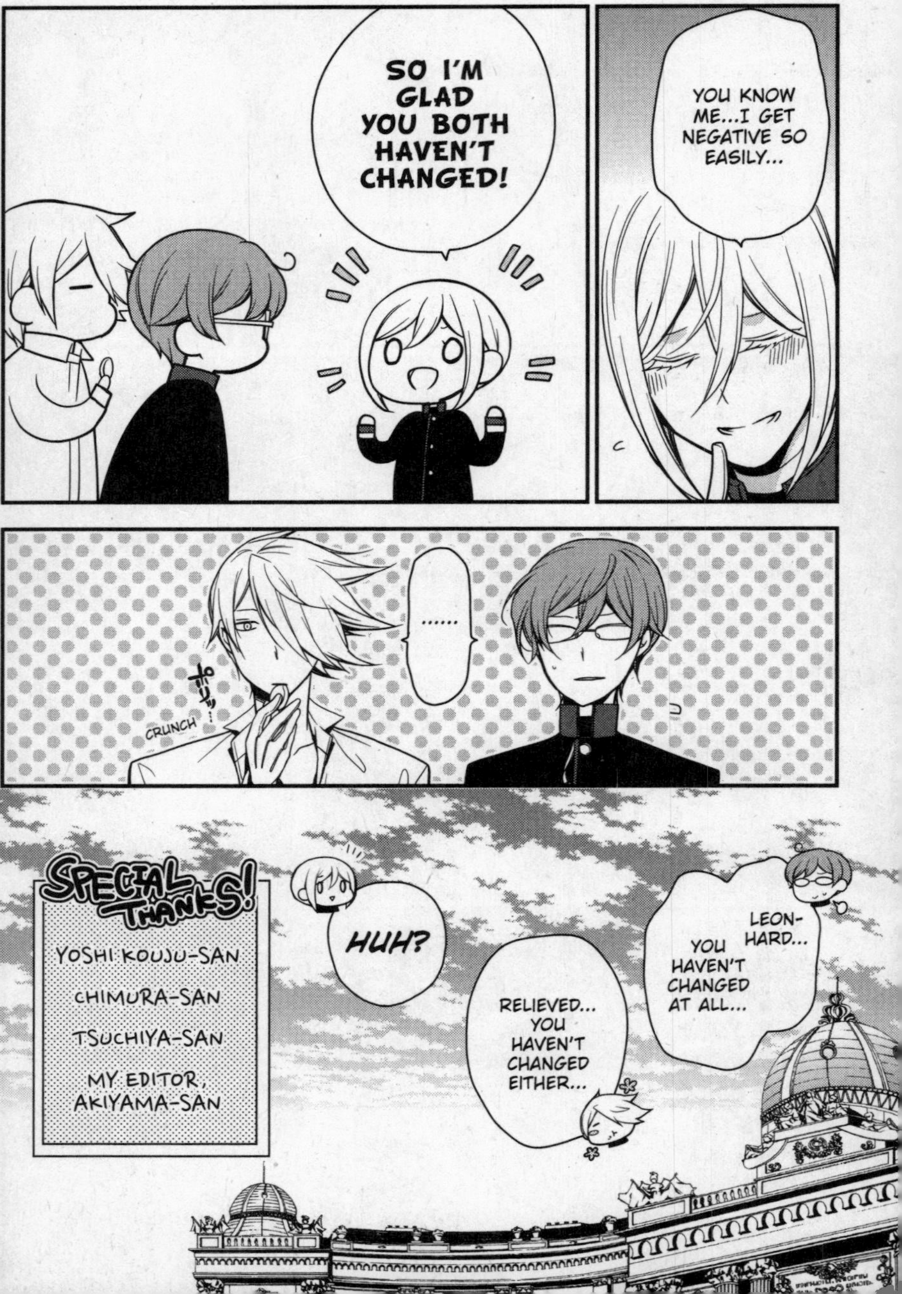
YOU KNOW ME...I GET NEGATIVE SO EASILY...
SO I'M GLAD YOU BOTH HAVEN'T CHANGED!
......
CRUNCH
LEON-HARD... YOU HAVEN'T CHANGED AT ALL...
RELIEVED... YOU HAVEN'T CHANGED EITHER...
HUH?
SPECIAL THANKS!
YOSHI KOUJU-SAN
CHIMURA-SAN
TSUCHIYA-SAN
MY EDITOR, AKIYAMA-SAN

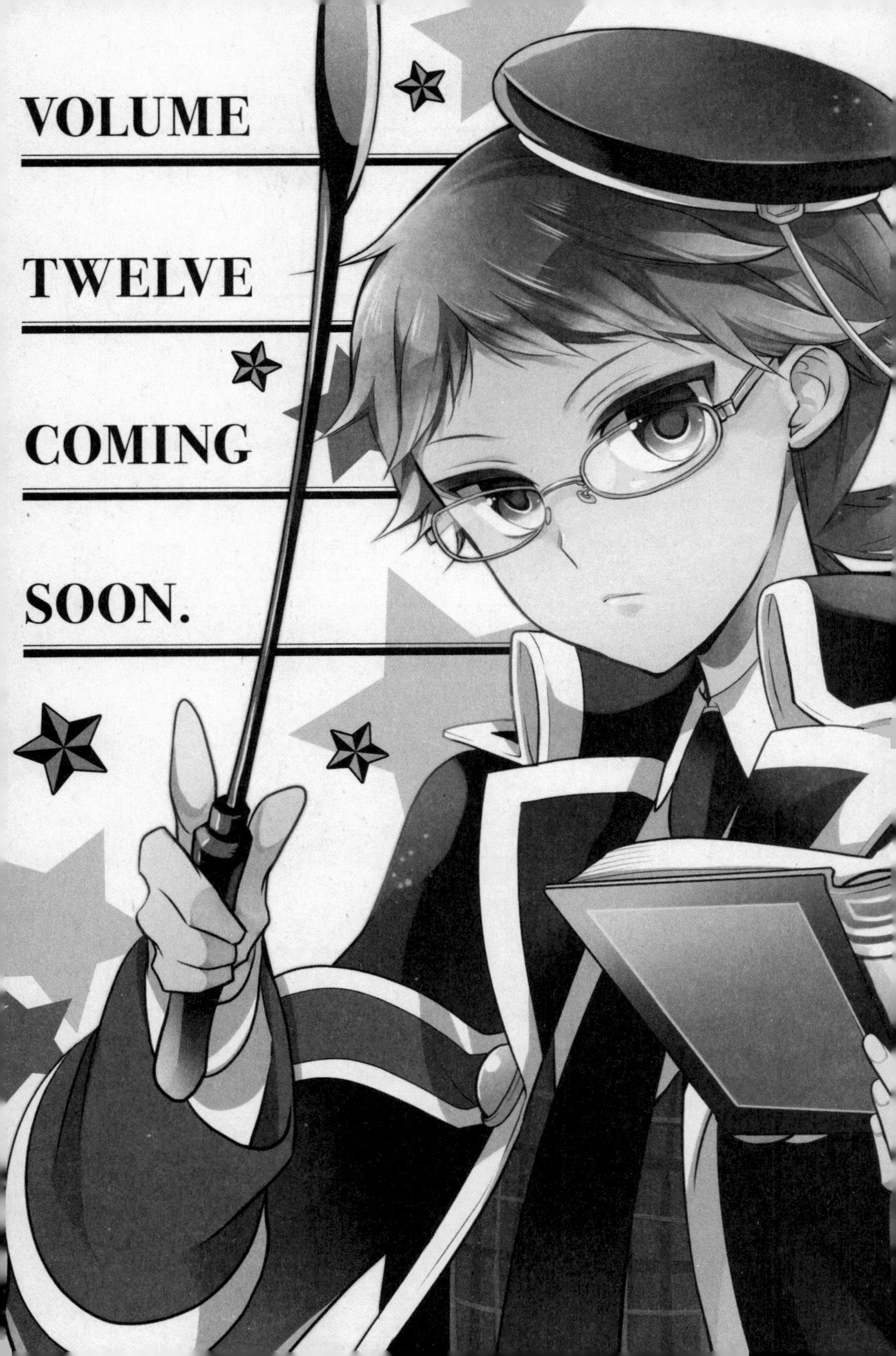
VOLUME
TWELVE
COMING
SOON.

The Royal Tutor ⑪

Higasa Akai

Translation: Amanda Haley • Lettering: Abigail Blackman

THE ROYAL TUTOR Vol. 11 © 2018 Higasa Akai / SQUARE ENIX CO., LTD. First published in Japan in 2018 by SQUARE ENIX CO., LTD. English translation rights arranged with SQUARE ENIX CO., LTD. and Yen Press, LLC through Tuttle-Mori Agency, Inc., Tokyo.

English translation © 2019 by SQUARE ENIX CO., LTD.

Yen Press
1290 Avenue of the Americas
New York, NY 10104

Visit us at yenpress.com
facebook.com/yenpress
twitter.com/yenpress
yenpress.tumblr.com
instagram.com/yenpress

First Yen Press Edition: April 2019
The chapters in this volume were originally published as ebooks by Yen Press.

Yen Press is an imprint of Yen Press, LLC.
The Yen Press name and logo are trademarks of Yen Press, LLC.

Library of Congress Control Number: 2017938422

ISBNs: 978-1-9753-3035-4 (paperback)
978-1-9753-3036-1 (ebook)

10 9 8 7 6 5 4 3 2 1

WOR

Printed in the United States of America